C. 41579

The Korean Economy Beyond the Crisis

The Korean Economy Beyond the Crisis

Edited by

Duck-Koo Chung

Professor, Graduate School of International Studies and Director, Research Center for International Finance, Seoul National University, South Korea, Former Vice Minister of Finance and Minister of Commerce, Industry and Energy of Korea, and Visiting Professor, Beijing University, China

Barry Eichengreen

George C. Pardee and Helen N. Pardee Professor of Economics and Political Science at the University of California, Berkeley, USA

Edward Elgar
Cheltenham, UK • Northampton, MA, USA

© Duck-Koo Chung and Barry Eichengreen 2004

All rights reserved. No part of this publication may be reproduced, stored in a retrieval system or transmitted in any form or by any means, electronic, mechanical or photocopying, recording, or otherwise without the prior permission of the publisher.

Published by
Edward Elgar Publishing Limited
Glensanda House
Montpellier Parade
Cheltenham
Glos GL50 1UA
UK

Edward Elgar Publishing, Inc.
136 West Street
Suite 202
Northampton
Massachusetts 01060
USA

A catalogue record for this book
is available from the British Library

Library of Congress Cataloguing in Publication Data
The Korean economy beyond the crisis / edited by Duck-Koo Chung, Barry Eichengreen.
    p. cm.
   Papers from an international conference convened in October 2002 by the Research Center for International Finance (RICF) of Seoul National University.
   Includes bibliographical references and index.
   1. Korea (South)–Economic conditions–1960–Congresses. 2. Financial crises–Korea (South)–Congresses. 3. Korea (South)–Economic policy–1960–Congresses. 4. Economic stabilization–Korea (South)–Congresses. I. Chung, Duck-Koo, 1948– II. Eichengreen, Barry J.

HC467.95.K6746 2004
330.95195–dc22

                                                           2003061587

ISBN 1 84376 603 5 (cased)

Typeset by Manton Typesetters, Louth, Lincolnshire, UK.
Printed and bound in Great Britain by MPG Books Ltd, Bodmin, Cornwall.

Contents

List of figures vii
List of tables viii
List of contributors x
Abbreviations xii
Foreword xv

1 Introduction 1
   Barry Eichengreen and Duck-Koo Chung
2 The Korean economy before and after the crisis 25
   Un-Chan Chung
3 What caused the crisis? A *post mortem* 48
   Won-Am Park and Gongpil Choi
   COMMENT *on Chapters 2 and 3* 69
   Ronald I. McKinnon
4 US policy toward the crisis 72
   Young-Kwan Yoon
   COMMENT *on Chapter 4* 87
   Justin Yifu Lin
5 The monetary policy response to the crisis 89
   Dongchul Cho
6 The fiscal policy response to the crisis 113
   Joosung Jun
7 Social impact of the crisis 137
   Joung-Woo Lee
   COMMENT *on Chapters 5, 6 and 7* 159
   Eduardo Borensztein
   COMMENT *on Chapters 5, 6 and 7* 164
   Gordon de Brouwer
8 Financial restructuring 172
   Joon-Ho Hahm
9 Corporate restructuring 194
   Sung Wook Joh

10	Changes in the labor markets and industrial relations	218
	Young-Ki Choi and Dae Il Kim	
	COMMENT *on Chapters 8, 9 and 10*	239
	Stijn Claessens	
	COMMENT *on Chapters 8, 9 and 10*	245
	Mitsuhiro Fukao	
11	Transparency and social capital	248
	Jaeyeol Yee	
12	Social realignment, coalition change and political transformation	267
	Hyun-Chin Lim and Joon Han	
	COMMENT *on Chapters 11 and 12*	286
	Dwight Perkins	
13	Recurrence of financial crises: cross-country patterns and implications for Korea	290
	Kiseok Hong, Jong-Wha Lee and Changyong Rhee	
14	Reform and the risk of recurrence of crisis	317
	In June Kim, Baekin Cha and Chi-Young Song	
	COMMENT *on Chapters 13 and 14*	338
	Masahiro Kawai	

References	344
Index	369

Figures

2.1	Macroeconomic indicators	29
3.1	Exchange market pressure index	60
3.2	Composite index	63
3.3	Conditional probability of crises	64
5.1	Exchange rate and call rate	90
5.2	Determinants of exchange rates and interest rates	93
5.3	Impulse responses from VARs using daily data	99
5.4	Variance decomposition of interest rates and exchange rates	100
5.5	Variables for calibration	104
5.6	Calibration results	106
6.1	Balance of the consolidated central government budget in Korea	116
8.1	The transition in corporate financing patterns	174
8.2	The transition in commercial bank portfolio structure	179
8.3	Indicators of the transition toward a market-based financial system	182
8.4	Pre-provision profit, provisioning and net profit of commercial banks	185
9.1	Accounting performance and capital structure before the crisis	198
9.2	Accounting performance and capital structure after the crisis	200
10.1	Job gains, job losses and net job gains during the crisis	225
10.2	Changes in employment type by firm size, 1997–2000	228
10.3	Percentage changes in wages, by decile, 1997–99	230
10.4	Wage growth vs union share, 1998–99	231
11.1	International comparison based on social typology	254
11.2	Corruption index, selected countries, 1995–2001	262
12.1	Trends in Gini coefficient and ratio of high- and low-income quintile	274

Tables

2.1	Growth factors, Europe and Japan vs Asia	31
2.2	Latent insolvency among firms subject to external audits	38
2.3	Proportion of manufacturing firms with earnings/interest ratios below unity	39
2.4	Changes in internal ownership of the 30 largest *chaebols*	41
2.5	Trends in nonperforming loans	43
3.1	Major economic indicators	51
3.2	Nonperforming loans at financial institutions	53
3.3	Financial indicators for 30 largest *chaebols*	55
3.4	Manufacturing sector statistics	56
3.5	Signals and crises	61
3.6	Performance of indicators	62
3.7	Within- and out-of-sample performance of the indicator model	65
3.8	Estimates of probit model	66
5.1	Summary of previous empirical research	95
6.1	Consolidated central government budget	118
6.2	Medium-term fiscal plan, consolidated central government	119
6.3	Divergences between planned and actual budgets	121
6.4	Government debt and debt guarantees	126
6.5	Interest payments and primary balance	127
6.6	Fiscal burden of restructuring	130
6.7	Liabilities of public pensions, 1998	132
7.1	Characteristics of sample households	139
7.2	Gini coefficients, all households	140
7.3	Size of middle class	142
7.4	Wage gaps before and after the crisis	144
7.5	Wealth inequality according to the existing literature	148
7.6	Inequality of wealth distribution	149
7.7	Distribution of land ownership	151
7.8	Net worth holdings by decile	153
7.9	Indices of social disorder	156
C.1	Autocorrelation and bias in revenue and expenditure forecast errors	168
8.1	Structure of corporate finance	177

Tables

8.2	Consolidation and performance of the commercial banking industry	184
9.1	Determinants of profitability of Korean firms	197
9.2	Output ratios by plant turnover status when size is measured by employees, assets and capital equipment, 1990–98	207
9.3	Review of special auditing, Daewoo-affiliated firms	208
9.4	Performance of the manufacturing sector, 1990–2000	210
9.5	Large *chaebols* under insolvency procedures	211
9.6	International comparison of creditor rights	214
10.1	Distribution of employment	227
10.2	Employment in sectors with strong unions	229
10.3	Indicators of union activity	232
11.1	Relational elements of the social system	249
11.2	Typology of social systems	251
11.3	Correlation of characteristics of social systems	254
12.1	Regional background of Cabinet ministers and vice-ministers, 1963–2000	272
12.2	Class structure in terms of income	274
12.3	Unionization and labor disputes	277
12.4	Votes by region, three presidential elections	280
13.1	Recurrence of crises by country	291
13.2	Macroeconomic variables during the crisis period	295
13.3	Conditional vs unconditional probabilities of crises	299
13.4	Probit estimates	301
13.5	Determinants of recurrence	304
13.6	Principal macroeconomic indicators	307
13.7	External balance	308
13.8	External, financial and corporate sector indicators	310
14.1	Selected indicators for commercial banks	321
14.2	Selected indicators of top 30 *chaebols*	327
14.3	Selected indicators for commercial banks	328
14.4	Profitability of manufacturing sector	329
14.5	Selected macroeconomic indicators	330

Contributors

Eduardo Borensztein, *International Monetary Fund*

Baekin Cha, *Korea Institute of Finance*

Dongchul Cho, *Korea Development Institute*

Young-Ki Choi, *Korea Labor Institute*

Gongpil Choi, *Korea Institute of Finance*

Duck-Koo Chung, *Seoul National University*

Un-Chan Chung, *Seoul National University*

Gordon de Brouwer, *Australian National University*

Stijn Claessens, *University of Amsterdam*

Barry Eichengreen, *University of California, Berkeley*

Mitsuhiro Fukao, *Keio University*

Joon-Ho Hahm, *Yonsei University*

Joon Han, *Yonsei University*

Kiseok Hong, *Ewha University*

Sung Wook Joh, *Korea University*

Joosung Jun, *Ewha University*

Masahiro Kawai, *Ministry of Finance, Japan*

Dae Il Kim, *Seoul National University*

In June Kim, *Seoul National University*

Jong-Wha Lee, *Korea University*

Joung-Woo Lee, *Kyungpook National University*

Hyun-Chin Lim, *Seoul National University*

Justin Yifu Lin, *Peking University*

Ronald I. McKinnon, *Stanford University*

Won-Am Park, *Hongik University*

Dwight Perkins, *Harvard University*

Changyong Rhee, *Seoul National University*

Chi-Young Song, *Kookmin University*

Jaeyol Yee, *Seoul National University*

Young-Kwan Yoon, *Seoul National University*

Abbreviations

ADB	Asian Development Bank
AMC	Asset Management Corporation
AMF	Asian Monetary Fund
APEC	Asia Pacific Economic Cooperation
BIS	Bank for International Settlements
CAMEL	Capital adequacy, Asset quality, Management, Earning and Liquidity
CBO	collateralized bond obligation
CCL	Contingent Credit Line
CES	Consumption Expenditure Survey
CMI	Chiang Mai Initiative
CPI	Consumer Price Index
CRA	Corporate Restructuring Agreement
CRCC	Corporate Restructuring Coordination Committee
CSIP	Capital Structure Improvement Plan
DERI	Daewoo Economic Resources Institute
DIF	Deposit Insurance Fund
EFF	Extended Fund Facility (IMF)
EIS	Employment Insurance System
EMBI	Emerging Market Bond Index
EPB	Economic Planning Board
ESAF	Enhanced Strategic Adjustment Facility
FDI	foreign direct investment
FKTU	Federation of Korean Trade Unions
FLC	forward-looking criteria
FRB	Federal Reserve Board
FSC	Financial Supervisory Commission
FSS	Financial Supervisory Service
GDP	gross domestic product
GKP	Grand Korea Party
GNP	gross domestic product
GRCH	Group Restructuring Coordination Headquarters
HERI	Hyundai Economic Research Institute
HLI	highly leveraged institution

xii

IBRD	International Bank for Reconstruction and Development
ICOR	incremental capital–output ratio
IFI	international financial institution
IMF	International Monetary Fund
ITC	investment trust company
KAMCO	Korea Asset Management Corporation
KCTU	Korean Confederation of Trade Unions
KDI	Korean Development Institute
KDIC	Korea Deposit Insurance Corporation
KICAC	Korea Independent Commission Against Corruption
KSSC	Korea Social Science Council
LIBOR	London Inter-bank Offered Rate
LPP	Livelihood Protection Program
M&As	mergers and acquisitions
MCI	monetary conditions index
MNC	multinational corporation
MOF	Ministry of Finance
MOFE	Ministry of Finance and Economy
NBFI	nonbank financial institution
NCNP	National Congress for New Politics
NIC	newly industrializing country
NMDP	New Millennium Democratic Party
NPL	nonperforming loan
NPS	National Pension Scheme
OECD	Organisation for Economic Co-operation and Development
OPEC	Organization of Petroleum-exporting Countries
P&A	purchase and assumption
PCA	prompt corrective action
PSI	private sector involvement
PVRP	proportional voting rights premium
RCIF	Research Center for International Finance (Seoul National University)
REER	real effective exchange rate
REIT	real estate investment trust
ROA	return on assets
ROE	return on equity
ROSCs	Reports of Standards and Codes
SAF	Structural Adjustment Facility (IMF)
SBA	Stand-by Arrangement (IMF)
SMEs	small- and medium-sized enterprises
SRF	Supplementary Reserve Facility (IMF)
SVAR	structural vector autoregression

TFP	total factor productivity
TLP	Temporary Livelihood Program
UHIES	Urban Household Income and Expenditure Survey
ULD	United Liberal Democrat (party)
VAR	vector autoregression
VAT	value added tax
WTO	World Trade Organization

Foreword

The winter of December 1997 was very cold in Korea. Chill winds seemed to blow directly out of Siberia, extinguishing everything that Korea had achieved economically in the course of preceding decades. The praise that the world once lavished on the country turned to derision. The new mood was encapsulated in the aloof gestures of the managing director of the International Monetary Fund, Michel Camdessus, as he laid out the conditions attached to the disbursement of emergency assistance. The volatility of international financial markets and the political uncertainty surrounding Korea's upcoming presidential election did not help to stabilize the already precarious situation. Capital took flight, the ratings of Korea's sovereign debt were cut, and the country found itself facing its gravest challenge since the Korean War.

The subsequent crisis reverberated throughout Korean society. Merely securing lines of credit did not suffice to stabilize the market. Korea inexorably headed into painful corporate and financial restructuring. Bankruptcies soared, paralyzing business activity and triggering job losses. With the corporate sector straining under an enormous debt burden, the high interest rates and fiscal austerity seen as necessary for restoring confidence transformed the shock from a liquidity shortage into a major credit crunch.

Although more than five years have passed since the onset of the crisis, important questions remain about its implications. In an effort to answer them, in October 2002 the Research Center for International Finance (RCIF) of Seoul National University convened an international conference bringing together experts from Korea and a variety of other countries. The results of their discussions can be found within the covers of this book.

My sincere gratitude goes to my co-editor Professor Barry Eichengreen of the University of California and my collaborator Dr Gongpil Choi of the Korean Institute of Finance, whose exhaustive efforts made possible the publication of this volume. In addition, this work would not have been possible without the steadfast contributions of Dr Shin Dongjin, Dr Lee Sangche, Mrs Jae Jung Im, and my faithful research assistants.

Duck-Koo Chung
President, RCIF
Seoul National University

1. Introduction

Barry Eichengreen and Duck-Koo Chung

Of all the countries to fall prey to the Asian financial crisis, South Korea was the most unexpected. Korea was an industrial and export powerhouse, by some measures the eleventh largest economy and twelfth largest exporter in the world.[1] It was one of the world's leading producers of semiconductors and computer disk drives. Its economic coming of age was acknowledged in 1996 by its admission to the Organisation for Economic Co-operation and Development (OECD), the club of high-income countries. That a country that had moved so far in the direction of economic maturity could be brought to its knees by a financial crisis pointed up doubts about the viability of the 'Asian model' of economic development and the 'Washington consensus' of economic and financial liberalization – or at least about their compatibility with one another.

The impact of the crisis was profound. This refers not simply to the sharp drop in output and the alarming rise in poverty and unemployment that occurred as events unfolded. At a deeper level the crisis provoked far-reaching changes in Korean economy and society. The Korean financial system was fundamentally reshaped by merger, consolidation and closure. A number of the country's leading industrial conglomerates were dismantled, and their viable lines of business were spun off to other companies. There was a transformation of Korean society, reflected in deepening class divides and a weakened labor movement.

Five years after the onset of the crisis, the Korean economy is recovering robustly. Growth is running in excess of 5 percent per annum, not far below the 'miracle' rates of the pre-crisis era.[2] Now the problem for the Korean authorities is not a weak exchange rate but an excessively strong one, as investable funds, attracted by what is once more an admirable record of economic performance, flood into the country.

This book is an attempt to better understand these three stages of the Korean crisis: the onset, the policy reaction, and the economic response. The goal, in a nutshell, is to explain how South Korea succumbed to the crisis, how it coped, and how it recovered.

THE HISTORICAL CONTEXT

Answers to these questions can only be framed by placing Korean economic development in its historical context. As late as 1960, South Korea was a heavily agrarian, desperately impoverished economy, most of whose residents lived close to the margin of subsistence. The country had little arable land, high population density and few natural resources. Still recovering from the effects of civil war and foreign military involvement, the South never felt entirely secure from the threat of renewed attack from the North.

Under these circumstances, growth naturally came to be viewed as a vehicle for achieving economic and geopolitical security. Not only might growth raise Koreans out of the mire of poverty and destitution, but a stronger economy would give the country the capacity to deter aggression from abroad. Hence, a government that delivered growth could count on the support, or at least the acquiescence, of large segments of Korean society. This was an important source of political legitimacy in a country where normal transfers of power were rare.

In attempting to jump-start the process of growth, successive Korean governments, staring with the Park Chung-hee government that took power in 1961, capitalized on the 'advantages of economic backwardness' (in the famous phrase of Alexander Gerschenkron, 1962). Officials encouraged companies to acquire proven technologies from abroad, mainly by importing the capital goods that embodied foreign science and techniques.[3] They pushed saving and investment to high levels, encouraging the capital formation needed to accelerate the process of technology transfer. They kept wages and exchange rates low in order to encourage exports, thereby capitalizing on the country's geographical proximity to Japan and its political proximity to the United States.[4] They espoused the 'ideology of growth,' another of Gerschenkron's concepts, uniting society behind the push for industrialization.

In initiatives that turned out to have important implications for the long term, officials encouraged the development of institutional substitutes for the missing prerequisites for growth.[5] The main institutional substitutes were the *chaebols*, the banks, and the government itself. The *chaebols*, Korea's closely held and widely diversified industrial conglomerates, substituted for the weakness of markets and contracts, internalizing transactions that were difficult to carry out at arm's length. The banks substituted for underdeveloped financial markets, cultivating connections with the *chaebols* and helping them to secure the funding essential for their expansion and development. The government orchestrated the process, deploying selective subsidies and import drawbacks to promote exports and using financial regulation to channel Koreans' savings to the banks, establishing public financial institutions to make loans for large-scale industrial projects, and instructing private financial institutions to extend such loans on a preferential basis. It applied special depreciation schedules to imported capital goods and encouraged the organization of unions within a centralized system designed to facilitate government control, secure labor peace, maintain competitiveness, and ensure high investment.[6] It encouraged the creation of general trading firms along Japanese lines.[7]

This model served Korea well for many years. Growth averaged more than 7 percent per annum between the early 1960s and early 1990s. Real GDP per capita at international prices rose ten-fold, from less than $1000 at the end of the 1950s to more than $7000 at the beginning of the 1990s. The share of exports in output rose from less than 3 percent to nearly a third. Savings rates rose from the negligible levels characteristic of a subsistence economy to nearly 40 percent. In this light, it is not hard to understand why the prevailing policies commanded support.

Why this model worked is no mystery. It suited the circumstances of the time. Korea was still at the stage of extensive growth, when the main challenge was to import and deploy foreign technologies – to do known things in known ways. In these circumstances, there was little cost to centralizing decision making in the hands of a few industry leaders and government bureaucrats.[8] Centralization and bureaucratic direction may not have been conducive to innovation – to pioneering products and processes not yet developed and implemented abroad – but innovation was not the issue; emulation was. Similarly, in a period when Korea was concentrating on heavy industries characterized by strong economies of scale, the *chaebol* system, which encouraged large firms at the expense of small enterprises, had more benefits than costs. The concentration and scale of industrial enterprise may not have been conducive to flexibility, but flexibility was not at a premium.[9] A tightly regulated and controlled banking system that channeled funds to industry underwrote the capital formation that was the vehicle for technology transfer and the engine of extensive growth. The government's influence over bank lending may not have encouraged a culture of arm's-length transactions, but this mattered little so long as both international and domestic financial markets and transactions were tightly regulated and repressed, appropriately for a period when the main task of financial markets was to mobilize resources for capital formation, not to help choose among alternative investment projects or provide corporate governance services.

With time, Korea, like other 'latecomers' before it, began to show signs of graduating from the stage of extensive growth. Having exhausted the opportunities for growth through catch-up, it sought to move up the ladder into the production of more technologically sophisticated goods. Innovation and flexibility began to figure more importantly in the growth equation. Meanwhile, workers, having shown restraint for years, grew impatient with the government's low wage strategy. There was an explosion of union militancy coincident with political liberalization in the second half of the 1980s; it became apparent that the low wage strategy would have to be abandoned and that production would have to be reoriented away from exports in favor of domestic demand.[10] With indications that savings would not remain high forever, as households sought to satisfy pent-up consumption demands, banks began to look abroad for funding, encouraging the government to contemplate the selective liberalization of international financial transactions.

By the early 1990s it was clear that a fundamental reorientation of the Korean economy was underway, away from heavy industry and toward high technology, away from brute force investment and toward innovation, away from exports and toward domestic demand, away from strict government direction of transactions and toward market liberalization. Yet resistance to this reorientation was strong. *Chaebol* owners were reluctant to give up concessionary finance. Banks were reluctant to give up their close ties to the planning bureaucracy. Bureaucrats and ministers were reluctant to relinquish the levers of control from which flowed their power and prestige.

Economic and social institutions are networks of interlocking relations. It is hard to change any one component so long as the others remain in place. Thus, it was hard to limit government influence over the banks so long as the *chaebols*, not to mention government officials themselves, strongly preferred the status quo. It was hard to counteract the dominance of the *chaebols* so long as the banks, having long-standing relationships with their largest customers, preferred the prevailing state of affairs. Given what President Kim himself referred to as 'the collusive intimacy between business and government,' it was all but inevitable that the evolution of the country's institutions would lag the evolution of economic conditions.[11]

At the deepest level, it was this tension between institutional inheritance and current economic circumstance that was at the root of the crisis. Having exhausted the scope for growth through catch-up, Korea needed to move toward a more flexible, innovation-friendly economic model. Yet its *chaebol*-, bank- and government-centered arrangements remained in locked in place, placing the prospects for continued growth at risk. It was this tension that set the stage for the crisis that erupted at the end of 1997.

THE CRISIS

But why in 1997, and not earlier, or, for that matter, later? And why in the context of the Asian crisis?

Indeed, some observers would insist that there were no flaws in the Korean model as it existed in the early 1990s – that the only mistake was to abandon some of the tenets of that model, notably the tight regulation of financial markets. The crisis, in this view, was simply an investor panic made possible by the decision to open Korean financial markets to international transactions. These initiatives allowed foreign money to first flow in and then be jerked back out when investors, perturbed by events in neighboring Thailand and Indonesia, lost their composure. The speed with which Korea recovered from the crisis once financial stability was restored is cited, in some circles, as confirmation of the validity of this interpretation.

An element of panic there undoubtedly was, but it is not the entire story. A more complete rendition would focus also on the mismatch between domestic financial development and international financial liberalization and on its role in the timing and shape of events. It was hardly coincidental that Korea began liberalizing the capital account hesitantly and unevenly in the early 1990s. With the model of extensive growth losing steam, it was necessary to devote progressively more resources to capital formation to keep the momentum going, and to achieve this by encouraging the banks to finance the *chaebols'* expansion into ever additional lines of business. Partially opening the capital account, starting with authorization to borrow abroad to finance capital goods imports in 1993, gave the financial sector additional resources with which to fund the activities of Korea's large corporations, putting off the day of reckoning.[12]

This pattern was not unique to Korea; it was a more general Asian response to the declining marginal productivity of capital and the increasing feebleness of the model of extensive growth. But the effects were accentuated by the extreme version of the model pursued in Korea, which placed an extraordinary premium on capital formation. According to the estimates of Hong (1981) and D. Cho and Koh (1996), the marginal productivity of capital declined from 35 percent in the 1960s to 25 percent in the early 1970s and less than 10 percent on the eve of the crisis.[13]

Because the elasticity of output with respect to capital is only on the order of a third to a quarter, this decline did not show up in the short run in an alarming decline in the rate of growth. Moreover, the decline in the marginal productivity of capital led officials to respond with policies designed to throw more investment at the growth problem. These still higher investment rates explain how a declining marginal productivity of capital, weak profitability and mounting financial problems could coexist with a seemingly impressive growth rate, observations which some economists have found difficult to reconcile and which have led them to some rather convoluted explanations for the Korean crisis.

Between 1994 and 1996, investment as a share of GDP rose by a further two percentage points, this despite the fact that domestic savings declined. The additional finance had to come from somewhere; hence, the authorities gave the banks access to offshore funding. Thus, the additional investment was financed by foreign borrowing. This was reflected in the current account deficit, which widened from 2 to 5 percent of national income, a level not reached since the crisis of 1980.[14] The current account deficit was financed by borrowing by the domestic financial sector, borrowing which rose by more than five percentage points of GDP over the same period. The banks were able to access such large amounts of external funding, if at short tenors, because their creditworthiness was seemingly secured by government guarantees.

So long as foreign capital flowed in, the economy's high rates of investment-led growth could be sustained. It could be denied that there were problems below the surface. But further increasing the capital intensity of an economy where the rate of return on capital had already fallen below international standards only compounded the fundamental problem.[15] Much of the additional investment flowed into sectors such as semiconductors where there already was excess capacity and productivity was low. Local observers were not oblivious to the problem; the stock market had been trending downward since 1996. This reflected disappointing rates of return on equity; for the 30 largest *chaebols*, rates of return had fallen from more than 10 percent in the mid-1980s to less than 6 percent in the early 1990s, and to less than 3 percent in 1996.[16] For the time being, foreign lenders had other things on their minds. But if they suddenly focused on the problem and capital flows turned around, as happened when the crisis erupted in Thailand and spilled over unexpectedly to Indonesia, the entire house of cards could come crashing down.[17]

There was pressure for international financial liberalization, to be sure, from the US Treasury and International Monetary Fund (IMF). Capital account convertibility was an obligation of South Korea as a newly minted member of the OECD.[18] But liberalization could have been phased in more gradually and sequenced more carefully. External pressures and constraints did not force the Korean authorities to free the banks' access to offshore funding while continuing to strictly control foreign access to Korean stock and bond markets and to limit inward FDI.[19] They did not dictate continuing to restrict Korean corporations' issuance of long-term debt and equity while at the same time allowing them to borrow abroad via the banks, thereby heightening their dependence on volatile foreign currency funding. In fact, discouraging the development of long-term debt and equity markets was important for maintaining the dependence of corporations on bank finance, where the banks were the lever with which government influenced the allocation of resources. In other words, it was the internal logic of the Korean model, and its growing strains as the scope for extensive growth was exhausted, that encouraged the authorities to liberalize the international accounts as they did. In turn, those actions largely explain the timing of the crisis – how it was put off for so long, and why it erupted when it did.[20]

The same mismatch between domestic financial development and international financial liberalization also explains why the fallout was so severe. With the banking sector heavily concentrated and sheltered from foreign competition, market discipline was limited. The banks, while privatized, had not yet shed the legacy of years of government involvement. They still took direction from the authorities on what products to sell and what priorities to set. Bank staff enjoyed guarantees of lifetime employment, mirroring the guarantee against failure that the banks themselves presumptively enjoyed as the quid pro quo for accepting the authorities' administrative guidance.

Believing that failure was not in the cards, the banks assumed heavy risks. They aggressively sought offshore funding, relying on short-term loans denominated in foreign currency. They did not keep on hand the dollar liquidity needed to repay their foreign-currency-denominated liabilities. They made illiquid loans to industry and held concentrated portfolios dominated by claims on a few *chaebols* without holding additional reserves against nondiversified risk.[21] They favored the politically connected – and the *chaebols* in particular – with preferential credit access. They did not do rigorous credit analysis or undertake careful loan reviews, relying instead on loans secured by physical assets, cross guarantees, and the word of corporate chairmen and directors.

The regulators did little to discourage this behavior. They did not demand rigorous credit analysis, loan classification, or provisioning. They did not require the banks to adopt international accounting and disclosure standards. They ignored evidence of excessive portfolio concentrations and risk taking.[22] They did not publish realistic, up-to-date figures on the extent of nonperforming loans. The government, for its part, limited the flexibility of the won, encouraging the perception that the exchange risk associated with dollar lending was minimal and inducing foreign banks to extend dollar credits to their Korean counterparts. There was the perception that the authorities were prepared to support them in the event of difficulties; this was the now-notorious problem of implicit guarantees.[23]

But it was not as if bank owners and regulators knew less than their counterparts in other countries about how to manage risks and supervise financial institutions.[24] Korean regulators were familiar with the Capital Adequacy Standards of the Basel Committee of Banking Supervisors and the CAMEL (Capital adequacy, Asset quality, Management, Earning and Liquidity) system devised by US regulators. The problem was not ignorance but the fact that relying on the banks to channel finance from households and, increasingly, foreign banks to Korean industry was seen as an integral and indispensable to the Korean growth model.[25] Even after the commercial banks were privatized in the mid-1990s, policy loans still accounted for nearly 20 percent of commercial bank lending, with window guidance presumably dictating the allocation of much of the rest.[26] The care and feeding of the *chaebols* required the continued support of the financial system. To suppress this one component of the mechanism without dismantling the rest would put the entire process at risk.

Banks are fragile, given that they operate in the information-impacted part of the economy and have maturity mismatches on their balance sheets. Because banks, securities markets and corporations are tightly linked, a banking crisis can disrupt the operation of the financial system and the entire economy. Problems in individual banks create problems for other banks, precipitating runs and cascading defaults and making the tangle of banking sector difficulties, once allowed to arise, immensely difficult to unravel.[27]

Thus, once the crisis erupted in Thailand and Indonesia, creating doubts about Korea's financial situation, foreign financial institutions refused to roll over their claims. The share of foreign loans rolled over fell from roughly 80 percent in October to 50 percent in November and 30 percent in December 1997.[28] The Bank of Korea pumped dollar liquidity into the system but found its reserves, even with replenishment by the IMF, inadequate to meet the needs of the banks. Interbank rates soared, and by late December the authorities found themselves having to choose between widespread failures of banks unable to meet their foreign obligations, uncontrolled depreciation of the won, and default by a government that assumed responsibility for the banks' liabilities.

Is the suggestion, then, that had Korea not liberalized its capital account while maintaining a heavy state presence in all financial transactions, the economy would have prospered? There is every indication that the maintenance of tight restrictions on capital account transactions, *à la* China or even Malaysia, would have insulated the economy from the financial crisis in the winter of 1997–98. After all, both of these countries avoided the worst financial aspects of the crisis. In particular, had there been no relaxation of the capital account restrictions that traditionally prevented Korean banks from borrowing offshore, there would have been no 90-day bank loans to roll over.

But keeping the capital account closed while maintaining a heavy state presence, not merely in the financial sector but the economy as a whole, would not have solved the country's deeper problems. Absent structural changes to encourage innovation and enhance flexibility, the marginal product of capital would have continued to fall. Growth rates would have continued to slow. Sooner or later, the poor profitability of industrial lending would have created mounting problems in bank balance sheets. Just as the banks were compelled by the government in the spring of 1997 not to force the liquidation of two troubled *chaebols* (Sammi and Jinro), they would have been forced to exercise yet additional forbearance as one *chaebol* after another experienced financial difficulties. Bank portfolios would have weakened further; bank earnings would have continued to decline. To put it another way, because the banks were the instruments of the government's industrial policy, an industrial policy encountering diminishing returns would have eventually created serious financial problems.[29]

The cost of recapitalizing the banks would then have punched a hole in the fiscal accounts, hobbling the public sector. Perhaps most importantly, there would have been nothing to ensure that the same problem would not recur. The Korean economy would still have had to be restructured sooner or later.

Would the situation have become untenable earlier or later in the absence of capital account liberalization? Initially, selective capital account opening allowed the *chaebols* to sustain higher rates of investment than would have been possible otherwise, in turn allowing the economy to run higher rates of growth. If the capital account had remained closed, this would have been harder. Growth would have been correspondingly slower. Perhaps a crisis – albeit a crisis of a different sort – would have erupted earlier. On the other hand, had the capital account remained closed, Korea would have been better protected from the Asian flu. Had the country been able to stagger on into 1997, with lower investment rates and slower growth but no other changes in its economic structure, it might have been able to stagger on for several additional years, given its insulation from financial turbulence elsewhere in Asia. In this scenario, the crisis would have occurred later. Later or earlier? No doubt debates over the appropriate counterfactual will occupy economists and economic historians for many years.

THE RESPONSE

The controversy over the response to the crisis centers on the stabilization program adopted under IMF auspices. It has been argued that the sharp interest rate hikes insisted on by the Fund with the goal of stemming reserve losses and restoring confidence among international investors were strongly destabilizing. Korea was special, the argument runs, because the country's corporations were so highly leveraged.[30] Interest payments as a share of business costs were three times as high as in the United States, and operating income before taxes was a scant 35 percent greater than debt service obligations. Since more than two-thirds of corporate debt was short term, higher interest rates pushed this last ratio down; they rendered many heavily indebted firms technically insolvent, dimming the short-term prospects for the economy and perversely encouraging foreign investors to get out. The fiscal cuts programmed by the Fund, it is further argued, depressed demand and therefore corporate profitability. They were superfluous, or so it is suggested, in a country that entered its crisis with a balanced budget and in which inflationary pressures were subdued. Moreover, the Fund waited too long to orchestrate negotiations with the foreign banks, rather than hoping that having large amounts of official money on offer would induce the banks individually to extend their loans.

In assessing the IMF program and the government's stance, it is again important to recall the context. The Korean crisis was unexpected; no one anticipated that the financial whirlwind would spread from Thailand and Indonesia. And when the storm blew up, it did so with exceptional speed, leaving scant time to craft the details of a stabilization program. An election was coming (on 18 December), and there was no clear front-runner. All that was certain was that there would be an extended interregnum between the election and installation of the new president. All three candidates had repeatedly declared that under no circumstances would they approach the IMF. This meant that the authorities were ill prepared to negotiate the details of a Fund program.

In the event, the program negotiated over the last week of November provided unprecedented amounts of financial support.[31] After initially expressing skepticism about its provisions, all three presidential candidates agreed to adhere to the IMF's recommendations. In its Letter of Intent to the Fund, the government agreed to raise interest rates and to maintain them at as high a level as needed to stabilize markets. The overnight call rate was immediately increased to 25 percent and raised again to 30 percent on 24 December after the initial increase failed to stem the tide. Corporate bond rates quickly rose to a matching 30 percent. The Fund calculated that slower growth would increase the budget deficit by 0.8 percent of GDP and that service on the additional government debt that would have to be issued to pay for recapitalization of the banking system would cost about the same again; it therefore programmed a 1.5 percent of GDP fiscal tightening for 1998, to be distributed evenly between tax increases and expenditure cuts.

This fiscal arithmetic was the instinctual reaction of Fund staff functioning under intense pressure of time. Given a few months to reflect, the Fund acknowledged that fiscal contraction in these circumstances was overkill. The Korean government had little debt (contingent liabilities notwithstanding), and its financial accounts were already in surplus when the balance in the social security funds was taken into account. In its 7 February 1998 revision of the Letter of Intent the IMF therefore agreed to additional social spending and a budget deficit of approximately 1 percent of GDP. In the second half of the year, with the economy clearly beginning to recover, the IMF relaxed its monetary and fiscal conditions further, and the government passed a supplementary budget.[32]

Whether a less stringent monetary policy would have been more effective remains controversial. Lower interest rates would have meant less pain for

Korea's highly leveraged *chaebols*; fewer corporations would have been thrust into bankruptcy, other things equal. But other things almost certainly would not have been equal; lower interest rates would have also meant a weaker exchange rate, since lower short-term returns would have given investors less compensation for staying in the country.[33] In particular, had the Korean government insisted on significantly lower interest rates, it would have found it more difficult to reach an agreement with foreign banks to roll over their maturing loans.[34] Some *chaebols* might have been spared, but the government would have been forced to default on the bank debts for which it had assumed responsibility. And default was something that the government, concerned to preserve its international good standing, was most anxious to avoid. The critics can argue that its objectives should have been different, but the high interest rate policy was consistent with the Korean government's own priorities.

Before long, interest rates began coming down, not as soon as the IMF had anticipated, perhaps, but in any case by the middle of 1998. By June they were again below pre-crisis levels. Industrial production fell by 15 percent over the first half of 1998 (on a seasonally adjusted basis) but was again running at pre-crisis rates by the end of the year. (By the end of 1999 it had reached 140 percent of those levels.) The exchange rate, having plummeted from 800 to 1800 to the dollar, recovered to 1100. All this provides some *ex post* justification for the monetary policy actions actually taken.

More controversial still were the long lists of microeconomic and structural conditions attached to the successive Letters of Intent. These specified, among other things, that the central bank would be made independent, that the country would adopt international accounting standards, that the *chaebols* would drop their traditional system of cross-subsidies and loan guarantees, and that domestic capital and motor vehicle markets would be opened up to foreign competition. These conditions have been criticized for emphasizing Korea's structural problems at a time when the priority should have been to restore confidence by talking up the economy's strengths. They have been criticized for doing more to delay than encourage structural reform by 'weakening ownership' – that is, for fostering the impression that these structural changes were being forced on the country from outside and thereby fueling popular resistance to change. They have been criticized for pandering to foreign interests, notably the interest of the US government in opening the Korean economy to foreign banks and producers. And they have been criticized for foisting on Korea one-size-fits-all advice – that is, for overlooking the fundamental strengths of the Korean model while attempting to remake the economy along Anglo-Saxon lines.

It is not hard to raise questions about particular conditions attached to the Letter of Intent. That the economy bounced back quickly from the crisis is no proof of the efficacy of the IMF's conditions; this could have instead reflected Korean society's heightened sense of solidarity in times of crisis, or the intrinsic strengths of the Korean economy. But to focus on the IMF's recommendations rather than the policies of the Korean government itself is, in any case, to lose sight of the point. It is not as if the government strongly opposed the IMF's recommendations. To the contrary, many government officials had already grown convinced of the need for far-reaching changes to prepare the country for the twenty-first century. It was Korean officials themselves who insisted on adding to the Letter of Intent conditions related to labor market reform, such as changes in regulation to permit layoffs and facilitate restructuring (Cumings, 1999). The newly elected president, Kim Dae Jung, was a long-standing critic of his country's *chaebol-* and bank-centered economic system, which he now sought to restructure root and branch.[35] The crisis was not welcome but, coinciding with Kim's electoral victory, it provided a window for implementing far-reaching structural and microeconomic reforms. It shattered the cozy system of mutual support that had held the Korean model in place, allowing the government to systematically address major problems in the banking and corporate sectors.

REFORM AND RECOVERY

Thus the lesson that the government drew from the crisis was the need to encourage flexibility, transparency and market discipline. The events of 1998 offered an extraordinary opportunity to advance that agenda. But doing so required surmounting the obstacles posed by the country's immediate financial difficulties. Perhaps 40 percent of Korean firms, including a number of the largest *chaebols*, had been rendered insolvent. Loan losses had destroyed the operating capital of many banks.[36] The question was whether the steps needed in the short run to get banks and firms back on their feet would be compatible with the fundamental reorganization of the Korean economy.

It proved easiest to push through changes in the structure of the financial sector, in part because the banks had long been under implicit or explicit government control. Central bank independence was buttressed. Statutes and regulations governing foreign bank ownership were liberalized. Prudential rules governing loan classification, provisioning, connected lending, short-term foreign borrowing and foreign currency exposures were tightened, and responsibility for supervision and regulation was consolidated in a single independent agency. Insolvent banks and nonbank financial institutions were nationalized, merged, or closed. And, to limit the economy's dependence on the banks, the authorities pursued initiatives to promote the development of domestic securities markets, introducing competitive bidding on initial offerings in the government bond market and promoting a futures market in bonds.

Most visibly, two of the largest commercial banks, Korea First Bank and Seoul Bank, were taken over by the government in December 1997, and six months later five smaller banks were closed. Within two years, the number of commercial banks had fallen by a third. Ten merchant banks were shut down in January 1998. Banks with liquidity problems were required to submit rehabilitation plans before being recapitalized; by the end of 2001 the government had injected 155 trillion won into distressed financial institutions (the equivalent of roughly 25 percent of GNP), mainly as a result of purchases of impaired assets. Nonperforming loans on the books fell to less than 4 percent of outstanding loans in 2001, down from 14 percent in 1998. In 2001 Korean banks returned to profitability for the first time in four years.[37]

Corporate reform was harder. Whereas banks were in the business of lending, the *chaebols* were involved in a myriad of activities. The authorities sought to address the complications by encouraging a series of 'Big Deals,' in which the *chaebols* swapped subsidiaries with the goal of eliminating excessive diversification and concentrating on their core competencies.[38] However, this addressed the symptom – inefficient scale and scope – rather than the fundamental problem – weak corporate governance that allowed managers to pursue size at the expense of shareholder value. The government sought to limit size by limiting indebtedness – specifically, by capping permissible debt/equity ratios – but limits on borrowing meant limits on investment, which threatened the recovery of industrial production. The *chaebols* being larger employers than the banks, initiatives to encourage restructuring that also slowed their recovery were resisted for their undesirable employment consequences.

And, more than the banks, the *chaebols* were still countervailing centers of political power. In many cases, they emerged from the crisis still under the control of their founding families.[39] The political influence of entrenched ownership made it difficult for the government to close down insolvent firms, replace management and strengthen the rights of outside shareholders. Not that the authorities didn't try, but progress occurred in fits and starts. The path of least resistance was first to restructure the financial sector, where government rather than family control prevailed, and then to use the reformed financial system to further the authorities' efforts to restructure the corporate sector.

This was why the authorities sought to rein in the *chaebols* by limiting their leverage. They adopted a target for debt/equity ratios of 200 percent, to be achieved by the end of 1999, and instructed the banks to adapt their lending practices accordingly. The dilemma, as noted, was that limiting borrowing meant limiting investment and thus slowing the recovery of employment. Since many Korean corporations already had high debt/equity ratios, a uniform ceiling imputed the same shadow price of finance to all producers, something that was not easily reconciled with market principles.

Ultimately, the market mechanism will determine the availability of credit to Korean firms only if the banks rely on their own calculations of profitability, not on government guidelines. The regulators therefore pressed the banks to undertake credit reviews and to limit the provision of additional external funding to firms with dubious repayment prospects – that is, to lend on economic criteria. But the banks, while under pressure from supervisors, felt pressure from corporates as well, particularly from distressed *chaebols* using debt to gamble for redemption.[40] Large borrowers were also able to substitute nonbank for bank credit, shifting their demands to investment trust companies over which they themselves had control.[41] Daewoo is a case in point: the company was able to significantly increase its borrowing in 1998 despite its dubious financial condition. Reflecting these pressures, bank reviews of 298 companies completed in 2000 identified just 50 companies whose credit should not be rolled over and which would therefore have to be sold, merged or liquidated.[42] Subsequent reviews of an additional 1100 or so companies, conducted under the auspices of the Financial Supervisory Service, added to this list fewer than 300 more firms. As of mid-2001, more than 20 percent of all bank loans were still to companies with negative earnings.[43] Concern that large companies were continuing to absorb a disproportionate share of bank credit then led the government to pressure the banks to roll over their loans to small and medium-sized firms and to establish a corporate restructuring fund and a public venture capital fund to extend concessionary finance to small enterprises.

Outside directors and shareholders are the other stakeholders with an interest in restructuring. In 1998, the Korean stock exchange required all publicly traded companies to have at least one outside director and by the end of 1999 to draw a quarter of its directors from outside.[44] The government strengthened the rights of minority shareholders, making it easier for them to inspect the company's books, file lawsuits, and table proposals at general shareholders' meetings.[45] It lifted limits on the voting rights of institutional investors with the goal of increasing the likelihood that management that failed to maximize shareholder value would be replaced.[46]

Accounting and reporting reforms have meanwhile made it easier for outside investors to determine what goes on inside the Korean corporation. Firms were required to adopt international accounting principles and standards in October 1998 and, starting in 1999, to produce consolidated financial statements that net out intra-group transactions and are audited by independent accountants. Transparency has been further enhanced by measures limiting cross-shareholdings to 25 percent of equity. While implementation of these measures remains uneven, the same can be said of other countries (including the United States, given what we have learned from Enron).

How should we evaluate the progress?[47] Corporate debt/equity ratios have fallen from 3.96 before the crisis to 2.11 at the end of 2000. Hyundai's break-up into several groups is proceeding.[48] Kia was sold to Hyundai. Samsung Motors was sold to Renault, a step that would have been almost inconceivable before the crisis. Following repeated delays, several Daewoo affiliates were finally split off or placed in receivership. The top *chaebols* have significantly reduced the number of their subsidiaries. Foreigners have raised their stake in companies listed on the Korean stock exchange from 13 percent in 1996 to 30 percent in 2001.

But not a few *chaebols* remain financially weak. As of the end of 2001, nearly a third of the top 30 conglomerates were in some form of workout.[49] A number of the top 30 continue to report negative returns on equity. More broadly, interest coverage (the ratio of operating profit to interest expense) has risen from barely unity in 1998 and 1999 to 1.6 in 2000 and 1.7 in 2001.[50] But as many as a third of manufacturing firms are still unable to meet their interest obligations, much less to repay principal, and remain dependent on the willingness of the banks to roll over their loans.[51]

That large parts of the Korean corporate sector have not yet returned to profitability reflects the severity of earlier difficulties, both the depth of the recession and the overhang of nonviable debt, which remains difficult to clear away. Post-1997 reforms placed tighter deadlines on court-supervised reorganizations and established a specialized bankruptcy court in Seoul. But the system remains overloaded, and companies still have as long as 18 months to submit and accept reorganization plans. The courts have limited ability to impose such plans on creditors seeking to block reorganization agreements or pressing for liquidation in their quest for a larger share of the enterprise's assets.[52] Cross-shareholdings continue to limit the scope for hostile takeovers. Even after seizing control, bank creditors remain reluctant to systematically restructure problem companies for fear of realizing additional losses.

Completing the picture requires observing that the uneven progress of reform has not obviously impeded the recovery of the economy. Growth rates have decelerated from the turbocharged 10 percent rate achieved in 1999–2000, when Korea bounced back from the crisis, but remain impressive even in the face of a global slowdown. Two indications are the fact that Korea had the best performing stock market in the industrial world in 2001 and that the government completed repayment of its IMF loan in August 2001, three years ahead of schedule. The country received an extraordinary double upgrade from the rating agencies in 2001 and graduated from the Emerging Market Bond Index (EMBI) in 2002.

The pace and character of structural reform are the key issues going forward. Korea is attempting to move to a more decentralized, atomistic corporate sector, a more competitive, market-based financial sector, a more flexible labor market, and a less interventionist public sector. It is too early to tell whether this is the right model for the post-crisis economy. And the question remains of whether, given Korea's historical experience and its deep-seated political and economic legacy, the goal is in fact achievable, or whether the country will eventually have to grope toward another, different development model. It seems safe to say that we have not yet seen the shape of the Korean economy in the twenty-first century.

A SYNOPSIS OF WHAT FOLLOWS

These are the questions taken up by the contributors to this volume. In Chapter 2, Un-Chan Chung provides an overview of the Korean economy before and after the crisis. Chung focuses on what is in a sense the key analytical issue, namely, how structural weakness could have coexisted with an extraordinary record of macroeconomic success. His answer emphasizes weak corporate governance and implicit government support that allowed the *chaebols* to maximize growth rather than profitability and shareholder value, and the deficient loan screening and allocation practices of financial institutions, which sustained growth in the face of mounting economic and financial strains. Chapter 3 by Won-Am Park and Gongpil Choi analyzes the consequences using the now conventional 'second generation' model of financial crises. The authors show that attempts to interpret the crisis purely in terms of flawed fundamentals or investor panic are too simple; rather, one needs a model with roles for both. Specifically, deteriorating fundamentals (in particular, slowing growth and mounting financial fragility, which were inevitable corollaries of the Korean model) moved the economy into a zone of vulnerability where a loss of investor confidence, brought about by events in Thailand and Indonesia, could lead to a debt run and to the rapid depletion of international reserves, precipitating a crisis that the authorities lacked the capacity to withstand.

The chapters that follow assess the macro policy reaction. Chapter 4 by Young-Kwan Yoon focuses on the US policy response. International assistance for Korea came mainly from the IMF but at the insistence of the US government, which is the Fund's largest shareholder. The US first torpedoed the Japanese proposal for an Asian Monetary Fund and the idea of unconditional bilateral support. It then pressed the IMF to come to Korea's aid when its crisis threatened the global financial system. And it took the lead in organizing negotiations with US, Japanese and European banks in the critical last week of December 1997. Yoon argues, contrary to conventional wisdom, that security considerations did not decisively influence the US decision. It was the perceived threat to the international financial system and fears of how an even deeper crisis would affect the US economy that drove the decision to extend extraordinary assistance. Treasury officials were also convinced of the necessity of remaking the Korean economy along Anglo-Saxon lines in order to lay the basis for renewed stability and growth, a fact which helps to explain the conditions attached to IMF programs. That conviction was more than incidentally reinforced, Yoon shows, by the knowledge that market liberalization and opening would benefit US banks and corporations seeking improved access to Korean markets.

Chapter 5, by Dongchul Cho, turns to monetary policy. The author starts with the controversy over high interest rates; like most previous studies his survey finds no evidence that the policy was ineffective or counterproductive. He does, however, suggest that the government stuck with high interest rates for too long: rates could have been lowered several months earlier, encouraging faster recovery, given the absence of inflationary pressures and the evident return of confidence. The most striking aspect of subsequent experience is how sharply rates fell and how stable they then remained. In part this is explicable in terms of the country's adoption of inflation targeting as its monetary policy framework: inflation targeting provided a nominal anchor for policy, creating the certainty and stability valued by market participants. That said, Cho suggests that the new monetary regime is not the entire story, that in addition other financial market reforms provide part of the explanation for the positive evolution of interest rates.

While early assessments of fiscal policy were sharply critical, Joosung Jun's analysis in Chapter 6, informed by more time and evidence, reaches a more favorable conclusion. The 1998 deficit of 4.2 percent of GDP, while a departure from the country's fiscal tradition of balanced budgets, appropriately sustained demand in the midst of a severe recession. When the economy then recovered, the authorities judiciously allowed the budget to return to surplus. The maintenance of a balanced budget and even surpluses on financial account going forward are critical, the author argues, given the government's contingent liabilities, pressures for increased social spending, and the aging of the population.

Chapter 7, by Joung-Woo Lee, then analyzes the social impact of the crisis. Inequality was not a major social issue before 1998, the land reforms of the 1950s and subsequent government policies having produced a strikingly even distribution of income. But this very fact heightened tension over the widening disparities that resulted from the crisis. Unskilled workers were the most likely to become unemployed once restrictions on layoffs were relaxed.[53] Members of the lower deciles of the wealth distribution saw their situation deteriorate as a result of rapidly growing debts, while the members of higher deciles did not; sometimes the latter were even able to improve their position by accumulating real estate in the period of severe financial distress. The net result was a reduction in the size of the middle class, aggravating social and political polarization. Those worries are reinforced by the observation that changes in technology had already raised the skill premium and by the prospect that further economic and financial liberalization will reinforce the trend toward greater inequality, as it evidently has in the United States.

The next two chapters, by Joon-Ho Hahm and Sung Wook Joh, review the results of financial and corporate restructuring. Hahm first describes how the pre-crisis pattern of credit allocation contributed to the investment spree of 1994–96 and heightened financial vulnerabilities. After summarizing post-crisis financial reforms, he shows how these policies affected the flow of funds in the restructuring period. While concluding that there has been progress in creating a more market-based financial system, Hahm predicts that further banking sector consolidation will be needed to cement these gains, as additional high-quality borrowers turn to the securities market, accelerating the process of disintermediation. It will be important for the regulatory authorities to reinforce market discipline and maintain the pressure for consolidation; otherwise, the banks, which still receive captive deposits, will respond to the loss of high-quality borrowers by pouring liquidity into high-risk property markets, as occurred in Japan in the late 1980s. Clearly, this is a precedent to be avoided.

Joh's chapter describes the environment that led to corporate sector problems such as high debt/equity ratios and low profitability. She examines the role of poor corporate governance and evaluates recent reforms in this light. Stock market data suggest that the influence of controlling shareholders has diminished, indicating some strengthening of minority shareholders' rights. In addition, limits on cross-shareholding and cross-debt guarantees show signs of having strengthened shareholder discipline, in that the daily returns on subsidiaries' stock prices vary more independently than before. The exception is the five largest *chaebols*, where implicit guarantees for subsidiaries have not been eliminated, or so the co-movement of stock prices suggests. The implication is that corporate sector reforms have yet fully to resolve the problems posed by the largest conglomerates.

Chapter 10, by Young-Ki Choi and Dae Il Kim, considers developments in labor markets in more detail. Unemployment insurance coverage has been broadened. The national pension system has been expanded. Temporary work has been allowed to increase. The government created a Tripartite Commission of representatives of employers, workers and government, charged with reaching a consensus on labor relations and ensuring that the burdens of restructuring were equitably shared. This Commission crafted a Social Agreement that permitted mass dismissals, something that was not happily received by the rank and file of the Korean Confederation of Trade Unions (KCTU). The leadership of the KCTU was criticized and replaced, and the new leadership withdrew from the Tripartite Commission in 1999. Labor market reforms remain contested, with uncertain implications for industrial relations. Rates of unionization have declined from formerly high levels, and industrial unions have gained ground at the expense of enterprise unions. The worry is that Korea enjoys neither the relatively centralized labor–management relations of some European countries nor the competitive labor markets of the United States. Occupying the middle of this distribution, the work of Calmfors and Driffill suggests, heightens the risk of labor–management strife and inadequate flexibility.[54]

In Chapter 11, Jaeyeol Yee looks more closely at how far Korea has gone in replacing family and political ties with market-based transactions. Much has been done to root out corruption, enhance the reliability of contract enforcement, increase transparency, and strengthen the play of market forces generally. The country adopted a new Anti-Corruption Law in July 2001 and created the Korea Independent Commission Against Corruption to fight the problem. It adopted a battery of disclosure, accounting and auditing requirements for banks and firms, as described above. Yet the government remains intimately involved in various structural and microeconomic aspects of the economy. Korea still ranks below other East Asian countries according to the PricewaterhouseCoopers index of opacity. Transparency International ranks it below other East Asian countries on its survey measure of corruption. While progress made in the last five years should not be underestimated, clearly much remains to be done.

The last of this series of chapters, by Hyun-Chin Lim and Joon Han, considers the impact of the crisis on social and political relations. As they describe, the attempt to remake the economy along more flexible, transparent and market-based lines has transformed state–societal relations. While the government continues to play a prominent role in, *inter alia*, shaping the restructuring process and developing a modern social safety net, its ability to guide political and social outcomes was much impaired by the crisis. Lim and Han worry that Korea has not yet figured out how to meet the diverse demands of society and to resolve the contradictions of its own policies. Specifically, it has not figured out how to build the more flexible, market-based economy that will be required for the maintenance of international competitiveness while at the same time preserving the equality, equity and social solidarity demanded by Korean society.

The last two chapters contemplate future prospects. Kiseok Hong, Jong-Wha Lee and Changyong Rhee use cross-country evidence to evaluate the risk of further crises. International experience suggests that this risk is minimized when a country strengthens its current account and fiscal balance, when its policies encourage the resumption of inward foreign direct investment, and when it successfully reduces its dependence on corporate indebtedness, short-term indebtedness in particular. The outlook for financial stability in Korea is favorable on this score: the country's current account and fiscal balances have strengthened impressively, inward FDI is on the rise, and debt ratios have been reduced, as noted above. To be sure, questions can be raised about the adequacy and consistency of measures to improve the climate for FDI and about whether indebtedness will be successfully maintained at its new lower level. Korea will not run current account surpluses forever; in particular, as the population ages, savings rates will come down, weakening the current account. Thus the authors' analysis points to the macroeconomic and financial aggregates that should be monitored by the markets and by vigilant government officials.

In the final chapter, In June Kim, Baekin Cha and Chi-Young Song take a broader look at the unfinished agenda. They warn that the risk of financial instability cannot be dismissed. There are still important unfinished tasks in the areas of financial and corporate sector reform, in particular. In a sense, it is economies in which the process of economic and financial reform and liberalization is underway but not yet complete where the risk of disruptions is greatest. And economies like Korea, which sought to restore investor confidence during the previous crisis by opening the capital account of the balance of payments still further, are especially susceptible to problems originating elsewhere in the region.[55] This is a reminder of the urgency for Korea of pushing ahead in order to exit the intermediate zone of incomplete reforms where such vulnerability is greatest.

NOTES

1. According to World Bank calculations, as published in the Bank's *World Development Indicators*.
2. The only faster growing Asian country is China. And China, clearly, is a special case. It is starting out far behind, and its catch-up growth is fueled by virtually unlimited supplies of low-cost labor.
3. Foreign capital goods suppliers sometimes provided training and scientific expertise to Korean purchasers, facilitating the associated technology transfer. In contrast, inward foreign direct investment (FDI) was discouraged by Korean policy, presumably on the grounds that it would undermine government control. In particular, this meant that foreign banks could not be allowed to enter the Korean economy, since this would undermine the effectiveness of directed lending. This perception had important implications subsequently, specifically in the mid-1990s when the capital account of the balance of payments was partially opened, allowing Korean banks to borrow offshore, but inward FDI (by bank and nonbank firms alike) continued to face formidable obstacles.
4. And using exports as a barometer of success in meeting the planners' economic goals. The currency was devalued by nearly 100 percent in 1964, and the country's multiple rates

Introduction 21

were unified. Then, starting in 1965 the government raised interest rates on deposits to mobilize domestic savings and began extending tax incentives to export-related industries. These, then, were the key years of the transition to what is now known as export-led growth.
5. Institutional substitution was yet another of Gerschenkron's famous analytical constructs.
6. The laws centralizing union structure were adopted at the beginning of the 1970s and loosened very slightly in the 1980s.
7. Why exactly Korea embraced this particular approach to economic development, itself a rarified version of Japan's state, bank and *keiretsu*-led model, continues to be debated. Several explanations have been suggested. In the 1960s, Japan was still the only example in Asia of a successful development experience. General Park had extensive contact with Japanese educational and military institutions (Noland, 2000). More than three decades of Japanese rule of the Korean Peninsula had left deep impressions, some positive as well as many negative, making Japan the obvious place to look when choosing a development model. The occupation also left an institutional legacy. It leveled the class system and bequeathed a financial system already structured along Japanese lines.
8. A neat theoretical model illuminating these points is Acemoglu et al. (2002).
9. Similarly, competition in domestic product markets may not have been intense, as the *chaebols* mastered the techniques of reciprocal dealing and market cornering, but this was of relatively little consequence in a period when the most technologically dynamic firms were producing for foreign, not domestic, markets.
10. To buy labor peace, the government imposed restrictions on layoffs and dismissals. By making industrial restructuring more difficult, this further locked in the prevailing structure of the economy.
11. Cited in Cumings (1999), p. 38.
12. In addition, there was pressure for capital account liberalization from small firms and other borrowers who felt disadvantaged by the favoritism the banks displayed toward the *chaebols*. But these lobbies did not obviously prefer the uneven order in which Korean capital account liberalization was phased in, with those very banks given exclusive access to foreign funding. Limited scope was also created in the first half of the 1990s for corporations to borrow offshore. In practice, most of their foreign borrowing was indirect, through the banks. This is not surprising; small firms in particular had little direct access to foreign finance.
13. Kwack (1999) instead computes total factor productivity (TFP) growth and finds that it began to slow from the 3 percent per annum characteristic of the 1970s and 1980s to less than 1 percent around 1990. There is no little controversy over estimates of TFP growth in Asia in the 1980s and 1990s, but, as Hsieh (2002) shows, the controversy does not extend to South Korea.
14. The Korean economy had grown overheated in the late 1970s as a result of the government's Heavy and Chemical Industries Drive. Attempts to stabilize were then made difficult by a drought which disrupted agriculture in 1978 and the second OPEC oil shock in 1979. Both stabilization, which eroded the competitiveness of Korean exports, and the oil shock contributed to the current account deficit, which rose to record levels in 1980 and growth turned negative for the first time in more than two decades. Eventually, a 20 percent devaluation of the won, supported by restrained monetary policies, restored export competitiveness, eliminated the current account deficit, and put the economy on the road to recovery.
15. Kwack (1994) and Pyo (1999) show that the rate of return on capital was below prevailing rates in the United States and even Japan. Krueger and Yoo (2002) show that rates of return in manufacturing were lower than in Taiwan (the other Asian 'tiger' with which Korea is frequently compared) throughout the 1980s and 1990s.
16. Krueger and Yoo (2002), Table 7. Returns for non-*chaebol* firms move in parallel, although the decline is less pronounced. There was a recovery in the rate of return in 1994–95, years when Korean growth accelerated, fueled by a sharp and ultimately unsustainable expansion of domestic credit (and by good times in the global electronics industry). Claessens et al. (1998) show that the rate of return on assets was lower in

Korea, on the eve of the crisis, than in the United States, Germany, and eight other Asian countries.

17. In retrospect, the only surprise is that earlier manifestations of the problem, such as the collapse of Hanbo Steel and Sammi Steel, two top-30 *chaebols*, in January and March of 1997, followed by the collapse of Jinro in April and the well-publicized problems of Kia Motors in the summer of the year, did not have this precipitating effect.
18. Prior to the crisis, the Korean authorities tabled a program of financial liberalization designed to bring the country into compliance with its OECD obligations, but few elements of this multi-year program were in place when the crisis struck. As Dobson and Jacquet (1998) and Noland (2000) note, countries are permitted reservations to the OECD code of financial liberalization, and the Korean government was not shy about taking advantage of this option.
19. Foreigners were prevented from purchasing the vast majority of corporate bond issues, for fear that this would undermine bank control. The share of stock issues that could be held by foreigners was initially limited to 10 percent in 1992 and then raised in a series of small steps, to the point where it had reached 18 percent in 1996. That foreign-eligible shares frequently traded at a premium is evidence of the binding nature of these restrictions.
20. The situation in certain other Asian countries, such as Thailand, bears no little resemblance, with the exception of the lesser importance there of family-owned and -controlled industrial conglomerates. But the Korean variant has some distinctive aspects, such as the uneven opening of the capital account which caused foreign finance to flow through the banking system, which was not so much the case in certain other Asian countries (Indonesia, for example). In this respect there were important parallels between the Korean and Thai cases, in both of which the capital account was opened unevenly and the banks were given favored access to international financial markets.
21. The problem of portfolio concentrations was especially evident in the large banks, which had the closest ties to the *chaebol*.
22. These problems were widespread in the commercial banking sector, but they were especially prevalent among the even more lightly regulated merchant banks, which expanded rapidly in the mid-1990s after the authorities attempted to clamp down on commercial bank lending to the *chaebols*. (Not a few of the merchant banks were in fact owned by the *chaebols* in question.)
23. Arguably, these guarantees extended to the banks' customers, namely, the *chaebols* – or so was the perception – since they too were the instrumentality of the government's industrial policy. This only aggravated the moral hazard problem (since it seemingly rendered the *chaebols* 'too big to fail') and helps to explain how they acquired the extraordinary levels of leverage that proved to be their albatross when the crisis struck.
24. One mistake the regulatory authorities did commit was to adopt in 1996 a mandatory deposit insurance scheme that made no provision for risk rating, which worked to further limit the market discipline felt by risk-seeking banks. In addition, it can be argued that it was a mistake to deregulate interest rates (a process that began in 1988). Given the otherwise distorted nature of the Korean banking system, the effect of interest rate deregulation was to allow the least solvent and most risk-tolerant banks to compete for deposits.
25. 'Policy lending' probably reached its peak in the 1970s, coincident with the Heavy and Chemical Industry Drive, when it is estimated to have accounted to as much as 60 percent of bank portfolios (S. Cho, 1994; J. Yoo, 1994; Noland, 2000). Not coincidentally, this was the period when the *chaebols* consolidated their hold on the economy (see Sakong, 1993), when the largest *chaebols* expanded at annual rates of 30 to 35 percent, and when the high debt/equity ratios that are among their distinguishing characteristics first began to emerge. The government subsequently sought to impose more discipline on *chaebol* borrowing by making a particular bank responsible for monitoring the borrower's business performance and overseeing its borrowing from all sources (in effect emulating the Japanese main bank system). In practice, the big conglomerates had as much leverage over the big banks as vice versa; *chaebol* borrowing was only weakly constrained. When in response the government placed a freeze on bank borrowing by the top *chaebols*, the latter shifted their borrowing to nonbank financial intermediaries.

26. Noland (2000), p. 53.
27. That the Korean banking system was characterized by an unusually high level of concentration (with six banks accounting for more than half of all domestic credit) heightened the danger that a few problem banks might bring down the entire financial pyramid. This too was no coincidence; regulatory barriers to entry, which supported high levels of concentration, were part and parcel of the government's policy of directed lending. That is, it was easier to give instructions to a few banks than to many, and if directed lending depressed profits, the resulting competitive pressure was less in an oligopolistic environment.
28. On some days in December the rollover rate fell to as low as 5 percent. Figures from Jwa and Huh (1998).
29. This is more than a counterfactual. In actual fact, rates of return on bank assets and equity almost halved in the period 1992–96, reflecting declining returns and mounting problems in the corporate sector.
30. Debt/equity ratios in manufacturing were in the range of 300–400 percent, in contrast to other industrial countries, where they were typically well below 200 percent (according to international comparisons by Krueger and Yoo, 2002). Thus, it is argued that the IMF's cookie-cutter advice failed to recognize this fundamental difference in the structure of the Korean economy.
31. Negotiations spanned the period 21 November–3 December. The government first attempted to obtain unconditional support from the US and Japanese governments, but the former in particular insisted that it go through the IMF and borrow subject to the usual conditions. The package included a $21 billion standby credit from the IMF, $10 billion from the World Bank, $4 billion from the Asian Development Bank, and an additional $22 billion from the United States, Japan and other countries. The size of the package reflected sudden awareness of the size of the short-term foreign bank credits coming due.
32. But, as Noland (2000) notes, the Ministry of Finance and Economy continued to resist aggressive stimulus on confidence-related grounds. Thus the idea that the IMF forced fiscal austerity on a reluctant Korean government is too simple.
33. A weaker exchange rate would not have made life easier for Korean banks and firms with dollar-denominated assets to service, but the main problem for the corporate sector, as distinct from the banks, was high debt gearing, which amplified the effects of high interest rates, not dollar-denominated debts. (Claessens et al., 1999 are in the minority in concluding that a weaker exchange rate did more to undermine the solvency and liquidity of Korean firms than higher interest rates.) It can be argued that lower interest rates, if they also meant fewer bankruptcies and less disruption to output, would in fact have made the exchange rate stronger rather than weaker (that there existed, in effect, an interest rate–exchange rate Laffer Curve), but econometric post mortems (for example Dekle et al., 2001) have found little empirical support for the existence of this nonlinear relationship.
34. On the complexities of Korea's restructuring negotiations, see Kim and Byeon (2001).
35. Speaking of the *chaebols*, Cumings (p. 38) writes, 'President Kim has been a lifelong critic of these firms, and they have reciprocated.'
36. At the end of 1997, 14 of 27 commercial banks had measured capital below the Basel Accord's 8 percent requirement, and their actual capital was certainly significantly lower than this.
37. The main shortcoming of the financial restructuring program was the authorities' reluctance to clamp down on nonbank financial institutions, notably investment and trust companies and insurance companies. Investment trust companies did not have to disclose their asset portfolios, and their accounts were not audited. See Y. Cho (2001a). This was hardly coincidental, since many of these companies were owned and operated by still-powerful *chaebols* (see below). This failure to deal with the nonbank financial sector allowed certain borrowers to gamble for redemption and led to the investment trust company crisis of 1999.
38. The authorities had responded in similar fashion to the previous crisis, in the early 1980s, but to limited effect.
39. Noland (2000) argues that family control was actually strengthened as a result of the crisis.

40. In addition, some banks have been reluctant to realize losses for fear of what this would do to their already fragile balance sheets.
41. See Y. Cho (2001b) for details.
42. Mako (2002), p. 23.
43. The banks might defend their practices on the grounds that many of these companies could be expected eventually to return to profitability, but after two and a half years of strong growth this interpretation is questionable; it is hard to believe that lobbying by the borrowers played no role in these lending decisions.
44. The Commercial Code and Securities Law was then amended to require large companies to appoint half of their directors from outside.
45. Changes in statute that increased the legal liability of controlling owners worked in the same direction.
46. In 2000, the principle of creditor takeover seemed in jeopardy when efforts to rescue some Hyundai companies preserved family interests. In 2001, financial restructurings again diluted or displaced family holdings, suggesting that the Hyundai episode may have been an aberration.
47. For another summary evaluation of corporate restructuring experience, see Mako (2001).
48. Notwithstanding the problems mentioned above.
49. Those workouts have generally proceeded under the auspices of a lead bank, and subject to extra-judicial rules for resolving disagreements as specified by the provisions of the 1998 Corporate Securities Law. Slightly different procedures have been followed for the five largest *chaebols*, the resolution of whose difficulties exceeds the capacity of even the largest banks.
50. Financial difficulties of some groups led debt/equity ratios to rise again in 2001; thus, Hyundai's ratio had risen to more than 475 percent at the middle of the year.
51. Eleven of the 15 top *chaebols* had interest coverage ratios of less than 1.0 in 2001.
52. Final approval of a reorganization plan still requires the approval of three-quarters of secured creditors and two-thirds of unsecured creditors.
53. Since firms sought to retain skilled workers, supervisors and technicians with firm-specific skills.
54. For a survey of the literature on the hypothesis of a hump-shaped relationship between the degree of centralization of wage bargaining and the flexibility of labor market outcomes, see Calmfors (1993).
55. One thinks, for example, of the possibility of a future Chinese banking crisis.

2. The Korean economy before and after the crisis

Un-Chan Chung

INTRODUCTION

The Korean economy has undergone many changes since the 1997 crisis. The closure of banks and other financial institutions shattered the belief that 'banks are forever.' The 'too big to fail' doctrine has been at least partially discredited by the placement of large conglomerates like Kia and Daewoo under court-supervised reorganization. The economy has regained some stability, the country having paid back its IMF loan in full ahead of schedule while amassing some foreign $100 billion of reserves. Yet not everyone is optimistic about its future, reflecting doubts about the adequacy of the country's restructuring program.

This chapter aims to clarify the nature and historical context of the 1997 crisis. It argues that the crisis was rooted in the Korean economic system's microeconomic and structural flaws; in other words, it contends that it was more than a temporary liquidity crisis. It then reviews subsequent developments, focusing on progress made in restructuring the economy and laying out the reform agenda.

THE ECONOMY BEFORE THE CRISIS

From the 1960s through the mid-1990s, the Korean government pursued economic policies heavily oriented toward growth. This approach can be dubbed 'centrally managed resource allocation' or 'structured competition.' The government told individual firms what industries were open to them and used the banking system as an instrument of industrial policy. In addition to allowing the authorities to guide the allocation of funding, this approach freed firms from the pressures of competition and allowed them to concentrate on growth.

The Korean economy was able to achieve in three decades the kind of economic transformation that had taken Western countries a century and more. But this accelerated growth came at the cost of distortions with significant long-term implications. On the real side, redundant investment undermined the economy's efficiency and flexibility. It led to overcapacity in many of the country's leading industries. On the financial side, deficient loan screening practices and the politicization of lending led to the accumulation of large numbers of nonperforming loans. The *chaebols*' unconstrained desire for expansion, coupled with the lack of due diligence and monitoring by the banks, allowed extraordinarily high corporate debt/equity ratios to develop. An economy with high leverage becomes very vulnerable even to a small external or internal shock and could easily collapse into a crisis situation if there is a loss of confidence in its economic prospects (Johnson, 2002). This is what Korea learned, at considerable cost, in 1997–98.

Not everyone agrees that these microeconomic and structural problems were at the root of the crisis that erupted at the end of 1997. Early skeptics of the micro-structural explanation (for example Sachs, 1997; Radelet and Sachs, 1998), while acknowledging that structural distortions can impede the process of economic growth, questioned whether they can also be responsible for a sudden loss of confidence and an abrupt collapse of currency and asset values experienced by Korea in 1997–98; these authors prefer to interpret the crisis as an investor panic brought about by the precipitous liberalization of the capital account of the balance of payments. Subsequent analysis has shown that this diagnosis is oversimple. Although structural distortions may not have precipitated the crisis, they helped to set the stage. Without them, the effects of the investor panic would have been by no means as devastating. That is, I argue in this chapter that it was those distortions that rendered the Korean economy so vulnerable to destabilization when investor confidence was disturbed.

THE ROOTS OF THE CRISIS

The principle underlying the market system is 'survival of the fittest.' Inefficient, unprofitable firms are forced to shut down, and only efficient and profitable firms are allowed to survive. It was this principle that was violated in Korea in both the real and financial sectors. For three decades, the country's large conglomerates, or *chaebols*, continued to expand by taking advantage of protection offered by growth-oriented government authorities.

Redundant Investment in the Real Sector

As the economy grew too large for effective hierarchical control, the result was a steady loss of economic efficiency.[1] A recent study by J.-W. Lee et al. (2002) shows that the relative efficiency of the *chaebols* declined steadily over the course of the 1980s and 1990s. The *chaebols*' inventory management practices broke down, and cash flow deteriorated badly, as they had difficulty in recovering invested funds in facilities. All this culminated in a sequence of *chaebol* failures that anticipated the 1997 crisis.

Why was the Korean economy so prone to redundant investment, and why did so many Korean firms – large firms in particular – display signs of chronic inefficiency? First, in Korea, firms were rated, by banks and other financial institutions alike, more according to size rather than profitability. In an advanced economy whose securities markets, banking system and venture capital industry are all well developed, small, newly established firms and not only their larger competitors are able to access external funding; that is, they are able to compete on an even footing. In contrast, in countries with underdeveloped market infrastructures, financial market structures in particular, external signals such as firm size are important determinants of the availability of external finance. Financial organizations have no choice but to rely on these criteria when it is impossible to rate corporate borrowers objectively according to such internal criteria as profitability. In Korea, large firms, or *chaebol*s, have more to offer as collateral and can expect the government to come to their aid in the worst case because they are 'too big to fail' and because they have long-standing political connections.

Cross-shareholding by the *chaebol*s was further conducive to redundant investment. The c*haebols*' founding families were often able to gain control of many subsidiaries at relatively low cost by using small shares of their own firm's assets to purchase substantial shares of the subsidiary. Moreover, the *chaebols*' influence over the key decisions of the subsisiary vastly exceeded their nominal holdings in the latter. That a *chaebol* owner's influence on the investment decisions of a subsidiary far exceeded his or her direct control rights reflected the *chaebol* owner's economic and political leverage. Moreover, the investment decisions of *chaebol* owners were frequently based not on the efficiency criteria but on other factors, such as the unconstrained desire of an owner to expand the range of businesses and industries in which the conglomerate had a hand.[2] With no mechanism to hold *chaebol* owners in check, redundant investment was the inevitable outcome.

Finally, there was moral hazard on the part of the government, financial institutions and the *chaebol*s themselves. When Korean banks suffered huge losses from failed investments in risky projects, the government had always made up for the losses, fearing that failing to do so might threaten the stability of the financial system. This pattern encouraged financial institutions naturally to ignore downside risks and to pay attention only to upside gain. This made for an atmosphere where inefficient, risky projects could still expect to be financed, regardless of their expected value, and ultimately at considerable cost to society.

NPLs (Nonperforming Loans) in the Financial Sector

The structure of the financial system added to these vulnerabilities. The role of financial institutions is to ensure that resources are efficiently allocated through the market. Efficient resource allocation requires that the screening by financial institutions be based on fundamental economic criteria such as profitability. In Korea, the importance of autonomous loan screening had become obscured over the three decades leading up to the crisis not just by the promise of government guarantees but also by the rosy hue of spectacular growth. Inadequate screening was not fatal to the stability of the financial sector so long as growth remained rapid. However, the financial sector's commitment to support economic growth inevitably resulted in inefficient allocation of funds and consequently unsound investment proliferated in the real sector. Although much of the blame must be shouldered by the firms that went ahead with flawed investment plans, financial institutions consorted in this behavior, abrogating their responsibility for due diligence and failing to screen out unpromising investments, as did government by creating an environment conducive to these practices.

The government's reluctance to release accurate statistics also played a role in compounding the nonperforming loan problem. The official pre-crisis figure for nonperforming loans as a share of total lending was in the range of 2 to 3 percent. However, this figure includes only the categories 'estimated losses,' where principal as well as interest is considered unrecoverable, and 'doubtful' loans, that is, cases where there was the need for a collection plan. If the 'fixed' category (collateral-secured loans with interest overdue by six months or more) had been included, as in Japan (which itself is hardly a country renowned for the adequacy of its reporting of nonperforming loans), the ratio would have been 7 to 8 percent. The US standard, which includes a 'precautionary' category for loans in arrears by 3 months or more, would have raised the ratio to more than 20 percent (compared to 1–2 percent in the United States). Before the crisis, neither the Korean government nor the banks were forthright in calculating and releasing such numbers, which aggravated matters during the crisis by fueling suspicion among foreign investors about the health of the country's financial institutions.[3]

CONUNDRUMS OF THE KOREAN ECONOMY

Macroeconomic indicators paint a remarkable success story for Korea. The average rate of growth since the 1970s was nearly 10 percent and dipped below 5 percent in only three years (Figure 2.1).[4] Inflation (as measured by the change in the GDP deflator) stayed in single digits from the early 1980s

Before and after the crisis

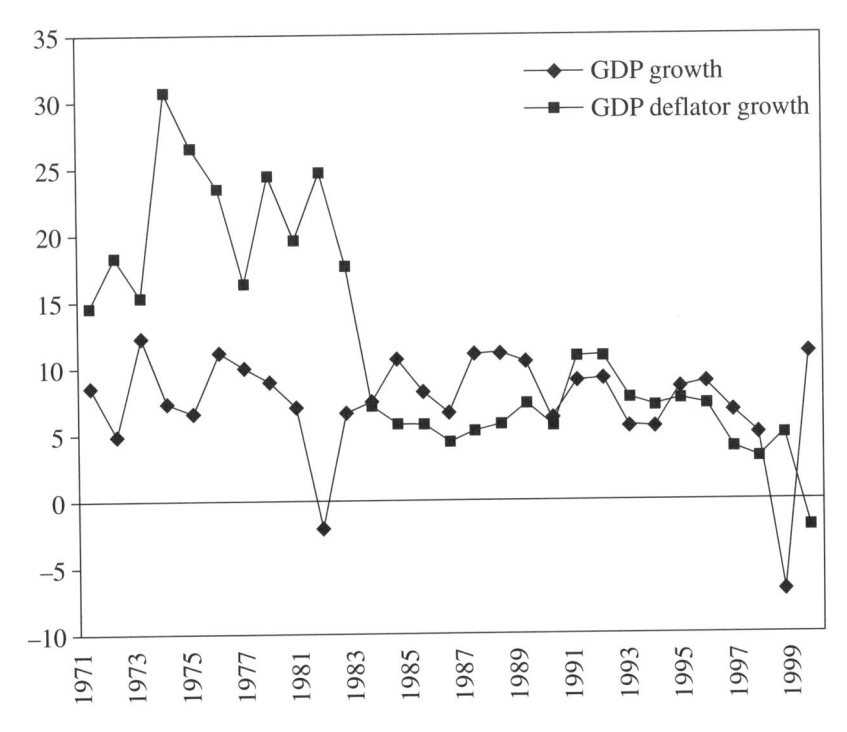

Source: Bank of Korea, *Monthly Bulletin* (various issues).

Figure 2.1 Macroeconomic indicators

through the mid-1990s, with the exception of 1990 and 1991 when it reached 10.8 percent.

Some have wondered how a structurally flawed economy could put up such stellar macroeconomic numbers. One answer is that it is possible for an economy in the early stages of industrialization to sustain extensive growth despite serious microeconomic and structural inefficiencies, as illustrated by the cases of the Soviet Union from the 1920s through the 1950s or China following its 1978 reform. When the technological gap between leader and follower is large, a country with a strong government can grow quickly if the latter is effective in encouraging high levels of investment, which serves as the medium through which foreign technological know-how is imported and implemented. Structural distortions that interfere with the operation of the market mechanism are of relatively little moment at this early stage of economic development. But as the technology gap closes, the efficiency of the market mechanism, and therefore the efficiency of the economy, becomes critical for sustaining economic growth. This, in a nutshell, explains how

Korea could grow so fast starting in the 1960s despite evidence of very significant structural distortions, and why those same distortions led to the collapse of the financial system and the growth miracle toward the end of the 1990s.

What, then, was the evidence for structural problems? Consider first the profitability of manufacturing. The return on assets (ROA) of Korean manufacturing firms has continually fallen since the 1960s, from 8.5 to 1.4 percent, to levels quite low compared to other countries. The immediate explanation for this low profitability relates to over-investment by the *chaebol*s, funded by indiscriminate lending by financial institutions. The problem deepened in the 1990s, when the balance of power between the government, financial institutions and *chaebol*s began to shift. The *chaebol*s' unchecked expansion and their redundant, excess investment reached dangerous levels as a so-called pro-market ideology was buoyed by haphazard financial liberalization starting in 1993. Financial liberalization fueled the *chaebol*s' expansion virtually without regard to profitability, reinforcing the influence of these large conglomerates over every sector of the economy. Meanwhile, small or medium-sized firms with good investment projects could not obtain access to investment funds, because the latter were almost completely depleted to finance the *chaebol*s' inefficient projects. This was when the seeds of the crisis were sown.

It is also important to note that the debt/equity ratios of the top 30 *chaebol*s were much higher and their profitability much lower than in the case of non-*chaebol* manufacturing firms (Joh, 2001a). The average debt/equity ratio of the six *chaebol*s that went bankrupt in 1997–98 was an astounding 1877 percent. Not surprisingly, these problems in the real sector made their way into the financial sector and created huge amounts of NPLs.

Some researchers argue that the compressed growth of the Korean economy was driven by factor accumulation to the almost total exclusion of technological progress. Table 2.1 summarizes the findings of studies comparing the growth experiences of Europe and Asia. It shows that, in contrast to the catch-up growth of Europe and Japan in the golden post-World War II era, the catch-up growth of Asia's newly industrializing economies was very heavily driven by factor accumulation, particularly capital accumulation.[5]

But it is no longer possible to expect this kind of spectacular performance now that factor accumulation alone no longer suffices to sustain the growth of the economy, unless the system's structural deficiencies are corrected. Sustained growth can only come from more efficient resource utilization.

In the past, Korea was able to achieve high growth despite its structural flaws for several reasons. It was easy to import foreign technology, mainly by importing foreign capital goods. Cheap, well-trained labor was available in abundance. The tasks of corporate management were relatively simple

Table 2.1 Growth factors, Europe and Japan (1950–73) vs Asia (1960–94)

	Capital	Labor	TFP	Output
1950–73				
France	1.6 (32)	0.3 (6)	3.1 (62)	5.0 (100)
Italy	1.6 (32)	0.2 (4)	3.2 (64)	5.0 (100)
Japan	3.1 (34)	2.5 (27)	3.6 (39)	9.2 (100)
UK	1.6 (53)	0.2 (7)	1.2 (40)	3.0 (100)
West Germany	2.2 (37)	0.5 (8)	3.3 (55)	6.0 (100)
1960–64				
Korea	4.3 (52)	2.5 (30)	1.5 (18)	8.3 (100)
China	3.1 (41)	2.7 (36)	1.7 (23)	7.5 (100)
Hong Kong	2.8 (38)	2.1 (29)	2.4 (33)	7.3 (100)
Indonesia	2.9 (52)	1.9 (34)	0.8 (14)	5.6 (100)
Malaysia	3.4 (50)	2.5 (37)	0.9 (13)	6.8 (100)
Philippines	2.1 (55)	2.1 (55)	–0.4 (–11)	3.8 (100)
Singapore	4.4 (54)	2.2 (27)	1.5 (19)	8.1 (100)
Taiwan	4.1 (48)	2.4 (28)	2.0 (24)	8.5 (100)
Thailand	3.7 (49)	2.0 (27)	1.8 (24)	7.5 (100)

Note:
* For China, figures are estimates for 1978–95.
** Figures in parentheses are percentage.

Source: Crafts (1999), p. 114.

and straightforward. And, finally, external conditions were favorable. The Korean economy benefited enormously in the 1960s from the United Nations' 'Decade of Development' Program and from the external demand generated by the Vietnam War. In the 1970s, there was the Middle East construction boom, on which Korean construction firms capitalized, and the recycling of petro-dollars. In the mid-1980s Korea benefited by the 'three lows' (low international interest rates, a low won–dollar exchange rate, and low oil prices). Cold war geopolitics played a role throughout the period, in so far as Korea could count on support from the United States. All of these factors made it possible to postpone the collapse of the model of accumulation-based extensive growth.

Since the late 1980s, however, technology transfers have become increasingly difficult, as developed countries have tightened restrictions on technology exports. Labor, especially skilled labor, is no longer abundant. Wages have risen dramatically, and corporate management has become more complex. As

Krugman (1994) pointed out, rapid growth fueled by increases in factor inputs is bound to lose momentum at some point. For Korea that point came in the 1990s.

ONSET OF THE CRISIS

The story of the Korean crisis is complex and has many aspects. However, it is particularly revealing to focus on the merchant banks, both because they played a pivotal role and because their actions and motivations are revealing of the economy's broader problems.

Most Korean merchant banks started as investment banks, established after the Decree of 3 August 1972 which aimed to legitimize the underground capital market. In 1994 and 1996, the Law Concerning Financial Institution Mergers and Transformation permitted the 24 existing investment banks to become merchant banks. However, unlike the six existing merchant banks, these 24 latecomers lacked experience in foreign currency operations and had weak business bases, which forced them to venture into risky activities in order to survive.

Merchant banks thus bought commercial paper issued by the *chaebol*s at discount, which they then resold to trust accounts at the commercial banks. Hard pressed to generate profits, they sometimes engaged in illegal operations. From 1995 to 1997, merchant banks increased their total commercial paper discounts and sales more than two-fold, from 42 trillion and 35 trillion won, respectively, to 90 trillion and 75 trillion won. As a result, the chain of *chaebols*' bankruptcies in 1997 left the merchant banks awash with unrecoverable debt. While nonperforming assets held by the 30 local merchant banks totaled 1.264 trillion won in December 1996, this figure had more than tripled, to 3.897 trillion won, by October 1997.[6]

The merchant banks borrowed cheap, short-term Japanese funds from Hong Kong to finance long-term loans at high interest to Russia, Thailand, Indonesia and other countries in a classic instance of the so-called 'carry trade.' This resulted in serious maturity mismatches, with 80 percent of debts being of short maturity but 70 percent of assets being long term. This maturity mismatch might have been sustainable had the merchant banks been able to maintain sound credit standing, enabling them to extend or roll over their maturing short-term debts. However, as soon as their international credibility plummeted, their branches in Hong Kong found it increasingly difficult to roll over their short-term debts. Ultimately, these banks had to resort to buying foreign currency on the foreign exchange market, using call loans in won from commercial banks, which worked to spread the problems of the merchant banks to the rest of the banking system.

Why were the merchant banks able to borrow so much both domestically and abroad? Part of the answer is that unified accounting standards and standards classifying assets as nonperforming did not exist, and external audits and supervisory monitoring were perfunctory at best. The merchant banks took advantage of this lack of market and regulatory discipline to lever up their bets.

In addition, the government was accustomed to managing the economy through the cozy symbiotic arrangement between the government, banks and corporations sometimes known as 'Korea, Inc.' and continued doing so even after Korea joined the WTO (World Trade Organization) and the OECD. Observing that the banks were finding it increasingly difficult to fund themselves abroad and that huge pressure for exchange rate depreciation existed in the foreign exchange market due to increased demands for US dollars, the government directly stepped in to peg the exchange rate at an unsustainable level. Consequently, the drain on foreign reserves became quite a severe problem. Finally, on 23 November 1997, the government was forced to ask the International Monetary Fund (IMF) for an emergency bailout loan.

THE KOREAN ECONOMY AFTER THE IMF

Korea's macroeconomic development over the last four years has been surprisingly good, given the severity of the preceding crisis. After contracting by nearly 7 percent in 1998, the economy rebounded strongly, growing by 10.7 percent in 1999 and 9.0 percent in 2000, thanks to a combination of resurgent exports and buoyant domestic demand. Per capita income recovered from US$6700 in 1998 to US$9900 in 2000, approaching the pre-crisis level of US$10 300 reached in 1997.

Post-crisis inflation fell to its lowest level in the 1990s, at 0.8 in 1999 and 2.2 percent in 2000, surprising those who had warned that depreciation of the won would set off an inflationary spiral. Due to a drastic fall in imports in the midst of the recession, the trade account shifted to a US$40 billion surplus in 1998 from the previous year's US$8.2 billion deficit, and it has remained in surplus ever since. Foreign reserves have grown dramatically, recovering from less than $4 billion in December 1997 to over US$100 billion by December 2001.

Similarly, interest rates, equity prices and the exchange rate have all recovered to or even surpassed their pre-crisis levels. Interest rates on corporate bonds soared more than 30 percent after the outbreak of the crisis, but began falling rapidly in the second half of 1998, before stabilizing at low, single-digit levels. The stock index plummeted to 280 immediately after the crisis, but recovered briefly to above 1000, reflecting the effects of fiscal stimulus and the popularity of investment funds that caught on in early 1999. The index subsequently fell, and hovered around 550 for about a year, but recently climbed back above 800. Meanwhile, the won–dollar exchange rate, after threatening to break above 2000 in early 1998, has declined steadily since then and stabilized at around 1300.

However, public finances have suffered badly. The budget deficit and government debt have grown rapidly, reflecting the spending increases needed to stimulate the economy and support the unemployed. Public debt, including that of local governments, reached 108 trillion won in 1999, driving up government debt as a percentage of GDP from 11 percent in 1997 to twice that level two years later. Interest payments have also soared because of public funds and government bonds issued for financial restructuring.[7]

This impressive short-term recovery has not left all observers sanguine about the prospects of the Korean economy. Corporate and financial sector reform remains incomplete. The economy's rapid recovery was a mixed blessing from this point of view, in that it reduced the perceived urgency of fundamental reform and strengthened the hand of entrenched interests opposed to far-reaching change.

THE REFORM AGENDA

What are the most critical remaining issues on the reform agenda? In the real sector, the success of restructuring hinges on closing down distressed firms, while in the financial sector, the problem of nonperforming loans must be urgently resolved.

Real Sector Restructuring

Forcing ailing firms to exit is at the core of restructuring, in the narrow sense that it corrects inefficient resource allocation decisions already made. It is also at the core of restructuring in the wider sense, in that exit reduces the probability of redundant, excess investment based on such criteria as size in the future. Also crucial to the success of restructuring is transparency in the financial reporting and transactions of corporations and financial institutions and in corporate governance. Without transparency, it is impossible even to begin to make accurate assessments of the financial health of firms and banks.

Real sector reform evolved around reform of the *chaebols*. The government's approach was based on the so-called '5+3 agenda.' In January 1998, then president-elect Kim Dae-Jung and *chaebol* owners agreed on five tasks for restructuring the *chaebols*. A year and a half later, three additional tasks were added to the original five. The original five elements include increasing transparency in corporate management, eliminating debt guarantees between *chaebol* subsidiaries, improving capital structures, establishing core competencies to prevent unconstrained expansion of the *chaebol*s through unrelated diversification, and increasing accountability of controlling shareholders and management. The three additional tasks are prohibiting the *chaebol* from holding controlling stakes in financial institutions, from conducting insider transactions, and from leaving improper bequests or gifts to the heirs of *chaebol* owners.

Thus, in February 1998 the owners of top the 30 *chaebol*s and the government agreed on a plan for reducing the conglomerates' extraordinarily high debt/equity ratios, leading to an agreement between the banks and *chaebol*s (the so-called Capital Structure Improvement Program). Under these provisions, the Korean government imposed a 200 percent limit on the debt/equity ratios for the top five *chaebol*s and asked them to meet that limit by the end of 1999.[8]

In addition, to encourage firms to focus on their core competencies and eliminate redundant capacity, the government used special tax concessions and financial support to promote a series of so-called 'Big Deals' – voluntary swaps of lines of business and subsidiaries – among the top five *chaebol*s. For other mid-sized *chaebol*s it pressed for workout programs (negotiations over debt restructuring between banks and *chaebol*s, outside the confines of formal bankruptcy procedures).

Corporate governance structures were also realigned. To strengthen minority shareholder rights, the government lowered the minimum level of shareholding in a listed company required for a derivative suit from 1 to 0.01 percent in May 1998. It also strengthened the outside director system. In December 1999, tax laws governing bequests and transfers were tightened as a way of limiting the persistence of family control. To increase transparency, the government required the 30 largest *chaebol*s to prepare *chaebol*-wide consolidated financial statements where all internal transactions between affiliates of the same *chaebol*s were subtracted.[9]

Financial Sector Restructuring

The core problem to be solved in the financial sector was the overhang of nonperforming loans (NPLs). On 29 June 1998 the government launched a financial sector restructuring program, dissolving five commercial banks. This was followed by an injection of public funds to restore stability to the remaining financial institutions. The government raised 64 trillion won in public funds in 1998, the entirety of which was injected into the financial sector by the end of 1999.[10] Public funds were raised by the Korea Asset

Management Corporation (NPL Management Fund) and the Korea Deposit Insurance Co. (Deposit Insurance Fund) through the issuance of government-guaranteed bonds.[11] Public funds are used for equity investment in ailing banks, for the purchase of NPLs, and to underwrite insurance payments for deposits at ailing banks.[12]

Including recovered funds that were recycled by selling off the assets of dissolved banks and 27 trillion won in government funds, the total amount injected into the financial system came to nearly 110 trillion won. In December 2000, the government raised an additional 40 trillion won of public funds and recycled an addition 10 trillion won, raising the total by an additional 50 trillion won. In all, some 104 trillion won has been raised in total as public funds, and the funds committed to financial restructuring to date add up to more than 175 trillion won.

Several other measures have been implemented to improve the soundness of the financial sector. The government pressed for bank mergers, foreign investment and equity increases designed to clear up the banks' bad loans and enhance their competitiveness. Korea's various supervisory agencies were consolidated into a unified Financial Supervisory Commission (FSC) in 1998. The FSC was empowered to request, recommend or order the restoration of depleted capital, the disposal of property holdings and the downsizing of business networks and organizations, to prohibit the holding of highly risky assets, and to order the suspension of all or part of business operations.[13]

EVALUATIONS OF REFORM

Clearly, the government has injected a massive amount of public funds in the course of its restructuring program. However, the restructuring program in both the real and financial sectors failed to transform the institutional environment in any real sense. This section asks why the process of restructuring has stalled and considers the ramifications.

Real Sector Restructuring

As pointed out earlier, the most important issue with regard to real sector restructuring was to establish the principle of the survival of the fittest by shutting down ailing firms. However, that principle was given short shrift in the political and economic arena. Even the 5+3 agenda for reform of the corporate sector focused on prohibiting the further expansion of the *chaebols* rather than on establishing the institutional environment to force the exit of insolvent firms. The restructuring of distressed firms since the crisis has focused on preventing large-scale corporate failures and widespread unemployment, by extending loan deadlines and offering favorable interest rates rather than financially distressed firms to be reorganized or closed down.

Why has restructuring stumbled in this way? The resolution of the Korean government to undertake painful and costly restructuring measures waned, while resistance from the *chaebols* and the rest of the business establishment grew stronger, as the Korean economy recovered from the crisis. Reform came to be seen as less pressing with signs that business was resuming. With growth providing the easy way out, the government concentrated on expansionary macroeconomic policy rather than structural reform. The fall of the Daewoo Group in 1999 coincided with the nadir of structural reform. The Daewoo case essentially resurrected the 'too big to fail' doctrine (Jun, 2002). Since the impact of Daewoo's collapse was so devastating to the system, the government tried to prevent any additional bankruptcies of that size. Most notably it did so in the case of Hyundai. When Hyundai Group experienced financial difficulties in 2000, the government mobilized such means as fast-track underwriting to prevent its bankruptcy.

The most compelling evidence for the failure of the reform process in the real sector was the high number of firms in latent insolvency (that is, firms that were technically insolvent but none the less allowed to continue operating by courtesy of the forbearance of the government and financial institutions). One measure of latent insolvency is the earnings/interest ratio (or interest coverage ratio) index.[14] Table 2.2 shows that, of the 6116 supposedly solvent firms at the end of May 1999, 31 to 33 percent (between 1874 and 2025 firms) were in fact insolvent according to their own financial accounts, although continuing to operate. This situation does not appear to have improved much subsequently. Table 2.3 shows that the proportion of firms with earnings/interest ratios below unity was still around 30 percent in the first half of 2001. Furthermore, the proportion of loans by these firms out of total loans in the manufacturing sector had risen to fully 50 percent.

Even more serious is the fact that, as of the end of 2000, some 4 percent of all manufacturing firms had earnings/interest ratios below unity for three consecutive years, despite the very rapid growth experienced over most of this period and the virtually complete recovery of levels of output to pre-crisis levels. This again shows the ineffectiveness of real sector restructuring.

Evidence like this of the lack of progress in real sector restructuring prompted the government to announce a list of 52 firms to be liquidated in the November 2000 restructuring program. However, many large distressed firms that threatened the efficiency of the Korean economy were not included in the list. Only those of relatively small importance were major targets of the program. With the postponement of the disposal of large distressed firms, real sector restructuring has reached an impasse.

Table 2.2 Latent insolvency among firms subject to external audits (based on financial data as of end 1998)

| | | EBITDA/(interest costs) ||| Earnings/interest ratio ||| |
		1 or above (A)	Below 1 (B)	B/(A+B)	1 or above (C)	Below 1 (D)	D/(C+D)	A+B (= C+D)
Top five *chaebols*	No. of firms	111	38	26%	105	44	30%	149
	Loans	142	24	14%	125	41	25%	166
Second-tier *chaebols*	No. of firms	233	196	46%	226	203	47%	429
	Loans	44	52	54%	41	55	57%	96
Independent firms	No. of firms	3898	1640	30%	3760	1778	32%	5538
	Loans	56	37	40%	54	39	42%	93
Total	No. of firms	4242	1874	31%	4091	2025	33%	6116
	Loans	242	113	32%	219	135	38%	354

Notes:
Loans in trillion won.
EBITDA (Earnings before interest payments and taxes plus depreciation and amortization) is the profit of a company before deducting interest and tax, plus depreciation and amortization. It shows a company's profit from the cash flow resulting from business operations.
EBIT (earnings before interest payments and taxes) is the same as EBITDA, except that is does not include depreciation and amortization.

Table 2.3 Proportion of manufacturing firms with earnings/interest ratios below unity (%)

	1995	1996	1997	1998	1999	2000	2001 (1st half)
By no. of firms	24.7	28.3	32.3	30.6	32.6	26.3	30.0
By loan amounts	–	21.9	25.7	32.8	62.6	50.0	50.0

Note: Data before 1998 report EBITDA/interest costs for 6116 manufacturing firms surveyed as of end 1999. From 1999, the figures are EBIT/interest costs for firms reporting total annual sales above 2 billion won to the National Tax Service in 1998.

Source: Bank of Korea, *Management Statistics*, with supplementary credit data from the Financial Supervisory Service.

The slowdown of real sector reform began in late 1998, when the government switched to a stimulative macroeconomic policy of low interest rates and ambitious public works programs. This policy was intended to alleviate corollary problems such as the failures among the *chaebols*' contractors that accompanied the process of restructuring. The restructuring program, which had proceeded despite the mass unemployment and corporate failures in early 1998, now took a back seat to the stimulus policy. Nonviable firms that should have been shut down found new life through the last-minute corporate bailout measures such as loan maturity extensions and preferential interest rates. These were essentially stop-gap measures that transferred corporate financial problems to the financial sector and avoided the realization of latent insolvencies by extending additional credit to distressed firms.

The real sector still lacks a system to force the exit of nonviable firms. This is because the government has failed to provide direction, leadership and commitment to fundamental principles. Even now the government is sticking to its corporate bailout policy rather than upholding the principle of the survival of the fittest. A particularly egregious example was the government's Fast-Track Underwriting Program of December 2000. This program was intended to stabilize the financial market by having the Korea Development Bank support the refinancing of corporate bonds on maturity, with the goal of insulating viable firms and subcontractors from the effects of a credit crunch. However, viable and nonviable firms not being easy to distinguish economically (and the latter often having disproportionate political influence), in practice the program has militated against the principle that nonviable firms should stop operating. The decision of whether to extend additional financial support should be left to the firm's primary bank, which presumably has the best information about the firm's finances and management. The Fast-Track

Underwriting Program, however, leaves the decision in the hands of the Korea Development Bank, which has political as well as economic motives.

Chaebol Reform

The unconstrained expansion of the *chaebols* was checked during the reform process, as evidenced by the drop in the number of affiliated companies in the top 30 *chaebols* from 819 in 1997 to 544 in 2000. But it is still too early to say that the *chaebols* are now focused on improving their efficiency and profitability. As Korea has begun to recover from its crisis, the *chaebols* have repeatedly requested the easing or removal of restrictions on them, to some effect. For example, the government agreed to loosen the restrictions on the total equity investment ceiling with the passage of a bill in December 2001. It is presumably not a coincidence that the number of *chaebol* subsidiaries increased from 544 in 2000 to 624 in 2001.

There has been significant progress in reducing the *chaebols*' debt/equity ratios, mainly as a result of the government's imposition of a 200 percent target ratio, to be met by the end of 1999. To cite one prominent example, Hyundai's debt/equity ratio was successfully reduced from 449 percent at the end of 1998 to 341 percent by the middle of 1999. However, there are reasons to doubt whether the observed reduction in the debt/equity ratios really represents an improvement in capital structures and underlying financial management practices. For example, Hyundai's total debt increased even while its debt/equity ratio decreased. Mako (2003) argues that the *chaebols* utilized a variety of subterfuges in order to meet the government's targets, for example pressuring their affiliates to issue additional equity, without achieving much in substance.

Table 2.4 shows how the internal ownership structure of the *chaebols* has changed since the crisis. It reveals that the controlling power of *chaebol* owners actually increased through shares held by affiliated companies even though their individual shares have been reduced, at least through 1999. Some observers question whether subsequent progress in reducing the concentration of control will be sustained, given the success of the *chaebols* in watering down de-control provisions in April 2002 (K. Kim, 2002).

Neither is there much evidence of a significant reduction in the product market power of the *chaebols*. The shares of Korean GDP accounted for by the top five and top 30 *chaebols* have not fallen significantly since the crisis. The Big Deals, the most prominent symbol of business sector restructuring and rationalization, did not achieve much in reducing excess capacity, enhancing efficiency or intensifying competition. In fact, the most prominent goal of the Big Deals, to allow individual *chaebols* to specialize in different strategic sectors and therefore to develop corresponding core competencies,

Table 2.4 Changes in internal ownership of the 30 largest chaebols (%)

Ownership	April 1997	April 1998	April 1999	April 2000	April 2001
Same person	3.7	3.1	2.0	1.5	1.9
Special relation	4.8	4.8	3.4	3.0	2.3
Affiliated company	33.7	35.7	44.1	36.6	35.9
Own equity share	0.8	0.9	1.0	2.3	4.2
Total	43.0	44.5	50.5	43.3	44.3

Note: POSCO was not included here since POSCO, while one of the top 30 largest business groups as of April 2001, is not a *chaebol*.

Source: K. Kim (2002).

was intrinsically anticompetitive. In the event, it was never realized anyway. The Big Deals also opened a door for more government intervention, which hardly set a useful precedent. Government intervention should have taken the form of establishing a legal and institutional environment conducive to the operation of the market mechanism. In the event, government officials preferred to exert their political muscle through direct involvement in the restructuring process, by encouraging Big Deals, rather than simply by setting rules of the game (Jun, 2002).

Transparency

The importance of transparency in accounting was demonstrated by the Daewoo bankruptcy in 1999, a case where inadequate information allowed a troubled *chaebol* to keep piling up more debt to the point where it almost single-handedly brought the reform program to a halt (D. Lee, 2003). Without transparency, one can hardly expect that loan assessments can be normalized and bad debts reduced. Neither can one expect the investor confidence needed for the development of a capital market. Furthermore, the lack of transparency abets excess investment and bubble formation by distorting resource allocation, as it impedes competition and compromises the signaling effect of prices.

Much effort has been made to enhance transparency since the 1997 crisis. The aforementioned requirement for Korean corporations to issue consolidated financial statements is an example. The amendment of the Securities and Exchange Act in 2000 stipulated that no less than a fourth of the directors of listed companies had to be outside directors. Some large companies were subject to even stronger constraints, with the number of outside directors set to at least three and comprising no less than half of the total number of directors. The rights of minority shareholders in a listed company were also strengthened. For example, as of 2002, the threshold to invoke the right to inspect the account book was lowered to 0.1 percent of outstanding shares. Those shareholders of a listed company who continued to hold no less than 1/10 000 of the total outstanding shares for at least six months could now file a derivative suit on behalf of the company. However, even with the various amendments, the effectiveness of the measures taken to increase the transparency of firms still needs to be proven. For example, in many firms, the role of outside directors is nominal rather than real. That said, much remains to be done.

Financial Restructuring

The massive injection of public funds contributed to clearing up the problem of nonperforming loans in the financial sector. However, even with the injection of public funds and steps by financial institutions to reduce NPLs, the problem has not been resolved because inadequate restructuring of the corporate sector has allowed the volume of NPLs at financial institutions to begin rising again. Table 2.5 shows their development over 1998–2001. The NPL ratio improved after the first injection of public funds in 1998 but worsened again in 2000. Subsequently, NPLs have fallen somewhat in 2001, thanks to the second injection of public funds, better performance by commercial banks as they focused increasingly on retail finance, larger deposit-loan interest spreads, and more decisive action by the banks to write off bad loans.

The NPL problem is most serious among non-banks. At the time of writing, merchant banks and insurance companies are in relatively good health, thanks to the stringent restructuring they have undergone in the last few years. Securities companies, mutual trust companies and leasing companies, in contrast, are in relatively poor shape. As of the end of September 1999, NPLs as a share of the assets of merchant banks and insurance companies were 8.5 and 28.3 percent, respectively, whereas comparable rates for securities companies, mutual trust companies and leasing companies were 48.2, 46.5 and 32.0 percent, respectively. Normal operation – and a positive contribution to the process of financial intermediation – can hardly be expected of financial institutions saddled with such massive burdens. Derivative of the problem of NPLs is the clustering of the arrival of maturity dates of the Deposit Insurance Fund (DIF) bonds used to raise public funds for financial restructuring. This clustering of the maturity dates could create major problems for Korean financial markets in the near future if DIF debt rollovers crowd out other debt issuance.

Table 2.5 Trends in nonperforming loans (trillion won)

		1998 End Jun.	1998 End Dec.	1999 End Jun.	1999 End Dec.	2000 End Jun.	2000 End Dec.	2001 End Jun.	2001 End Sep.
Banks	Total loans (A)	471.6	443.4	439.2	474.2	02.5	526.1	529.4	543.7
	NPLs (B)	40.0	33.6	37.1	61.2	56.5	42.1	30.2	27.4
	Ratio (B/A)	8.5%	7.6%	8.4%	12.9%	11.3%	8.0%	5.7%	5.0%
Non-banks	Total loans (A)	153.2	133.9	120.9	116.7	105.0	95.3	92.2	92.4
	NPLs (B)	23.5	26.6	26.3	28.6	26.0	22.5	19.6	18.9
	Ratio (B/A)	15.3%	20.0%	21.8%	24.5%	24.8%	23.6%	21.3%	20.5%
Total	Total loans (A)	624.8	576.5	560.1	590.9	607.5	621.4	621.6	636.1
	NPLs (B)	63.5	60.2	63.4	88.0	82.5	64.6	49.8	46.3
	Ratio (B/A)	10.2%	10.5%	11.3%	14.9%	13.6%	10.4%	8.0%	7.3%

Notes: 'NPLs (B)' refer to the sum of loans classified as fixed, doubtful and estimated loss. The forward-looking criteria were adopted in late 1999.

Source: Financial Supervisory Service, *Financial Supervision Information*, various issues.

Another reason for the poor progress in financial restructuring can be found in the government's reluctance to dissolve distressed banks. The essence of the second financial sector restructuring program launched in late 2000 was to encourage mergers between banks in relatively better financial shape, and to consolidate nonviable banks under financial holding companies. Considering the realities of the Korean financial system, it is doubtful whether the bank mergers or the establishment of financial holding companies alone can be expected to yield the intended results. The financial institutions consolidated under the umbrella of holding companies are, without exception, in very poor shape. In the United States, the rationale for creating bank holding companies was to allow healthy financial institutions to pursue lines of business traditionally dominated by bank and nonbank institutions – that is, to exploit economies of scope. In contrast, in Korea the holding company system is being used to disguise the residual problems that continue to lurk in the merged banks. There is no reason to expect that the economic and financial condition of unsound banks will improve simply as a result of consolidating them into a holding company. The holding company system appears to be an attempt to restore the financial health of troubled intermediaries simply by slimming down their organization and personnel. Clearly, this is only one of several elements needed to enhance the banks' long-term performance.

In November 2001 the Ministry of Finance and Economy proposed a bill to amend Korea's banking laws to relax restrictions on the ownership of banks by the *chaebols* while at the same time strengthening financial supervision, as a way of preventing the re-emergence of connected lending. The bill was enacted in 2002. The new Banking Act, effective on 28 July 2002, permits an individual (including any other person acting in concert) to hold shares of a bank up to 10 percent of outstanding shares while the original ceiling was 4 percent. It is also possible for anyone to hold more shares than the ceiling with the permission of the supervisory authority. In reality, the major beneficiary of the relaxation of restrictions on the ownership of banks is mainly the *chaebol*-related entity, since very few individuals could increase holdings of shares up to 10 percent at a time.[15] In addition, the new Banking Act facilitates *chaebols*' acquisition of banks by revising Clause 3, Article 11 of the Financial Holding Company Act of October 2000 which prohibited a *chaebol* firm from engaging in the banking business unless five years had passed since the firm dis-affiliated itself from the *chaebol* group. However under the new law, a *chaebol* firm could own a bank merely by providing a plan to transform itself into a dis-affiliated firm within two years.

The purpose of this amendment is to facilitate the recovery of public funds by early sales of banks taken over by the state during the restructuring process. This is a risky strategy, given Korea's still underdeveloped system of prudential supervision and regulation, the *chaebols*' past performance, and the observed consequences of allowing them to effectively control nonbank financial institutions.[16] All these raise serious doubts as to whether the government has any credible intention or concrete idea for implementing financial reform.

ECONOMIC REFORM: SETTING THE COURSE

The measure of the success of the reform should be whether Korea succeeds in establishing a legal and institutional framework conducive to the operation of a competitive market economy. The success of reform cannot be judged by the performance of immediate macroeconomic indicators alone. Rather, it should be judged by how efficiently the market is operating. And how efficiently the market is operating depends, in turn, on how rigorously the 'survival-of-the-fittest' principle is being followed, and in particular on whether market forces are allowed to compel the closure of unprofitable firms.

In countries with well-developed market systems, a firm's profitability seals its fate. In Korea, in contrast, it has always been firm size rather than profitability that has shaped a firm's interaction with the market. Because the market evaluated firms by external rather than internal criteria (by size rather than profitability), the 'too big to fail' principle prevailed. Firms therefore concentrated on maximizing size rather than profits, inevitably resulting in over-investment and poor financial health.

The role of the financial sector, and specifically of the commercial banks, is important in this regard. The survival-of-the-fittest principle cannot take root unless banks tighten up their loan screening practices, and other financial institutions produce more meaningful corporate credit ratings for use by other financial market participants. This is why financial sector restructuring is important – why the survival-of-the-fittest principle must be applied there as well. This means that insolvent banks should be closed even if they are very large, or at least that their owners' stakes should be eliminated when they are recapitalized.

Besides curing past ailments, restructuring must also aim to build up an economic system that will be both efficient and stable. This principle applies to both the real and financial sectors. Transparency must be enhanced to achieve this end. Stronger accounting standards must be introduced. The core financial data published by intermediaries – such as paid-in capital ratios, NPLs and net profits – must acquire more economic content. A particular problem in this context is loan accounting, including standards for credit classification and loan loss provisions, all of which are notoriously inaccurate. Financial supervision is meaningless without reliable data. When combined with improper financial market practices, this lack of transparency makes it nearly impossible to establish clear lines of accountability.

Thus measures to enhance market discipline and transparency are the key components of the reform agenda to create a more efficient, competitive market economy in Korea. Viewed from this perspective, the transformation has only begun.

NOTES

1. Korea's economic growth, which created the *chaebols* that became too large for government control, has been likened to Dr Frankenstein's creation (*Economist*, 1995).
2. For example, it is well known that a *chaebol*'s decision to enter the already-overcrowded car industry was related more to the owner's personal enthusiasm for the industry than to the profitability of the investment project itself.
3. This is why foreign investors are pressing for greater transparency to be the first priority in Korea's economic reform agenda.
4. The figures are for 1972 (4.9 percent), when the matter of distressed companies surfaced as a serious issue; 1980 (−2.1 percent) which saw the Kwangju uprising; and 1998 (−6.7 percent), when the economy suffered the worst from the 1997 crisis.
5. Hsieh (2002) questions the validity of the low TFP estimates of the NICs (newly industrializing countries), especially that of Singapore, based on his dual estimates of productivity growth. Young (1998) acknowledges that TFP estimates could be sensitive to the estimation procedures and the data used. However, it is undeniable that the TFP estimate of Korea is much lower than those of advanced countries.
6. Nonperforming assets are defined here as promissory notes that are past due or subject to court receivership, plus loans in arrears for over six months.
7. Total government bond issuance was about 2.9 trillion won in 1997, but increased to 13.3 and 17.3 trillion won in 1998 and 1999, respectively, as government spending expanded. As a result, fiscal expenditures on interest on public funds and existing government bonds increased from 2.3 trillion won in 1997 to 5.9 trillion won in 1999, and 3.3 trillion won in the first half of 2000.
8. Refer to the section beginning on p. 40 for the consequences of the plan.
9. For complete coverage on what kind of measures have been taken, refer to K. Kim (2002) and Joh (2002).
10. A sum of 64 trillion won amounts to 13.8 percent of the average GDP of 1998 and 1999. The GDP of the Korean economy was 444.4 (in trillion won) in 1998, 482.7 in 1999 and 517.1 in 2000.
11. The guarantee of interest and principal requires the approval of the National Assembly.
12. Although public funds do not require immediate government expenditure, the burden falls on the government if the two funds cannot pay for the bonds at maturity. 'Government funds' in this case (note: the direct translation from the Korean is also public funds) refer to funds borrowed for financial sector restructuring from the IBRD (International Bank for Reconstruction and Development) and ADB (Asian Development Bank), plus equity investment by state-run banks and funds borrowed by KAMCO (Korea Asset Management Corporation) and KDIC (Korea Deposit Insurance Corporation). These funds do not require approval by the legislature, but are otherwise identical to public funds in nature and usage.
13. Jun (2002) provides a complete discussion on the changes in the legal environment around the 1997 crisis.
14. An index value of less than 1 implies that the firm's operating profit does not cover even its interest costs. Firms are generally rated as sound when the index exceeds 3.

15. As far as the *chaebols* are concerned, they cannot exercise the voting right in excess of 4 percent of outstanding shares even if they hold more shares than that. However, many are still worried that there may be many other informal ways available to the *chaebols* to control banks once they are allowed to own a bank. For example, suppose a *chaebol*-related entity owns 10 percent of the shares of a bank. Even though control right is still 4 percent in this case, as soon as a *chaebol*-related entity sells its shares to a non-*chaebol*-related entity, the purchaser obtains 10 percent of control right immediately. Thus even when a *chaebol*-related entity could only have 4 percent voting right, its influence is substantial if it owns a large portion of shares.
16. Refer to S. Kim (2002).

3. What caused the crisis? A *post mortem*[1]

Won-Am Park and Gongpil Choi

INTRODUCTION

Since the devastating crisis of 1997–98, the Asian economies have shown remarkable resilience. While early *post mortems* cited structural weaknesses in the affected countries as the principal cause of the crisis, the speed and vigor of the subsequent recovery sits uneasily with this explanation emphasizing deeply flawed economic and financial structures. The rapid turnaround, epitomized by Korea, is widely attributed to the fundamental strength of the Asian economies. Indeed, it can be argued that the recovery was due more to the restoration of the old system, reinvigorated by macroeconomic policy stimulus and the shedding of excess capacity in heavy industry, than to any fundamental change in economic structure. All this is seen as casting doubt on the structural-flaws explanation for the crisis and as supporting instead an interpretation emphasizing volatile capital flows and erratic investor sentiment.

To be sure, the post-crisis recovery has a transient element. There is a tendency for growth to exceed sustainable rates in the short run, as the economy begins to spring back from the crisis. This is a specific instance of a general point: growth performance in Asia over any short horizon must be placed in the context of the boom-and-bust cycles experienced by the economies of the region. It follows that any effort to identify the causes of the Asian crisis must adopt a broader perspective and a longer time frame.

More than five years after the crisis, there remains considerable disagreement about why the crisis occurred and how it should have been resolved. For the sake of simplicity, the academic community may be divided into two camps. The first camp focuses on problems of illiquidity in Asia and emphasizes instability in international financial markets, along with sudden shifts in market expectations and confidence, as factors triggering the crisis.[2] Defenders of this view argue that a new international financial architecture should be created feature expanded support facilities extended through the international financial institutions (IFIs), orderly international workout procedures, and systemic safeguards. This view also holds that the merits of high interest rates and other policies of austerity as measures to resolve a crisis should be reconsidered, as these may do more to compound than to ameliorate a country's economic and financial problems, and that they may fail to improve policy makers' credibility with the markets.

Members of the opposing camp, which includes the IMF, stress structural weakness and policy distortions in the countries in question, and in particular moral hazard in both the corporate and financial sectors. This view emphasizes the need for fundamental restructuring to create a macroeconomic and financial basis for sustainable growth.[3] In Korea, it is said that the crisis reflected lax financial supervision and inadequate financial regulation and the resulting mismatch in the sources and uses of funds. In short, Korea's relatively strong macroeconomic fundamentals compared with other East Asian countries could not prevent it from succumbing to crisis, given these structural weaknesses.

Our own view is that the Asian crisis resulted from the interaction of internal structural weaknesses with the instability of the international financial markets (an interpretation that can also be found in, *inter alia*, Eichengreen, 1999 and Chopra, et al. 2001). These two causes are interrelated rather than mutually exclusive, because structurally unsound economies tend to be more vulnerable to instability in financial markets. In particular, the high-growth strategy and the associated exchange rate regime rendered the financial sector vulnerable to erratic shifts in investor sentiment, more so with the progress of financial opening.

The remainder of this chapter develops these points. It examines the causes of the Korean crisis, with special attention to the role of the exchange rate regime in creating financial vulnerability. In the next section, we describe various aspects of economic vulnerability and account for the economy's susceptibility to contagion and so-called self-fulfilling speculative attacks. In the following section, we test the empirical power of the competing explanations for the Korean crisis. Concluding remarks are provided in the last section.

ANATOMY OF THE CRISIS

We start by describing the seeds of Korea's crisis and proceed to the financial market and policy failures.

The Debt-financed High-growth Strategy

Following its inauguration in February 1993, the administration of President Kim Young-sam embarked on an ambitious plan to revive the economy and bolster sagging investor confidence through a campaign for a 'new economy.'

Investment picked up in 1994-95, due largely to measures taken to liberalize the financial system and the economy. The increase in productive capacity was dramatic, especially in Korea's five major industries (that is, shipbuilding, semiconductor, steel, auto and petrochemicals). Korea's accession to the OECD in 1996 was significant in this context, because it lent further momentum to the liberalization of the financial system and the current account. Capital account liberalization rendered Korea more vulnerable to a crisis because it introduced new sources of shocks, including potentially shocks to capital flows, to which the country's slowly responding heavy-industry-based economy could not easily adjust. This became evident as early as 1995–96 (the period *before* capital flows declined), when Korea experienced a deterioration in its terms of trade. Faced with heavy debt service obligations, Korean industry, rather than adjusting, maintained production levels even in the face of declining shipments, resulting in a sharp rise in the inventory/shipment ratio in 1996. Meanwhile, high levels of investment in heavy industry caused the country to incur large current account deficits beginning in 1994, deficits that had to be financed by increasing the country's reliance on capital inflows. Those deficits widened with the depreciation of the Chinese yuan that same year, which further squeezed Korean export prices. Although the volume of exports remained steady, declining unit prices contributed to the further deterioration of the current account balance.

To make matters worse, a huge mismatch between assets and liabilities arose as a result of borrowers' increasingly heavy reliance on low-interest, short-term financing. Poorly sequenced liberalization of the capital account of the balance of payments, in conjunction with inadequate supervision by the prudential authorities, allowed excessive short-term borrowing overseas. Korea became involved in a vicious cycle of misplaced investment in low-profit heavy industries fed by excessive short-term external borrowing. Ironically, those short-term capital inflows placed pressure on the won to appreciate even while the fundamental underlying position of the country's export industries deteriorated.

Early indications of the impending crisis surfaced in 1996 as economic growth began to slow. The declining growth rate contrasted with the current account deficit, which widened to 4.8 percent of GDP in 1996, from less than 2 percent in the two preceding years. The weakening of the Japanese yen in 1995–96, following depreciation of the yuan in 1994, exacerbated this source of weakness. All the while, the burgeoning external deficit was financed by inflows of foreign capital, especially short-term flows, a maturity structure that was itself a reflection of declining foreign confidence in Korea's ability to sustain its competitiveness.

Foreign investors were not oblivious to the deterioration in the external position. As their confidence began to crumble, the won began to weaken.

Table 3.1 Major economic indicators (%)

	1991	1992	1993	1994	1995	1996	1997
Gross domestic product	9.1	5.1	5.8	8.6	8.9	7.1	5.5
Consumption	9.3	6.8	5.3	7.0	7.2	6.9	3.5
(Private)	9.5	6.6	5.7	7.6	8.3	6.8	3.1
(Public)	8.5	7.6	3.0	4.2	1.0	7.8	5.7
Fixed investment	12.6	−0.8	5.2	11.8	11.7	7.1	−3.5
(Construction)	13.0	−0.6	8.9	4.5	8.7	6.2	2.7
(Equipment)	12.1	−1.1	−0.1	23.6	15.8	8.3	−11.3
Exports	11.8	11.0	11.3	16.5	24.0	13.0	23.6
Imports	19.2	5.1	6.7	21.7	22.0	14.8	3.8
Savings and investment							
Gross savings/GDP	35.9	34.7	35.1	35.2	35.9	34.5	34.2
Gross investment/GDP	38.9	36.6	35.1	36.1	37.0	38.2	36.1
Current account/GDP	−2.8	−1.3	0.3	−1.0	−1.8	−4.8	−1.9
Compensation of employees/NI	60.2	61.0	60.4	60.0	61.2	63.3	–
Consumer price index	9.3	6.2	4.8	6.3	4.5	4.9	4.4
Producer price index	4.7	2.2	1.5	2.8	4.7	2.7	3.8
Inventory/shipment ratio	1.10	1.12	1.09	1.03	1.04	1.11	1.10

Source: Bank of Korea, *National Income* (various issues).

There was a steep decline in short-term trade credit early in the second half of 1996, with strong expectations of declines to follow, reversing the increase that had occurred in the first half of the year. Traders paid back credit early in order to avoid incurring rising debt burdens due to a weaker won in the future (G. Choi, 1999); this contributed further to the weakness of the balance of payments.

Other signs of system fatigue began surfacing in early 1997. Investors began to question the lender-of-last-resort capacity of the government, effectively terminating the era of debt-financed high growth. A number of companies, starting with Hanbo Steel, collapsed under their huge debt burdens early in the year. The next high-profile bankruptcy was Kia, in July. These failures signaled a break from the government's practice of supporting large groups through various schemes, such as coordinated lending and bridge loans arranged through the application of political pressure. The abrupt withdrawal of government support, while consistent with the desire to place greater reliance on market forces, was not helpful for confidence. As in

52   *The Korean economy beyond the crisis*

Mexico in 1995, it placed the authorities in the awkward position of emphasizing the market principle at a financially sensitive time, while also struggling with the reality that the country's largest enterprises might still be 'too big to fail.'

Fragile Financial System and Lax Supervision

The financial system in Korea was quite well adapted to the high-growth strategy, which emphasized measures to promote the expansion of the *chaebols*, but less well adapted to the new, more diversified environment for growth. The exchange rate regime was also better suited to the past than the present; that regime focused on stabilizing currencies against the dollar (McKinnon, 2000) and sustaining old industries through exports to the United States, which encouraged unhedged foreign borrowing by minimizing perceived exchange risk, rather than on facilitating adjustment and promoting prudent risk management. The persistence of these old practices in a new environment led to excessive investment in several key industries, which squeezed cash flows and undermined the quality of the assets held by Korea's commercial banks.

Financial repression had long been justified because it led to high growth, but by the mid-1990s it had clearly lost much of its effectiveness. With financial opening, the Korean economy began to experience a serious mismatch problem (Chung, 2002). These facts did not escape Korean policy makers, who sought to upgrade the economic system to accommodate the more liberalized financial environment. For the first time, profitability received the same emphasis as growth and market share. Increasingly it was acknowledged that input-driven growth without systemic restructuring resulted in serious mismatches between market expectations and corporate performance. But efforts to upgrade the system were hampered by the fragility of market structures. There was enormous concern for the stability of the system – a stability that might be undermined if reform proceeded too quickly. This concern delayed the implementation of fundamental solutions.

Needless to say, the insolvencies of several large corporations even before the crisis compromised the soundness of financial institutions with large exposures to heavy industry. The total volume of nonperforming loans (NPLs) at commercial and merchant banks as of the end of 1996 stood at about 13 trillion won and more than tripled to 43 trillion won by December 1997.[4] Merchant banking corporations, which were not closely supervised because they had only recently been upgraded from small finance companies, held a total of 3.9 trillion won in NPLs by the end of October 1997, nearly three times the 1.3 trillion won the levels of end 1996. By the end of March 1998, the nonperforming loans of the consolidated financial sector (nonbank financial

Table 3.2 Nonperforming loans at financial institutions (trillion won)

	Dec. 1996	Dec. 1997	Mar. 1998	June 1998
Precautionary Loans of Banks	– –	42.8 (9.4)	57.7 (13.0)	72.5 (16.3)
Non-Performing Loans of Banks and Merchant Banks (A)	13.5 (3.2)	43.6 (9.6)	59.6 (13.4)	63.5 (14.3)
NPL of Banks	12.2 (2.6)	31.6 (6.9)	38.8 (8.5)	40.0 (8.7)
NPL of Merchant Banks	1.3 (0.3)	12.0 (2.6)	20.8 (4.7)	23.5 (5.3)
Total Loan of Banks and Merchant Banks (B)	434.4 (103.8)	647.4 (143.0)	668.7 (150.5)	624.8 (140.6)
A/B (%)	3.1	6.7	8.9	10.2

Notes:
Figures in parentheses represent nonperforming loans as a percentage of nominal GDP.

Source: Ministry of Finance and Economy, *Press Release* (1998) and Bank of Korea, *Bank Supervisory Service* (1996–98).

institutions as well as banks) had risen to 59.6 trillion won, the equivalent of 13 percent of GDP. Clearly, declining international competitiveness and then the imposed crisis had a crushing burden on an already fragile financial sector. What was notable was that this increased vulnerability was not reflected in macroeconomic indicators, which allowed some observers to remain blissfully oblivious of underlying weaknesses. Indeed, the indicators suggested by so-called 'first-generation' models of financial crises, which emphasize the roles of monetary and fiscal policies, still suggested that the Korean position was fundamentally sound.

Inadequate Transparency

Gaps in the information environment further explain why so many failed to appreciate the underlying risks. Many of the relevant data were not easily available due to the Korean economy's inadequate transparency. Figures provided by the government and private corporations were not indicative of the true economic situation. In the industrial sector, conglomerates composed of many seemingly independent affiliates had been the major drivers of the country's growth since the 1960s. Their profitability was often overstated as a result of related-party transactions and cross-payment guarantees. Because such guarantees were not illegal and internal transactions were not reported, the supervisory authorities could not prevent or even effectively monitor these practices.

The situation of Korean financial institutions was also less healthy than it appeared on the surface. As a result of cross-payment guarantees, bad loans were understated. To make matters worse, the figures for banks' nonperforming loans excluded substandard loans. While a serious deterioration in profitability in financial institutions had occurred well before the crisis was under way, neither the authorities nor investors were in a position to detect it. Since the figures as reported did not reflect the true condition of the country's corporations and financial institutions, the authorities had no basis on which to take prompt corrective action.

Market Principles Ignored

At a deeper level, the problem in Korea was the paralysis of the market mechanism. Market principles, to put it simply, were not applied. Moral hazard due to implicit government guarantees was widespread; it affected corporations, financial institutions, workers and bank depositors alike. Corporations, especially large-scale enterprises, including the *chaebols*, had long enjoyed official protection and operated under the shelter of generous import restrictions. They could borrow at low interest rates, creating strong incentives to expand without proper consideration of risks and returns; this encouraged the sharp rise in debt/equity ratios. By the end of 1997, the 30 largest Korean conglomerates had an average debt/equity ratio of 387 percent, in contrast to 154 percent in the US, 193 percent in Japan, and 86 percent in Taiwan. High leverage was a major factor in the vulnerability of large enterprises in 1997.

The weakness of market discipline allowed Korean firms to pursue growth rather than profitability or efficiency. In this sense, the crisis was a result, not a cause, of the low profitability of Korean enterprises. As most Korean firms had little cushion against external shocks, their survival depended upon sales volume. Since most of their operating costs were fixed, typical of companies in heavy industry, any temporary shortfall in cash flow could only be satisfied by further borrowing, which resulted in still higher leverage ratios over time. Many firms' investment outlays were financed exclusively by borrowing, not also through retained earnings or cash flows as in major corporations in advanced countries.

Neither were market principles observed in the financial sector. The government often operated supposedly 'private' financial institutions as *de facto* government banks, regulating personnel management and day-to-day opera-

Table 3.3 *Financial indicators for 30 largest* chaebols *(trillion won, %)*

Excess guarantees of major conglomerates (end February 1998)

	Loans (A)	Debt guarantees	Guarantee offers	Sum(B)	Excess guarantees (B–A)	Ratio (B/A)
Total	25.3 (5.7)	33.5 (7.5)	6.9 (1.6)	(40.4) (9.1)	15.1 (3.4)	159

Debt ratio and number of affiliated companies of 30 top conglomerates

	1995	1996	1997	1998
Debt ratio (%)	355.7	347.5	386.5	518.9
Number of affiliated companies	623	669	819	804

Note: Figures in parentheses show percentage ratio to nominal GDP.

Sources: Korea Fair Trade Commission, *Corporate Strategy for Financial Institutions to Resolve the Corporate Debt Guarantee Problem* (1998a) and *Large Business Groups and Designation of Business Groups with Debt Guarantee Restrictions* (1998b).

tions. This did not allow banks and financial institutions to be run as profit-maximizing concerns, rendering it unsurprising that they ultimately accumulated massive volumes of nonperforming loans. Counterparty discipline was weak; the banks allowed firms to waste resources through inefficient and redundant investments. Government-controlled financial institutions had weak profit motives and merely channeled funds from foreign sources to domestic enterprises without conducting due diligence.

These problems were of little concern so long as economic growth was high and jobs were plentiful. The independent media, the only outlet which might have exposed the true situation, was suppressed or marginalized with the advent of *chaebol* media groups, which mainly promoted the interests of elite groups and the captains of industry. These links began to fray once Korea attained OECD membership and the government pursued economic and financial liberalization. Heavy reliance on external sources of financing also served to gradually break down the close ties among Korean power groups, since foreign creditors demanded independent monitoring and supervision.

These capital market distortions had important implications for investor behavior in the period leading up to the crisis. In an environment where risk

Table 3.4 Manufacturing sector statistics (%)

Manufacturing sector	1992	1993	1994	1995	1996	1997
Equity to total assets	23.9	25.3	24.8	25.9	24	20.2
Debt ratio	318.7	294.9	302.5	286.8	317.1	396.3
Total borrowings and total assets	47.2	46.8	44.5	44.8	47.7	54.2
Current ratio	92.8	94.1	94.6	95.4	91.9	91.8
Fixed ratio	227.4	218.5	220.2	212.5	237	261.1
Ordinary income to sales	1.5	1.7	2.7	3.6	1	–0.3
ROE	3.7	4.2	7.6	11	2	–4.2
ROA	0.9	1	1.9	2.8	0.5	–0.9

Semiconductor industry						
Export unit price (2000=100)	664.1	664.1	743.9	766.9	329.6	243.3
(growth rate, %)	(–)	(0.0)	(–12.0)	(–31.0)	(–57.0)	(–26.2)
Growth rate of exports	21.1	3.1	54.3	68.7	–15.6	13.2
ROE	–	–	18.4	48.9	5.9	14.5
ROA	–	–	4	16.4	2	2.9
Net barter terms of trade (%)	0.1	–1.6	3.4	1.2	–9.5	–2.6

Source: Bank of Korea, *Financial Statement Analysis* (various issues).

was given short shrift or even ignored, banks were free to expand their balance sheets and accumulate high-risk/high-return assets. There was no regulatory mechanism to prevent reckless behavior or to monitor the banks' on- and offshore activities in a comprehensive fashion. The implicit government guarantee militated against market-based risk management, and more generally disabled the market mechanism.

This situation was in some sense an unavoidable corollary of Korea's cultivation of a bank-centered financial system. The authorities restricted the ability of corporations to borrow on the international markets, while banks were freed to borrow abroad, rendering the *chaebols* dependent on their debt.

In retrospect, the country's financial weakness could have been contained if limits had been imposed on the intermediaries' access to external funding. The authorities' failure to do so not only heightened financial fragility but also consolidated the tripartite superstructure of the bureaucracy, banking sector and politicians, in effect locking in the problem.

Contagion

Along with the structural and financial vulnerabilities associated with the high-growth strategy, contagion is widely cited as an important element in the Korean crisis, as in the spread of emerging-market financial crises more generally.[5] In fact, external conditions worsened with the slowdown in the global electronics industry, appreciation of the dollar from the lows of early 1995, and the rise of competition from China. Viewed from this angle, the roots of the crisis go back to 1994, when China devalued the yuan by some 40 percent, provoking the competitive depreciation of the Japanese yen by more than 25 percent in 1994–95. Although joint US–Japanese intervention in 1995 first halted and then reversed the excessive strengthening of the yen, the Asian region remained under serious stress, and Korea's inflexible exchange rate system worsened the country's current account balance as its terms of trade deteriorated. Pressure on the won began to build, and suspicion mounted with regard to the sustainability of the external disequilibrium.

The combination of a bank-dominated financial system and a managed exchange rate heightened financial vulnerabilities and magnified financial stress, especially once misalignments between the dollar, yen and yuan became serious after 1994. The financial sector did not develop along with the economy, as evidenced by low profitability, high NPLs, and the general lack of oversight and transparency, while the choice of exchange rate regime encouraged moral hazard and increased the scope for contagion.

Pressure in the foreign exchange market intensified with the outbreak of turmoil in Thailand, Indonesia and Malaysia, and then with the Hong Kong market crash.[6] Japanese banks began cutting their credit lines and withdrawing money from the crisis countries, including Korea, in a scramble to restore their liquidity and capital adequacy. Even if Japanese banks were not the immediate trigger of contagion, their actions contributed to the spillover effects through the 'common lender channel' (Kaminsky and Schmukler, 1999; Masson, 1998). In this sense, a lack of financial cooperation in the region contributed importantly to the spread of the crisis.

As the country's foreign reserves declined, under pressure from currency depreciation in Thailand, Indonesia and Taiwan, confidence deteriorated in the won. While it was already widely anticipated in November that the Korean authorities would scrap the daily exchange rate trading band of ±2.25

percent, the impact on confidence when this finally happened was more devastating than anticipated. The widening of the daily trading band to ±10 percent on November 16 led to a steep decline. The won hit the maximum 10 percent limit on four consecutive trading days, forcing the suspension of foreign exchange trading.

The damage to confidence owing to the currency's abrupt collapse raises the question of why the authorities did not move in the direction of greater exchange rate flexibility at an earlier date. Even when signs of trouble, such as a massive current account deficit, had appeared in 1996, the authorities continued to insist on a stable exchange rate. They cited the need for the business community to become competitive on the world market in other ways than merely by taking advantage of a weak won. They emphasized the importance of stable exchange rates for exports and capital-market access. Whatever the case, the incompatibility of monetary independence, a stable exchange rate, and free capital mobility manifested itself in growing stress and heightened vulnerability. In retrospect, an exchange rate regime intended to maintain current account competitiveness backfired when financial opening rendered the capital account as important as the current account. In this context, a policy of stabilizing the exchange rate created even greater moral hazard for financial institutions and encouraged excessive investment in heavy industry.

There can be no doubt that the exchange rate regime was instrumental in the development of the imbalances that were at the root of Korea's structural weaknesses, and that it heightened the economy's susceptibility to contagion. In particular, limited exchange rate flexibility encouraged unhedged, short-term borrowing by merchant banks from overseas. In addition, the interdependence of Asian currencies, as a result of common adherence to the *de facto* dollar peg, contributed to the synchronicity of business cycles and the spread of the crisis.

Policy Failures

Why, then, did policy fail to respond? In fact, the government implemented a number of policy reforms. But its response was piecemeal and ineffective. Owing to inappropriate timing and internal inconsistency, it sent mixed and conflicting signals to the market. Take for example foreign exchange rate policy. Pegging is dangerous when a weak financial system experiences increased capital inflows and when, as a consequence, external competitiveness is undermined. In hindsight, if the daily fluctuation band had been widened earlier, the sudden and massive fall in the exchange value of the Korean won toward the end of 1997 might have been avoided.

Another example of policy inconsistency is the way in which the problem of distressed enterprises was addressed. The authorities repeatedly declared that troubled enterprises would be subject to market discipline. In practice, however, their problems were addressed through a variety of nonmarket mechanisms, such as court mediation or the application of the Bankruptcy Prevention Accord.[7] The authorities' failure promptly to address the problems of Kia, the country's eighth largest conglomerate, heightened distrust on the part of foreign investors. The Kia episode was taken as evidence that the authorities were not really prepared to deal with such issues openly, and that they had not assimilated the consequences of their policy of opening the financial system to international influences. The absence of a clear legal framework for resolving the problems of insolvent firms, the lack of adequate bankruptcy procedures, and the politically sensitive nature of these issues effectively rendered coherent policy responses infeasible. Politically, it was impossible to alter the exchange rate regime and address problems in the financial system in an orderly fashion when signs of stress began to appear.

Meanwhile, the government emphasized at every turn the fundamental soundness of the economy. This served to deepen distrust on the part of those international investors who had insight into the weaknesses of the economic and financial system. Confidence was seriously tested in the second half of 1997 as the authorities maintained an easy stance in the face of the spreading crisis infecting the rest of the Asian region. The decisions to convert Kia into a public enterprise and to guarantee the payments of foreign currency liabilities of Korean financial institutions were also made in the mistaken belief that such public intervention would improve international creditworthiness rather than undermine it. In fact, these actions disappointed international investors, who wanted market-based solutions. Government intervention only served to raise the level of uncertainty surrounding the Korean situation.

QUANTITATIVE ANALYSIS

This section turns to a quantitative analysis of the causes of the Korean economic crisis. In particular, we attempt to identify the relative roles of economic vulnerability and financial fragility. We adopt the indicator approach popularized by authors such as Kaminsky et al. (1997) and Kaminsky (1998). We also use a probit model to estimate the contributions of different factors, and attempt to test for self-fulfilling aspects of the crisis.

The Indicator Approach

Kaminsky et al. (1997) propose a number of indicators and a methodology useful for predicting a crisis. While most of empirical studies use multi-country data, we use only Korean data on the presumption that Korea's crisis experience was unique. We regard the Korean crisis as, first and foremost, a currency crisis and utilize exchange market pressure as a measure of its severity. A currency crisis is said to occur when we observe high values of an index exchange market pressure (*EMP*), which is a weighted average of won depreciation (Δe), percentage point changes in the interest rate (Δi), and percentage changes in foreign reserves from the previous year (ΔR). The weights of the components are the inverse of the standard deviation of each variable.

$$EMP = \frac{1}{\sigma_e} \times \Delta e + \frac{1}{\sigma_i} \times \Delta i - \frac{1}{\sigma_R} \times \Delta R \qquad (3.1)$$

The sample period is January 1990–November 1997 (the period December 1997–September 2000 is reserved for out-of-sample forecasts). Figure 3.1 shows the change in this index. *EMP* began to increase in 1996 and peaked in January 1998, after a brief decline around the middle of 1997. It then declined very rapidly until January 1999, when it turned upwards again. A crisis is defined to occur when the deviation of *EMP* from its mean exceeds 1.1 times the standard deviation of exchange market pressure.[8] This makes the

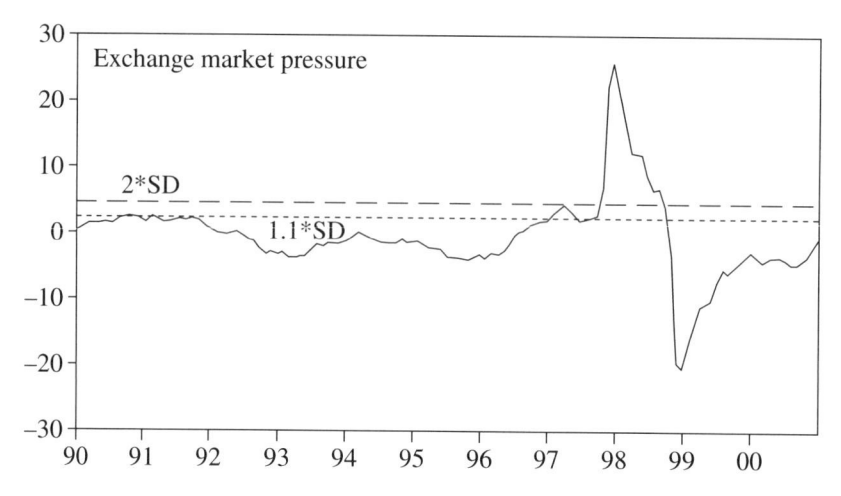

Note: Exchange market pressure is measured by a weighted average of the change in the won/dollar exchange rate (year on year), changes in corporate bond yields (y-o-y), and (negative) changes in reserves (tot), with weights determined by the inverse of the standard deviation of each variable.

Source: See text.

Figure 3.1 Exchange market pressure index

crisis months October–December 1990, February–June 1997 and November 1997.[9]

An indicator issues a signal for economic vulnerability when it crosses a certain threshold. Four combinations of signals and crises are shown in Table 3.5. A 'good' signal is one in which a crisis occurs within a certain period of time (here 12 months) after a signal is issued. The 12-month window allows time for the triggering mechanism and propagation. Since propagation is most likely when the economy is structurally weak, this methodology should pick up the self-fulfilling nature of a crisis to some extent. The Type I error of rejecting the null hypothesis of crisis when in fact there is a crisis is $C/(A+C)$, while the Type II error is $B/(B+D)$. The noise-to-signal ratio is defined as Type II error divided by one minus Type I error. The threshold of an indicator is defined in terms of the percentiles of the distribution of the indicator. An 'optimal' threshold for each indicator is set by minimizing the noise-to-signal ratio (the 'adjusted' ratio of false signals to good signals).[10]

Table 3.5 Signals and crises

	Crisis within 12 months	No crisis within 12 months
Signal was issued	A	B
No signal was issued	C	D

Source: See text.

Table 3.6 lists 22 indicators and shows the performance of each during the sample period of January 1990–November 1997. It is notable that such indicators as the terms of trade, the stock price index, exports, domestic credit/GDP, and the M2 multiplier predict the crisis quite accurately. Observe that, except for the interest differential, capital account/GDP, current account/GDP, and budget deficit/GDP, these indicators are expressed as year-on-year rates of growth.[11] Most of the data were obtained from the Bank of Korea database, except for the real effective exchange rates, which were obtained from JP Morgan. Since the noise/signal ratio of a random signal is one, we exclude from the list industrial production, the service price/manufacturing price, and foreign debt/total debt of those monetary institutions whose noise/signal ratios are in fact higher than one.

A composite indicator can be constructed by combining the signals issued by different indicators. We use the negatives of the noise/signal ratios rather than the inverse of the noise-to-signal ratios as weights, because the noise/signal ratios of some indicators are zero.

Table 3.6 Performance of indicators

	A/(A+C)	B/(B+D)	Noise/signal ratio [B/(B+D)]/ [A/(A+C)]	Threshold interval (x)	A/(A+B)
Terms of trade	45.5	0.0	0.00	4*	100.0
Industrial production**	21.2	25.8	1.22	1*	30.4
Inventory index/shipment index	45.5	12.9	0.28	1	65.2
Stock price**	36.4	8.1	0.22	7*	70.6
Dishonored bill ratio	12.1	9.7	0.80	12	40.0
Service price/manufacturing price	6.1	25.6	4.26	1	11.1
Capacity util. ratio in manufacturing	12.1	9.7	0.80	15*	40.0
Foreign exchange reserves**	42.4	14.5	0.34	2*	60.9
Capital account/GDP	18.2	6.5	0.35	15	60.0
Interest differential**	24.2	21.0	0.86	2	38.1
Current account/GDP	21.2	6.5	0.30	14*	63.6
REER**	18.2	12.9	0.71	7	42.9
Exports**	33.3	6.5	0.19	10*	73.3
Depreciation of Asian competitors	24.2	3.2	0.13	14	80.0
External debt/foreign reserves	39.4	14.5	0.37	2	57.1
Budget deficit/GDP	18.2	14.5	0.80	8	40.0
Domes. credit/GDP**	51.5	0.0	0.00	5	100.0
M2 multiplier	57.6	0.0	0.00	2	100.0
M2/foreign reserves	36.4	16.1	0.44	1	54.5
Foreign debt/total debt of monetary inst.	21.2	25.8	1.22	1	30.4
For. debt/for. res. of financial inst.	33.3	16.1	0.48	3	52.4
S&P credit rating	6.1	0.0	0.00	1	100.0

Notes:
Growth from the year earlier except for the interest differential (percentage point change) and capital account/GDP, current account/GDP, budget deficit/GDP (all at current levels). A through D represent the cell in Table 3.5. The threshold interval represents the corresponding interval among the upper 25% and upper 10% that minimizes the noise/signal ratio.
* Indicates the negative sign of the corresponding variable.
** Indicates the indicator listed in Kaminsky et al. (1997).

Source: See text.

What caused the crisis? 63

$$I_t = \sum_{j=1}^{n}(1-\omega^j)S_t^j \qquad (3.2)$$

where S_t^j is equal to 1 if indicator j crosses the threshold in period t and zero otherwise, and ω^j is the noise-to-signal ratio of variable j.

The number of signals was highest in January–February 1997 and January 1998, when 12 out of the 19 indicators used in this exercise issued warning signals. In contrast, no signal was issued in May–June 1995 or July 1999. The composite index as defined in equation (3.2) also reached high levels in January 1997, but fell to zero in May–June 1995 and July 1999.

The composite index (shown in Figure 3.2) seems to lead the index of exchange market pressure (shown in Figure 3.3). Note, however, that the composite index peaked in January 1997 and then declined until July, when it began rising again. If the composite index had stayed at a high level in the first half of 1997, it would have been easier to predict the crisis.

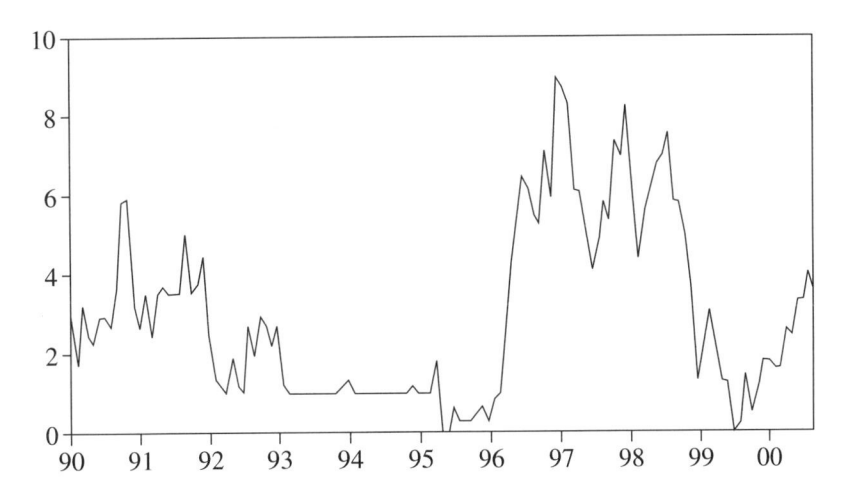

Source: See text.

Figure 3.2 Composite index

In order to measure the explanatory power of the composite index, we define the conditional probability of crisis as the relative frequency of crisis within 12 months at a certain interval of the composite index.[12]

$$P(C_{t,t+h}|I_i < I_t < I_j) = \frac{\text{months with } I_i < I_t < I_j \text{ and a crisis within } h \text{ months}}{\text{months with } I_i < I_t < I_j} \qquad (3.3)$$

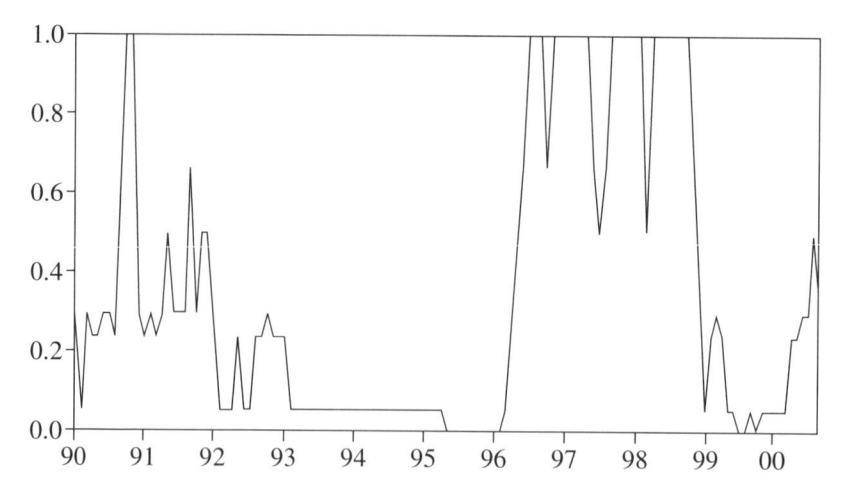

Figure 3.3   Conditional probability of crises

where *P* denotes the probability of the occurrence of a crisis within *h* months ($C_{t,t+h}$) in the composite index interval [I_i, I_j] and *h* is set to 12.

Figure 3.3 shows the conditional probability of a crisis as defined in equation (3.3). It reaches 1 in the periods identified as crisis months in Figure 3.3, that is, when the exchange market pressure rose above its mean plus 1.1 times the standard deviation.

Table 3.7 shows the within- and out-of-sample predictive power of the composite index.[13] As the cutoff probability rises, Type I error increases but Type II error declines. Since the noise/signal ratio is dominated by Type II error, other criteria of goodness of fit are also applied. The noise/signal ratio and percentage of signals incorrectly called are very low in both the within-sample and out-of-sample exercises, while the percentage of observations correctly called is very high. If the indicators listed in Table 3.6 are the relevant measures of economic vulnerability, we can say that the Korean crisis erupted because of the economic weaknesses.

Probit Analysis

The probit model can be used to test the statistical significance of individual indicators, taking into account their correlation. Exchange market pressure is modeled as normally distributed and as a function of a vector of explanatory variables chosen from the preceding list of indicators. This probit model has both advantages and disadvantages in comparison with the indicator model.

Table 3.7 Within- and out-of-sample performance of the indicator model

	Within sample Jan. 1990 ~ Dec. 1997	Out of sample Dec. 1997 ~ Sep. 2000
Cutoff probability 0.5		
(A+D)/(A+B+C+D)	0.84	0.94
A/(A+C)	0.58	0.91
D/(B+D)	0.98	0.96
B/(A+B)	0.05	0.09
[B/(B+D)]/[A/(A+C)]	0.03	0.04
Cutoff probability 0.25		
(A+D)/(A+B+C+D)	0.82	0.79
A/(A+C)	0.82	1.00
D/(B+D)	0.82	0.70
B/(A+B)	0.29	0.39
[B/(B+D)]/[A/(A+C)]	0.22	0.30
Cutoff probability 0.75		
(A+D)/(A+B+C+D)	0.81	0.97
A/(A+C)	0.45	0.91
D/(B+D)	1.00	1.00
B/(A+B)	0.00	0.00
[B/(B+D)]/[A/(A+C)]	0.00	0.00

Note: A through D represent the corresponding cell in Table 3.5.

Source: See text.

It has the additional merit that we can now test the statistical significance of each indicator, assuming normal distribution of *EMP*, and the estimated coefficients on the individual indicators can be used as weights for forming the composite indicator. The disadvantage is the strong assumption of normality.[14]

Table 3.8 shows the results. Of the 22 indicators, only three (exports, stock price and domestic credit/GDP) are statistically significant at standard confidence levels.[15] Even with only three explanatory variables, it turned out that the probit model predicted crisis as well as the indicator model within sample, but not quite as well as the indicator model out of sample.

The probit model can be used to shed light on the self-fulfilling prophecies interpretation of the Korean crisis. Suppose the probability of a crisis increases dramatically when fundamentals enter the crisis zone. Then the slope and intercept shift significantly when the economy breaches the threshold.

Table 3.8 Estimates of probit model

Constant	Export	Stock price	Domestic credit/GDP	McFadden R^2
−0.856*	−0.067*	−0.037*	192**	
(−2.312)	(−2.481)	(−2.333)	(3.096)	0.54

Notes:
z-statistic is in parentheses.
*   Significant at 5%.
** Significant at 1%.

Source: See text.

The dummy variables put to the slope will be significant. We therefore ran the probit model assuming that the threshold for each explanatory variable was the same as that in the indicator model that minimizes the noise-to-signal ratio.[16] It turns out that neither the slope nor the intercept changes significantly.[17] We conclude that self-fulfilling expectations (or panic) did not play the key role in triggering the crisis. Rather, the Korean crisis was predictable to a large degree by the movement of key economic variables.

CONCLUDING REMARKS

This chapter has sought to shed new light on the controversy over the causes of the Korean crisis, and specifically on the debate between two schools of thought emphasizing deteriorating economic fundamentals and self-fulfilling speculative attacks. Our account emphasizes the interaction of capital flows, the exchange rate regime, and the financial system in setting the stage for the crisis. While these interactions are also emphasized by those who subscribe to so-called 'second-generation models' in which speculative attacks are of the self-fulfilling variety, our analysis highlights the roles of economic and financial fundamentals. One way of putting our conclusions is that self-fulfilling dynamics can only come into play when deteriorating fundamentals have already moved a country into the financial danger zone. Economic fundamentals are still important for understanding second-generation crises in which there is a role for self-fulfilling dynamics, in other words, since those fundamentals affect both investor sentiment and the scope for policy measures to restore confidence once it is disturbed.

The evidence laid out in this chapter thus suggests that Korea was not simply an innocent victim of an unwarranted attack. The crisis in Korea was a result of the interplay of weak fundamentals and fragile investor confidence. This synthetic view emphasizes that the potential for a crisis is importantly affected by the exchange rate regime, and that a group of countries that share a similar exchange rate regime may be particularly vulnerable.

NOTES

1. The chapter benefited from comments received at seminars at the Korea Institute of Finance, Korea Development Institute, Kookmin University and Hongik University.
2. R. Chang and Velasco (1998) and Radelet and Sachs (1998) asserted that the Asian crisis was primarily caused by illiquidity brought to a head by the panicked, herd behavior of international investors and creditors.
3. Studies emphasizing economic fundamentals as the primary cause of the financial crisis in Asia are Corsetti et al. (1998a, 1998b), Fischer (1998a), Kaminsky (1998) and Krugman (1998). In the case of Korea, see also W.-A. Park and Choi (1998b).
4. Sum of substandard, doubtful and estimated loss loans.
5. Specifically, given the level of vulnerability, the economy can enter the crisis region of multiple equilibria by self-fulfilling expectations. Multiple equilibrium models are categorized into three types by Masson (1999). First, the balance sheet models of Aghion et al. (2000) and Cespedes et al. (2000) typically emphasize the role of expectations of crisis, such as the possibility of devaluation and default. Second, the financial panic models emphasize changes in expectations and the withdrawal of funds from the banking sector (R. Chang and Velasco, 1998; Tornell, 1999; Furman and Stiglitz, 1998; Radelet and Sachs, 1998). Third, the information cascade model asserts that the herd behavior is a result of an information asymmetry (Barberis et al., 1998).
6. In this vein, it is important to note that Taiwan's decision to depreciate its currency in October 1997, possibly for political reasons, greatly ratcheted up the pressure on Hong Kong (Bergsten, 1997). Taiwan's action, taken after only a minimal defensive effort, prompted renewed depreciation of the Korean won and damaged market sentiment throughout Asia.
7. This accord was introduced in April 1997 to prevent a chain of insolvencies. If an ailing firm's application for protection under the accord was approved, banks would defer the default of its bills.
8. Kaminsky et al. (1997) apply 3 standard deviations, but we use 1.1 standard deviations considering the sample size. W.-A. Park and Choi (1998a) did sensitivity analysis on different thresholds to define the crisis, but found no significant sensitivity.
9. The crisis period is extended to January–December 1990 and February 1996–November 1997 with the application of a 12-month window, which will be explained later.
10. The noise-to-signal ratio has merit in that it increases with both Type I and Type II error, but it has the drawback of being more influenced by Type II error than Type I error.
11. This is appropriate, given the unit root in these series.
12. The composite index is divided into 10 intervals: 0–1, 8 equally divided intervals between 1 and 8, and an interval larger than 8.
13. A weakness of indicator models is that indicators are estimated *ex post*. To show that the model performs well beyond the sample period, both within-sample and out-of-sample predictability is reported.
14. The *p*-value of the Jacque–Bera statistic of exchange market pressure is 0.35, thus accepting the hypothesis of normal distribution.
15. The small number of statistically significant variables is not peculiar to Korea. In the probit model built by the Developing Country Studies Division of the IMF, only five of 18 indicators were significant (Berg, 1999).
16. Berg and Pattillo (1998) use the piecewise linear probit model to test the usefulness of the

threshold concept in the indicator model. We consider their model as one that can show the validity of self-fulfilling expectations, following Sachs et al. (1996).
17. The period dummy is simpler and more popular than the threshold dummy (Sachs et al., 1996). If the period dummy for all of 1997 or the second half of 1997 is used, it turns out to be insignificant.

Comment on Chapters 2 and 3

Ronald I. McKinnon

As an outsider, I enjoyed reading both the Chung and Park–Choi chapters. The authors' assessments of the structural flaws that made the Korean economy so vulnerable to the 1997–98 currency attack, and then what progress was made subsequently to correct these flaws, are remarkably candid. Both chapters suggest that the crisis was not merely a currency panic brought on by contagion from Korea's East Asian neighbors. Rather the underlying financial and industrial structure of Korea's economy had become too unbalanced to support further high growth. And because of such candor, serious economic reform has been possible.

Both the Chung and Park–Choi chapters emphasize the steep fall in the return to capital in Korea for almost a decade before 1997. Korea's large conglomerate firms, the *chaebols*, over-expanded by acquiring more and more affiliates with apparently lower and lower profitability. This over-expansion was abetted by banks extending too much credit, and by the government sponsoring loans. In this connection, both chapters emphasize the lack of due diligence in assessing loan quality, and the general lack of accounting transparency in the *chaebols* and in the banks themselves.

Park and Choi actually use the expression 'financial repression' to describe the government intervention to direct the flow of credit in the economy, and to pressure the banks to keep lending. In the mid-1960s, when Edward Shaw (my senior colleague at Stanford) and I visited Korea, the flow of credit was even more controlled by the government than in recent times. Shaw began to use the term financial repression to describe the situation. Later, we published parallel books (Shaw, 1973; McKinnon, 1973) suggesting that financial repression was distressingly general in developing countries – and the term is now used extensively. But our earlier Korean experience was the catalyst.

Although domestic capital markets remained repressed, in 1994 Korea applied to join the OECD. But a condition for membership was the abolition of capital controls. In the subsequent negotiations, the Korean delegation opted to relax controls over short-term capital flows first, while deferring the elimination of long-term ones. Clearly, this relaxation was the wrong way round – and it led to massive short-term borrowing in foreign exchange. In 1995–97, the absence of tight rules against net foreign exchange exposure led commercial banks to overborrow in dollars or yen at short term in the international interbank market. This was compounded by the complete loss of regulatory control over the so-called merchant banks, which dramatically increased their foreign exchange exposure. The rest is history. (When visiting China, I always advise my Chinese colleagues 'Don't join the OECD!')

Does currency risk, with substantial net foreign exchange exposure, still exist in the Korean economy? Surprisingly, neither chapter addresses this important issue. With the restructuring (after nationalization) in 1998 of Korea's dollar debts to lengthen their term to maturity and with Korea's recent large trade surpluses, I would guess that significant net short-term foreign currency exposure is less of a problem. However, these restructured dollar debts are still coming due. Thus a comprehensive quantitative analysis of the remaining foreign exchange risk in today's Korean economy could be very useful. A permanent feature of Korea's regulatory structure should be strong sanctions against banks and similar financial institutions borrowing in foreign exchange in order to make loans in the domestic currency.

Apart from the foreign exchanges, I was surprised to learn from Chung how incomplete were the purely domestic structural reforms of the *chaebols*, smaller firms and financial institutions – despite the massive cost of the bank bailout. He notes:

1. The *chaebols* have again stepped up their acquisition of affiliated companies. The reduction in their debt-to-equity ratios is something of a mirage: debt was not reduced but new equity was issued – often purchased by affiliated companies.
2. About 30 percent of firms are still latently insolvent in the sense that their current earnings are insufficient to cover interest payments.
3. The nonperforming loan (NPL) problem has not really been resolved but rather shifted more to securities, mutual trust and leasing companies.
4. The recent relaxation of ownership restrictions on the banks raises concern that *chaebols* will once again be the beneficial buyers.

The post-crisis boom, in Chung's view, is due to expansion of domestic demand – by government spending and the loosening of restraints on consumer credit, and by export expansion from the undervalued currency. Thus he views the post-crisis recovery as a one-time affair that is unlikely to be sustained until the underlying structural imbalances are corrected. No wonder economics is called the 'dismal science'! However, I find much that is persuasive in Chung's argument.

In the Park–Choi chapter, I will not comment on the cross-country econometric model for predicting banking and currency crisis. This is virtually a separate chapter.

However, I do question Park's and Choi's interpretation of the foreign exchange pressure on Korea that triggered the 1997–98 crisis. They mentioned China's devaluation of early 1994 when the consolidated exchange rate settled at 8.3 yuan per dollar after the official rate had been 5.5. However, the effect of this devaluation was muted. First, much of China's trade had already been at the higher swap rate of 8.7. Second, China had higher price inflation from 1994 into 1996. This inflation was sufficient to offset, or more than offset, the effect of the net nominal depreciation of the renminbi (RMB) in early 1994. What worsened the crisis was the sharp depreciation of the yen from 1996 through early 1998, when it touched 147 yen per dollar after peaking at 80 yen per dollar in 1995. The impact of this yen depreciation on the smaller East Asian economies was far stronger than anything that China had done.

Instead, China was the savior of the system by not devaluing in 1997–98 despite feeling great deflationary pressure from the devaluations going on around it. China recognized that its size was sufficient that a depreciation of the RMB would worsen the crisis in its neighbors – and China maintains 8.3 yuan per dollar to the present day. This, then, has helped crisis economies like Korea, with undervalued currencies in the post-crisis era, to recover much faster.

Finally, Park and Choi refer to Korea as a 'small open economy'. Korea is certainly open, and more so than it was before the crisis. However, it is not 'small' in the East Asian context. Being much richer per capita, its GNP is of the same order of magnitude as China's. Thus any future depreciation of the won would have sharp negative impacts on its neighbors.

In conclusion, exchange rate policies in the ever more integrated East Asian countries should be considered jointly because the spillover effects from one country to another are so large. Exchange rate stability is a public good for the region. Thus in the Asia Pacific Economic Committee (APEC) or the Ching Mai Initiative (CMI) negotiations, mutual exchange rate stability should have center stage. Fortunately, China at 8.3 yuan, Hong Kong at HK$7.8, Malaysia at 3.8 ringgit to the US dollar provide a natural fixed point relative to which the other East Asian countries could – and should – establish benchmark dollar 'parities' for their currencies.

4. US policy toward the crisis

Young-Kwan Yoon

INTRODUCTION

Since 1998, numerous books and articles have been written on the causes of the Korean crisis. They have considered the pros and cons of the International Monetary Fund's prescriptions for the Korean economy and the social impact of the crisis, among other topics. By comparison, less attention has been devoted to and less progress has been made in understanding US policy toward the crisis. This is unfortunate, for the United States was the major actor which almost single-handedly orchestrated the international response.

The crisis in Korea came as a surprise to most US policy makers. The Korean economy was the eleventh largest in the world and the fifth largest trading partner of the United States. The standard economic indicators had not been sending out warning signals. To all appearances, the geostrategic importance that the US policy makers attached to Korea caused much concern among key high-level officials about the impact of the crisis. As Secretary Rubin observed, 'we have a tremendous national security interest in maintaining a stable South Korea and not creating the kinds of problems we have in that peninsula in the context of instability.'[1]

This chapter focuses on the following questions. What were the main goals of the US government in responding to Korea's crisis? In particular, was US policy motivated mainly by security interests, as the preceding statement by Secretary Rubin seems to imply, or were economic considerations actually paramount? In answering these questions, I seek to clarify why the US government intervened in the crisis management process in the manner it did and how it attempted to achieve its goals. The analysis suggests some implications for the future of the global financial order, which I draw out in the conclusion to the chapter.

US RESPONSE TO THE THAI CRISIS AND THE ASIAN MONETARY FUND

When the peso crisis broke out in early 1995, Treasury Secretary Rubin and his aides rushed to aid the Mexican economy. They were concerned that, if the Mexican government defaulted on its debt and economic conditions in Mexico deteriorated further, there might be a flood of illegal immigration to the United States, provoking a protectionist backlash which might cause the crisis to spread to other Latin American countries. Encountering reluctance to cooperate on the part of the House of Representatives, Rubin decided to use the Exchange Stabilization Fund, which did not require Congressional approval. This money was added to the $40 billion loan package assembled by the IMF. After the crisis, however, Senator Alfonse D'Amato of New York amended an appropriations bill so as to place conditions on the Treasury Department's use of this fund to extend further loans to emerging markets without Congressional approval.[2]

The US response to the Thai crisis was very much influenced by these constraints. When the Thai crisis broke out in July 1997, Rubin did not initially consult with Congress. Instead, he and his deputy, Lawrence Summers, discussed the problem with Alan Greenspan, chairman of the Federal Reserve Board (FRB) and decided not to commit American money to the Thai economy. The State Department and the National Security Council argued that the United States should contribute a modest amount of money to Thailand so that the US could consolidate its image as a leader in this region.[3] Rubin, however, rejected this idea. He and his aides considered the Thai crisis as primarily a regional problem, and in any case he was loath to approach Congress for its approval.[4]

When the United States refused to extend bilateral assistance in response to the spreading crisis, Japan quickly offered $4 billion to Thailand, matching the loans arranged by the IMF. The Japanese government also committed $5 billion to Indonesia and added $10 billion to the $57 billion IMF-led rescue package subsequently arranged for South Korea. In effect, Japan sought to fill the power vacuum left by the United States.[5] At an IMF meeting in Hong Kong in September 1997, the Japanese Finance Minister proposed a $100 billion Asian Monetary Fund (or AMF). The concept was developed by the Vice Minister of Finance for International Affairs, Eisuke Sakakibara, who had long been a fervent defender of the government-led Japanese economic model.[6]

US officials did not respond favorably to the idea of an AMF. According to Secretary Rubin, the existence of two separate funds (an AMF and an IMF) would 'provide an opportunity for reform shopping.'[7] Rubin thought that the creation of an AMF would in practice make it very difficult for the IMF to urge debtor countries to adopt rigorous reform programs, even if the two funds ostensibly cooperated with each other.

Thus, on 17 September Rubin and Greenspan sent letters to their counterparts in Asian countries emphasizing their opposition to an AMF. Two of their aides, Timothy Geithner (Assistant Secretary of the Treasury for International Affairs) and Edwin Truman (Director of the FRB's Division of International Finance), visited Asian capitals for the same purpose. In the end, US opposition succeeded in stalling the campaign for the AMF.[8]

THE US GOVERNMENT AND THE CRISIS

Developing an Approach to the Asian Crisis

By September, Asian countries such as Indonesia, Malaysia and the Philippines had witnessed massive declines in their currencies and/or their stock markets. Rubin and his aides became increasingly concerned about the impact of the worsening situation in Southeast Asia on US exports and about the possibility of a protectionist backlash. They were further concerned that the crisis, if left uncontained, might spread to other countries, such as Korea, Brazil and Russia.

These fears led US policy makers to contemplate new approaches to the Asian crisis. Rubin, Greenspan and their deputies reportedly hammered out the contents of their new approach on a flight to Hong Kong for the IMF and World Bank's annual meetings in September.[9] According to Rubin and Greenspan's letter to their Asian counterparts, US officials believed that the IMF and other multilateral institutions should take the lead in providing rescue funds and that these funds would be sufficient to contain the crisis.[10] However, Asian policy makers still doubted that the funds offered by the multilaterals would suffice. Although they did not accept the idea of an AMF, US policy makers were forced to acknowledge the need to mobilize additional funds.

This was how the concept of 'the second line of defense' was developed. The essence of this strategy was that 'the US should lead the rescue, through the IMF where possible, by providing conditional support …' but that it should also provide additional bilateral assistance where multilateral finance did not succeed in dousing the flames.[11] This approach was accepted by Asian officials at the Manila conference of deputy finance ministers from Asia and the United States in November 1997 in what came to be known as 'the Manila framework.' As a result, the idea of an AMF never came to fruition, and the IMF, now equipped with a new loan window, the so-called the 'Supplemental Reserve Facility,' remained the pivotal institution for handling crises. IMF support would be supplemented, as necessary, by loans from other multilateral institutions. And a second line of defense would also be available, in the form of bilateral loans, if the first line turned out to be insufficient.

The 3 December 1997 Decision to Rescue Korea

By the middle of November, it had become evident to US officials that Korea faced a serious financial predicament. The magnitude of the problem was brought home to the government when the Washington representative of the Bank of Korea, Lee Keun Yung, informed Charles Siegman, Senior Associate Director of the Fed's Division of International Finance, that the Bank of Korea was seriously short of usable hard-currency reserves. This revelation led to a high-level meeting the day before Thanksgiving with the attendance of Alan Greenspan, Robert Rubin, David Lipton (Undersecretary of Treasury for International Affairs), Timothy Geithner, Caroline Atkinson (Deputy Assistant Secretary of the Treasury for International Monetary and Financial Policy), and Daniel Zelikow (Deputy Assistant Secretary for Asia, the Americas and Africa). The mood was pessimistic. Officials thought that Korea was very close to default, that its short-term debt was dangerously high, and that it was reluctant to change its traditional ways in the manner needed to regain the confidence of the markets.[12]

Geithner, for one, emphasized that Korea was too important from the strategic and economic points of view to be allowed to default on its debt. Rubin resisted this logic on the grounds that 'you can't let some perceived imperative of action dictate your choices, and you may not have alternatives that are a plausible response to the problem ...'[13] Thus, discussions continued while Korean reserves continued to hemorrhage out of the coffers of the central bank.

In conference calls on Thanksgiving Day, top national security and foreign policy officials argued that the United States should help South Korea. National Security Adviser Samuel (Sandy) Berger expressed his fears about the consequences of a default. Berger believed that should the South Korean economy collapse, North Korea might attempt to capitalize on the social turmoil in the South by launching dangerous military adventures. Madeleine Albright, Secretary of State, also argued in favor of bailout, presumably with similar motivation.

For Rubin, however, simply pouring money into Korea would not solve the problem. An ineptly designed IMF rescue program formulated with inadequate consideration of the probability of success, he argued, would only damage the effectiveness of the IMF. And only the IMF could instill confidence among bankers and investors and restore stability to the international economy.[14]

Eventually, the economic and security branches of the government reached an understanding. As James Steinberg, one of the participants in the conference calls, recalled, 'What was mutually arrived at was that it was no good to do something if it was absolutely futile. We accepted that there had to be some degree of probability of success, and Treasury accepted that it didn't have to be just a high probability. If there was some chance it would succeed – even if it was less than fifty–fifty – there was a political value in having tried.'[15]

Several hours of conference calls on Thanksgiving Day eventually led to the formulation of a $57 billion package. The Clinton Administration itself decided to make $5 billion available for South Korea (Senator D'Amato's restriction on the use of the Exchange Stabilization Fund having, by this time, expired). This second line of defense was designed to back up the $35 billion provided by the IMF (which contributed $21 billion), the World Bank (which added $10 billion), and the Asian Development Bank (which added $4 billion). The second line was to be made available only if the initial $35 billion provided insufficient. The Japanese government also pledged $10 billion of immediate relief. The total package of $57 billion was larger than the $17 billion offered to Thailand, the nearly $40 billion lent to Indonesia, and the $48 billion offered to Mexico in 1997.

Once the US government assembled this package and the IMF entered into negotiations with the Korean government, the principal concern of Rubin and his team at the Treasury became to press for structural reform in Korea. There was some disparity of views on this question between the Rubin team and IMF staff. According to Paul Blustein, IMF staff were not entirely enthusiastic about the idea of requiring extensive structural reform. They thought that the structural changes which the US government was eager to impose on Seoul would not necessarily help to halt the panic – to the contrary, some feared, emphasizing the country's structural weaknesses might only further undermine investor confidence. Some IMF officials were cynical about the Treasury's motives. A member of the Asia and Pacific Department of the IMF was quoted as saying that '[t]he US saw this as an opportunity, as they did in many countries, to crack open all these things that for years have bothered them.'[16]

Be that as it may, there is no question that Rubin regarded Korea as 'a firewall that could not be breached for fear of other "teetering" dominoes like Russia – and even Japan.'[17] As he put it, 'We have a vital national economic and security interest in helping Korea to restore market stability as soon as possible.'[18]

However, the negotiations surrounding the IMF rescue package revealed clearly how eager Secretary Rubin and his aide David Lipton were to pressure the IMF into insisting on tough conditionality. They were especially enthusiastic about having the Korean negotiating team accept the request for market opening. Lipton was dispatched to Korea for the purpose of monitoring the negotiation. According to Blustein, 'some on the mission team fumed that they couldn't get to see [Hubert] Neiss [the chief of the IMF mission] because when he wasn't locked in negotiations with the Koreans, he was spending so much time with Lipton.'[19] On the morning of 3 December, in the final stages of the negotiation, Secretary Rubin himself called Michel Camdessus, the IMF's Managing Director, who had just arrived in Seoul to conclude the process, making clear that the United States would not support a weak IMF program.[20]

Pressure from Republicans in Congress was another reason for Rubin to impose a tough program requiring market opening. The Treasury wanted to provide the IMF with more financial resources so that the Fund would be equipped with enough fire power to bail out future crisis countries. However, Congressional Republicans criticized the Administration's request for more funds for the IMF. Texas Republican Ron Paul argued that the bailouts of these Asian countries would put US taxpayer money at risk and negatively impact the economy by weakening the dollar and fanning inflation. US workers and taxpayers would pay the price for insulating bankers and other investors from losses.[21] Some Democrats, for their part, wanted to tie international assistance to improvements in human rights and working conditions.

Administration officials sought to persuade Congress by arguing that IMF assistance and US back-up funds would enable the US government to require significant changes in Korea's financial and economic system. The Korean government would have to abstain from pressuring financial institutions to make loans to troubled companies and to those with political connections. Conditions attached to the IMF package would also require Korea to open her markets wider and foster a favorable environment for foreign investment in Korean companies, including in commercial banks. Clinton Administration officials insisted that the US government would agree to provide additional back-up funds:

> ... only after determining that the IMF package was tough enough on the Koreans to restore market confidence in their economy while reassuring American taxpayers that the Treasury Department was not throwing good money after bad ... And it would be released only if Seoul continues to meet all the requirements of the IMF program and if the Treasury Department thinks it will be repaid.[22]

But strict conditionality also had a paradoxical aspect. One of Rubin's former aides was quoted as characterizing the Korean package as 'an experiment in trying to make something look as real as possible without ultimately having to spend the money. It had a sort of Catch-22 quality to it: If you don't need the money, you don't get it. And if you do need it, then you probably haven't met the conditions for disbursal.'[23]

In short, the US officials attached strict conditions to the $3.5 billion package in order to garner support from Congress for strengthening the position of the IMF. The Korean negotiators and the IMF mission team at last entered into the final agreement on the afternoon of 3 December.

The 24 December Decision to Rescue Korea

Although a great deal of effort went into preparing the rescue package, it did not produce the hoped-for effects. The reforms promised by the Korean government did not progress as smoothly as anticipated, and the Korean economy did not regain the confidence of the international investors. By the time Secretary Rubin held a small dinner meeting at the Jefferson Hotel on the evening of 18 December, the foreign currency reserves of the Bank of Korea were all but exhausted. Given the rapid depletion of the remaining reserves, at a rate of $1 billion a day, it looked as if Korea would be forced into default by the end of the year.

The participants at the meeting were extremely concerned, given the importance of Korea as the eleventh largest economy in the world. According to the recollection of one, the prevailing view was that the US government had only two alternatives. One was to let Korea fail while still trying 'to save the rest of the world.' The other was to have the IMF expedite the process of releasing the loan to Korea while also making the second line of defense available.[24]

Yet a third option, first developed in a conference call on 20 December by a group headed by Summers, Geithner and Truman, aimed at persuading international creditors to roll over their loans to Korea as a condition for the US government to approve disbursal of the IMF money together with their second line of defense, if necessary.[25] It is uncertain whether the IMF did more than simply accept and help to implement the idea initiated by the US government. But there is no question that the IMF facilitated the subsequent negotiations, between Korea and a group of foreign creditor banks, with the goal of operationalizing this plan.[26]

US officials, Treasury officials in particular, felt uncomfortable about arm-twisting the private sector to alter their loan contracts. Secretary Rubin discussed this problem with William J. McDonough, the president of the Federal Reserve Bank of New York, for four hours by phone. McDonough then called the major US creditor banks, while his central-bank counterparts in the UK, Germany, Japan and France held synchronized conversations with bankers in their respective countries. Banks in all five countries then agreed to roll over their Korean credits.[27] The Treasury thus worked, directly or indirectly, with banks on three continents, leading them to recognize the importance of cooperating in the readjustment of Korea's debt.[28]

Meanwhile, on 19 December, Lipton met with Kim Dae-jung, who had been elected president just the preceding day. The President-elect gave Lipton a positive response, saying that he would meet the conditions attached to US assistance and pursue the goal of reform, even if it came at the cost of widespread layoffs and social unrest. With these pieces in place, the second Korea rescue plan was announced on Christmas Eve.

An important question is why the rollover option was not adopted at an earlier stage of the crisis. By early December, almost every dollar flowing into Korea as the result of the IMF rescue package flowed back out, ending up in the hands of the creditor banks. This was the so-called 'bailout problem' that caused much concern about the moral hazard and ineffectiveness with IMF lending.[29] As DeLong and Eichengreen explain, there existed a collective action problem for creditor banks and governments that had to be surmounted in order to implement the rollover program.[30] Surmounting it took time. However, if the US government had tackled the crisis more aggressively by adding the rollover option to the IMF package at the time of the first Korean rescue, unnecessary costs for both debtors and creditors might have been avoided, and the second-round crisis might have been prevented.

THE GOALS AND THE MEANS OF THE US POLICY TOWARD THE CRISIS

The Central Position of the Treasury

When we look back on decision making by the US government, the central position of the Treasury Department is clear. This centrality of the Treasury was due partly to general circumstances at the end of the cold war. The State Department carried less sway once geopolitical tensions were defused. The rapid growth of international financial markets heightened the importance of the financial issues that were the Treasury Department's domain. The United States experienced a long economic boom, and many international economic issues such as currency intervention had become much more salient and politicized than before.

Another factor that provided the Treasury with more influence than other agencies was Rubin's relationship with Alan Greenspan. From his first day as Treasury Secretary, Rubin tried not to interfere with the Fed's management of monetary policy, defusing the traditional tension between the two agencies. Nor did Rubin threaten the State Department by attempting inroads into foreign policy. Thus, there was little competition over prerogatives between the Treasury and the State Departments.[31] Hence, when the Asian crisis broke out, senior bureaucrats of the State Department and other members of the US foreign policy apparatus let the Treasury take the lead in formulating the US response, despite the obvious implications of the crisis for US foreign policy.[32] Pressure from Congress was still a restraining factor, but Rubin attempted to handle this through compromise rather than confrontation.

The Goals and Means of US Policy

Indicative of the dominance of the Treasury, US policy reflected the economic and, especially, financial interests of the United States more than security concerns. To the extent that policy was not informed about these aspects of the picture, it became the subject of some criticism on the part of independent opinion leaders in the United States.[33]

To be sure, officials of the National Security Council and the State Department raised security concerns. However, North Korea's dire economic situation and the regime's presumed awareness that provocation would certainly lead to devastating American military retaliation allowed security considerations to take second place.[34] There was not much evidence that security was a major factor in the US government's decision to help Korea financially.

Several bits of evidence suggest that economic considerations were key. First, maintaining US economic prosperity had always been a paramount goal of the Clinton Administration. President Clinton believed that the economic boom benefited the poor and the middle class in the United States even more than many of his social programs.[35] In this regard, the Administration was greatly concerned about the potential threat to this prosperity posed by the crisis in Asia. And, in order to sustain economic prosperity, it was important in turn for the Administration to cultivate the confidence of financial markets. This led to the development of close connections between the Treasury and Wall Street. As former Labor Secretary Robert Reich once put it, 'Bob has done an able job keeping Wall Street happy and confident … And in today's world, their confidence is critically important to the success of the economy. But is it necessary to accept a world in which Wall Street has that much influence over both economics and politics?'[36]

To be sure, the relationship between Treasury and Wall Street was not a one-way street. As we have noted, Treasury pressure for cooperation from Wall Street was key to the success of the second Korean rescue. Indeed, Blustein and Chandler suggest that it was only after the creditor banks agreed to roll over their loans to Korea that Rubin and his team in turn agreed to provide official assistance. In their words,

Although the banks' willingness to accept deferred payments was still not a sure thing, word that they were considering granting such relief came as enormously welcome news to the Clinton Administration – and not only because of the benefits it offered the South Koreans. By showing that private lenders were bearing some of the burden of the rescue, White House and Treasury officials believed they could deflect criticism that taxpayer money was being used to bail out rich bankers ...[37]

Thus, the so-called 'Wall Street–Treasury complex' was important for advancing the goal of US economic prosperity, in this instance by rescuing Korea and thereby preventing the crisis from spreading to other regions. The Fed was the bridge between the Treasury and the banks.

This episode is one instance of the general increase in the influence of financial interests in US economic policy making, which can in turn be understood as a result of the 'financialization' of the US economy. The Reagan–Thatcher revolution in economic policy had brought about a sharp change in attitudes toward the desirability of financial liberalization and globalization, not just in the US and the UK, but worldwide. As the financial sector became more important to the US economy, the Treasury, as the obvious political representative of US financial interests, became more influential in the formulation of US policy. To be sure, the Treasury did not act alone. In the case of the East Asian economic crisis, we can think of it as part of a policy network that included also Wall Street interests, the Federal Reserve Board and Federal Reserve Banks, and Congress and its staffers. This was the so-called Wall Street–Treasury complex through which cooperation between policy makers and market participants was achieved.

The other goal of US policy was to encourage structural reform and market opening in Korea. Rubin and his staff regarded the Korean crisis as the result of Korea's pursuit of the Japanese economic model. The Treasury had long been pressuring Korea to open its financial markets and the government to abandon the Japanese model. The driving force behind this pressure was lobbying by US financial firms.[38] US financial firms might make inroads into the Korean market if the Korean government removed restrictions on foreign competition and permitted Korean firms to purchase bonds from and sell stock to foreigners.

US officials also sought to eliminate barriers to merchandise imports and exports. The Treasury specifically demanded that the IMF play the role of 'battering ram' for American interests, by pressuring the Korean negotiating team into opening domestic markets to imports.[39] According to Kapur, IMF sources acknowledged that 'conditions such as the one asking Korea to speed up the opening of its automobile and financial sectors reflected pressures from major shareholders (Japan, and the United States).'[40]

In encouraging market opening, the IMF was acting as an agent for its principal shareholder, the government of the United States. This should be no surprise, when we recall that the US, by virtue of its 18 percent voting power in the Fund, has effective veto power over its decisions. This also meant that the IMF had to cultivate the support of the US government when it sought to augment its own financial capacities. The Clinton Administration, in turn, had to carefully manage the campaign for an IMF quota increase in order to overcome Congressional opposition. Secretary Rubin repeatedly expressed his support for the Fund when the latter became the target of criticism during the crisis. He defended the IMF as preferable to an AMF when the Japanese government tabled its proposal for the latter.[41]

The reforms imposed by the IMF as conditions for the extension of financial assistance effectively forced Korea to abandon its traditional state-led development model. As Bruce Cumings has observed, 'the deep meaning and intents of the American and IMF response to the Asian liquidity crisis are to close the historical chapter in which the sheltered "developmental states" have prospered.'[42] Cumings also noted Alan Greenspan's statement that the result of the Asian crisis was 'a worldwide move toward "the Western form of free market capitalism".'[43]

The Treasury–IMF complex differed from the Wall Street–Treasury complex. The latter can be characterized as a structural relationship that manifested itself as a policy network, while the former was purely instrumental – it was an instrument for carrying out the goals formulated by the Wall Street–Treasury complex. While the Treasury and Wall Street maintained a relationship based on equality and mutual respect, the IMF could not significantly influence or change the direction of Treasury policy. It is thus important to emphasize the fundamental difference in the nature of these two relationships.[44]

CONCLUSION

In responding to the Korean crisis, the goals of US policy were defined mainly in terms of US economic interests. The Wall Street–Treasury and Treasury–IMF complexes were the main instruments enabling the US government to advance those interests. Contrary to conventional wisdom, security considerations do not appear to have played a major role in US decision making. While they were undoubtedly at the back of decision makers' minds, the more immediate concern in November and December was the economic threat posed by the developing-country debt and financial crisis and its implications for US economic relations.

In this sense, the traditional statist interpretation of US foreign policy making has little power in explaining US policy toward Korea at the time of the crisis.[45] Rather than being formulated by the state in isolation from social interests, policy was shaped in interaction with them. The Treasury and Wall Street influenced one other. The State Department and the National Security Council, which tended to define and represent US national interests on a more autonomous basis and were less vulnerable to the influence of the private sector, were marginal in shaping the decision-making process. It is also clear that the Treasury–IMF complex was the main tool mobilized by the US government to pressure Korea into opening her markets and abandoning her traditional state-led development model.

It is one thing to identify the foreign policy goals of the United States, but another to evaluate the results and implications of the associated policies. It behooves us to avoid becoming entrapped in the oversimplified debates between neoliberal defenders of US policy on the right and critics of the US and IMF on the left. Joseph Stiglitz, for example, has argued that the IMF's orthodox prescriptions for debtor countries lacked careful consideration of the social and political context of each individual country.[46] We have also seen how the 'economistic' prescriptions of the IMF imposed on Indonesia led to political and social upheaval.[47] But the problem for the critics is that they have not yet offered a viable alternative to the developmental state. While criticizing the neoliberal prescription of the US government and the IMF, they implicitly assume that Korea should stick to its traditional model of state-led development. Yet it has become clear that the traditional model based on the coalition of the state and the *chaebols* is no longer viable, due to the changing nature of Korea's own economy.

The policies and prescriptions recommended by the United States and the IMF may have been insufficiently sensitive to these dilemmas. But it is also true that the shock of the crisis provided Korea itself with an important opportunity to eliminate an inheritance of debilitating structural distortions. This does not mean that Korea must accept the Anglo-Saxon model of capitalism outright. Rather, the crisis may have brought about an opportunity for the country to develop a more rational but still uniquely Korean model of capitalist organization.

One undoubted lesson of the Korean crisis and response is the dangerous nature of the gap between rapid financial globalization and the slow development of crisis management practices and methods. This is shown in the present instance by the way in which the US government dealt with the Asian crisis country by country, on an *ad hoc* basis.

More than a few Asian observers insist that the current international financial system is inefficient and inequitable. The burden of adjustment, they argue, falls on the shoulders of debtor countries, whereas creditors who make poor decisions when offering loans to ultimately uncreditworthy countries get off scot-free. Secretary Rubin did not offer a definitive solution to this problem in a speech made at Georgetown University, observing that

Foreign investors injected an extraordinary amount of capital into these flawed systems without due weighting of the risks involved ... I would not give one nickel to help any creditor or investor ... Unfortunately, there was no way to restore growth and stability without sheltering some investors.[48]

Although there have been many discussions in recent years about how to strengthen the international financial architecture, there has been disappointingly little concrete progress. In some sense, policy makers in the leading Western nations remain prisoners of the ideology and institutions of global capitalism.[49] Ultimately, they must free themselves from this prison in order to build a more stable and equitable global financial system.

NOTES

1. PBS Online Newshour, 'Newsmaker: Secretary Rubin,' 16 January 1998. (http://www.pbs.org/newshour/bb/asia/jan-june98/rubin_1-16.html).
2. Jacob Weisberg, 'Keeping the Boom From Busting,' *The New York Times*, 19 July 1998.
3. Paul Blustein, *The Chastening: Inside the Crisis that Rocked the Global Financial System and Humbled the IMF* (New York: PublicAffairs, 2001), p. 78.
4. CRS Report 97-1021, *The 1997–1998 Asian Financial Crisis*, by Dick K. Nanto (updated 6 March 1998), p. 7.
5. Blustein, *The Chastening*, p. 79.
6. Blustein, *The Chastening*, p. 166.
7. Secretary Rubin's Speech on US Response to Asian Financial Crisis, 21 January 1998, Georgetown University.
8. The confrontation between the US government and the Japanese government on the issue of the AMF indicates that the nature of the Asian economic crisis goes beyond a simplistic economic interpretation focusing on the economic variables. We need to take a broader perspective. The Asian economic crisis was nothing but an expression of the confrontation that had been going on between two economic models, that is, between the Anglo-Saxon model and the East Asian model as explained in Young-Kwan Yoon, 'The East-Asian Economic Model and the World Capitalism: Focusing on the Concepts of the Market, State, and Institutions,' in Young-Kwan Yoon and Kwang-il Paik (eds), *East Asia: The Political Economy of Crisis* (Seoul: Seoul National University Press, 1999), (in Korean), pp. 424–5.
9. Weisberg, 'Keeping the Boom From Busting.'
10. Blustein, *The Chastening*, p. 167.
11. Weisberg, 'Keeping the Boom From Busting.'
12. Blustein, *The Chastening*, pp. 132–6.
13. Ibid., p. 137.
14. Ibid., pp. 138–9.
15. Ibid., p. 139.
16. Ibid., p. 143.
17. *The New York Times*, 10 December 1997.
18. 'Crisis in South Korea: The Bailout,' *The New York Times*, 4 December 1997.
19. Blustein, *The Chastening*, p.145.
20. Ibid., p. 147.
21. 'Crisis in South Korea: The U.S. Role,' *The New York Times*, 4 December 1997.
22. Ibid.
23. Blustein, *The Chastening*, p. 179.
24. Weisberg, 'Keeping the Boom From Busting'.

25. Ibid.
26. IMF, 'The IMF's Response to the Asian Crisis,' a factsheet, 17 January 1999. (http://www.imf.org/External/np/exr/facts/asia.HTM). Also see, Hubert Neiss, 'In Defense of the IMF's Emergency Role in East Asia,' *International Herald Tribune*, 9 October 1998.
27. Weisberg, 'Keeping the Boom From Busting'.
28. Secretary Rubin's speech on 21 January 1998.
29. J. Bradford DeLong and Barry Eichengreen, 'Between Meltdown and Moral Hazard: The International Monetary and Financial Policies of the Clinton Administration,' in Jeffrey A. Frankel and Peter R. Orszag (eds), *American Economic Policy in the 1990s* (Cambridge, MA: MIT Press, 2002), p. 225.
30. Ibid., p. 225–6.
31. Weisberg, 'Keeping the Boom From Busting'.
32. CRS Report 98-74, 'Asian Financial Crisis,' p. 16.
33. See for example Zoellick's comment. Robert B. Zoellick, 'A Larger Plan for Asia,' *Washington Post*, 6 January 1998.
34. If there were concerns about the security effects of Korea's economic crisis, they were rather directed toward other issues. According to Cronin the more likely threat to American security interests was the possibility that South Korea might be unable or unwilling to keep its financial commitment to the KEDO light-water reactor project or its possible cancellations of arms purchases from US defense contractors. CRS Report 98-74, 'Asian Financial Crisis,' pp. 12–13.
35. Weisberg, 'Keeping the Boom From Busting'.
36. Ibid. Weisberg who had interviewed Secretary Rubin intensively, concluded that Rubin, having tried his utmost to resist Wall Street's influence on a number of issues, recognized that 'his move from Wall Street to Washington has turned out to be less of a departure than expected.'
37. Paul Blustein and Clay Chandler, 'Behind the S. Korea Bailout: Speed, Stealth, Consensus,' *The Washington Post*, 28 December 1997.
38. Blustein, *The Chastening*, p. 143.
39. Bruce Cumings, 'The Asian Crisis, Democracy, and the End of "Late" Development,' in T.J. Pempel (ed.), *The Politics of the Asian Economic Crisis* (Ithaca: Cornell University Press, 1999), p. 28.
40. Devesh Kapur, 'The IMF: A cure or a curse?' *Foreign Policy*, **111** (Summer 1998), p. 123.
41. Comments by Stanley Fischer, 'International Economic Policy Under the Clinton Administration,' Harvard University, 27 June 2001. (http://www.imf.org/external/np/speeches/2001/062701.htm).
42. Cumings, 'The Asian Crisis,' p. 24. A high-level Korean negotiator also mentioned in an interview that 'it was clear that the U.S. goal at the time of the crisis was to take advantage of the crisis situation to prevent Korea from becoming a second Japan in the future.'
43. Cumings, 'The Asian Crisis,' p. 29.
44. For example, Robert Wade and Frank Veneroso, 'The Asian Crisis: The High Debt Model vs. the Wall Street–Treasury–IMF Complex,' *New Left Review* (March–April 1998).
45. There have been heated debates on the nature of the linkage between the state and the private sector in the US foreign economic policy-making process. For instance, the statists argue that the US national interest has been defined independently of the pressures of the private interest groups. They regard the state as an autonomous entity. Stephen D. Krasner, *Defending the National Interest* (Princeton, NJ: Princeton University Press, 1978), p. 5. On the other hand, the interest-group liberalists deny this view on the nature of the state and argue that politics is nothing but competition of interest groups. They assert that US foreign policy is 'the resultant of effective access by various interests.' David D. Truman, *The Governmental Process: Political Interests and Public Opinion*, 2nd edn (New York: Knopf, 1971), p. 507. Another camp of political theory, Marxists (especially instrumental Marxists), claim that US foreign policy has been and will continue to be determined, reflecting the dominant capitalist interest. Joyce and Gabriel Kolko, *The Limits of Power: The World and United States Foreign Policy, 1945–1954* (New York: Harper & Row, 1972).

46. Joseph Stiglitz, 'Globalization and Its Discontents: How to Fix What's Not Working,' Joseph Stiglitz Lecture, IDPM, University of Manchester, UK, 4 April 2001. (http://idpm.man.ac.uk/idpm/stiglitz.html).
47. I use the term 'economistic' keeping Karl Polanyi's criticism of blind belief in a self-regulating market mechanism. See Karl Polanyi's classical work, *The Great Transformation: The Political and Economic Origins of Our Time* (Boston, MA: Beacon Press, 1957).
48. Weisberg, 'Keeping the Boom From Busting'.
49. See, for example, John Ruggie, 'International Regime, Transactions, and Change: Embedded Liberalism in the Post War Economic Order,' in Stephen D. Krasner (ed.), *International Regime* (Ithaca: Cornell University Press, 1983), pp. 195–232; Polanyi, *The Great Transformation*; Dani Rodrik, 'The Global Fix,' *The New Republic*, 2 November 1998.

Comment on Chapter 4

Justin Yifu Lin

The chapter by Professor Yoon on US policy toward the Asian financial crisis is very informative and insightful. There have been many discussions about the International Monetary Fund's conditionality and its effects on the crisis-hit countries. However, less attention has been paid to the decision process and motivation behind the IMF's rescue package. The US, by virtue of its 18 percent voting power in the Fund, has effective veto power over the Fund's decision. The chapter shows convincingly that the US government's responses to the Asian crisis were mainly determined by its economic interests instead of geo-strategic consideration and how the so-called Wall Street–Treasury Complex used the IMF as an instrument to achieve the Wall Street interests of securing the repayment of loans and opening financial markets, and the Treasury's goal of eliminating trade barriers to US exports. The analysis from the political aspect in the chapter is a valuable contribution to the conference. I have three suggestions for further explorations or future research:

1. It is not surprising that a country's policy response toward an international event is conditioned by the country's, or more specifically the decision-making coalition's, concerns and benefits. However, the chapter has not provided enough analysis of how much the US's change in its response to the Asian crisis from the traditional geo-strategic objective to the economic benefit was due to the end of cold war and how much to Treasury Secretary Rubin's personal relationship to Wall Street. If the latter is the main reason for the change of the US response to the Asian crisis, it would be interesting to explore how the change from the Clinton Administration to the Bush Administration could have affected US policy in a future crisis. Alternatively, if the former was the main reason, it would also be interesting to see how the events of 11 September and the anti-terrorism strategy would affect the US response to future crises.
2. IMF conditionality was a bitter pill for the Korean economy to swallow. The Korean government implemented it decisively. The Korean economy weathered the crisis and has bounced back quickly. However, the conditionality caused the Indonesian economy to collapse and resulted in

great difficulties for society. I believe the situation in Indonesia to be bad for the US strategic position in Asia as well as for its long-term economic interests. It would be interesting to have some comments on how the consequences could have affected US policy thinking about its response to a similar future crisis in Asia as well as in other regions and how IMF conditionality may be modified.
3. The US opposed Japan's idea of setting up the Asian Monetary Fund when the Asian financial crisis erupted in 1997. However, financial crises due to structural or liquidity problems may recur in Asia in the future. The Chiang Mai Initiative has proposed bilateral currency swaps in case a crisis occurs in the future. It would be interesting to include some discussion about the US position on the Chiang Mai Initiative and whether the US has changed its position on the Asian Monetary Fund.

Finally, no matter what the main concern of US policy will be in the future, a crisis is extremely costly and painful for a country. Korea should be congratulated for having taken decisive action and recovered so quickly and strongly from the crisis. However, as Joung-Woo Lee's chapter shows, even for Korea the social costs of the crisis are high. The inherent instability of the international financial system is one reason for the Korean crisis. Nevertheless, as argued in the chapters by Chung and by Park and Choi, the internal structural weakness of the Korean economy is the main cause. The state-led development model worked extremely well in Korea in the past. However, in my opinion, this development model encouraged the Korean economy to develop over-ambitiously and invest heavily in sectors that deviated from Korea's comparative advantages. The state's protection of *chaebols*, the corruption, the financial sector problems, the trade barriers and so on are the consequences. When economy in such a situation liberalizes its financial sector, the capital account in particular will be vulnerable to unstable international capital flows. In an integrated international financial system, it is important for a country to follow closely its comparative advantage in the development of industries and technology so that the economy will be more competitive in international markets and develop resilience to external shocks. The differences in the performance of Taiwan and Korea in the Asian crisis demonstrate the above point. Most developing countries in the past were influenced by the state-led development model and have some degree of structural problem in their economies. It is therefore important for the developing countries to have the correct sequence of financial liberalization. While long-term foreign direct investment should be welcome, the opening up of the capital account and permission for unchecked short-term capital flows should be carried out with extreme caution.

5. The monetary policy response to the crisis[1]

Dongchul Cho

INTRODUCTION

Korean history will probably record the last three years of the twentieth century as a period of dramatic economic policy experiments. Reforms affected virtually the entire economy, from financial and labor markets to the corporate and government sectors.

Macroeconomic policy was no exception. Immediately following the outbreak of the crisis, the fiscal authority decided to mobilize funds totaling more than 12 percent of GDP for purposes of financial sector restructuring. But this was nothing compared to the revolution in monetary policy. In November and December 1997, when the currency crisis was triggered, stabilization of the exchange rate had been the foremost policy objective. Before the crisis, the fluctuation of the currency was limited to a narrow range, and a variety of restrictions were maintained on capital inflows and outflows. The crisis led to a complete change: the exchange rate was allowed to float freely, and the capital account was liberalized. Inflation targeting was introduced as a legal mandate, and the intermediate target of monetary policy was shifted from the monetary aggregates such as M2 to short-term interest rates.[2]

Perhaps the most dramatic and controversial aspect was interest rate policy. Overnight interbank call rates were raised to more than 30 percent from the previous level of 12 to 13 percent in order to attract capital inflows and limit outflows. Partly in response, the GDP growth rate plunged to –8 percent (year-on-year) in the second quarter of 1998, and the unemployment rate skyrocketed to over 8 percent, from less than 3 percent before the crisis. A large number of firms, unable to bear the now higher costs of servicing their debts, were plunged into bankruptcy, and the volume of nonperforming loans in the financial sector rose dramatically.

Eventually, the foreign exchange market stabilized, and the call rate was lowered to 8 percent by the end of September 1998. On 30 September the Bank of Korea lowered the call rate target by 100 basis points, signaling that

90   *The Korean economy beyond the crisis*

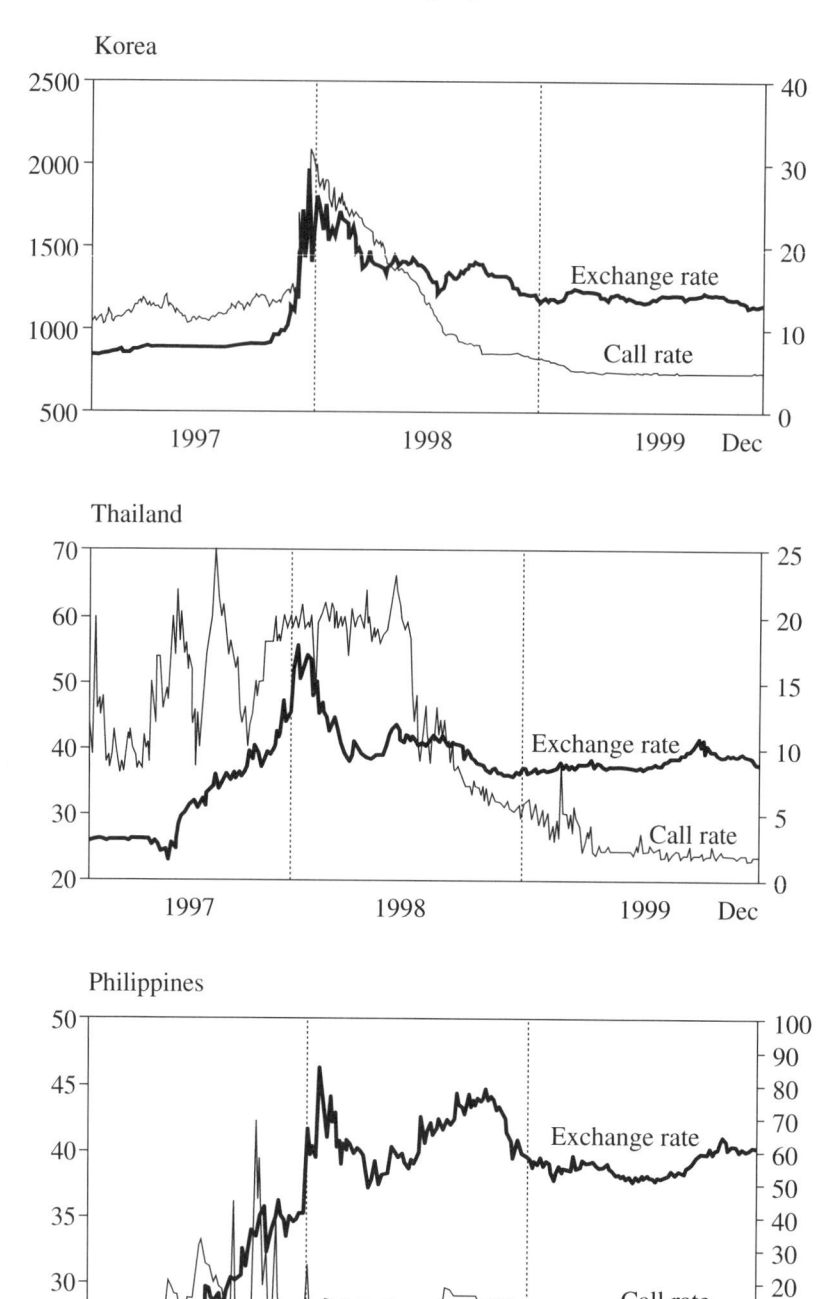

Source: D. Cho and West (2000).

Figure 5.1   Exchange rate and call rate

the goal of monetary policy had shifted from stabilizing the currency's value to boosting the economy. The call rate continued to be reduced until it hit historically low levels of 4 to 5 percent, inaugurating the era of 'super-low interest rates.' The path of interest rates is shown in Figure 5.1, together with the won/dollar exchange rate, and along with the corresponding variables in Thailand and the Philippines.

There has been no shortage of arguments criticizing and defending the interest rate policies adopted in response to the crisis. The relevant literature is already very large. Rather than survey this terrain again, in this chapter I focus on two issues that require further clarification and that would benefit from additional research. These issues are whether the high interest rate policy was effective in stabilizing the exchange rate and whether post-crisis interest rate policy was too tight or too loose when judged from the vantage point of the literature on optimal interest rate rules.

THE HIGH INTEREST RATE POLICY

Interest rate policy was at the center of the crisis program designed by the International Monetary Fund and implemented by the Korean government. The country's agreement with the Fund essentially declared that the immediate goal was to stabilize the exchange rate (not inflation or the level of output) and that the interest rate would be raised substantially to achieve this end.[3]

Theoretical Underpinnings

Along with questions about whether this focus on stabilizing the exchange rate was justified as a way of restoring confidence in financial markets and stability to the Korean economy, the presumption that interest rate hikes were the appropriate device for achieving that goal was also challenged in the literature on the Asian crisis countries (see, for example, Furman and Stiglitz, 1998). The conceptual framework laid out by D. Cho and West (2003) is helpful in addressing this question. That framework starts with the uncovered interest parity condition, which can be written as:

$$i_t = E_t s_{t+1} - s_t + d_t, \qquad (5.1)$$

where i_t is (net) domestic interest rates; s_t is the log of the spot exchange rate (with higher values indicating depreciation); E_t denotes expectations; and d_t is a risk premium that incorporates the fluctuation of foreign interest rates. The orthodox relationship follows directly: if i_t is increased, but $E_t s_{t+1}$ and d_t are unchanged, then s_t must fall (the exchange rate must appreciate).

This channel may be offset, however, in so far as increases in the interest rate are associated with increases in the risk premium. That is, the effect of i_t on s_t depends on the indirect but endogenous movement of d_t, which may be represented by:

$$d_t = di_t + u_{dt}, \qquad (5.2)$$

where d is a parameter and u_{dt} is a disturbance term. The conventional view would be $d < 0$ or $d = 0$. In an alternative view, such as that of Furman and Stiglitz (1998), $d > 0$, and higher interest rates are associated with higher risk.

It is important to note that while the monetary authority sent consistent signals that the high interest rate policy was temporary, it also indicated that the timing of its abandonment would depend on the movement of the exchange rate. Since investors in the currency market were forward looking, they presumably incorporated this information into their expectations. This idea can be captured by modeling i_t as endogenously determined through the policy reaction function:

$$i_t = aE_{t-1}s_t + u_{mt}, \qquad (5.3)$$

where a is a parameter and u_{mt} is a disturbance term. The IMF's preferences can be modeled by assuming $a > 0$; in other words, the monetary authority leans against expected exchange rate depreciation.

Equations (5.1)–(5.3) can be used to derive solutions for the three endogenous variables, i_t, s_t and d_t, under the stability assumption $0 < b \equiv [1 + a(1 - d)]^{-1} < 1$. In order to make the implications more transparent, assume that both u_{dt} and u_{mt} follow AR(1) processes with the AR coefficients $0 < \phi_d < 1$ and $0 < \phi_m < 1$, respectively: $u_{dt} = \phi_d u_{dt-1} + \varepsilon_{dt}$ and $u_{mt} = \phi_m u_{mt-1} + \varepsilon_{mt}$, where ε_{dt} and ε_{mt} are innovations. The Appendix uses these assumptions to derive explicit solutions for the effects of exogenous variables. Figure 5.2 summarizes those solutions intuitively.

Suppose that there was a shock to the risk premium term, ε_{dt}, at time 0. (This can be thought of as capturing the impact of the crisis elsewhere in Asia on Korea.) This unanticipated increase in risk causes the exchange rate to depreciate and the interest rate to rise (that is, both i_t and s_t rise). In Figure 5.1, this is represented by an upward shift of the interest rate–exchange rate frontier which connects the equilibrium values of s_t and i_t (where the parameter a is still to be determined).[4] If it is assumed that the risk premium is persistent (that is, that $\phi_d > 0$) and that the system is stable ($0 < b \equiv [1 + a(1 - d)]^{-1} < 1$), then the frontier gradually shifts back to the origin following the shock. One may justify this persistence by the fact that the restoration of market confidence or foreign reserves takes time.

The monetary policy response 93

$$(1 - d)i_t + (1 - \phi_d)s_t = \phi_d^t \varepsilon_{do}$$

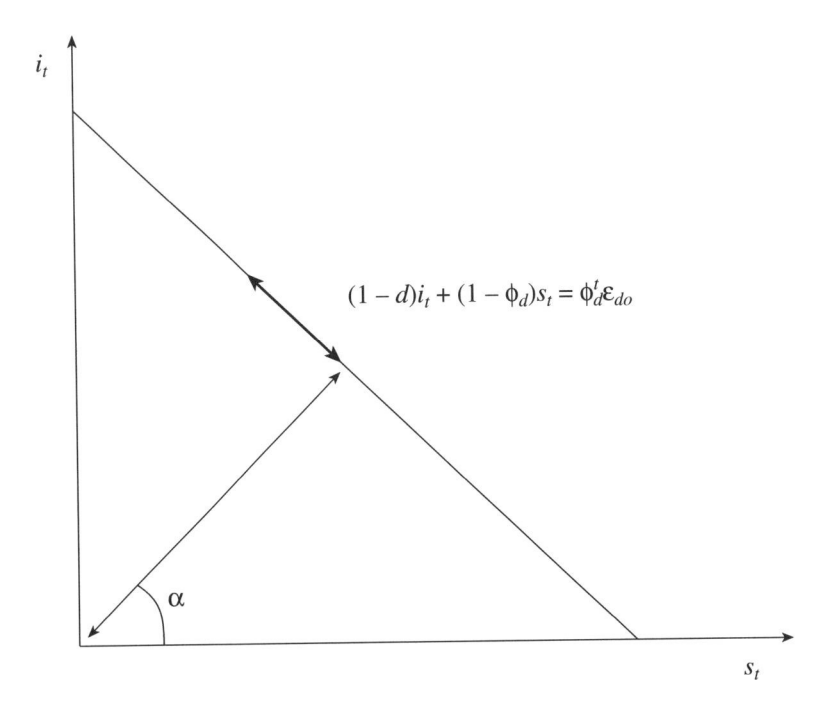

Source: See text.

Figure 5.2 Determinants of exchange rates and interest rates

Given this frontier, a monetary authority for which the level of the exchange rate appears in the objective function can resort to two tools. First, it can operate on investors' expectations by announcing a monetary policy rule. This can be captured by assuming an increase in the parameter a, and by the upward rotation of the diagonal line in Figure 5.1. By announcing their policy rule, the monetary authority chooses a value of a, which pins down the economy's position (in other words, it pins down a particular equilibrium pair of s_t and i_t along the interest rate–exchange rate frontier). In the extreme case where a approaches infinity, we have the case of a currency board system as in Hong Kong. At the other extreme, as a approaches zero, only s_t adjusts, while i_t is fixed. By raising a, the case in question, the monetary authority declares that interest rate policy will henceforth more closely target fluctuations in the exchange rate. If credible, this policy announcement can feed into the investors' expectations about the future path of the interest rates, which will be stabilizing immediately. This is the 'signaling effect.'

The monetary authority's second tool is to adopt a policy stance that is even more contractionary than anticipated by the market. This is represented by a positive value for ε_{mt} and by movement in Figure 5.1 along the interest rate–exchange rate frontier in a northeast direction. As shown in the Appendix, a contractionary monetary shock (under the assumption of stability) causes the interest rate to rise and the exchange rate to appreciate; again, this is the orthodox effect. By this interpretation, the collapse of Korea's exchange rate was caused by an increase in the perceived level of risk, and the exchange rate would have collapsed still more dramatically than was actually the case had the monetary authority not pursued a policy even more contractionary than anticipated by the market.

One important point to note from this discussion is that the goal of the high interest rate policy taken to stabilize the exchange rate was not just to surprise the market with an unusually tight monetary policy, but also to impress upon investors the intentions of the monetary authorities. That is, the authorities sought to stabilize the exchange rate by exploiting what is referred to above as the signaling effect. The repeated announcements of the Korean government and the IMF regarding the stance of monetary policy suggest that the policy makers were attempting to utilize this signaling channel.

Unfortunately, this analysis suggesting that the high interest rate policy was indeed effective in stabilizing the exchange rate is contingent on the validity of the stability assumption – in other words, that $0 < b \equiv [1 + a(1 - d)]^{-1} < 1$. If the risk premium is sufficiently responsive to the interest rate ($d > 1$), then the model becomes unstable and the preceding logic breaks down. In this case, the appropriate policy for stabilizing the exchange rate is to reduce interest rates ($a < 0$). This may be the case that Furman and Stiglitz (1998) had in mind – that higher interest rates so increased the cost of servicing the heavy debt loans of Korean banks and firms that investors began worrying about the possible bankruptcy of Korean enterprise, leading them to demand a higher risk premium for holding Korean assets. This, then, is the heterodox result. While the preceding model helps by identifying the issues and assumptions on which the controversy turns, that controversy can be resolved only by examining the data.

Empirical Findings

Table 5.1 summarizes empirical research on the impact of interest rates on the exchange rate in the context of the Asian crisis. General conclusions are evidently difficult to draw. Indeed, there may be good reasons why empirical work in this area is inconclusive. First, the high interest rate policy was maintained for only a limited time, six months to a year depending on the country concerned. Even if weekly data are available, this still provides only

Table 5.1 Summary of previous empirical research

Authors	Data	Methodology	Conclusion
Goldfajn and Baig (1998)	Various data including daily time-series data Five Asian crisis countries (1997–98): Indonesia, Korea, Malaysia, Philippines, Thailand Five other crisis countries: Mexico (1982), Chile (1982), Sweden (1992), UK (1992), Mexico (1994)	Estimation of real exchange rates, real interest rates, and real interest parity relation	The evidence is mixed, but on balance favors the view that the higher interest rates were associated with appreciations in crisis-hit Asian countries
Park and Choi (1999)	Daily time-series data Korea (1/4/97–30/10/98) Indonesia (3/1/97–24/7/98) Malaysia (3/1/97–24/7/98) Thailand (20/1/97–24/7/98)	Single equation regression using forward exchange rates as control variables	High interest rates appear to cause exchange rate appreciation except for Malaysia
Dekle et al. (1999)	Weekly time-series data (1997–98) Korea, Malaysia, Thailand	VAR	Interest rate hikes led to exchange rate appreciation, though with long and variable lags.
Goldfajn and Gupta (1999)	Cross-country data for the countries that have undergone currency crises during the period 1980–98	Panel data regressions with various descriptive measures	Dramatic increases in interest rates have been associated with currency appreciation. But there was no clear association for a subsample of countries that have undergone a banking crisis along with a currency crisis

Table 5.1 continued

Authors	Data	Methodology	Conclusion
Tanner (1999)	Monthly time-series data (Jan. 1990–Dec. 1998) Indonesia, Korea, Thailand, Brazil, Chile, Mexico	VAR whose variables include the exchange market pressures (the sum of exchange rate depreciation and reserve outflows), monetary policy stance (domestic credit growth), and the differential between domestic and foreign interest rates	Contractionary monetary policy helps to reduce exchange market pressure
Gould and Kamin (2000)	Weekly time-series data Five crisis-hit Asian countries (1997–98): Indonesia, Korea, Malaysia, Philippines, Thailand	Use measures of international credit spreads and of domestic stock prices as proxies for investor concerns about creditworthiness and country risk	Unable to find a reliable relationship between interest rates and exchange rates
Cho and West (2003)	Daily time-series data Korea (17/12/97–30/6/99)	Single equation regressions and vector error correction model	Although the major driving force of exchange rate stabilization seems to be the recovery of the foreign currency liquidity position, the high interest rate appears to have contributed to stabilizing the exchange rate

Barsurto and Ghosh (2000)	Monthly time-series data (Jan. 1990–Dec. 1998) Indonesia, Korea, Thailand	Identify the risk premium by the difference between the actual exchange rate and the (pure monetary model based) theoretical exchange rate, and relate thus defined risk premium with the interest rate policy	Tighter monetary policy was associated with appreciation of the exchange rate, and there is little evidence of higher interest rates contributing to a widening of the risk premium
Kraay (2000)	Data for speculative attack periods in a sample of 75 developed and developing countries over the period 1960–97	Examine the behavior of interest rates around successful and failed speculative attacks	There is no systematic association between interest rates and the outcome of speculative attacks
Cho and West (2001)	Weekly time-series data Korea (17/12/97–16/12/98) Philippines (23/7/97–22/7/98) Thailand (23/7/97–22/7/98)	Estimate structural parameters of the model composed of two equations, a monetary policy reaction function and an interest parity relationship	Point estimates indicate that exogenous increases in interest rates led to exchange rate appreciation in Korea and the Philippines, depreciation in Thailand, but confidence intervals are huge

Source: See text.

25 to 50 observations and few degrees of freedom for empirical work. Daily data provide more degrees of freedom but contain substantial amounts of noise.

Second, there is the problem of identification (whether we are observing the impact of monetary policy on the variable or variables of interest – the exchange rate, for example – or the effect of those other variables on monetary policy). Although identification problems are pervasive in empirical macroeconomics, identification is likely to be particularly difficult in currency crisis periods, which feature large disturbances and structural shifts.

Nevertheless, there is some evidence of the orthodox effect of high interest rates in Korea. D. Park and Choi (1999), Dekle et al. (1999), Tanner (1999), Barsurto and Ghosh (2000), and D. Cho and West (2000, 2003) all find evidence for the orthodox effect in the Korean data, although their findings for other Asian countries are more mixed. As an experiment, Figure 5.3 shows the impulse responses estimated from bivariate vector autoregressions (VARs) for the exchange rate and the interest rate, country by country.[5] Bearing in mind all the reservations about why VARs like these should be regarded cautiously, the left-hand figure for each country can be interpreted as showing the effect of an increase in the interest rate on the exchange rate. These results suggest that Korea was the only country where interest rate hikes led to appreciation of the exchange rate.

Why then was the result different in Korea? There are several potential explanations. The first of these is destructive: it is the possibility of misidentification. Specifically, there is the danger of misattributing to monetary policy the effects of two important country-specific events that may have significantly affected the investors' expectations in the currency market and thereby the exchange rate. The first such event was the announcement by the US government on 24 December 1997 that a second line of emergency loans from G-7 countries would be made available. The second was the successful completion of the negotiation in February 1998 between the Korean government and foreign creditors for converting more than $20 billion in short-term debt into long-term debt. These two events occurred soon after the interest rate was raised, complicating efforts to isolate the effect of the high interest rate policy.

A second possible explanation for the contrast with other countries is that the high interest rate policy was more credible in Korea. In comparison with Thailand and the Philippines, the interest rate in Korea moved far more closely with the exchange rate (Figure 5.1). The simple correlation between the two variables is 0.300 for Korea but only 0.064 for Thailand and –0.135 for the Philippines. The impulse responses estimated in Figure 5.3 show that the interest rate rose (or, more precisely, was raised by the monetary authority) in response to the increase in the shock to the risk premium only in

1. Korea

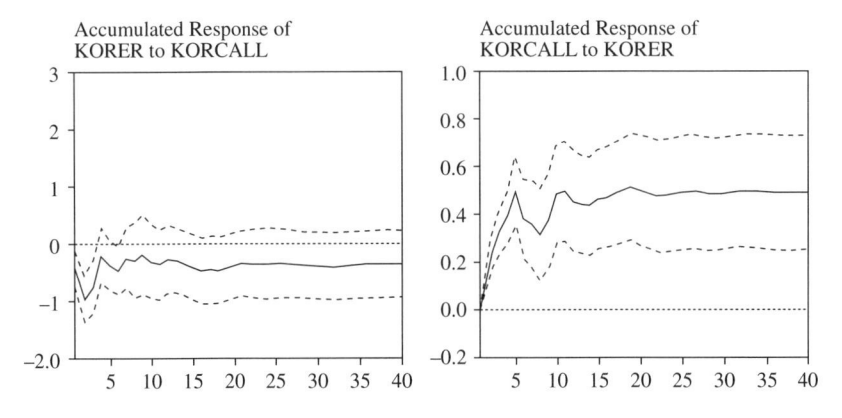

2. Thailand

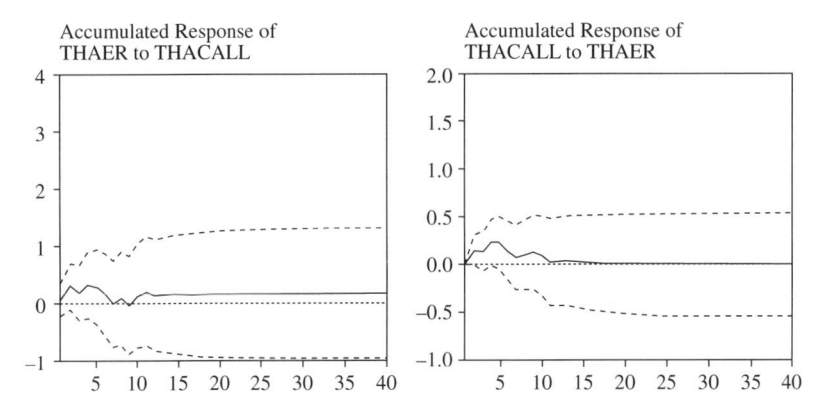

3. Philippines

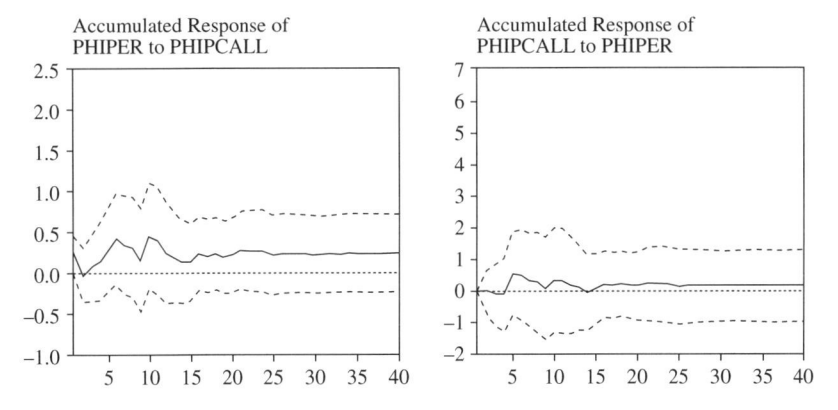

Source: See text.

Figure 5.3 Impulse responses from VARs using daily data

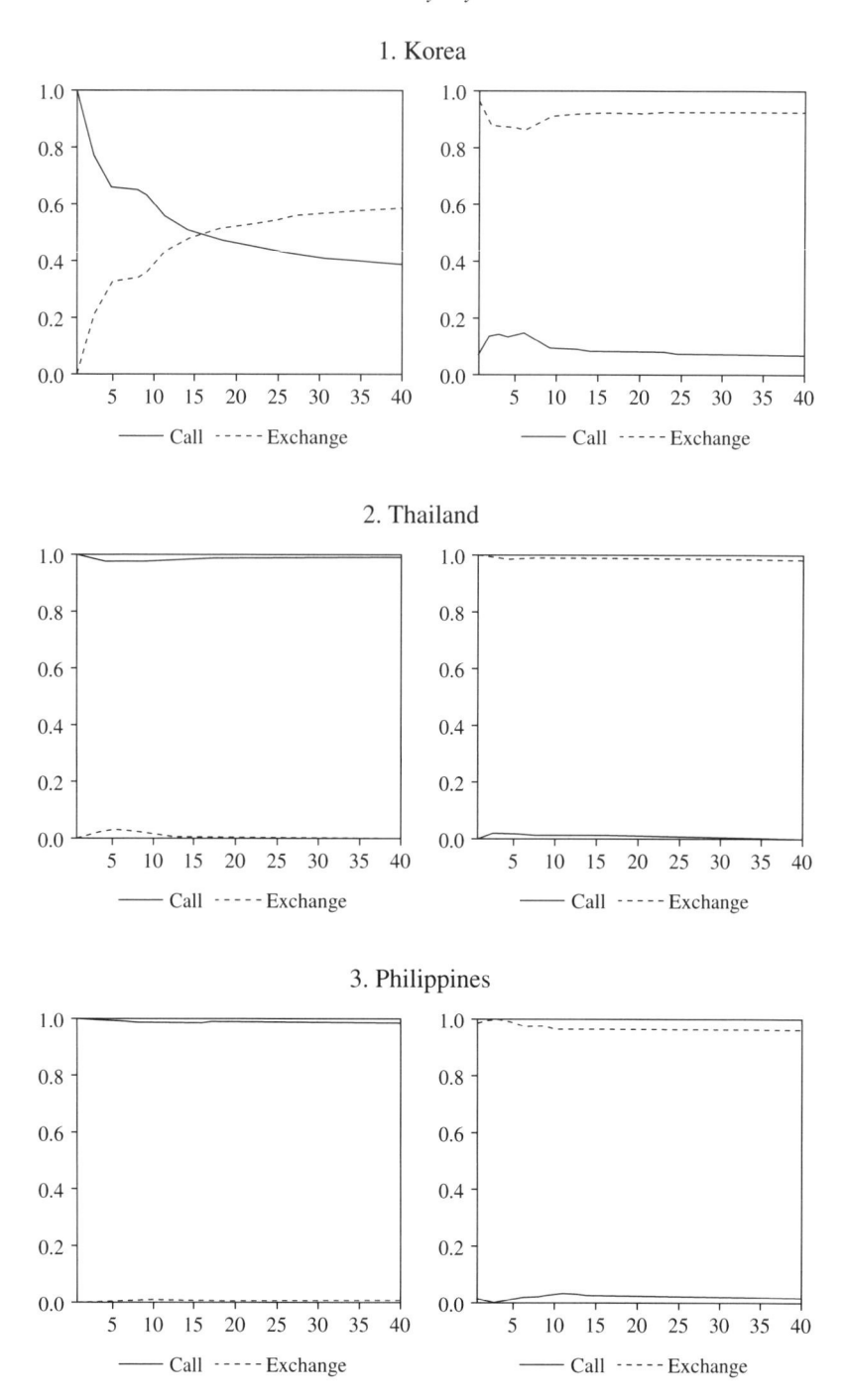

Figure 5.4 Variance decomposition of interest rates and exchange rates

Korea. The variance decompositions in Figure 5.4 also suggest that the interest rate was largely determined by the exchange rate shock in Korea, while it was determined independently in the other countries. That is, the announcement by the government and the IMF that interest rates would be raised and kept at higher levels for as long as needed to stabilize the exchange rate appears to have been more credible in Korea, at least *ex post*. Investors may have come to believe that the Korean monetary authority was very serious about achieving its goal of exchange rate stabilization while continuing to regard skeptically the policy announcements of other countries.[6]

Although this evidence is less than definitive, it is also true that many arguments critical of the high interest rate policy are equally or perhaps even more questionable. For example, there is criticism that high interest rates actually aggravated the problem of capital outflows in December 1997, but this criticism overlooks the fact that an even larger capital outflow (reflecting the actions of domestic as well as foreign investors) might have resulted had interest rates not been raised. In this regard, it may be noteworthy that, while foreign banks drastically reduced their exposures to Korea in December 1997, a substantial amount of foreign currency flowed into Korea seeking high interest rates. For example, net private transfers, which had been slightly negative until October 1997, increased sharply to approximately 2 percent of monthly GDP in December 1997, and then gradually declined to zero as the call rate was lowered.

MONETARY POLICY AND STANDARD POLICY OBJECTIVES

If the high interest rate policy was ineffective or, rather, contributed to further depreciation of the exchange rate after the crisis, it was a mistake. But even if the policy helped to stabilize the exchange rate, as suggested by the preceding evidence, it still does not follow that the policy was optimal. In other words, the question is whether stabilization of the exchange rate should have been the intermediate target of policy – that is, whether it was an efficient means of achieving the ultimate goals of concern to the authorities.

Policy Objectives and the Optimal Policy Rule

A standard way of modeling optimal policy is to assume that the monetary authority minimizes a loss function of the form:

$$\text{Min. } (1 - \alpha)(\pi - \pi^*)^2 + \alpha(y - y^*)^2, \tag{5.4}$$

where π and y are the inflation rate and the level of output, respectively, * denotes the target levels of these variables, and α is a parameter that reflects the preferences of the authorities (the relative weights they attach to these targets). The standard assumption, then, is that stable output and low inflation are the ultimate goals of policy. Strictly speaking, a central bank with a legal mandate to target inflation, like the Bank of Korea after the crisis, should set $\alpha = 0$.[7] In practice, however, most countries expect the monetary authority to be concerned with the stabilization of business cycles within an 'acceptable' range of inflation; that is, the monetary authority is expected to set α such that $0 < \alpha < 1$, since economic activity would experience severe fluctuations otherwise. Thus, while the Bank of Korea announced a medium-term inflation target of 2.5 percent in 1999, annual inflation was allowed to deviate from that target by ±1 percent.

One implication of this formulation is that exchange rate stabilization, in and of itself, is not the ultimate goal of economic policy. For a small, open economy like Korea, Ball (1999) shows that the optimal monetary policy rule relates a linear combination of the interest rate and exchange rate (what is referred to in the literature as the monetary conditions index, or *MCI*) to the two gaps in the preceding objective function:

$$MCI = w(r - r^*) - (1 - w)(e - e^*) = \beta'(\pi - \pi^*) + \gamma'(y - y^*), \qquad (5.5)$$

where r and e are the real interest rate and log of the real exchange rate, respectively, and w, β' and γ' are the parameters that depend on the underlying economic structures and the policy maker's preferences.[8] Ignoring the distinction between control and state variables and the distinction between expected and actual inflation, rearranging this equation yields an expression for the nominal interest rate, $i \equiv r + \pi$;

$$i = (\pi + r^*) + \beta(\pi - \pi^*) + \gamma(y - y^*) + \delta(e - e^*), \qquad (5.6)$$

where the parameters β, γ and δ are appropriately transformed from equation (5.5).[9]

According to equation (5.6), the interest rate should be raised, even if there has been no change in current levels of inflation and output, in response to depreciation of the currency. Currency depreciation boosts aggregate demand, which implies both faster inflation and higher levels of output in the future. Optimal policy today will respond to this information about economic conditions tomorrow – information conveyed by the exchange rate – even though the level of the exchange rate itself is not a policy objective. Ignoring the distinction between nominal and real variables, which is sensible for the very short-term, equation (5.3) can be interpreted as a special case of equation (5.6), where $a = \delta$ and u_{mt} comprise the remaining inflation and output gap terms. Intuitively, interest rate policy in response to the crisis had to be tied to the fluctuation of the exchange rate fluctuation because the latter was the dominating factor determining macroeconomic fluctuations.

Calibration

Even if there is some theoretical justification for using high interest rates to defend the exchange rate following the shock of the crisis, there remains the question of whether the authorities' response was too much or too little. Were interest rate responses optimal, in other words? Or were there alternative interest rate paths that would have resulted in a lower social loss, as measured by equation (5.4)?

One way of addressing this question is by calibrating the optimal interest rate rule of equation (5.6). Doing so is useful not just for assessing the high interest rate policy adopted in response to the crisis, but also for analyzing the 'super-low' interest rate environment established once confidence had been restored. (Compared with pre-crisis levels of around 12 percent, call rates were reduced to approximately 4 percent, depths that had not been experienced in Korea since the 1960s.)

I imposed a value of 5 percent for r^*, reflecting the commonly cited potential growth rate of Korea after the crisis, and 2.5 percent for π^*, the medium-term target declared by the Bank of Korea in 1999. As for π, there are important issues. The first issue is which inflation indicator should be used. An obvious candidate is core CPI, the official inflation target variable used by the Bank of Korea since 1999, which excludes irregular elements such as the prices of agricultural products and petroleum. However, a GDP deflator that covers a wider range of prices than the CPI or core CPI better represents aggregate economic conditions. After the crisis, in particular, there were significant discrepancies between the core CPI and GDP deflator due to the deterioration of the terms of trade (as shown in Figure 5.5). In 1999, for example, the core CPI inflation rate was more than 2 percent, while the GDP deflator inflation rate was negative. Therefore, I used both indexes in the following calibration.

A second issue is whether to use data on *ex ante* expected inflation or *ex post* actual inflation. Expected inflation is conceptually preferable (particularly when calibrating the real interest rate), but it must be estimated. And, in practice results are likely to differ substantially depending upon the techniques used in estimation. I therefore used the *ex post* (year-on-year) inflation rate in the benchmark case and an estimate of expected inflation for comparison.

For the core CPI and GDP deflator, respectively, Figure 5.5 compares the actual with expected inflation rates.[10] According to Figure 5.5, expectations

104   *The Korean economy beyond the crisis*

Actual vs expected inflation (Core CPI)

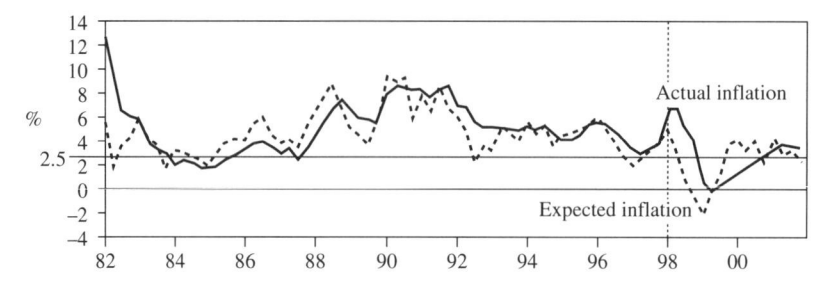

Actual vs expected inflation (GDP deflator)

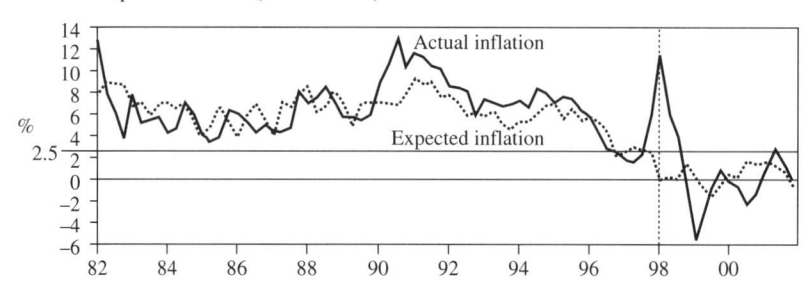

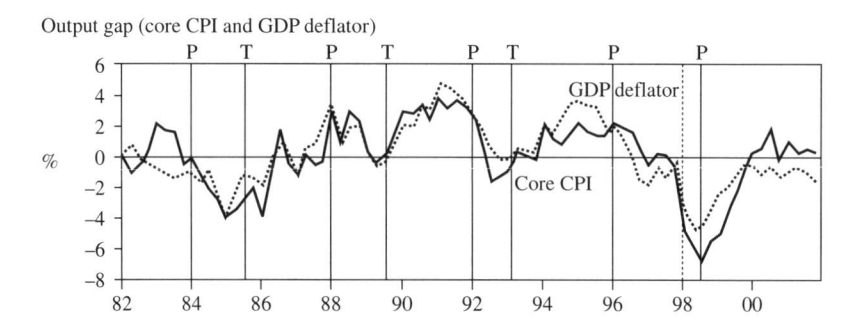

Output gap (core CPI and GDP deflator)

Real effective exchange rate (won vs dollar and yen)

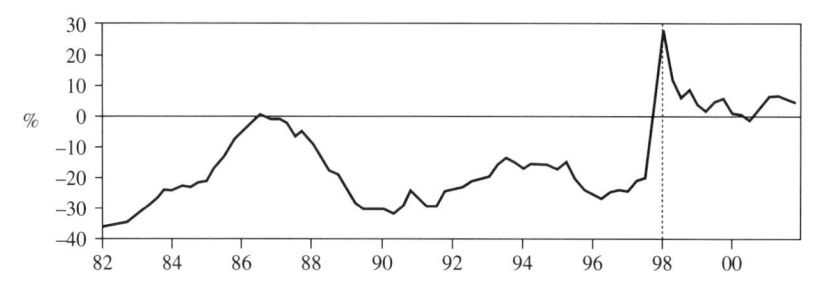

Source: See text.

Figure 5.5   Variables for calibration

of inflation (in terms of the core CPI) had turned negative by the end of 1998, before gradually returning to 2 to 4 percent rates of expected inflation thereafter. Another feature of this figure is that expected inflation leads actual inflation, especially in the post-crisis period.

An even more dramatic contrast between the actual and expected inflation rates is shown in Figure 5.5. While the actual inflation rate (in terms of the GDP deflator) exceeded 10 percent in the first quarter of 1998, expected inflation remained at zero, according to these estimates. Expected inflation is far smoother than the actual inflation and remains continually below the target level of 2.5 percent.

It is common in the literature to calibrate $y - y^*$ as the deviation of actual output from the hypothetical level that would have obtained in the absence of demand-side shocks. In order to obtain this output gap, I applied the structural vector autoregression (SVAR) methodology of Blanchard and Quah (1989), using seasonally adjusted real GDP and price index (core CPI or GDP deflator) data from 1980:I to 2002:I, and eight lags of the respective variables.[11] Figure 5.5 shows the estimated output gap series, the GDP component that is driven by the demand shock alone, along with the peaks and troughs officially defined by the Statistics Bureau of Korea. According to these estimates, the output gap plunged to historically unprecedented depths in 1998, but recovered to approximately zero by 2000. After the crisis, the output gap estimated using the GDP deflator appears to be lower than that estimated using core CPI, reflecting differences in the behavior of the two price indexes.

For $e - e^*$, I constructed a simple real effective exchange rate (REER) index based on two currencies, the US dollar and the Japanese yen, with equal weights of 0.5.[12] Figure 5.5 plots this REER series in percentage changes from the base year of 2001. According to this series, the exchange rate in the first quarter of 1998 was approximately 30 percent undervalued.

With these variables in hand, the parameters β, γ and δ still need to be calibrated. Although this calibration should in principle be based on estimates of the relevant parameters derived from the Korean data, this chapter simply borrows values from Ball (1999). For both β and γ, Ball assumes a range from 0.5 to 2.0. (The value of β becomes smaller as the weight on the inflation fluctuation in the loss function becomes smaller.) For δ, Ball (1999), Freedman (1994) and Gerlach and Smets (2000) all recommend a value of 0.3, although estimation results in D. Cho (2002) suggest that a value of 0.1 is more plausible in the Korean case.

Results and Discussion

Figure 5.6 shows calibration results using actual inflation rates and $\beta = \gamma = \delta = 0$, along with the actual call rate (measured as a quarterly average). When

Actual inflation, $\beta = 0$, $\gamma = 1$, $\delta = 0$

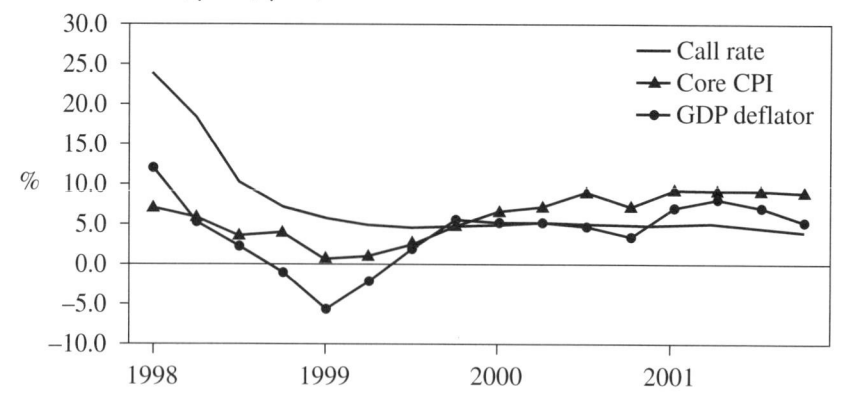

Actual inflation, $\beta = 0$, $\gamma = 1$, $\delta = 1$

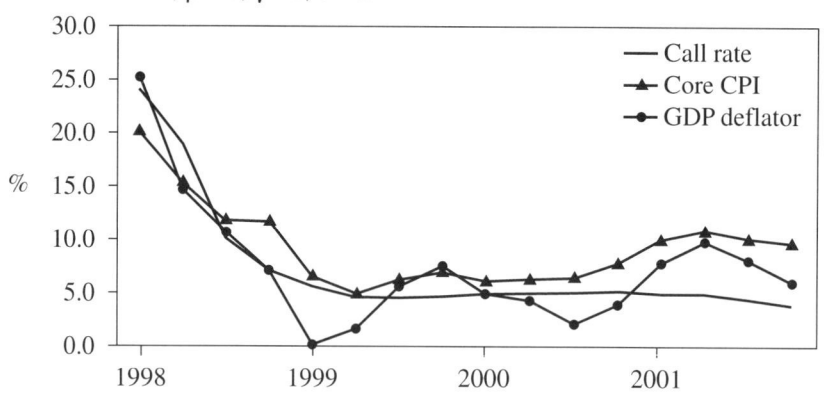

Actual inflation, $\beta = 1$, $\gamma = 1$, $\delta = 0.3$

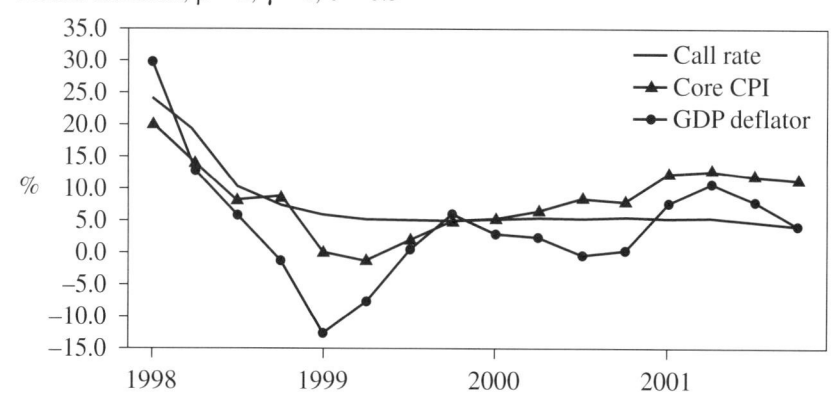

Source: See text.

Figure 5.6 Calibration results

Actual inflation, $\beta = 0$, $\gamma = 0$, $\delta = 0$

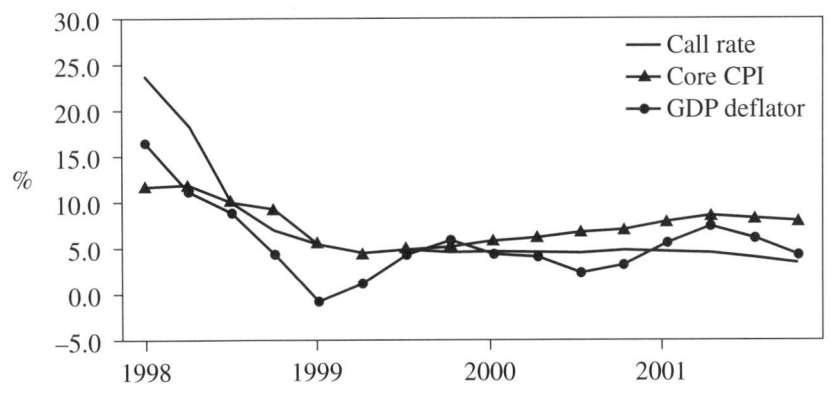

Actual inflation, $\beta = 0$, $\gamma = 0$, $\delta = 0$

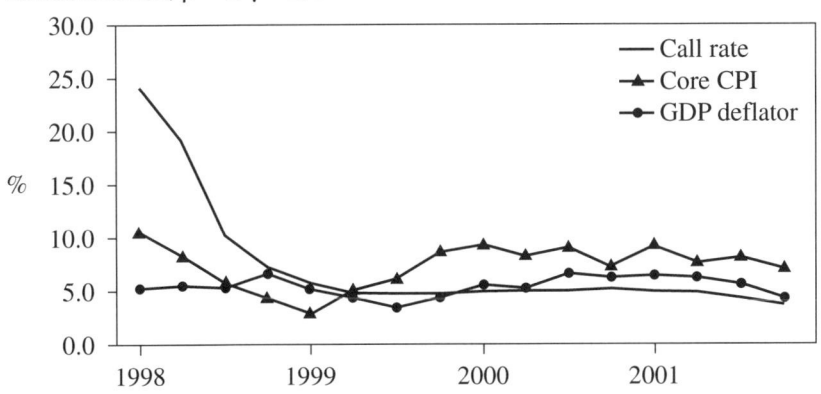

Actual inflation, $\beta = 1$, $\gamma = 0$, $\delta = 0$

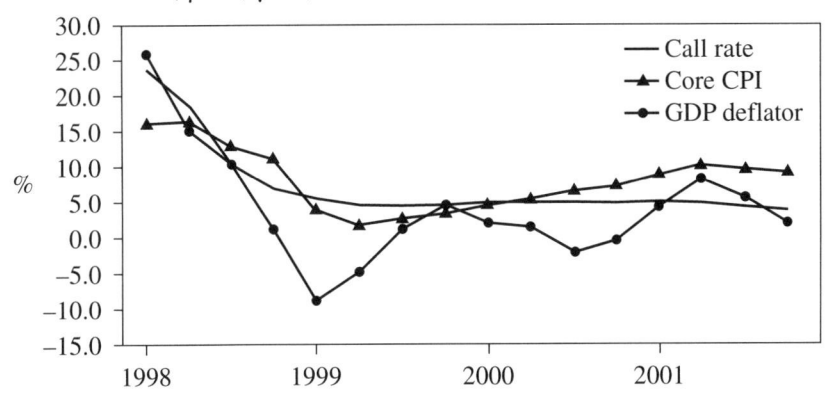

Figure 5.6 continued

the core CPI is used to measure inflation outcomes, actual interest rates appear to have been too high in the first two quarters of 1998 but too low in 2000 and 2001. When the GDP deflator is used, in contrast, call rates appear to be too high throughout all four quarters of 1998, before falling to roughly appropriate levels in 2000 and 2001. That is, the 'super-low interest rates' since 1999 do not appear to be too low if the GDP deflator accurately captures inflationary conditions.

However, call rates immediately following the outbreak of the crisis are too high no matter which price index is used. This finding is placed in relief in Figure 5.6, where expected inflation (estimated from a VAR) is used in place of actual inflation. Here optimal interest rates do not exceed 10 percent even in 1998, which contrasts with the 30 per cent rates actually observed.

In contrast, Figure 5.6 shows that the high interest rate policy in the first half of 1998 may have been justified, had the authority actively tried to stabilize the inflation or exchange rates and judge the inflation conditions by the actual GDP deflator. In these cases, however, the optimal interest rate falls below zero in the first quarter of 1999, which raises doubts about this policy response.

In short, the key assumption on which assessments of post-crisis interest rate policy appears to turn is which index of inflation is the appropriate guide to policy outcomes, rather than the particular parameter values that are assigned. The question, in other words, is whether Korean policy makers should care about core CPI inflation or the GDP deflator and whether they can formulate reliable estimates of expected inflation. Using expected inflation rates, no reasonable combination of parameter values can justify an interest rate as high as 15 percent in the first half of 1998. The crucial issue when judging the low interest rate policy put in place after 2000 is whether the core CPI or GDP deflator should be used. Using core CPI, it is again the case that no combination of reasonable parameter values can justify the authorities' decision to cut interest rates to less than 5 percent after 2000.

The question of which index of inflation is more relevant and reliable is not easily answered. However, the actual year-on-year inflation rate used in calibration has a clear shortcoming, despite the fact that the year-on-year changes are commonly used in Korea to calculate baseline inflation rates. For example, while the level of the GDP deflator rose substantially in the first quarter of 1998, it then declined significantly in the second quarter. These wide fluctuations quarter to quarter will not be picked up by the year-on-year inflation rate. Although the volatility of annualized quarter-to-quarter inflation rates (actual, not expected) obtained using the calibrated model raise questions of reliability, taken at face value, they can justify the high level of interest rates actually observed only in the first quarter of 1998, not thereafter (and recall that interest rates were maintained at high through 1998:II and only gradually reduced in the second half of the calendar year).

Of course, data on current macroeconomic conditions become available only with a lag, and monetary policy must be formulated on the basis of uncertain forecasts. In practice, however, it is hard to invoke uncertainty as a justification for the maintenance of high interest rates beyond the first quarter of 1998. Few if any macroeconomic indicators signaled the danger of accelerating future inflation after March; if anything, most variables pointed to the danger of deflation. The exchange rate, which was the leading indicator of short-term price movements during the crisis, began stabilizing in February 1998. Nominal wages, which may be a more informative guide to medium-term inflationary pressures, actually fell in 1998 relative to the preceding calendar year. In short, it is hard to justify the maintenance of the high interest rate policy after the first quarter of 1998, unless one sticks to a possibly deficient indicator like the year-on-year inflation rate.

It is always difficult to determine an appropriate monetary policy, not just ex *ante* but also *ex post*. But, in the Korean case, evidence suggests that had the authorities begun lowering interest rates earlier, they would not have been forced to shift monetary policy so dramatically in October 1998. Had they started reducing interest rates earlier and more gradually, they might have helped to avoid a deflationary recession in 1998 and a bubble-like recovery in 1999. They would have avoided what turned out to be the largest business cycle fluctuation experienced in Korea in nearly four decades.

SUMMARY AND CONCLUSIONS

This chapter has discussed Korea's post-crisis monetary policy, focusing on whether the high interest rate policy adopted immediately after the outbreak of the crisis was effective in stabilizing the exchange rate and whether post-crisis interest rate policy can be justified in light of the literature on optimal monetary policy. While it is impossible to determine conclusively whether tight monetary policy was effective in stabilizing the exchange rate, if there is any country in Asia for which the policy worked, that country was Korea. As to whether post-crisis monetary policy was too tight, too loose, or just about right, the answer hinges on which index of inflation is appropriate for such calculations. The high interest rate policy maintained in the first quarter of 1998 can be justified if the actual (year-on-year) inflation rate as opposed to the expected inflation rate (estimated from vector autoregressions) is used. The low interest rate policy in place since 1999 can be justified if the GDP deflator rather than the core CPI is used. But whatever uncertainty remains about the advisability of raising interest rates to observed heights in the first quarter of 1998, the analysis suggests that the authorities should have started moving to reduce them at an earlier date. In fact, there appears to have been considerable latitude for interest rate reductions starting in the second quarter of 1998.

This chapter has also revealed that many important issues related to the conduct of monetary policy in Korea remain unresolved. It will have succeeded even if it only provokes more active discussion of them.

NOTES

1. I am grateful for the research assistance of Yoon-Ki Kim and Jong-Man Yoo.
2. Detailed explanations about the evolution of monetary policy scheme in Korea after the crisis can be found in D. Cho (2002).
3. The Letter of Intent (http://www.imf.org/external/country/KOR/index.htm) stated that '[m]oney market rates will be allowed to rise sufficiently and will be maintained at that level or higher as needed to stabilize the market'(3 December 1997); 'Raise call rates to 30 per cent, or above if needed, to stabilize the exchange rate' (24 December 1997); 'Call rates have been at around 30 per cent since Dec. 26 and will be kept high until the foreign exchange situation improves' (January 1998); 'With the mitigation of the immediate foreign exchange crisis, call rates will be cautiously allowed to ease, in line with continued exchange rate stabilization' (February 1998); 'Interest rate policy will continue to be conducted in a flexible and symmetric manner. Subject to the objective of maintaining stability in the foreign exchange market, call interest rates will continue to be lowered, in line with market conditions' (May 1998); 'Interest rate policy will continue to be conducted in a flexible manner with upward and downward adjustments as necessary' (July 1998); 'Easy monetary stance will be maintained …' (November 1998).
4. This frontier, $(1-d)i_t + (1-\phi_d)s_t = \phi_d' \varepsilon_{d0}$, is derived by eliminating a from the solutions for i_t and s_t, for $\varepsilon_{mt} = 0$ for all t. I call this line the interest rate–exchange rate frontier in the sense that the monetary authority cannot alter it.
5. Sample periods for the VARs were one year after the outbreak of the crises: 1 December 1997–30 November 1998 for Korea and 1 July 1997–30 June 1998 for Thailand and the Philippines. Ten lagged variables, or approximately two weeks, were included in the VAR, and the exchange rate was put first in the Cholesky decomposition. Differenced data were used in estimation, but the impulse responses were calculated for the levels. Dotted lines indicate 95 percent confidence bands in each graph.
6. The legal introduction of inflation targeting in 1998 might have served to raise Korea's monetary policy credibility, but this does not seem to be the major factor behind the success in exchange rate stabilization. Inflation targeting had not yet become standard practice in 1998, and many international investors were worried about the possibility of deflation rather than inflation.
7. The new Bank of Korea Act (passed by the National Assembly in December 1997 and took effect on 1 April 1988) declares that the primary goal of monetary policy is price stability instead of multiple, obscure objectives such as the soundness of the banking system and economic growth. Since 1999, the Bank of Korea has announced the next year's inflation target at the end of every year, and the Board of Governors convenes every month to set up the policy directions (mostly the level of call rate as the operating target) in accordance with the announced inflation target.
8. In fact, Ball (1999) proposes a policy rule that considers the short-term effect of the lagged exchange rate, but I did not include this effect for two reasons. First, this rule appears to be sensitive to an *ad hoc* specification about economic structures. Second, I applied this part in the calibration exercises, but the results did not change much.

9. Strictly speaking, equation (5.6) is not a formula describing the optimal interest rate rule in the sense that the right-hand side includes an endogenous variable, e: when i changes, e changes too.
10. Since the data frequency is quarterly, the expected annual inflation rate needs forecast values of up to four quarters ahead.
11. As for the application of the Blanchard and Quah (1989) methodology to the Korean data, Kim (1996) has already reported detailed estimation results. The most critical identification assumption of this technique is that the demand shock does not change the output level in the long-run, while the supply shock does. The only deviation of this chapter's estimation from J.-I. Kim (1996) is that I used the core CPI instead of the GDP deflator.
12. D. Cho (2002) shows that this simple index is similar to a far more complex index based on 16 trading partners' currencies using the relative portions of trading volumes as the respective currencies' weights.

APPENDIX: SOLUTIONS OF THE MODEL

The reduced-form solutions to the system in the text are:

$$E_{t-1}s_t = b\sum_j \{b^j E_{t-1}[u_{dt+j} - (1-d)u_{mt+j}]\},$$

$$i_t = aE_{t-1}s_t + u_{mt},$$

$$s_t = [-(1-d)i_t + E_t s_{t+1} + u_{dt}].$$

An unanticipated risk shock: with respect to a unit shock to ε_{dt} at time 0, both the interest rate and the exchange rate both jump initially (s_0 and i_1), but both variables decline smoothly thereafter.

$$i_0 = 0,$$

$$s_0 = 1/(1-b\phi_d) > 0,$$

$$d_0 = 1 > 0,$$

$$i_t = a\, s_t > 0, \qquad\qquad \text{for } t > 0,$$

$$s_t = \phi_d^t b/(1-b\phi_d) > 0, \qquad \text{for } t > 0,$$

$$d_t = f_m^t adb/\{1-bf_d)+1\} > 0, \quad \text{for } t > 0.$$

An unanticipated monetary shock: with respect to a unit shock to ε_{mt} at time 0, the interest rate rises and the exchange rate appreciates initially, after which both gradually approach zero over time.

$$i_0 = 1 > 0,$$

$$s_0 = -\{(1-d)/(1-b\phi_m)\} < 0,$$

$$d_0 = d > 0,$$

$$i_t = \phi_m^t b(1-\phi_m)/(1-b\phi_m) > 0, \quad \text{for } t > 0,$$

$$s_t = -\phi_m^t b(1-d)/(1-b\phi_m) < 0, \quad \text{for } t > 0,$$

$$d_t = \phi_m^t bd(1-\phi_m)/(1-b\phi_m) > 0, \quad \text{for } t > 0.$$

6. The fiscal policy response to the crisis

Joosung Jun

INTRODUCTION

Fiscal conservatism has long been a touchstone of Korean macroeconomic policy. From this point of view the 1997–98 crisis was a major shock. When the crisis hit, the International Monetary Fund called on Korea to maintain its traditional conservative fiscal stance. A tighter fiscal policy, it argued, would facilitate macroeconomic adjustment, allow for the financing of restructuring, and help to restore investor confidence. Once the magnitude of the crisis became known, however, fiscal conservatism was abandoned in favor of a more activist stance with the goal of boosting economic activity and strengthening the social safety net.

In 1998, the budget deficit reached 4.2 percent of GDP, reflecting declining tax revenue and the expansion of spending during the post-crisis recession. At the time, doubts about the speed and vigor of recovery led the authorities to conclude that an expansionary fiscal policy would have to be maintained for some years. Since late 1998, however, Korea has staged an impressive comeback, with macroeconomic fundamentals improving markedly. With recovery well underway, in 2000 the fiscal authorities shifted toward medium-term consolidation with the goal of restoring fiscal balance by 2003. Their efforts were even more successful than they imagined, as by 2000 the country had already achieved a surplus of 1.3 percent of GDP.

This chapter examines these developments and reflects on the appropriateness of the fiscal policy during and after the crisis. No discussion of the fiscal response to the crisis would be complete without revisiting the controversy over the initial IMF prescription. With the benefit of hindsight, most analysts now agree that the depth of the recession should have been more adequately taken into account. But since the IMF acknowledged this mistake and modified its insistence on fiscal austerity in 1998, criticism of the Fund on the fiscal policy front has been significantly muted.

Consequently, this chapter focuses instead on whether the Korean authorities were right to insist on the restoration of a balanced budget even before the recovery of the economy was complete. There is evidence that, even before the outbreak of the crisis, Korean fiscal policy was not adequately countercyclical – that the authorities' determination to 'spend within revenue' weakened the operation of the country's fiscal stabilizers. According to modern 'tax-smoothing' theories of fiscal policy, spending within revenue is not social welfare maximizing. While fiscal policy was expansionary in 1998–99, its use as a tool of macroeconomic stabilization in the subsequent period was inadequate. This problem was compounded by unreliable revenue forecasting and by the authorities' associated reliance on supplementary budgets, which together resulted in significant and unintended deviations between planned and realized outcomes – deviations that, in the present instance, were strongly procyclical. Thus, in 2000 the difference between the proposed deficit and the actual surplus was a full 4.4 percentage points of GDP. This gap between intentions and outcomes inadvertently rendered fiscal policy even more destabilizing than would have been the case otherwise.

Fiscal fine-tuning is more art than science. That said, there is little question that the government's plan for fiscal consolidation – and specifically its goal of limiting the growth of nominal expenditures to two percentage points below that of nominal GDP in the short run – distorted budgetary priorities by preventing necessary spending and paralyzing the countercyclical function of the budget. Looking further into the future, the government's plan ignored the continued burden of restructuring costs and the underfunding of public pensions. This suggests that reining in expenditures alone will not achieve the long-run goals of fiscal consolidation; it will also be necessary to increase revenue in the medium term.

The most immediate concern is the budgetary cost of financial sector restructuring. That cost could raise government debt by about ten percentage points of GDP even if economic recovery remains on course. This may not be cause for serious concern in so far as the official debt-to-GDP ratio in December 2000 was 23 percent, far below the OECD average (of 72 percent). However, the official debt-to-GDP ratio may not provide an accurate guide to Korea's debt dynamics, in so far as it does not incorporate the government's contingent liabilities.[1]

In particular, in the aftermath of the crisis the government implemented a number of fiscal measures to provide income security for those who have lost their jobs and are in need of social support. Outlays in this area rose further as a result of the passage of the National Basic Livelihood Protection Law in late 2000. The public pension scheme is also giving rise to higher expenditures. As the Korean population ages, reliance on family support will become less important and will be increasingly supplanted by formal pension arrangements. Without changes to the present configuration of generous benefits and low contribution rates, the pension system will face serious financial problems.

Absent large ongoing deficits, rising debt is not a problem so long as the economic growth rate exceeds the real interest rate, as was the case throughout Korea's high-growth era. Unfortunately, this favorable configuration of parameters is less likely to obtain in the future, with the decontrol of interest rates and the diminished scope for catch-up growth. Fiscal stabilization will require both containing expenditures and mobilizing additional revenues. Considering the pressure on expenditures from financial restructuring, reinforcement of the social safety net, and the prospect of Korean reunification, concerted efforts will be required to raise additional revenue by closing tax loopholes, expanding the tax base, and simplifying the tax code.

The remainder of this chapter develops these points. The next section examines fiscal developments in the wake of the crisis, with a focus on shifts in the fiscal stance and discretionary policy measures, including social welfare programs and tax incentives. The following section then analyzes the prospects for fiscal consolidation, presenting estimates of the costs of restructuring the financial sector and of funding public pension programs. The final section concludes by suggesting directions for fiscal reform.

THE FISCAL POLICY RESPONSE TO THE CRISIS

Fiscal policy was transformed by the crisis that erupted in 1997, as Korea's long-standing fiscal conservativism gave way to a more activist approach in response to economic weakness and soaring unemployment. This section reviews major developments in this period.

Shifts in the Fiscal Stance

Korea has long pursued a conservative fiscal policy. Spending commitments have typically been limited to anticipated revenues. Consequently, budget deficits were not a major problem in the period leading up to the crisis. The consolidated central government budget had remained more or less in balance throughout the period 1990–97 (Figure 6.1).[2] Because fiscal policy was not used as an instrument of demand management, the cyclically adjusted fiscal balance did not deviate much from the financial measure.[3] The gap between the primary and conventional balances was slight because the public debt was small and interest payments accounted for only a small share of the budget.

The government's strong financial position reflected fiscal consolidation efforts undertaken in the 1980s. The government had run deficits in the 1970s, reflecting its active support for investment in the heavy and chemical industries and transfers to the agricultural sector. In the early 1980s it then

116   *The Korean economy beyond the crisis*

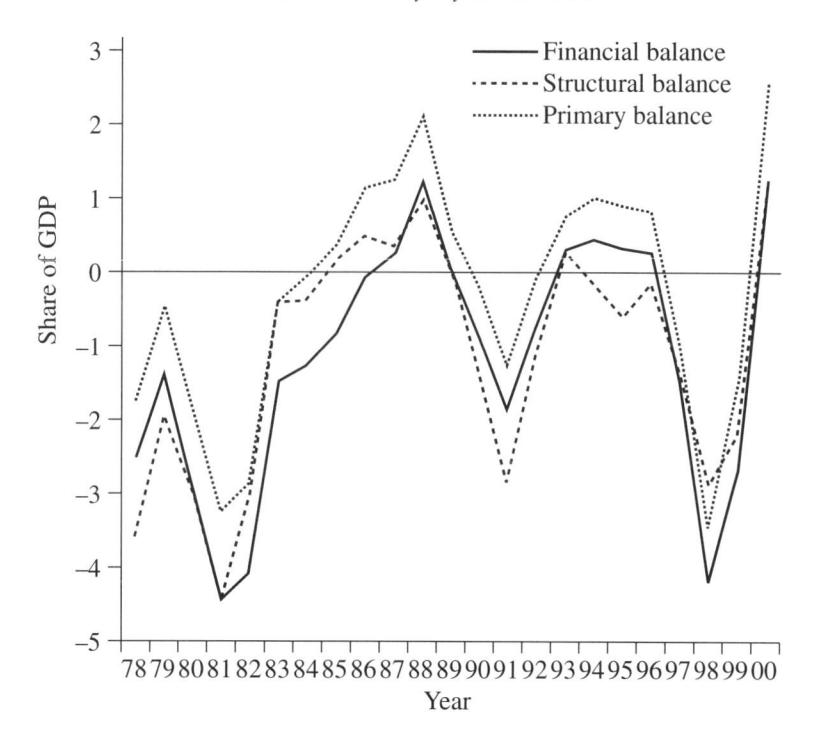

Note: The structural balance is estimated according to IMF methodology.

Source: Author's calculation based on Ministry of Finance and Economy, *Government Finance Statistics in Korea* (various issues).

Figure 6.1   Balance of the consolidated central government budget in Korea

began to focus on macroeconomic stability in response to the acceleration of inflation and economic stagnation in the aftermath of the second oil shock and political turmoil in 1979.[4] Fiscal policy became tight, and a conservative tone was maintained through most of the 1980s and the 1990s.

When the crisis hit, the IMF called for a further tightening of fiscal policy.[5] In the face of massive capital outflows, it believed that additional public saving was needed to contribute to the adjustment of the current account. A worsening fiscal position would have placed a heavier burden on monetary policy in bringing about this adjustment, which might have created intolerable pain for Korea's highly leveraged corporations. In addition there was the need to raise funds for financial sector restructuring. The interest on restructuring bonds was directly borne by the budget, while their redemption was guaranteed by the government. Finally, a tight fiscal policy was seen as necessary for restoring confidence in financial markets, since the tighter the fiscal policy, the less the likelihood that budget deficits would have to be monetized.

The original 1998 budget, passed in November 1997, targeted a surplus of 0.24 percent of GDP. As the crisis deepened, however, spending demands arising from the recession became heavier than anticipated. The 1998 budget was planned on the assumption of 6 percent growth, whereas the economy actually contracted by 6.7 percent. This forced the government, still committed to fiscal conservatism, to make changes. Late in 1997, selected expenditures (for example the salaries of civil servants) were frozen or reduced, while excise and oil taxes were raised. The government also considered a hike in VAT rates as a way of maintaining the flow of revenue.

As the extent and nature of the crisis became clear, there was growing doubt about the appropriateness of this strategy. The sharp drop in aggregate demand and greater-than-expected currency depreciation improved the current account balance more than expected but further weakened the fiscal position. Critics argued that a tight fiscal stance would exacerbate the economic contraction and perversely reduce investor confidence.[6] In early 1998 the authorities embraced a more flexible position, reflecting their growing concern over the sharp downturn in economic activity and the excessive hardships faced by the unemployed and the poor. Their focus shifted from reducing the current account deficit to accommodating the effects of economic conditions on the budget balance, and subsequently to actually augmenting those effects, which were countercyclical, through expansionary measures such as direct stimulus to the economy and expanding the social safety net.

Supplementary budgets were passed in March and September of 1998. These contained expansionary measures such as public work programs, expansion of the employment insurance system, and assistance to small and medium-sized enterprises. By the end of 1998, the deficit reached 4.2 percent of GDP (Table 6.1), indicative of the reversal of fiscal strategy since the original budget was drafted.

The planned deficit rose to almost 5 percent of GDP in 1999, a clear indication of the government's continued commitment to an activist fiscal policy. There were further increases in spending on the social safety net and support for small and medium-sized enterprises.[7] Once again two supplementary budgets were passed, this time to provide additional assistance to the unemployed, the poor, salaried workers, business start-ups, and the victims of Typhoon Olga.

The deficit in 1999 was smaller than forecast because the economic recovery was stronger than expected. The economy grew by a remarkable 10.7

Table 6.1 Consolidated central government budget (trillion won, %)

	1996	1997	1998	1999	2000	2001
Revenue	85.5	93.4	96.7	107.9	135.8	142.1
Growth rate	17.5	9.2	3.5	11.6	25.8	4.6
Share of GDP	20.4	20.6	21.8	22.4	26.0	24.6
Expenditures	84.4	100.3	115.4	121.0	129.3	142.5
Growth rate	18.0	18.8	15.1	4.9	6.9	10.2
Share of GDP	20.2	22.1	26.0	25.1	24.8	24.6
Balance	1.1	−7.0	−18.8	−13.1	6.5	n.a.
Share of GDP	0.3	−1.5	−4.2	−2.7	1.3	n.a.
Balance planned	−0.7	−1.0	1.1	22.7	−16.5	−0.4
Share of GDP	−0.2	−0.2	0.2	−4.7	−3.2	−0.1

Source: Ministry of Finance and Economy, *Government Finance Statistics in Korea* (various issues).

percent, and the deficit shrank to 2.7 percent of GDP. Strong growth diminished the need for increased spending on the social safety net, as unemployment fell to little more than half of earlier levels. Entering 2000, the economy continued to rebound, and the need to assist the unemployed and the poor diminished further. One fiscal liability which had not yet been addressed, however, was the restructuring of the financial sector. While only interest on government-guaranteed restructuring bonds was explicitly brought into the budget, potential losses stemming from the repayment of the principal were expected to raise the level of public debt substantially.

In 2000, the focus again became medium-term fiscal consolidation. The government originally sought to restore fiscal balance by 2004, by holding the growth in nominal expenditures to two percentage points below the growth of nominal GDP. But whereas the 2000 budget targeted a deficit of 3.6 percent of GDP, the outturn was a surplus of 1.3 percent of GDP. Because of the strong recovery, the government shortened its deadline for realizing a fiscal balance by one year, now targeting 2003, as shown in Table 6.2.

Assessment

As noted above, there were two major shifts in fiscal stance following the crisis. First the collapse of aggregate demand forced the government to break from its tradition of fiscal conservatism and to engage in deficit financing to counteract the contraction of the economy. Then after two years it moved back toward fiscal conservatism as the public debt and contingent liabilities increased.

Table 6.2   Medium-term fiscal plan, consolidated central government

	1998	1999	2000	2001	2002	2003	2004
Real GDP growth	−6.7	10.7	8.0	6.0	5.9	5.6	5.3
Nominal GDP growth	0.7	8.9	10/11	8.5	8.5	8.0	7.6
Spending growth	13.1	9.6	4.7	6.0	6.0	6.0	6.0
Budget balance (% of GDP)	−3.2	−2.7	−2.0/−2.5	−2.0	−1.0	0.0	0.5

Source: Ministry of Planning and Budget (2002).

In both cases the authorities and their critics disagreed over the appropriateness of these shifts. The first question is whether fiscal policy should have been more expansionary at an earlier stage. Critics argue that the standard IMF prescription of fiscal and monetary tightening did not duly take into account the state of the Korean economy.[8] Noting Korea's high savings rate and the temporary nature of the budget deficits created by the recession, Feldstein (1998) questioned the need to raise taxes and cut spending. As he argued, the combination of higher private savings and lower business investment was already releasing resources sufficient to largely eliminate the current account deficit. Moreover, the country's low level of public debt allowed fiscal policy to be used to stimulate the economy without creating worries about future debt sustainability. With the benefit of hindsight, even the IMF has acknowledged that the fiscal policy prescriptions of the initial program had perhaps been excessive, considering the deeper-than-expected recession and the need to strengthen the social safety net.

Standard tax-smoothing theories of fiscal policy imply that efficiency costs are minimized when tax rates are constant over time.[9] If tax rates are held constant, temporary deficits will occur during recessions, when revenues are temporarily depressed and spending on social programs is unusually high, whereas budget surpluses will occur during boom periods when revenues rise even faster than public spending. Fiscal policy will then be countercyclical: it will tend to counter temporary fluctuations in private spending. In other words, the fiscal balance will tend to automatically stabilize the level of aggregate demand. But tax smoothing will not be possible if the government adheres to a policy of 'spending within revenue' like that which had been practised in Korea for many years.[10] The inadequacy of the social safety net, especially the unemployment insurance system, had also until quite recently limited the working of automatic stabilizers.

Korean fiscal policy had not in fact been strongly countercyclical. In most of the 1980s and 1990s, neither the fiscal stance (the structural budget balance) nor the fiscal impulse (as measured using IMF methodology) moved in a countercyclical fashion.[11] Between 1989 and 1990, for example, when the GDP gap (the gap between potential and actual output) fell by 2.8 percentage points, reflecting the rapid expansion of the economy, both the fiscal stance and the fiscal impulse indicate a loosening of fiscal policy. A similar pattern is evident for a variety of other pre-crisis years. In the years following the crisis, however, fiscal policy appears to have played a stabilizing role.[12]

The government redirected fiscal policy toward medium-term consolidation in 2000, and the economy began to slow late that year. Noticing that the budget balance turned out to be a surplus of 1.3 percent of GDP, critics accused the government of reverting too quickly to a conservative stance.[13] The surplus in 2000 was due mostly to the unexpected rise in revenue rather than intentional adjustments. Whereas a 12 percent increase in revenue was forecast in the initial budget, actual revenue growth was more than twice as high, as shown in Table 6.1.[14] Whereas expenditure growth was rather modest (6.9 percent) compared to past years, the seemingly destabilizing fiscal stance in 2000 was only partly attributable to the government's consolidation initiative.[15]

The government was not immune to criticism of its plans for fiscal consolidation, however. The goal of restraining the growth of nominal expenditures to 2 percent lower than the growth of nominal GDP (Table 6.2) was seen as excessively optimistic and as preventing necessary spending and paralyzing the countercyclical function of the budget.[16] Furthermore, when the government and its supporters celebrated the return to a budget balance four years ahead of schedule in 2000, they ignored the impending burden of restructuring costs and the underfunding of public pensions. Given these impending costs to the budget, it is unlikely that expenditure restraint alone will be enough to achieve the objectives of fiscal consolidation; efforts will also be needed to raise additional revenue.

Two serious concerns regarding fiscal stabilization in Korea are the unreliability of revenue forecasting and the practice of issuing supplementary budgets, which have repeatedly led to significant deviations between planned and realized budgets. Table 6.3 illustrates the extent of those deviations between 1982 and 2000. The first two columns show the percentage difference between the planned and the actual budgets, while the next three columns show those same measures, and the budget balance, as shares of GDP. Note that the actual budget balance in 2000 was 4.4 percentage points of GDP, far different than that targeted in the initial budget. The average absolute deviation of revenue, expenditures and the balance as a percentage of GDP during 1991–2000 were 1.52, 1.05 and 1.63, respectively. The variability for revenue and expenditures during the period 1982–1990 was a bit higher than during the 1990s. Thus the increase in the deviations of the budget balance between

Table 6.3 Divergences between planned and actual budgets

	[(Final−Planned)/Planned]*100		[(Final−Planned)/GDP]*100		
Year	Revenue (1)	Expenditure (2)	Revenue (3)	Expenditure (4)	Balance (5)
1982	0.28	9.40	0.06	2.28	−2.22
1983	4.41	0.84	0.87	0.18	0.69
1984	11.66	14.52	2.25	2.98	−0.73
1985	−21.31	−16.94	−4.06	−3.38	−0.69
1986	−22.02	−16.41	−3.93	−3.19	−0.74
1987	−18.97	−24.76	−3.22	−4.15	0.92
1988	−4.58	−15.01	−0.80	−2.44	1.64
1989	−3.39	−7.60	−0.60	−1.34	0.74
1990	3.05	3.45	0.55	0.66	−0.10
1991	−4.92	0.71	−0.85	0.14	−0.99
1992	1.95	0.85	0.35	0.16	0.19
1993	−13.61	−18.03	−2.53	−3.30	0.77
1994	−8.60	−15.01	−1.64	−2.80	1.16
1995	3.55	0.12	0.69	0.02	0.66
1996	3.58	1.48	0.73	0.30	0.43
1997	−2.89	3.25	−0.60	0.72	−1.32
1998	−9.97	8.84	−2.17	2.30	−4.47
1999	5.90	−2.67	1.32	−0.67	1.99
2000	16.55	−0.45	4.31	−0.11	4.42
(average absolute values)					
1982–1990	9.96	12.10	1.82	2.29	0.94
1991–2000	7.15	5.14	1.52	1.05	1.64

Source: Author's calculations based on budget figures.

these two periods was mostly attributable to the unexpected fiscal outcome in the aftermath of the crisis.

Significant uncertainty over revenue and spending implies the advisability of a cautious approach to discretionary spending to prevent the latter from inadvertently becoming destabilizing from a cyclical point of view. If neither fiscal conservatism nor discretionary policy serves to stabilize the economy properly, the less harmful choice for the time being is probably the former.[17]

Expanding the Social Safety Net

Before the crisis, public spending on social welfare was very low, reflecting Korea's low rate of unemployment, its declining poverty rates, and the limited provision of social services. Social welfare has generally been perceived to be the responsibility of families and companies (the severance allowance provided by companies upon retirement had been the major form of retirement plan before public pensions were introduced), and the economy's high growth rate, combined with a relatively equal and stable distribution of income, contributed to a steady reduction in the ranks of the poor.[18] A health care system was introduced in 1977, followed by a national pension plan and unemployment insurance in 1988 and 1995, respectively. But these schemes had very limited coverage at first, and beneficiaries could only become eligible after a minimum contribution period.

The Livelihood Protection Program (LPP) was the country's major social assistance scheme. It covered living expenses, medical care and educational expenses of the poor. Because of relatively strict eligibility requirements, only 1.5 million people, or 3 percent of the population, received benefits under this program in 1997.[19] In addition, the maximum livelihood benefit was set at 60 percent of the minimum cost of living, and the benefit was available for only six months a year for an able-bodied person capable of working.

The crisis led to a sharp increase in unemployment and a drop in real wages.[20] The government implemented a number of fiscal measures to provide income security for those who lost their jobs and were in need of social support. Expenditures on the social safety net soared. The total budget for labor market programs amounted to 2.3 percent of GDP in 1998 and 3.2 percent of GDP in 1999. The corresponding figure for LPP benefits was only 0.3 percent of GDP.

Unemployment insurance coverage and benefits were similarly expanded. Before the crisis, the Employment Insurance System (EIS) covered only firms with more than 30 workers. In the face of rapidly rising unemployment, the government expanded the coverage of the EIS in 1998 to include all firms.[21] Consequently, the percentage of wage workers covered by the insurance system rose from 33 percent to 70 percent. The government also shortened the required contribution period for eligibility and lengthened the duration of benefits.[22] As joblessness increased and the insurance coverage expanded, both the volume of benefit payments and the number of beneficiaries increased dramatically.[23]

Despite the expanded coverage of the EIS, there were still limitations on eligibility, because a major percentage of the unemployed were from small firms and were not adequately insured. Due to the strict means-test and the earning capacity provision, many of these uninsured jobless were not eligible for the existing Livelihood Protection Program (LPP) either. The government took several temporary measures to address this problem.

Public works programs became an integral part of assistance, providing temporary jobs in street cleaning, parking control, forest conservation, and the like. About 1 trillion won ($0.8 billion) was allocated for public work projects in 1998, and the budget was more than doubled the following year.[24] The government also instituted the Temporary Livelihood Program (TLP) to alleviate distress among low-income workers who had recently lost their jobs. This program covered 310 000 new beneficiaries in 1998, in addition to those 1.2 million beneficiaries who had already been receiving benefits under the existing Livelihood Protection Program.

A variety of other job creation, income support, and vocational training programs was implemented in 1998–99. Targeted loan programs were launched to help the unemployed cover their living, housing, educational and medical expenses. Start-up fund subsidies were made available for venture businesses. Some of these labor initiatives, notably public work programs, were phased out in 2000 as the recovery gained strength. As a result, spending on labor market programs plummeted to 1.1 percent of GDP.

The temporary assistance programs, along with LPP and EIS, helped alleviate distress among the unemployed and the poor during the crisis. Due to their *ad hoc* nature, however, benefits were sometimes inadequate or poorly targeted.[25] There were too few social workers to manage the system. In order to ensure adequate benefits and enhance the efficiency of the screening and monitoring process, in August 1999 the government enacted the National Basic Security Livelihood Law.

The new system, which became effective in October 2000, increased benefit levels substantially, bringing recipients' incomes up to the minimum cost of living.[26] It made social welfare a right of all eligible individuals. The number of social workers was increased to improve administrative efficiency. And, in order to prevent excessive reliance on the social safety net, beneficiaries able to work were required to actively search for jobs in addition to undergoing vocational training and accepting job placements offered by the social welfare office. The number of beneficiaries was estimated at around 1.5 million in 2001, roughly equivalent to the number under the previous system.[27]

While this new system has several positive elements, there has been concern over the potential for moral hazard on the part of the recipients and the cost to taxpayers. Some recipients may choose not to work because the benefit level for a single household is not much lower than the minimum wage, and some marginal recipients may have a strong incentive to underreport their income in order to pass the means-test.[28]

124   *The Korean economy beyond the crisis*

Reflecting the increased level of benefits, the budget for the Livelihood Protection Program rose by some 60 percent, from 1.7 trillion won in 2000 to 2.7 trillion won in 2001. This upward trend in welfare spending combined with the underfunding of public pension schemes, has added to the concern about rising government debt.

Tax Incentives for Consumption, Investment and Restructuring

The government introduced various tax measures after the crisis to boost economic activity, facilitate restructuring of the corporate and financial sectors, and promote foreign direct investment and capital inflows.

Wage and salary earners received tax relief in the form of increased deductions and a cut in the marginal tax rates. Deductions for earned income, educational expenses and charitable contributions have been raised, and deductions for pension income were introduced. The elderly and disabled receive additional deductions and tax-exempt saving opportunities. Income tax rates were reduced by 10 percent across the board.[29] The tax burden on the self-employed was reduced by exempting income and value added taxes on sales through credit card transactions. To encourage private consumption, special consumption taxes have been reduced or eliminated.[30]

To stimulate investment, tax incentives were provided to small and medium-sized enterprises, including tax exemptions on capital gains and stock options in venture capital businesses. Temporary investment tax credits were reinstated, and eligibility for them was expanded. Global taxation of capital income was suspended in 1999 and 2000 to prevent negative impacts on financial markets.[31] The personal capital gains tax rate was reduced by ten percentage points in order to boost the real estate market.

In an effort to promote the inflow of foreign investment, tax preferences were introduced and expanded. Foreign investors and firms investing in high technology or investing more than $100 million in a Foreign Investment Zone were made exempt from personal and corporate income taxes for seven years and granted a 50 percent reduction for a further three years. Additional tax incentives for such investments were made available by local governments in the form of reduced property, acquisition and registration taxes.

With regard to restructuring, the focus of changes in the tax code has been on reducing the costs of asset and equity transactions and debt payments. Taxes on revaluation profits following mergers and acquisitions have been deferred; taxes on capital gains on asset and equity transactions for restructuring have been put off; acquisitions, registration and securities transactions taxes have been exempted on transactions related to restructuring; and taxes on capital gains accruing to assets that were sold to repay debt were exempted. Tax relief was also provided for financial sector restructuring. To facilitate the closure of nonviable financial institutions, proceeds from their liquidation, merger or sale of assets have been exempted from taxation.

While these measures were intended to alleviate the adverse effects of the crisis and to facilitate restructuring, they also added to the complexity of the tax system, which was already overly complex, inefficient and inequitable. In the face of rising government debt and the growing cost of financial sector restructuring, fiscal consolidation has become a major policy objective, as discussed in the following section. Taking into account the potential costs of reunification and soaring welfare expenditures stemming from the rapid aging of the population and the maturing of public pensions, the tax burden will likely increase over the next several decades. Therefore, the top priority for taxation is to expand the revenue base in an efficient and equitable manner.[32]

FISCAL CONSOLIDATION

Previous sections have noted the rise in government-guaranteed debt, the bulk of which was incurred by issuance of bonds to raise funds for financial sector restructuring. The underfunding of public pensions will also impose financial pressures over the next several decades. And then there is the prospect of reunification. All this has rendered fiscal consolidation a major policy goal. This section examines the dynamic nature of this process.

Overview

Korea's fiscal condition was relatively sound before the crisis. In 1998, the Korean government began to run a deficit, and the debt mounted at a rapid rate. As shown in Table 6.4, the gross debt of the central government reached 23.1 percent of GDP in 2000, almost twice the 1996 level. This increase was largely due to accumulated budget deficits and to the loans received from international financial institutions. The debt figure is not a cause for concern in and of itself, since it is well below the OECD average of about 72 percent in 2000 (OECD, 2001). More alarming is the sharp rise in government-guaranteed debt from 1.8 percent of GDP in 1996 to 13.7 percent of GDP in 2000. Government debt and guaranteed liabilities together amounted to 194.2 trillion won, or 37.6 percent of GDP in 2002.

A major portion of the debt guarantees is attributable to the issuance of restructuring bonds, which could become an additional fiscal burden because the public agencies that issued these bonds are not likely to be able to redeem them in full.

A simple, intuitive method of assessing debt sustainability is to look at the trend of the debt-to-GDP ratio.[33] This trend is determined primarily by the

Table 6.4 Government debt and debt guarantees (trillions of won)

	Dec. 1996	Dec. 1997	Dec. 1998	Dec. 1999	Dec. 2000
Government debt	53.2	69.6	90.0	107.7	119.7
(% of GDP)	(12.7)	(15.3)	(20.0)	(22.3)	(23.1)
Debt guarantee	7.6	13.0	72.0	81.5	74.5
(% of GDP)	(1.8)	(2.9)	(16.0)	(16.8)	(13.7)
Total	60.8	82.6	162.0	189.2	194.2
(% of GDP)	(14.5)	(18.1)	(36.0)	(39.1)	(37.6)

Note: Debt figures are from the end of each year.

Source: Ministry of Finance and Economy (2001b).

initial size of the debt, real interest rates, the economic growth rate, and the behavior of expenditures and revenue. As the initial debt increases, real interest rates rise, economic growth slows, and budget deficits increase, the debt-to-GDP ratio will likely rise. This relationship can be conveniently described by the dynamic equation:

$$\dot{d} = (r-g)d - p, \qquad (6.1)$$

where d is the debt-to-GDP ratio, r is the real interest rate on government debt, g is the real economic growth rate, and p is the primary, or non-interest, balance to GDP ratio. Intuitively, interest payments on old debt and the current non-interest deficit will be financed by new debt, and the debt-to-GDP ratio will fall as the growth rate rises.

Note how debt sustainability is affected by the difference between the real interest rate and the growth rate. If r is greater than g, then the system becomes unstable, and the debt-to-GDP ratio rises exponentially unless the difference is offset by primary surpluses. In past decades, the growth rate in Korea had generally been higher than the real interest rate.[34] During the 1982–89 period, the average yield on five-year-maturity national housing bonds was 13.69 percent, while the average nominal growth rate was 14.85 percent (Table 6.5). However, the gap narrowed during the 1990s and reversed after the outbreak of the financial crisis in 1997. Moreover, the growth rate will probably not continue to exceed the interest rate in the future. Consequently, an increasing debt burden may impose additional pressure on Korean financial markets, which are already beset by structural weaknesses.

Table 6.5 Interest payments and primary balance (%)

	Interest/ GDP (1)	Primary balance/ GDP (2)	Nominal growth rate (3)	Interest rate (national bonds) (4)	(3)–(4) (5)
1982–89	1.04	−1.26	14.85	13.69	1.16
1990–96	0.57	0.27	14.26	13.49	0.77
1997	0.50	−1.04	8.30	15.32	−7.02
1998	0.76	−3.46	−2.00	7.59	−9.59
1999	1.22	−1.49	8.60	10.07	−1.67
2000	1.32	2.57	7.10	7.04	0.06

Note: The interest rate on national bonds is the yield of the five-year-maturity national housing bonds.

Source: Bank of Korea (2001).

Of course, the variables in equation (6.1) are not independent of one another. As the debt increases, interest rates might rise as government creditworthiness deteriorates and the crowding out of private investment becomes more serious. Excessive crowding out of investment will almost certainly reduce economic growth. Low growth, in turn, will cause the balance of the consolidated budget to worsen, since revenues are likely to decline.

In order to avoid a sustainability problem, fiscal adjustments are therefore needed. From equation (6.1), the primary surplus needed to stabilize the debt-to-GDP ratio ($\dot{d}=0$) at the current level d_0 when r is greater than g is:

$$p^* = (r-g)d_0 \ ^{35}. \qquad (6.2)$$

In a previous study (Jun et al., 2000), I concluded that the government debt in Korea is likely to be sustainable as long as there is high to moderate growth.[36] The debt-to-GDP ratio will rise indefinitely only if the real interest rate exceeds the growth rate by more than five percentage points. It should be noted, however, that this conclusion is based on relatively optimistic assumptions in the government's medium-term fiscal plan. For example, the primary budget was assumed to be in balance or surplus in the years after 2002.[37] The realism of this assumption hinges on the state of the economy, however. A prolonged recession will increase the costs of restructuring, reduce the growth rate, and worsen the fiscal deficit. In addition, the rising expenditures for the social safety net will threaten fiscal stability unless there is a tax hike and a cut in other expenditures.

The Fiscal Cost of Financial Sector Restructuring

The cost of financial sector restructuring is a major threat to fiscal consolidation. In order to rescue ailing financial institutions, the government had injected 156 trillion won into the financial sector by June 2002. These public funds were used to purchase nonperforming loans (NPLs) from ailing financial institutions and to help the latter to recapitalize themselves and pay off their liabilities. The Korea Asset Management Corporation (KAMCO) is in charge of purchasing and recovering NPLs, while the Korea Deposit Insurance Corporation (KDIC) pays off deposits and recapitalizes financial institutions.

The funds needed for these activities were raised mainly by issuing restructuring bonds. A total of 104 trillion won ($87 billion or 20 percent of GDP in 2000) in restructuring bonds was issued by KAMCO and the KDIC. The government guarantees the repayment of these bonds and pays the interest accruing to them from the budget. An additional 20 trillion won was raised through other means, and the government recycled some recovered funds for additional uses.[38] A quarter of the total funds or 39 trillion won was spent for the purchase of NPLs, 38.5 percent (60 trillion won) for recapitalization, 26.9 percent (42 trillion won) for repayment of deposits and other liabilities, and 9.6 percent (15 trillion won) for the purchase of assets and subordinated debt.

The full 156 trillion won used for financial restructuring does not show up in the government budget. But there are still important implications for government liabilities, actual and contingent. The actual impact of restructuring on fiscal policy can be estimated by summing annual interest payments on restructuring bonds issued and the realized losses of the principal from the sale of collateral, assets and shares acquired during NPL purchases, the assumption of net liabilities, and recapitalization costs. That interest burden depends on the future level of interest rates on public bonds, while realized losses will be affected by the state of the economy and the effectiveness of recovery efforts.

We can estimate the realized losses of the principal by assuming a range of recovery rates, defined as the ratio of the amounts recovered eventually over the amounts raised initially. Note that a significant amount of restructuring funds went through cycles of injection, recovery and then reuse. Since we are interested in the incidence of restructuring costs on the budget, we must estimate the final recovery rate. Since the recovery rates are likely to vary across alternative uses of funds, we need to estimate them separately according to each use.

The fiscal policy response 129

In a previous study (J. Jun, 2001), I estimated these rates based on a detailed breakdown of the sources and the uses of funds available in a White Paper published in June 2001.[39]

Recovery rates for funds used for the assumption of deposits and other liabilities were estimated to be low. Since recovery from paying off deposits and assuming liabilities relies mostly on proceeds from the sales of assets of distressed or bankrupt entities, the amounts recovered have typically been small. Recovery from recapitalization depends on the prices of acquired shares, which has remained depressed but might rise when financial restructuring is complete. The recovery rate from the sale of NPLs was estimated to be higher than from the assumption of liabilities and from recapitalization. This is because the government's financial restructuring strategy was to purchase NPLs at low prices and cover the consequent bank losses by means of recapitalization or assumption of liabilities.

I apply these rates to the 104 trillion won of restructuring bonds to estimate the realized losses of principal for each use of the funds as well as alternative states of the economy.

Table 6.6 presents the results.[40] The interest burden based on the maturity schedule was provided by the authorities.

In the neutral scenario, estimated losses amount to 52.3 trillion won, or about a half of principal. This means that the national debt as a share of GDP could rise by about ten percentage points if the restructuring bonds are redeemed as scheduled.[41] The total fiscal burden, defined as the sum of interest and principal losses, would reach 94.9 trillion won, or 18.4 percent of GDP. The total loss could reach 67.8 trillion won if the recovery effort is less successful (13.1 percent of GDP, or a loss rate of 65 percent). In this pessimistic scenario, the total fiscal cost (110.4 trillion) exceeds the amount of bonds issued (104 trillion won). Even in the optimistic scenario, the total fiscal burden is estimated to be 79.43 trillion won, or 15.4 percent of annual GDP.

The estimates reported in Table 6.6 are subject to various qualifications. Since these estimates were based on restructuring funds raised through the issuance of government-guaranteed bonds, they do not reflect the full burden of restructuring borne by the public sector. One potentially important source of uncertainty is NPLs. If the volume of NPLs rises, then the cost of restructuring also increases.[42] In addition, our estimates depend on assumptions about parameter values and debt-restructuring schedules.[43]

The Burden of Public Pensions

An additional source of concern is the prospect of the rising burden of pensions. The public pension system includes the National Pension Scheme

Table 6.6 Fiscal burden of restructuring (trillion won, %)*

	Recovery rates			Principal loss (Share of GDP)	Interest** (Share of GDP)	Total
	Purchase of NPLs	Liability payments	Recapitalization			
Optimistic	95	45	70	36.83	42.60	79.43
				(7.1)	(8.3)	(15.4)
Neutral	80	35	50	52.30	42.60	94.90
				(10.1)	(8.3)	(18.4)
Pessimistic	65	25	30	67.78	42.60	110.38
				(13.1)	(8.3)	(21.4)

Notes:
2000 nominal GDP was 517.1 trillion won.
* The fiscal cost calculation is done for the 104 trillion won of bonds issued, for which the central government is responsible with regard to interest payments and the repayment of the principal.
** Total interest costs on restructuring bonds estimated by KAMCO and KDIC.

(NPS) and special programs for civil servants, military personnel and private-school teachers. As the Korean population ages and the coverage of the NPS expands, expenditures on public pensions will increase significantly in the coming decades.[44] Since these schemes currently have low contribution rates relative to benefit levels, the resulting imbalance may pose a serious problem in the future.

Pension expenditures are projected to increase mainly because the number of recipients under the NPS is expected to rise sharply in the future. The Korean population has been aging rapidly, reflecting declines in both fertility and mortality rates. The government projects the ratio of persons over 65 to those between 20 and 64 years of age to reach 30 percent by 2030, a sharp increase from the current level of 10 percent. In addition, coverage of the NPS has been steadily expanded since the scheme was implemented in 1988. It now covers nearly all firms and the self-employed.[45] The number of insured persons jumped from 4.4 million in 1988 to 16.3 million in 1999, or from 25.6 percent to 75.6 percent of the labor force.[46]

Because the NPS is relatively new, it is currently recording an annual surplus of around 2 percent of GDP, with an accumulated reserve of about 10 percent of GDP. According to projections, however, it will start recording a deficit in 2030, and the reserve fund will be exhausted by 2040 (Suk, 2002). Currently, the contribution rate for employees is 9 percent of monthly wages, divided evenly between employers and employees.[47] Experts recommend that this rate be doubled. The weak compliance of the self-employed is another factor threatening the stability of the scheme. Many self-employed under-report their income, which reduces the size of their pension contribution.

The financial problems of the occupational pension schemes also must be solved.[48] The civil service and military personnel schemes rely on government subsidies to finance pension payments.[49] Their financial deficits are basically due to their generous benefit structure. Benefit accrual rates are higher than those under the NPS and have been indexed to wages rather than consumer prices. Civil servants also receive a lump-sum allowance upon retirement, equivalent to 60 percent of their final monthly salary for each year of their employment. Although the contribution rates have been raised to 17 percent and other reform measures have been implemented recently, benefit levels remain to avert financial problems in the near future.[50]

Table 6.7 shows a global estimate of the underfunding of public pensions (Y.-H. Kim, 2000). As of the end of 1998, the net liabilities amounted to 208 trillion won (46.8 percent of GDP), almost twenty times annual contributions. About half of the total shortfall is attributable to the NPS, while underfunding appears to be more serious in the occupational schemes.

Table 6.7 Liabilities of public pensions, 1998 (billions of won)

Liabilities	Military personnel	Civil servants	Private-school teachers	The NPS	Total
Reserve	9 318	67 292	13 537	164 676	254 823
Net liabilities	414	4 784	3 443	37 465	46 106
(A)	8 904	62 508	10 094	127 211	208 717
Contributions (B)	261	1 974	448	7 923	10 606
(A)/(B)	34.1	31.7	22.5	16.1	19.7

Source: Y. Kim (2000).

CONCLUSIONS

This paper has examined fiscal developments in Korea during and after the crisis. Fiscal policy has been actively used as a means of economic stimulus and to strengthen the social safety net. Public funds raised through the issuance of government-guaranteed bonds have been essential in the process of financial sector restructuring. The fact that Korea had been running surpluses in earlier years allowed these aggressive fiscal measures to be pursued.

Few would dispute that the pressing fiscal task for coming years is consolidation. The ongoing costs of financial sector restructuring, the rise in social welfare spending, and looming reunification costs all add to the concern over fiscal sustainability. Expenditure restraint and piecemeal tax changes alone will not suffice to address the situation. While the resources available to the government should be more efficiently allocated, opportunities to increase revenue also need to be effectively exploited.

In addition, the opacity and complexity of the current budget system need to be addressed. The consolidated central government budget consists of a general account, 22 special accounts and 43 public funds. Since public funds are not subject to legislative approval, the ministries can exercise discretion, often to an excessive degree, in raising and allocating resources.[51] In addition, funds are not transferable among accounts, lowering overall allocative efficiency. The number of public funds should be reduced by incorporating many of them into the general account. The budget should be made more predictable by improving revenue forecasting and curtailing the use of supplementary budgets. Unless the predictability of fiscal outcomes is improved, fiscal policy could again become destabilizing.

One of the most challenging tasks will be to overhaul the tax system so as to ensure adequate revenue to cover rising expenditures, minimize distortions in resource allocation, and enhance equity. For this purpose, the tax base should be broadened, eliminating unnecessary deductions and exemptions in the personal income tax, corporate income tax, and the value added tax systems. Enforcement should be improved by increasing the number of audits and imposing higher penalties for evasion, as well as through more efficient sharing of information among government agencies.

Of particular urgency is achieving greater compliance in sales and income reporting on the part of the self-employed. The issue of horizontal equity has often been raised with regard to the taxation of wage earners, salary earners and the self-employed. Many of the deductions and allowances of the personal tax system have been justified as means of alleviating the relatively high taxes on salary and wage workers.[52] Thus, unless the taxation of the self-employed is strengthened, loopholes in the personal tax system will not likely be reduced. Under-reporting by the self-employed could be corrected by eliminating the special allowance provisions of the value added tax system and by stepping up enforcement through audits and imposing higher penalties.

Capital income taxation also needs to be streamlined. While the global taxation of capital income was reinstated in 2001, dividend and interest income for investors with capital income below a certain threshold is taxed separately, and financial capital gains are exempt from personal taxation. As a result, the effective tax rate on capital income may differ significantly according to the source of income and tax status of investors. This distorts saving and portfolio decisions, erodes the tax base, and increases compliance costs.[53]

Lastly, the underfunding of the public pension system must be urgently addressed. The NPS will face a serious deficit problem unless the current structure of low contributions and high benefits is changed. Options for reform include cutting benefit levels, increasing contribution rates, raising the age of eligibility, improving the management of funds, and taxing pension income. Moreover, the occupational pension schemes, most of which have already suffered underfunding, could be integrated into the NPS, and the role of private pension schemes should be expanded. One possibility is to transform the current severance payment scheme into a corporate pension that could be a fully funded and defined-contribution scheme. Individual pension accounts should also be improved, possibly by including investment incentives.

Korean fiscal policy makers have made impressive progress in restoring budget balance since the disruptive crisis of 1997–98. But while the immediate task of fiscal consolidation has been completed, the longer-run imperative of ensuring debt sustainability will require continued efforts.

NOTES

1. Interest on these restructuring bonds has been borne by the central government budget.
2. Other measures of fiscal conditions show a similar pattern.
3. The structural balance and fiscal impulse measures used in this chapter were calculated according to IMF methodology (Schinasi and Lutz 1991).
4. President Park Chung-Hee was assassinated in October 1979.
5. Even if fiscal imbalances were not a major part of the problem, fiscal adjustment could still be an integral part of the solution.
6. See Feldstein (1998), for example.
7. A detailed description of social safety net expenditures is presented below.
8. Stiglitz called it a standard 'one-size-fits-all' response to a financial sector crisis. His book (Stiglitz, 2002) contains a fairly detailed description of his criticism of the IMF.
9. This is because efficiency costs associated with a distortional tax are convex.
10. Using US data, Bayoumi and Eichengreen (1995) found that fiscal restrictions could reduce the responsiveness of budgets to the cycle by up to 40 percent.
11. An expansionary stance is denoted by a year-on-year decrease in the structural balance or a positive fiscal impulse measure.
12. During this period, the social safety net was significantly expanded, and various tax incentives were implemented to boost consumption and investment. A discussion of this issue follows in this section.
13. The targeted balance in the original budget was –3.2 percent of GDP.
14. A significant portion of this extra tax revenue was from corporate taxes.
15. The lower-than-expected spending on unemployment benefits was also partly responsible for the modest increase in spending.
16. In recent years, for example, infrastructure spending was restricted to allow for other spending priorities.
17. Feldstein (1992) addresses this point.
18. The Gini coefficient hovered around 0.29 for the two decades leading up to 1997.
19. An applicant has to pass a means-test, on an annual basis, based on family assets, income and earning capacity.
20. Income distribution deteriorated as well, with the Gini coefficient rising from 0.28 in 1997 to 0.32 in 1998.
21. In March 1988, the EIS was expanded to cover enterprises with five or more employees. In October 1998, the coverage was extended to all enterprises, part-time workers and temporary workers.
22. The minimum duration of benefits increased from one month to three months while the maximum duration period increased from seven months to nine months.
23. To help cover the increased costs, the contribution rate was raised from 1.5 percent to 3 percent of wages in 1999.
24. Separate projects were available for those incapable of hard labor, such as the elderly and women.
25. Some public works funds were used for unproductive projects or unqualified persons. The subsidies from different government branches for venture enterprises sometimes overlapped.
26. Note that under the previous system, the benefit level was set at a maximum of 60 percent of the minimum cost of living.
27. This is because the eligibility requirements are similar under both schemes.
28. In addition, local officials may now have weak incentives to strictly enforce the eligibility requirements since the right to assistance is now guaranteed by law, thus making any pre-set budget limits meaningless. Previously, the central government imposed very strict limits on the budgets that could be dispensed by local governments.
29. The marginal tax rates were reduced from 10–40 percent to 9–36 percent effective in 2002.
30. Special consumption taxes are excises imposed on some luxury goods. In 1999, special

excises on electronic goods (TV sets and refrigerators!), food and beverages, and other necessities were eliminated.
31. Instead, withholding taxes were imposed on dividends and interest at the source.
32. The concluding section suggests a direction for tax reform.
33. Fischer and Easterly (1990). For a more detailed discussion of fiscal sustainability, see Chalk and Hemming (2000).
34. If g continues to exceed r, the government could possibly continue borrowing to pay principal and interest on the existing debt, a kind of Ponzi scheme.
35. From equation (6.1), the debt-to-GDP ratio at the present time d_0 is determined as:

$$d_0 = \int_0^{+\infty} pe^{-(r-g)t}dt.$$

36. While this calculation considered the cost of restructuring, the interest on restructuring bonds is not adequately taken into account. The increase in interest payments in recent years was largely attributable to interest on restructuring bonds. At the time of writing, restructuring bonds are counted as a contingent liability, which is excluded from the official debt measure, interest on these bonds is included in the budget. Thus the initial debt position used in this study was effectively understated.
37. In fact, the primary balance reverted to a surplus in 2000. Tax revenue increased unexpectedly in 2000. During the period 1990–96, the primary budget was generally in a slight surplus.
38. These include contributions from the public capital management fund, government property management special account, Bank of Korea account, and loans from the ADB (Asian Development Bank) and IBRD (International Bank for Reconstruction and Development).
39. Korea Ministry of Finance and Economy, Public Fund Management Committee (2001).
40. Note that these figures represent a crude approximation, making no present-value adjustments with regard to interest payments and the principal value.
41. GDP in 2000 was used as a denominator (Jun, 2001).
42. Several huge companies are currently in trouble. Many firms are still in the debt workout program. This will increase the overall strain on financial institutions.
43. We assumed that all restructuring bonds would be retired when they mature.
44. Heller (1997) estimated that population aging may increase pension expenditures by four percentage points by 2035.
45. The coverage of the NPS was originally limited to employees at firms with more than ten employees. Firm with more than five workers were included in 1992. The coverage was extended to the self-employed in rural areas in 1995 and in urban areas in 1999. The former include farmers and fishermen.
46. Given that the NPS is only 14 years old and that the minimum contribution period is ten years, there are presently relatively few pension beneficiaries. As the scheme matures, however, the number of pension recipients will increase sharply.
47. The contribution rate for the self-employed was only 3 percent until 1999. Beginning in 2000, the rate has been increased by one percentage point each year, and it will continue to rise until it reaches 9 percent in 2005.
48. These schemes now cover about 1.3 million persons. Pension is transferable within the occupational schemes but not between them and the NPS.
49. The civil servant and military personnel schemes were implemented in 1960 and 1963, respectively. So both schemes are now fully matured, with 33 years of maximum contribution. The civil servant system first ran a deficit in 1995 and began to rely on government subsidy in 2001, while the reserve fund of the military personnel scheme was exhausted in 1977.
50. For example, the indexation of benefits was shifted from wages to prices, and the minimum pension ages were established for the civil servant scheme.
51. The funds are subject only to Cabinet approval.
52. After the crisis, deductions and credits were expanded in an effort to mitigate the distress on wage and salary earners.

53. In addition, the use of earmarked taxes and 'quasi-taxes' (fees and charges) should be reduced. The education tax, the transportation tax, and the special tax for rural development together account for about 18 percent of total tax revenue. Eliminating them would require overcoming vested interests, including bureaucrats, who favor the use of these special taxes and fees.

7. Social impact of the crisis

Joung-Woo Lee

INTRODUCTION

Without question, the social impact of Korea's economic and financial crisis was profound. 'Restructuring,' a concept unfamiliar to Koreans who for several decades had been accustomed to robust economic growth and full employment, became a household word. The shock of large-scale unemployment cast a pall over society.

The greatest shock was probably the crumbling of the myth of sustained economic growth and heightened certainty about whether government-led growth would resume. Corporate bankruptcies, rising unemployment, and the widening gap between rich and poor were prominent features of the Korean landscape in the years following the crisis. Although the government announced at the end of 2000 that it would repay the IMF loan ahead of schedule, many citizens remain unconvinced that substantial economic improvement has taken place and regard the crisis as still underway.

Korea was not the only country to experience profound economic changes after turning to the IMF. Income inequality became more severe and poverty became more widespread in many of the countries that have turned to the IMF for help (Chossudovsky, 1997; Pieper and Taylor, 1998; Pastor, 1987; Garuda, 2000; Vreeland, 2001). There is a question, of course, of whether the IMF program causes the poverty, or whether the shock to the economy that forces the government to turn to the IMF is in fact responsible for the deterioration in living standards and the rise in inequality. But there is no question about the existence of the correlation.[1]

Chen and Ravallion (2000) have estimated that the Asian crisis in 1997 increased the incidence of poverty by four percentage points, or 22 million people. The World Bank has affirmed that poverty increased sharply in Korea. Of the four Asian countries that experienced crises, it has shown the greatest rise in unemployment (Haggard, 2000).

Before the crisis, the distribution of income was not a major issue in Korea. Although inequality had become somewhat more pronounced as a result of land speculation in the 1980s, the gap had begun to narrow after the

137

real estate bubble burst in the early 1990s. What is more, poverty rates had shown a long-term tendency to decline (Kwon et al., 1998). These trends were reversed by the crisis. For the first time in Korean history, the gap between rich and poor became a serious issue. Society became more polarized, heightening the sense of imminent social disintegration. The Presidential Committee for Quality of Life acknowledged the gravity of the situation and submitted to the president a report entitled *How to Improve the Structure of Income Distribution* (2000).

Although there has been much discussion of the reasons for the growing gap between rich and poor, a clearer understanding of the problem is required. The purpose of this chapter is to examine the social impact of the crisis, with special reference to poverty and changes in the distribution of income and wealth. With this analysis in hand, I suggest some directions for future policy.

DATA AND METHODOLOGY

Virtually all research on inequality around the time of the crisis has relied on the *Dosi Gagye Yonbo* (the Urban Household Income and Expenditure Survey, or UHIES), conducted by the National Statistical Office. Although there are some slight variations, earlier research studies have all reached broadly similar conclusions because earlier researchers have all relied on the same data. Research using the UHIES shows that the distribution of income deteriorated markedly following the crisis. Measured by the Gini coefficient, inequality rose by three to four percentage points. The poverty rate was 7 to 8 percent before the crisis but rose to 16 percent in 1998.

Despite its many strengths, the UHIES falls short of providing a complete picture because it excludes farm and single-person households. In addition, it provides no information on the incomes of employers, the self-employed, unemployed persons, and persons without jobs.

To address these problems, I use two new data sets: the panel survey data of the Daewoo Economic Research Institute (DERI) and the Social Equity Surveys of the Korea Social Science Council (KSSC). The DERI survey covers six years starting with 1993; it spans the years immediately preceding and following the crisis of 1997 and covers the entire country. My second source is the Social Equity Survey designed by the Korea Social Science Council and conducted in 1990, 1995 and 2000. The sample is not large, only around 2000 households, but it is valuable because it covers the entire country and contains income information on all households.

Table 7.1 presents the characteristics of sample households covered by the DERI survey over the six-year period 1993–98 (for more details see J.-W.

Table 7.1 Characteristics of sample households (mean [standard deviation], %)

	1993	1994	1995	1996	1997	1998
Sample size	4248	3551	2910	2616	2419	2164
Age of household head	43.4	46.3	47.4	48.6	49.4	51.4
	(12.4)	(13.5)	(13.4)	(13.4)	(13.4)	(12.2)
Household size	3.69	3.53	3.59	3.55	3.47	3.42
	(1.20)	(1.28)	(1.29)	(1.32)	(1.33)	(1.39)
Household income	136.2	145.2	169.6	189.4	203.6	173.2
(10 000 won)	(123.7)	(102.6)	(122.8)	(165.1)	(144.0)	(159.1)
Labor income	68.3	67.8	78.5	79.6	92.4	71.2
	(84.9)	(81.6)	(96.5)	(98.4)	(115.1)	(103.6)
Business income	42.5	48.0	59.5	63.3	64.7	49.8
	(102.7)	(95.1)	(111.2)	(121.2)	(119.6)	(97.2)
Farm income	5.5	8.0	6.9	13.1	12.1	13.7
	(30.9)	(28.9)	(27.8)	(70.6)	(47.4)	(97.6)
Non-regular	8.9	10.2	11.6	13.6	13.9	13.7
	(24.2)	(28.7)	(32.1)	(35.9)	(40.2)	(34.3)
Moonlighting	0.8	0.7	0.8	1.5	1.3	1.5
	(7.4)	(6.9)	(6.6)	(10.6)	(11.4)	(41.8)
Interest	3.1	3.6	6.0	7.1	8.5	11.9
	(14.3)	(10.4)	(20.9)	(20.1)	(37.6)	(41.8)
Rent	4.1	4.4	2.3	5.9	3.9	4.1
	(37.5)	(23.2)	(14.3)	(82.5)	(20.4)	(21.3)
Transfer income	2.8	2.4	4.0	5.3	6.7	7.3
	(14.3)	(9.2)	(13.7)	(16.5)	(24.2)	(25.4)
Male	3869	3215	2624	2348	2144	1897
	(91.7)	(90.5)	(90.2)	(89.8)	(88.6)	(87.7)
Female	351	336	286	268	275	267
	(8.3)	(9.5)	(9.8)	(10.2)	(11.4)	(12.3)

Source: DERI panel surveys (1993–98).

Lee and Lee, 2001a). The DERI data capture 94 per cent of average household income in the national accounts. According to Atkinson et al. (1995), a survey's income data are of good quality if they capture more than 90 percent of the income reported in the national accounts.[2] Judged on these criteria, the DERI survey is quite reliable.

In examining changes in income distribution and poverty, I use the concept of equivalent income. Equivalent income is similar to per capita income but is calculated by dividing household income by the square root of the number of the household members ($\sqrt{N}$), instead of the raw number (N). Dividing household income by the number of household members ignores economies of scale in household consumption.

INCOME INEQUALITY

Changes in Income Distribution

There is evidence, based on analyses of the UHIES, that income distribution in Korea had been improving up to the mid-1990s. Evidently, however, the economic crisis reversed that trend. This has been the conclusion of many recent researchers (see, for example, G.-P. Choe et al., 1999; Moon and Yoo, 1999; Kakwani and Son, 1999; Cheong, 2001). However, Kakwani and Prescott (2001) emphasized the stability of the Gini ratios of consumption of urban households in the period from 1990 to 1998. They prefer to analyze the distribution of consumption rather than the distribution of income, on the grounds that the income data of the UHIES are not available or reliable. Given the different findings of investigators who focus on income versus consumption, further analysis is clearly required.

Using panel data from the DERI, I have computed Gini coefficients for the period 1993–98. The higher the Gini, the less equal is income distribution. Table 7.2 shows that the Gini coefficient for household income rose from 0.36 in 1997 to 0.40 in 1998.[3] When the Gini coefficient is computed for earned income only, it shows a three percentage point increase, from 0.34 to 0.37.

It is noteworthy that the Gini for household income climbed to 0.4 in 1998. Compared to previous research based on the UHIES, which found the Gini hovering around 0.3, this is a large difference. However, considering that the DERI data capture only 23 percent of household financial income, that the government imposed record high interest rates at the request of the IMF, and that high-income families held significant financial assets, there is a strong possibility that the Gini was underestimated in my earlier analysis. Likewise,

Table 7.2 Gini coefficients, all households

Year	Household income	Equivalent income	Earned income	Expenditure	Per capita expenditure
1993	0.377	0.364	0.329	0.311	0.300
1994	0.376	0.364	0.321	0.322	0.317
1995	0.373	0.362	0.282	0.312	0.301
1996	0.372	0.356	0.340	0.353	0.334
1997	0.363	0.346	0.344	0.341	0.324
1998	0.404	0.384	0.373	0.343	0.323

Source: DERI panel surveys (1993–98).

studies obtaining a Gini of 0.3 using UHIES data probably also underestimated the level of actual income inequality.

Even though the DERI data are better than the UHIES data in some respects, they are not available after 1998. The only source of information about subsequent changes in income distribution is the UHIES data. G.-J. Yoo (2001) analyzes recent trends in income distribution using this source: he finds that the Gini increased by three to four percentage points in 1998 and remained stubbornly high thereafter.

Shrinking Middle Class?

Recently, the phrase 'collapse of the middle class' has often appeared in the headlines. In the United States, the possibility of a shrinking middle class has been widely discussed since the late 1980s as a corollary of the growing gap between rich and poor (Strobel, 1993). But defining and measuring the middle class is not straightforward. Usually, the middle class is defined relative to the upper and the lower classes on the basis of income, occupation and social status. In this chapter, I define the middle class based only on income, the practice generally adopted by economists.

One way of defining the middle class is to divide the population into five groups by income level and define the middle three quintiles, or 60 percent of the population, as middle class.[4] While this allows us to analyze income fluctuations within the middle three quintiles, the size of the middle class is assumed fixed. Another method is to define the middle class by annual income. For example, in his 1992 presidential election campaign Bill Clinton defined the middle class as households with a yearly income between $20 000 and $65 000. This method is intuitive, but its downside is that the definition needs to change constantly with fluctuations in prices and incomes.

In this chapter, I use several methods to define the middle class. First, I identify median income and define households within a certain range of the median as middle class. Some researchers employing this method use a range from 80 to 125 percent of median income, while others use a 66.7 to 133.3 percent range. The OECD uses a 50 to 150 percent range, while the US Census Bureau adopts a 50 to 200 percent range. I estimated the size of the middle class for each of those four ranges. According to all four methods, the size of the middle class shrank sharply in 1998, falling five percentage points or more from 1997 levels (Table 7.3). That such a big drop occurred within a year suggests that the economic crisis dealt a hard blow to the middle class. Table 7.3 also shows that more people slipped into the lower class than ascended to the upper class.

The collapse of the middle class and the emergence of a more bi-polar society is consistent with the public perception, as reflected in social surveys

Table 7.3 Size of middle class (%)

	Definition 1			Definition 2			Definition 3			Definition 4		
Year	Lower class	Middle class	Upper class	Lower class	Middle class	Upper class	Lower class	Middle class	Upper class	Lower class	Middle class	Upper class
1993	33.5	32.5	34.0	26.0	44.0	30.1	17.4	59.6	23.0	17.4	72.2	10.4
1994	35.7	31.2	33.2	26.6	45.0	21.2	17.8	61.2	28.5	17.8	72.6	9.9
1995	38.2	29.1	30.5	28.6	41.8	26.4	19.3	58.5	20.2	19.3	70.8	9.0
1996	36.0	31.0	33.0	22.8	43.7	28.6	18.1	60.8	21.2	18.1	73.9	8.0
1997	36.8	30.5	32.7	27.5	43.6	29.0	18.7	58.7	22.5	18.7	71.6	9.6
1998	38.8	24.6	36.6	31.8	35.9	32.3	21.0	53.0	26.0	21.0	66.6	13.4

Notes: The figures are based on equivalent incomes. The middle class is defined differently across the four categories of definition. In Definition 1, it is defined as households whose incomes range from 80 to 125% of the median income. In Definition 2, households earning 66.7 to 133.3% of the median income are grouped under the middle class. In Definitions 3 and 4, a 50 to 150% range and a 50 to 200% range are used respectively.

Source: DERI panel surveys (1993–98).

conducted during the crisis period. According to a survey conducted by the Hyundai Economic Research Institute (HERI, 1998), 20 percent of those polled responded that they had fallen out of the middle class. Only 34.8 percent thought of themselves as belonging to the middle class, a record low since the first such survey was taken in Korea in the 1960s. Before 1998, the size of the middle class as measured in this way had been in the order of 50 to 65 percent (Seok-Joon Kim, 1999). Although the size of the middle class based on such self-appraisal rose to 45 percent in the next survey (HERI, 1999), this was still a historically low figure.

Winners and Losers

One common criticism is that the poor have borne the brunt of the economic distress due to high unemployment, while the crisis has proven to be an unexpected bonanza to the rich, typically creditors who have benefited from high interest rates. Stephan Haggard (2000) asserts that in Korea, 'the crisis ... affected precisely those emergent, transitional, weakly organized "striving classes" ...' (p. 198). However, it is not clear what he means by 'emergent, transitional, striving classes'. An earnings function analysis can render these suppositions more concrete. Both personal characteristics (variables such as sex, education and age) and market variables (like industry, region, occupation and firm size) are used in the analysis. To reveal the wage gaps between groups as clearly as possible, all variables are specified as dummies.

The DERI data cannot be used in this analysis because the occupational codes were changed between 1997 and 1998. The data used for this analysis are therefore from the Social Equity Survey conducted by the Korea Social Science Council (KSSC) in 1995 and 2000. Although the size of these surveys, a little less than 2000 households, is limited, they paint a suggestive picture.

The results are in Table 7.4. The R^2 of the regression is 0.30; in other words, about 30 percent of the variance of earnings is explained by seven variables. The wage gap between men and women, after controlling for education, age, occupation, industry, region and firm size, is high, at 14 percent, although it is widely believed to have been narrowing over time. The results also show the trend of declining wage disparity between the sexes, from 16 percent in 1995 to 14 percent in 2000.

The Korean labor market has traditionally been characterized by a seniority wage system *à la* Japan, with a very steep age–earnings profile. However, it is possible that this system has come under serious stress as a result of the crisis to the extent that the restructuring and downsizing of firms have mainly targeted older employees. Our analysis supports this conjecture. The wage premium for workers older than 50 relative to those in their twenties was 17

Table 7.4   Wage gaps before and after the crisis

	1995 Parameter (s.e.)	1995 t-value	2000 Parameter (s.e.)	2000 t-value
Constant	1.998 (0.034)	58.042***	2.220 (0.062)	35.664***
Sex				
Female	−0.162 (0.041)	−3.963***	−0.139 (0.045)	−3.065***
Age				
30–39	0.109 (0.026)	4.255***	0.007 (0.050)	1.447
40–49	0.175 (0.029)	6.097***	0.155 (0.051)	3.034***
50 +	0.169 (0.032)	5.370***	0.124 (0.057)	2.167**
Education				
Middle school	−0.025 (0.026)	−0.969	−0.180 (0.050)	−3.611***
Technical colleges	0.036 (0.032)	1.117	0.065 (0.046)	1.404
Colleges	0.063 (0.026)	2.412**	0.060 (0.037)	1.600
Occupation				
Professional	0.105 (0.043)	2.446**	0.109 (0.050)	2.181**
Administrative	0.249 (0.038)	6.622***	0.129 (0.055)	2.362**
Clerical	0.063 (0.025)	2.514**	0.072 (0.042)	1.724*
Sales	0.011 (0.048)	0.222	0.131 (0.091)	1.449
Services	0.040 (0.047)	0.857	0.038 (0.079)	0.478
Industry				
Agr. fishing	−0.372 (0.173)	−2.153**	−0.029 (0.217)	−0.132
Mining	−0.132 (0.124)	−1.070		
Utilities	−0.024 (0.080)	−0.296	−0.132 (0.221)	−0.596

Table 7.4 continued

	1995 Parameter (s.e.)	*t*-value	2000 Parameter (s.e.)	*t*-value
Construction	0.0278 (0.030)	0.915	0.002 (0.049)	0.033
Distribution, hotels	0.032 (0.031)	1.023	0.063 (0.072)	0.879
Transportation and communication	−0.023 (0.029)	−0.796	−0.004 (0.046)	−0.079
Finance and real estate	0.055 (0.035)	1.578	0.017 (0.049)	0.336
Services	−0.041 (0.028)	−1.479	−0.044 (0.039)	−1.136
Region				
Inchon and Kyungki	0.010 (0.023)	0.440	−0.044 (0.038)	−1.153
Gangwon	0.136 (0.071)	1.908*	−0.027 (0.099)	−0.274
North Choongchung	−0.010 (0.064)	−0.165	−0.073 (0.065)	−1.127
South Choongchung	0.069 (0.051)	1.341	0.007 (0.053)	0.125
North Jolla	−0.003 (0.059)	−0.051	−0.089 (0.067)	−1.324
South Jolla	0.131 (0.034)	3.830***	−0.216 (0.052)	−4.145***
North Kyungsang	0.0231 (0.033)	0.704	−0.099 (0.046)	−2.146**
South Kyungsang	−0.0004 (0.025)	−0.179	−0.065 (0.045)	−1.465
Firm size				
Less than 50	−0.029 (0.023)	−1.238	−0.074 (0.036)	−2.071**
50–499	−0.036 (0.022)	−1.642*	−0.019 (0.039)	−0.499
Adj. R^2		0.374		0.292
F-value		9.462***		5.003***

Notes: Omitted alternatives are male, younger than 30, high school graduates, blue-collar, manufacturing sector, Seoul and big firms (more than 500 employees). The dependent variable is the natural logarithm of the household income of the workers.
*** $p < 0.01$, ** $p < 0.05$, * $p < 0.10$.

Source: See text.

percent in 1995 but only 12 percent in 2000. It is widely believed that the seniority wage system in Japan and Korea is giving way to an American type wage system that places more emphasis on the jobs and individual abilities of workers. Our regression results suggest that such a transition may indeed be going on in Korean firms.

The wage gaps between individuals with different educational backgrounds, which had long been eroding before the crisis, appear to have widened thereafter. As of 1995, there was no difference in pay between middle school and high school graduates, and the wage premium of technical college and university graduates was also minimal (in the vicinity of 5 percent). After the crisis, however, the wages of middle school graduates appear to fall short of those of high school graduates by as much as 18 percent, and the premium received by technical college graduates as against high school graduates has also risen substantially.

A widening wage gap between workers with high and low educational backgrounds has also been observed in the United States in recent years and interpreted as a corollary of the 'new economy,' which puts a premium on skilled labor. One clue that the same influences are being felt in Korea is rising income differentials between those with different educational backgrounds, already evident in 1995, before the crisis.

Workers in administrative occupations possess the greatest wage advantage over blue-collar workers, but this wage premium declined from 25 percent in 1995 to 13 percent in 2000. The premiums enjoyed by professionals and clerical workers relative to blue-collar workers, meanwhile, remained unchanged at 11 and 6 percent, respectively. Although service sector jobs as a whole offer more or less the same pay as blue-collar jobs, one notable difference is the extraordinarily high wage premium received by sales workers in 2000.[5]

As for wages by sector, the most significant change is the decline of relative wages in the finance and real estate sectors, which had traditionally paid the highest wages. Agriculture, forestry and fisheries have seen the most improvement in relative wages; while these were traditionally the sectors with the lowest wages, they are now paying almost the same wages as manufacturing. The exodus of workers from the cities back to the countryside after the beginning of the economic crisis may be partly a result of the movement of the relative wages of the farm sector.

The two most important findings from the table are the increase in relative manufacturing wages and the flattening of inter-industry wage disparities. Evidently, Haggard is right in saying that construction workers were particularly vulnerable. He is on shakier ground, however, when he says that manufacturing was also vulnerable.

The outstanding feature of regional wage differentials is the rise of Seoul relative to the provinces. While in 1995, several regions – Kyungki, North

Choongchung, North Jolla, North and South Kyungsang among them – paid the same wages as Seoul, many other regions did not. In 2000, every province except South Choongchung paid substantially lower wages than Seoul. It is worth mentioning in this connection that both North and South Jolla Province have been falling behind: while nearly every region has fallen behind Seoul, the decline in relative wages in South and North Jolla has been especially pronounced. Considering that this has occurred at a time when Korea had its first president from Jolla Province – and that there were widespread complaints about the appointment of people from this region to high government offices – the relative retreat of wages in Jolla Province is quite surprising.

Finally, we find that there was a widening wage gap between large and small firms (more than 500 employees versus fewer than 50 employees) in 2000, but a narrowing gap between large and medium-sized firms (between 50 and 500 employees).

To sum up, there is clear evidence of changing wage structures around the time of the crisis. Wage differentials have widened between sexes, ages and occupations have narrowed, while those among different educational backgrounds, regions and firm sizes. The major losers are older workers with low educational backgrounds working in small firms in the provinces. Not all of these changes should be ascribed to the economic crisis itself, but there is no doubt that the crisis played a major part.

What Caused the Inequality?

How, then, should we interpret the worsening inequality observed in the post-crisis years? One interpretation is as a corollary of business cycle fluctuations. In a downturn, joblessness increases and income distribution worsens for at least three reasons. First, as the income of the unemployed falls to near zero, the gap with others naturally widens. Second, the probability of job loss is not equal among all workers; it is highest for the unskilled and low-paid. Because companies are more inclined to regard skilled workers, supervisors and technicians as fixed assets, they are reluctant to lay them off in difficult economic times. Third, the oversupply of unskilled laborers due to rising unemployment causes the income gap between skilled and unskilled workers to widen further. According to studies of the UK and the United States, cyclical factors such as inflation and the unemployment rate strongly affect the income distribution. One difference between the 1998 recession and its predecessors, and between Korea and these other countries, is that this recent episode was marked by IMF intervention and the fiscal and monetary austerity that the IMF required, which may have shaped the distributional outcomes.

WEALTH INEQUALITY

The Importance of Wealth Distribution

Along with income, wealth is the most important indicator of economic welfare for individuals and households. None the less, there are few surveys of wealth and, as a result, little research on wealth distribution. In Korea, land prices, which had been trending upward for half a century until the early 1990s, have played an important role in the economic disparity between classes.[6] Furthermore, Korea has a unique form of wealth concentration due to the existence of the *chaebols*, or business conglomerates. Wealth inheritance and transfers from the founders of these business groups to their offspring have become a controversial social issue.

Table 7.5 summarizes findings on wealth distribution as revealed by a 1988 Korean Development Institute (KDI) survey and the 1990 and 1995 KSCC surveys. According to the KDI survey, while the Gini coefficient of income inequality was 0.40, that of asset inequality stood at 0.58. A few years later, a World Bank research team compared the KDI survey results with analogous results for other countries and concluded that wealth inequality was equal to or less than that of developed countries 20 to 30 years earlier (Leipziger et al., 1992). Thus, whereas popular opinion tended to regard wealth as very unevenly distributed, international comparisons tended to paint a different picture. A possible explanation is the failure of the 1988 KDI survey used by the World Bank team to measure wealth adequately. The wealthiest group may have been undersurveyed, resulting in the underestimation of inequality.

Table 7.5 Wealth inequality according to the existing literature (Gini coefficients)

Year	Research institute	Income	Wealth	Sample size
1988	Korea Development Institute	0.404	0.579	5107
1990	Korea Social Science Council	0.362	0.578	1792
1995	Korea Social Science Council	0.299	0.539	1865

Sources: Kwon et al. (1992); and Seok (1997), p. 111.

A New Estimate of Wealth Inequality

We can test the validity of this conjecture using other sources, like the DERI survey. The DERI survey contains information on household property taxes for buildings and aggregate land taxes, as well as details on financial assets.

Social impact of the crisis 149

From 1996 onward, it also collected data on the value of real estate owned by households. Therefore, the DERI data allow us to analyze asset distribution among households. (In this chapter, I use the term 'household wealth' synonymously with 'assets.' Assets are defined as the combination of financial assets and real estate holdings, and they are referred to as total worth.)

To check the reliability of the DERI survey, I evaluated data for the ten wealthiest households in each year. The average total worth of the top ten households was about 500 million won ($750 000) in 1993 (the first survey year) and 1.3 billion won ($930 000) to 2.1 billion won ($1.5 million) in 1998 (the final survey year), which was much lower than expected. This leads one to suspect that many of the wealthiest households either were not included in the survey or, if they were surveyed, under-reported their wealth.[7] Since it is highly probable that many super-rich were omitted from the survey, we should remember that measures of inequality calculated using these data are likely to be downward biased.[8]

The resulting estimates of the distributional inequality of assets among Korean households from 1993 to 1998 appear in Table 7.6. Real estate, land and financial assets were distributed disproportionately, with the degree of disparity slightly higher than according to other studies. Real estate holdings were more unequally distributed than financial assets.[9]

Total worth has a lower degree of disparity than other categories of assets; this might be due to rent deposits. In Korea there is a peculiar system of renting a house, where the renter pays the owner of the house a large deposit which he takes back when the rental contract expires. (The occupant does not in addition make monthly rental payments.) However, the owner of the house

Table 7.6   Inequality of wealth distribution (Gini coefficients)

	Including insurance policy holdings			Excluding insurance policy holdings		
Year	Net worth	Total worth	Real estate	Financial assets	Total worth	Financial assets
1993	0.571	0.451	0.689	0.593	0.451	0.578
1994	0.573	0.492	0.675	0.633	0.501	0.667
1995	0.577	0.488	0.657	0.600	0.499	0.634
1996	0.570	0.470	0.633	0.593	0.479	0.624
1997	0.600	0.488	0.652	0.610	0.501	0.648
1998	0.655	0.462	0.602	0.630	0.473	0.678

Source: DERI panel surveys (1993–98).

can collect monthly payments by investing the deposit during the period of renting contract. And the renter, for his part, often has to borrow money in order to make the deposit. This is one reason why total worth, which does not take liabilities into account, is only a crude measure of household economic status. This causes many investigators to use net worth when analyzing wealth distribution.

In addition, whether or not insurance policy holdings are included in financial assets has a sizable impact on inequality. A majority of Korean households hold insurance policies, and differences in the value of insurance policy holdings across social classes are not very great.

Concentration of Land Ownership

Land is the largest single component of inherited wealth, accounting for 60 percent of the total.[10] DERI has two types of data on land ownership: land tax data, and responses regarding real estate ownership. The former are available from 1993 to 1998 and the latter from 1996 onward. For the period before 1996, I calculated land values from the aggregate land tax collection data.

Table 7.7 shows the findings on land ownership distribution. As expected, land ownership was highly concentrated. In 1993, half of the surveyed households owned no land, while the other half owned at least some land, most of which was held by the top 5 percent. The top 10 percent of households owned 58 percent of the nation's land. The Gini coefficient for land ownership by all households was 0.76, slightly lower than that calculated by Hyun (1995) and Yoon et al. (1999).[11]

In a panel survey, people who own a house change their residency less frequently; consequently, they are more likely to remain in the sample. In the DERI survey, more respondents without land or houses left the sample over time, resulting in some pseudo-equalization of land ownership status. This inference is supported by the figures in Table 7.7. Comparing across deciles, the proportion of households without land was equally large among the five lowest groups in 1993, but by 1998 only the lowest three groups had no land.

The distributional inequality of real estate (land and houses combined) is shown in Table 7.7. The Gini coefficient (based on the estimates produced from the aggregate land tax data) was 0.69 in 1993 but only 0.60 in 1998. However, given that this result may reflect the tendency for respondents without a house to drop out of the sample over time, we must be cautious in concluding that this indicates a decline in inequality in real estate holdings over time.

Table 7.7 Distribution of land ownership (10 000 won, %)

Year	3rd decile	4th decile	5th decile	6th decile	7th decile	8th decile	9th decile	10th decile	Top 5%	Top 1%	Gini coefficient
1993											0.761
Mean	–	–	–	327	1 000	1 000	2 299	6 406	9 297	14 786	
Owning land (%)	–	–	–	3.8	9.0	9.0	20.7	57.6	41.8	13.1	
1994											0.749
Mean	–	–	181	504	787	1 750	2 802	8 439	12 076	22 598	
Owning land (%)	–	–	1.2	3.4	8.0	11.8	18.9	56.8	40.6	15.0	
1995											0.738
Mean	–	–	454	814	1 663	2 205	3 585	11 706	15 278	34 588	
Owning land (%)	–	–	2.2	4.0	8.1	10.8	17.5	57.3	37.2	16.4	
1996											0.703
Mean	–	192	555	1 253	1 753	2 685	3 770	11 436	15 016	34 713	
Owning land (%)	–	0.9	2.6	5.8	8.1	12.5	17.4	52.8	34.5	16.0	
1997											0.711
Mean	–	223	545	1 193	1 750	2 623	3 866	12 028	15 776	37 951	
Owning land (%)	–	1.0	2.5	5.4	7.9	11.8	17.4	54.1	35.5	16.8	
1998											0.671
Mean	–	318	826	1 285	1 874	2 661	4 234	10 074	14 054	29 893	
Owning land (%)	–	1.5	3.9	6.5	8.8	12.5	20.0	47.3	33.0	13.9	

Note: The Gini coefficients in the last column represent the disparities of land ownership of all households, including those without any land.

Source: DERI panel surveys (1993–98).

Economic Crisis and Increasing Indebtedness

How do poor families who do not own a house or land secure long-term rent deposits which often approach the value of houses themselves? Presumably, many rely on credit. To test this hypothesis, we need to compute not only the total wealth distribution but the distribution of net worth, which takes liabilities into account. This is done in Table 7.8.

The results show that the distribution of net worth is quite different from that of total wealth. While the Gini coefficients of net worth are generally higher than those of total worth, there is no fixed pattern in their relationship. The Gini of net worth was 0.57 in 1993, the year believed to reflect the real estate distribution most accurately. Subsequently, the coefficient rose. This is noteworthy because the increase in the Gini coefficient of net worth distribution against the backdrop of a steadily decreasing Gini coefficient of real estate distribution is a clear sign of a widening gap between the rich and poor.[12]

A reasonable conjecture is that the Gini coefficient of net worth distribution rose sharply in 1998 because the poor fell deeper into debt. The net worth of the lowest decile was negative in both 1997 and 1998.[13] This seems to have less to do with a decrease in the assets of the group than with an increase in its debts. Table 7.8 sheds further light on this question. The poorest (first decile) group suffered a drop in net worth, from –8 million won in 1997 to –20 million won between 1997 and 1998. Another group that experienced a large change in net worth was the richest decile; it registered an increase of 7 million won in net worth over the same two-year period. The increase in net worth was greater for the richest 5 percent, and it was even greater still for the richest 1 percent. Real estate holdings contributed to the increase in their net worth more than financial assets. Considering that real estate prices were falling nationwide, we can infer that there was a net increase in real estate owned by members of the highest deciles.

In the early days of the crisis, newspapers reported that the rich were getting richer and the poor were getting poorer because of the differential impact of high interest rates and the rising unemployment. The popular perception (HERI, 1998) was not much different from the reality, Table 7.8 suggests.

The net worth of the poorest decile fell due to an increase in debts rather than a decrease in assets. Borrowing was for many poor Koreans an important component of the safety net. The problem is that there are both economic and financial constraints on the use of this form of self-insurance in a crisis. This makes it important for the government to extend the social safety net before another crisis strikes (Ferreira et al., 2000).

Table 7.8 Net worth holdings by decile (based on real estate survey results)

Year and category	1st decile	2nd decile	3rd decile	4th decile	5th decile	6th decile	7th decile	8th decile	9th decile	10th decile	Top 5%	Top 1%
1997												
Net worth	−797	1 582	2 846	3 960	5 202	6 761	9 002	11 670	16 728	38 088	52 047	95 829
Liabilities	2 146	347	430	401	521	780	558	699	949	1 350	1 841	2 394
Total assets	1 350	1 930	3 727	4 362	5 723	7 540	9 560	12 369	17 677	39 437	53 888	98 223
Financial assets	692	1 250	1 947	2 420	2 002	2 110	2 069	2 653	2 981	4 856	6 014	10 983
Real estate	658	680	1 330	1 942	3 721	5 431	7 491	9 716	14 696	34 581	47 874	87 240
1998												
Net worth	−1 998	1 582	2 740	3 906	5 116	6 614	8 599	11 304	16 700	44 915	64 137	132 862
Liabilities	3 741	648	499	542	807	755	698	691	975	1 374	1 680	2 096
Total assets	1 743	2 233	3 245	4 451	5 927	7 369	9 295	12 000	17 686	46 282	65 810	134 964
Financial assets	645	1 228	1 702	2 022	1 962	1 958	2 044	1 972	3 286	5 423	6 621	7 440
Real estate	1 098	1 005	1 543	2 429	3 965	5 411	7 251	10 027	14 400	40 860	59 189	127 524

Source: DERI panel surveys (1997–98).

POVERTY

While journalists take poverty seriously, there is not much academic analysis of it, reflecting the paucity of systematic data. Most research on poverty in Korea after the crisis has relied on the Urban Household Income and Expenditure Survey (UHIES). As mentioned above, while of good quality and available for a long period, these data do not cover the rural sector or single-person households, and do not provide any information on the incomes of employers and self-employed. Research using this source has concluded that poverty has increased since the crisis in 1997, although the magnitude of the increase differs according to different authors (see Moon and Yoo, 1999; Jin-Wook Kim and Park, 2000; Rew, 2000).

Rew (2000) made a special effort to estimate the size of the poor population among the single-person households, and she concluded that the total number of the poor in Korea rose from 6 million in 1997 to more than 10 million in 1998. This was a huge figure, fully 24 percent of the total population. Bark et al. (1999) utilized a new data set, the 1996 Consumption Expenditure Survey (CES), to fill the gaps in the Urban Household Income and the Expenditure Survey (UHIES), and concluded that the poverty rate more than doubled, from 7 percent in 1997 to 16 percent in 1998–99.[14] The largest increase is reported by Kakwani and Prescott (2001), who estimated the head-count ratio of both consumption poverty and income poverty using the UHIES. They found that consumption poverty increased from 8.6 to 19.2 percent of the total population. These authors broke down the population of poor into the 'ultra-poor' (with incomes of less than 80 percent of the poverty line) and the 'marginal poor' (with incomes between 80 and 100 percent of the poverty line). Among the 19 percent of the population who were regarded as poor in 1998, 9 percent were ultra-poor, while 10 percent were marginal poor. The head-count ratio of income poverty turned out to be much smaller than that of consumption poverty: it rose from 2.6 percent in the last quarter of 1997 to 6.1 percent in the first quarter of 1998.

Finally, J.-W. Lee and Lee (2001b) used the DERI data to estimate the extent of poverty before and after the crisis. They found that the poverty (head-count) ratio rose from 10.2 percent in 1997 to 15.5 percent in 1998.

More reassuringly, the income necessary to lift all the poor to the poverty line was only 1 percent of total household income in 1997, although it rose to 2.3 percent in 1998. Sen's poverty index, a composite measure of poverty containing information on the head-count ratio, poverty gap and the Gini ratio among the poor, doubled from 4.6 to 9.0 percent between 1997 and 1998.

Poverty becomes more severe as we move from big cities to small cities and the countryside. In 1998, more than a fifth of individuals living in the countryside could be classified as poor. Considering the dislocations caused by the liberalization of trade in agricultural products in the mid-1990s, this is hardly surprising. At the same time, the rise in poverty after the crisis was less pronounced in the countryside than in the cities because the countryside was relatively insulated from the effects of the financial crisis and the recession. This can be seen in Table 7.1, where farm income shows no sign of decline in 1998.

Because the DERI survey was discontinued after 1998, to analyze more recent trends one must look to other sources. Using the UHIES, Whang (2001) reports that absolute poverty peaked at 10.5 percent in the first quarter of 1999 and declined gradually thereafter to 5.6 per cent in 2000:IV. This contrasts with income inequality, which has remained stable at higher levels despite the improvement in general economic conditions.

OTHER SOCIAL IMPACTS

The crisis was jarring for a society that had long been accustomed to rapid economic growth. Large-scale job losses created a great deal of stress among laid-off workers; the social shock to those who lost their jobs was substantial. It is hardly surprising to find that the physical and mental health of the unemployed deteriorated.

Based on interviews of 150 people who had lost their jobs during the 1997 crisis, S.-O. Chang (1999) found that many were experiencing health problems, identity crises and loss of self-esteem. Major effects of the crisis were felt by the household. Ahn (1999) showed that the domestic difficulties were more serious in households where the husbands had been laid off. The greatest difficulties were experienced in households where the housewives entered the labor market to seek new careers.[15] In addition, there was a change in gender roles between laid-off men and their spouses. Most notably, husbands became more tolerant of their wives working. However, the attitudes of husbands toward housework have changed little, so the net result has been a heavier burden for their wives. Evidently, the precise impact of job loss on a family depends on the type of family. H.-K. Chang and Kim (1999) emphasize that the greatest difficulty is experienced by the vertical-type family, in which husbands had wielded authoritarian control.[16]

While there had been a gradual rise in divorces even before 1998, the crisis seems to have left its mark here as well. The number of the couples filing for divorce for 'economic reasons' rose substantially. Divorces filed on other grounds, 'bad relationships,' for example, also increased since 1998; some of these cases presumably also stemmed from the economic distress accompanying the crisis.

Finally, crime increased, with crimes committed for 'economic reasons' up the most. The well-known case of the burglar who broke into a house and stole a bag of rice, leaving a short note of apology and asking mercy for a hungry family, testifies to the social atmosphere. While crimes cannot solely be explained by economic pressures narrowly defined, the rise in distrust between people under circumstances of extreme uncertainty may have also been a factor. There is some evidence of a decline in trust and social capital after the crisis (Yong-Hak Kim, 1999). Social breakdown rears its ugly head in the rise in drug addiction as well; there was a noticeable increase in the drug problem after 1998.

The most extreme manifestation of the despair and stress brought on by the crisis is the number of suicides (Suh, 2001). As Table 7.9 shows, the suicide rate suddenly jumped from around 6000 before the crisis to about 8500 thereafter.

Table 7.9   Indices of social disorder

Year	Divorces	Crimes	Crimes per 100,000	Drug addicts	Suicides
1996	79 895	1 494 846	3 282	6 189	5 777
1997	91 159	1 588 613	3 454	6 947	5 957
1998	116 727	1 765 887	3 803	8 350	8 496
1999	118 014	1 732 522	3 697	10 589	7 014

Source: National Statistical Office (1997–2000).

SUMMARY AND POLICY IMPLICATIONS

In this chapter, I examined the social impact of the 1997–98 economic crisis in Korea. The findings clearly support the conclusion that income distribution, which had been improving before 1997, deteriorated in the crisis. The major losers were older workers outside Seoul with little education. In addition, poverty almost doubled during the crisis, as an additional 5 percent of the population fell below the poverty line.

Changes in wealth inequality were even more extreme. Because this effect of crises is commonly observed in other countries, it does not come as a surprise. However, it should be pointed out that our figures for wealth concentration are probably underestimates, due to the limitations in the data. In other words, the distributional problem in Korea, as reflected in the distribution of wealth, may be even more serious than suggested here. The two most notable characteristics of the Korean wealth distribution are the importance of real estate holdings in household assets and a wide disparity in real estate holdings across social strata. This chapter has revealed that wealth distribution became steadily more unequal in the 1990s. It thereby supports media reports that the gap between the rich and the poor widened during the crisis and shows that this was largely due to a rapid increase in indebtedness among the poor combined with growing real estate holdings among the rich.

Another important finding is the collapse of the middle class. This result should be interpreted cautiously; the same phenomenon can be observed in the United States, although it has unfolded more slowly, over a period of 15 to 20 years. In Korea, in contrast, the economic crisis struck suddenly, and the change in the relative position of the middle class was extremely rapid. It is not surprising that income inequality widened and poverty increased as society was experiencing a serious economic recession. We can therefore conclude that the most effective policy for improving distributional equity and reducing poverty would be one that flattens the business cycle, maintains a robust economy and creates more jobs.

Growing inequality in Korea in recent years is a different phenomenon than that observed in the United States. Economists view US inequality as resulting from a combination of globalization, job loss from the decline of smokestack industries, the digital divide, and the weakening of labor unions (Danziger and Gottschalk, 1995; Freeman, 1999; Ryscavage, 1999). On the one hand, since Korea's growth strategy is broadly similar to that pursued by other market-oriented economies like Europe and the United States, it is not surprising that we observe similar trends. On the other hand, Korea has a more limited welfare state, so the distributional impact of these changes in the economy is likely to be even more profound.

Maintaining growth, stabilizing the business cycle and creating jobs are crucial for improving the distribution of income and reducing poverty, but expanding the social safety net is also important. Social spending, despite significant increases in recent years, is still low in Korea compared to other countries with similar per capita incomes, not to mention the advanced nations. This fact could be overlooked so long as the Korean economy was doing well and poverty could be reduced through growth and employment expansion. While it is true that growth is good for the poor (Dollar and Kraay, 2001), it will be difficult for Korea to match the pace of past growth in the future. The poor coped with the recent crisis by taking on greater debt. It goes without saying that this kind of individually provided safety net is fragile and incomplete. Perhaps the most important lesson we should draw from the harsh experiences of the economic crisis in 1997–98 is that Korea needs to develop a viable social safety net before its economy and society are tested by another serious disturbance.

NOTES

1. The World Bank claims that, due to the 1997 crisis, East Asian countries experienced increasing disparities in income distribution, but that such disparities were not as great as those of South American nations (World Bank, 2000a). Comparing the Gini coefficients of between 0.5 and 0.6 in Latin American countries and the coefficients that are generally less than 0.5 in Asian countries as reported in the *World Development Report*, 2000, this comment seems plausible (World Bank, 2000b).
2. It is of moderate quality if it reaches 70 to 90 percent of those of the national accounts; and it is of questionable quality if it is under 70 percent.
3. This finding is almost identical to those of prior studies using UHIES data, in which the Gini coefficient also moved up three to four percentage points.
4. Gregory Duncan defines the middle 70 percent of society as the middle class.
5. Note, however, that the difference between sales workers and blue-collar workers that year is not statistically significant.
6. Land is at the heart of wealth distribution in Korea. Some studies, such as Hyun (1996), and Yoon et al. (1999), calculated inequality exclusively according to land holdings. Hyun estimated land ownership inequality using the raw data of aggregate land taxes levied in 1993. According to his study, the Gini coefficient of land ownership was 0.803 among landholding households, and the corresponding figure was 0.861 for all households in the nation, including those owning no land. Yoon et al. (1999) reached a very similar estimate.
7. To remedy this sort of problem, some researchers (for example Keister, 2000) oversample the wealthy. It is regrettable that the DERI survey did not follow this procedure.
8. Responses to surveys on income and wealth often suffer from problems as under-reporting and concealment. This is especially true of surveys on wealth. Respondents do not remember their wealth as accurately as they do their income, and at times they attempt to conceal their wealth more than they do their income. But while the DERI data may have reliability problems, wealth surveys are rare in Korea.
9. This contradicts the 1988 KDI findings but is more consistent with common-sense knowledge of Korea.
10. The cost of land per acre in Korea seems to exceed even that in Japan. Even though statistics on land are not collected systematically in Korea, it is not difficult to establish that Korea's land prices are comparatively high. In terms of total value, they seem to be surpassed only by Japan and the United States. This means that Korea probably has the most expensive land in the world.
11. The difference may be partly due to the methodology employed in the DERI study. After 1994, the Gini coefficient continued to decline, falling to 0.67 in 1998. Some might interpret this as a result of equalizing land ownership, but that was actually not the case.
12. The Gini coefficient for net worth rose from 0.57 in 1993 to 0.65 in 1998, but the actual change may have been even greater. Obviously, if the downward bias in the disparity of real estate ownership – due to many households dropping out of the sample – had been considered, the Gini coefficient of net worth distribution in the years after 1994 would have been higher than the figures computed here, and the upward adjustment value would have been slightly higher from one year to the next. I believe that the Gini coefficient for 1998 (0.65) was underestimated, and the real value might be close to or higher than 0.70.
13. The values changed depending on whether real estate was estimated or actually surveyed, but the trend did not.
14. When comparing the poverty rate in urban areas, the finding of Bark et al. (1999) is very close to Moon and Yoo (1999) cited above.
15. In this respect, the assertion by Sohn (1999) that the major victims of the economic crisis were women along with the elderly and the young makes some sense.
16. They found that horizontal-type families that had relative equality in power and responsibility between the spouses could overcome the economic crisis more easily with help and cooperation from the members of the family.

Comment on Chapters 5, 6 and 7

Eduardo Borensztein

The three foregoing chapters provide valuable insights into the macroeconomic management of the Korean crisis and some of its consequences. In the first chapter, Cho analyzes monetary policy after the collapse of the won in December 1997. The tight monetary policy stance of the Bank of Korea has been criticized on the grounds that it imposed an excessive burden on corporates that were already under financial stress. Even worse, the effectiveness of tightening monetary policy and increasing interest rates in stabilizing the exchange rate has been questioned by the 'unorthodox' view, which states that the relationship between monetary policy and the exchange rate is not as in the standard textbook case but in fact the opposite: an increase in domestic interest rates (or, equivalently, a tightening of domestic monetary policy) weakens the currency instead of strengthening it.

Cho presents a simple and insightful model to analyze the relationship between monetary policy (interest rates) and the exchange rate under conditions of exchange market pressure. The model allows for the risk premium on domestic assets to react perversely to monetary policy, the basic argument of the unorthodox view. Cho shows that stability of the model rules out the unorthodox view. Indeed, the implication of the unorthodox view is that the monetary authority could increase the value of the domestic currency just by printing more of it. It is not surprising that, in a formal framework, such an assumption would lead to an unstable result. Next, Cho briefly reviews the empirical literature on the subject, which largely finds the right association between interest rates and exchange rates, although often with weak statistical significance. In the case of Korea, Cho presents results from bivariate vector autoregressions that yield the right effect of interest rates on the exchange rate, although the size of the effect is small and the statistical significance not overwhelming. This result, however, attests more to the difficulty of identifying the structural relationship between interest rates and exchange rate because of endogeneity problems than to an actual tenuous effect of monetary policy. The exchange rate appreciates when interest rates are raised, but a depreciation of the exchange rate causes the central bank to respond by increasing interest rates.

It is extremely difficult to disentangle these two effects even with high-frequency data.

It is noteworthy that monetary management during the Korean crisis was, as in many other crisis countries, quite pragmatic. The Bank of Korea raised interest rates but also carried out large sterilized intervention operations, and the international community cooperated with Korea in putting together an effective 'private sector involvement' effort that yielded a rollover agreement with international commercial banks. The sterilized intervention policy was not operated in the standard way but instead consisted of dollar-denominated loans by the Bank of Korea through a special foreign exchange window to private banks that had to make loan repayments. These operations were equivalent to the Bank of Korea selling foreign exchange to the banks and then sterilizing the monetary impact through loans to those same banks. The currency of denomination of the loans (US dollars instead of won) is perhaps atypical but the monetary implications of the Bank of Korea operations are exactly the same as in a standard sterilized intervention operation. Lending by the Bank of Korea through this foreign exchange window amounted to about $23 billion (although part of it took place in November, just before the crisis). By comparison, all the external support disbursed by international financial institutions in 1997 and 1998 amounted to some $26 billion. And the interest rates charged on the Bank of Korea loans (LIBOR plus 400 basis points, later gradually raised to LIBOR plus 1000 basis points) were certainly much lower than those that would have been necessary to preserve the same level of the exchange rate by tightening monetary policy alone. The importance of the rollover agreement with commercial banks for the stabilization of the foreign exchange market cannot be overstated. Despite the IMF program of 4 December, international commercial banks were unwilling to roll over short-run loans to Korean banks, and the pressures on international reserves from the repayment of those loans were mounting. Absent the rollover agreement with commercial banks, international reserves wouldn't have been sufficient to finance the repayment by Korean banks, and the depreciation of the won and/or increase in domestic interest rates would have been much more dramatic.

What about the claim that high interest rates were responsible for widespread bankruptcies and a deeper recession? The fact is that exchange rate depreciation hurt the finances of the corporates to a much greater extent, probably four to six times more. According to data in Hallward-Dreimeier (2001) the debt/equity ratio of Korean corporations was close to 3, and foreign debt was about 37 percent of total debt, which means that the foreign debt/equity ratio was about unity. This means that, for a nontraded goods producer, the roughly 50 percent devaluation of the won (a doubling of the price of foreign exchange) represented a loss equivalent to 100 percent of equity. Assuming nontraded-goods-producing firms were prudent in their financial decisions and had a foreign debt share three times lower than the traded firms, say about 20 percent of total debt, the devaluation would still wipe out 60 percent of equity. By comparison, the interest rate effect is quite modest. The increase in interest rates affected mostly short-term rates. According to Hallward-Dreimeier (2001) data, short-term debt was about 50 percent of total debt, or 1.5 times equity, in the typical Korean corporate. Even under the extreme assumption that all short-term debt had to be rolled over at the highest interest rate, this means a loss equivalent to less than 20 percentage points annually (the approximate increase in nominal interest rates, assuming they are equal to real rates for a nontraded goods firm), which would be equivalent to about 15 percent of equity. Hence the conclusion that corporate losses on account of the exchange rate depreciation were easily four to six times as high as losses on account of the higher interest rates. While the specific assumptions behind this calculation are tentative, the conclusion that the effect of the sharp depreciation was several times higher than that of the increase in short-term interest rates appears fairly robust.

In Chapter 6, Jun presents a comprehensive and insightful analysis of fiscal policy in the Korean crisis. He focuses on the policy response to the crisis and the longer-run implications for debt sustainability and fiscal reforms. As the crisis unfolded, fiscal policy was tightened, but this action was quickly reversed, and the fiscal policy stance became quite expansionary in 1998. There is broad agreement now that the initial tightening was a mistake. Yet the decision to tighten fiscal policy was not baseless. The measure was intended to help improve the current account and support external confidence. Although government debt was quite low, private debt was high, and private debt has a tendency to become public debt in crises. Moreover, the large expected support to the financial sector provided a quasi-fiscal expansionary impulse and implied the need for fiscal consolidation at some point. And, most importantly, a much shallower recession was expected. In the event, the recession was much worse, the current account improvement was enormously higher than expected, external confidence proved hard to bolster by fiscal measures, and the cost of bank restructuring fell short of the most pessimistic scenarios. As this situation started to become apparent, the fiscal tightening was promptly reversed.

The response to the crisis also left a number of lasting changes in fiscal policy in Korea. Notably, the social safety net that had to be put together hastily in 1998 was successful in fulfilling pressing needs. The various programs put in place provided social support equivalent to about 2 percent of GDP in 1998 and 3 percent in 1999. Yet the consequences of the system for the labor market and public finances over the longer term will need to be studied carefully.

Another legacy of the crisis is the significant increase in government debt that resulted from the cost of financial sector restructuring and the expansionary stance in 1998–99. Although the full extent of the cost of financial sector restructuring will only be known over the next few years, Jun presents some estimates that would put Korea's debt-to-GDP ratio close to 40 percent. In comparison to OECD levels, he argues, Korea's debt is quite low. Moreover, the high growth rate and low interest rates currently enjoyed by Korea (in fact the growth rate exceeds the interest rate at the time of writing) imply a favorable dynamics, reinforced by the switch back to fiscal conservatism that has resulted in budget surpluses since 2000. While this view may indeed be correct, a note of caution is appropriate. Volatility in emerging markets is generally much higher than in OECD countries, and the correlation between macroeconomic variables tends to be unfavorable. For example, a negative shock to external demand for an emerging market country's exports would typically cause a depreciation of the exchange rate, which increases the burden of external debt; an increase in interest rates on account of the higher country risk; and an economic slowdown or recession owing to the export decline, which reduces tax revenues and increases the budget deficit. Each of these factors tends to worsen the debt-to-GDP ratio, and their combined effect can result in sizable increases in debt in a short time. Debt sustainability analysis requires the evaluation of all vulnerabilities of this sort, without which it is not possible to conclude that a certain debt-to-GDP level is safe.

In Chapter 7 Lee analyzes the impact of the crisis on income distribution and poverty. Among the evidence presented by Lee, I find two most interesting pieces: the changes in different types of income as reflected by household survey of the Daewoo Economic Research Institute (DERI), and regressions showing the determinants of the wage structure for 1995 and 2000.

The sharp recession during the crisis affected incomes across all social brackets. Poverty rates increased because previously nonpoor households fell below the poverty line, even if the revamping of the social safety net, mentioned above, helped to ameliorate the situation. But it is not obvious *a priori* that the financial crisis and associated depreciation should change income distribution (say as measured by Gini coefficients) in favor of the rich. Lee argues that the high level of interest rates during the first half of 1998 was responsible for the income redistribution because the upper segments of the income ladder benefited from high interest on their savings. Conceptually, that seems at best an incomplete argument. High interest rates benefit savers but hurt borrowers, who are mostly businesses and higher-income consumers. Furthermore, recessions are bad for employment and real wages but also bad for profits. And while the depreciation reduced real wages, it also caused large financial losses to corporates with foreign debts. In fact, the structural changes in the financial sector implied bankruptcies and reorganization for many of the top *chaebols*, which can't be good for the income of the richest group of consumers.

Indeed, Table 7.1 presents a mixed picture of the income changes for different groups in 1998. For example, business and labor income fell by the same rate, 23 percent. Farm income went up, probably helped by the higher food prices brought about by the depreciation of the won. Interest income rose sharply, but it had been on an upward trend since 1994. At least at this level of aggregation, there isn't a clear story that can be told on income distribution during the Korean crisis. The Gini coefficient on household income did increase from 0.37 to 0.4, but the Gini coefficient on household expenditure remained constant. Overall, these data do not suggest a dramatic shift in income distribution in 1998.

The analysis of wage determinants uncovers many trends that are perhaps not consequence of the crisis but may have been helped by some of the corporate and structural reforms that were initiated as a response to the crisis. The most notable change in 2000 relative to 1995 is the increase in the education premium and the decline in the seniority premium. This would seem to be a welcome trend, as labor markets in Korea, as well as elsewhere in East Asia, tend to display a bias in the direction of rewarding seniority excessively and performance too little. But it should be noted that many coefficients are not statistically significant and the point estimates are small. For example, the increase in wages expected from a complete college education over high school education is 5 percent. By comparison, estimates in advanced countries cluster around an average of 6 to 7 percent per year, that is, more than four times higher than in the wage regression for Korea in 2000.

Comment on Chapters 5, 6 and 7[1]

Gordon de Brouwer

These three chapters are a commentator's dream and reflect well on the intellectual strengths of Korea. They introduce new material, they are analytically rigorous and passionate, and they canvas some of the key challenges facing policy makers, not just in Korea but elsewhere in the region and beyond. The topics are, however, big enough to give others room to comment.

Let me do this in three steps, first by looking at the three chapters as a whole, then by making links between a couple of them, and finally by exploring some analytical or policy issues particular to each.

At the most general level, the chapters are a powerful record of the damage caused by economic and financial crises. As Cho and Jun show, the economic costs of the crisis, including the consequences of some policy mistakes, are great. As Lee shows, the social costs, in terms of personal suffering and tragedy, are enormous; the dimension of human loss that Korea experienced is more what you expect from war. We have to avoid crises.

How do we avoid crises? This is not straightforward. We do not live in a nice neat world. There seem to be aspects of instability in markets, such as an inherent tendency for herding and overshooting in financial and asset markets. And, for open economies, events and problems in other countries can spill over and affect the domestic economy. National policy makers cannot do a lot about these things, except perhaps try to use international processes to mitigate and resolve their consequences. But they can reduce the likelihood of these things spiraling out of control and creating a crisis by getting basic economic structures right.

'Getting things right' has two elements. It means ensuring that clear, accountable and robust policy structures are in place. This helps because policy makers are more likely to have consistent frameworks in which to deal with unexpected events without panicking, and because they are less likely themselves to make domestic policy mistakes (which is the source of many woes). It also means that the economy itself has to be sufficiently flexible to deal with the many various disturbances or shocks that it faces, to minimize their negative impact on living standards. Apart from good luck, my own country,

Australia, only weathered the adverse economic and financial consequences of the East Asian financial crises of 1997 and 1998, maintaining 4 per cent real growth, because it had got its basic structures right before the crisis.[2]

With this general comment in mind, I look in more detail at the chapters presented here. There are a number of connections between them that can be teased out.

The first is the connection between Cho's chapter on monetary policy and Jun's on fiscal policy. Neither mentions the relevance of the other policy arm. When I was an undergraduate student, macroeconomic stabilization analysis was mostly about the policy mix: how to coordinate monetary and fiscal policy. Of course, we subsequently learned about the inflation bias of politically controlled monetary authorities and the deep-seated political and timing problems of using fiscal policy as a demand-management tool. We now have independent central banks which focus primarily on inflation[3] and finance ministries which focus primarily on medium-term fiscal sustainability. But as Jun shows, there is also increasing scope in Korea for using fiscal policy as a tool for managing the business cycle. So where does that leave us in terms of coordinating separate and independent arms of policy?

Some would say that we are better off with the two arms of policy kept separate. Andrew Kilpatrick argues, for example, that, at least in the case of the United Kingdom, there never was proper coordination in the old days. He reckons that *de facto* coordination will now occur so long as central banks and finance ministries have clear and stable policy functions with each side taking account of the reaction of the other in setting policy. That may be right if objective functions and reaction functions are stable, but we do not know yet whether this is the case. This is also not an argument against explicit coordination: coordinated actions are more efficient than uncoordinated ones in the presence of uncertainty, all else given.

The modest way to address the issue of coordination, or lack of it, is to have someone from the finance ministry on the central bank board, either with voting power (as in Australia) or without (as in the United Kingdom). But this itself is no guarantee of coordination. What we also have to do is monitor and scrutinize our institutions to make sure that they cooperate. And we need to reassure our central banks that talking with the finance minister and his ministry about the relative merits of monetary or fiscal action is not a sign of the absence of independence but is rather a strong indication of its presence.

There are other ways to address the policy coordination issue. Economists like Larry Ball and Nick Gruen say that we should also make the countercyclical elements of fiscal policy independent from politicians, establishing a statutorily independent fiscal agency. To ensure policy coordination, the fiscal and monetary authorities would need to share some overlap in management, perhaps at the board level. This is a shocking idea but it is no more radical than the idea of independent central banks; we are just not accustomed to it. Adopting this measure, however, would be a sad reflection of the inability of our politicians to govern. It would also give even more power to officials and we would need to be confident that they would be sufficiently accountable to voters.

As a final observation on the issue of monetary and fiscal coordination, I would like to stress that it is important because monetary and fiscal policies are not perfect substitutes. They can have different interest rate, exchange rate, economic and distributional effects. Fiscal policy – and financial supervisory policy, for that matter – can be a far more finessed instrument than monetary policy: fiscal policy can be directed at a particular sector; monetary policy is always a general and blunt instrument. The upshot is that the assignment of instruments is important and we need to ensure that some coordination occurs.

Lee's chapter can also inform the question raised by Cho in relation to which price index the monetary authorities should focus on, the implicit GDP deflator or core CPI. Implicit in Lee's chapter is the basic notion that the ultimate focus of policy makers must be on the wellbeing of the people. Neoclassical economists would agree. In terms of material wellbeing, this means that our central bankers must focus on stability in the value of people's consumption. The core CPI, not the GDP deflator, is the right measure.

I now consider some specific issues raised by each chapter.

MONETARY POLICY

Cho draws two tentative conclusions from his thorough empirical analysis. First, raising interest rates at the start of the crisis helped the Korean authorities to stabilize the exchange rate; it did not in Indonesia and Thailand. This makes him cautious about accepting casual arguments that are critical of the high interest rate policy. Second, if the Bank of Korea was targeting base CPI inflation, then monetary policy was too high for most of 1998 and probably too low in 2000 and 2001.

The first point looks pretty reasonable. The motivation for raising interest rates in a currency crisis is to make domestic financial assets more attractive to resident and non-resident investors alike, and to demonstrate policy makers' commitment to 'go the hard yards' to earn credibility (even if that means self-inflicted pain!). Whether this works or not depends partly on the price elasticity of investor demand. If investors just want to get out and so are completely price insensitive in that market, then raising interest rates will have no effect. This is by now well-trodden ground. The only point I would like to make is that people talk too readily about the East Asian financial crisis as a single uniform event. It was not. It was a series of crises over 15 months, with a range of triggers, speculative positions, and fundamental factors that varied substantially between countries, and within countries, over time.[4] It is not reasonable to expect a standard policy response to work in all conditions, especially in the more extreme ones.

The second point is interesting and provocative. In defense of the central bankers, they were working in highly uncertain circumstances and some excessive tightness/easiness at times would hardly be surprising. Taken at face value, Cho's results suggest that the reaction function of the Bank of Korea was not stable in the crisis and post-crisis periods. The models that best fit 1998 are those in which the central bank is sensitive to exchange rate movements, in addition to inflation deviating from its target and to the output gap. The models that best fit 1999 and 2000 are those where the central bank no longer responds to the exchange rate, and focuses on inflation deviating from target. That also sounds pretty reasonable given that the authorities were dealing with a currency crisis in 1998.

But the results are highly sensitive to calibration, and to accept the results and interpretation, one has to believe that the parameter calibrations are right. Cho uses one set of Ball's calibrations for the US economy, with parameters set to 1 or 0 in most cases. They are different to the rough calibration of 0.5 on both the inflation deviation and output gap terms in John Taylor's 1993 reaction function for the Fed. I don't know how the implied optimal call rate would change if Taylor's calibrations were used for the inflation deviation and output gap, or whether indeed Ball's or Taylor's numbers are the right ones for Korea. What I would rather see is direct estimation of the reaction parameters for Korea and a comparison of the fitted call rate to the actual.[5]

FISCAL POLICY

Jun has written a very comprehensive and accessible chapter. I have two comments and three questions.

Jun is critical of the Korean fiscal authorities for a number of reasons, including the big forecast errors they make in revenue, expenditure, and the net balance of spending. He presents these figures in Table 6.4 and provides a measure of their accuracy (in terms of average absolute values). The issue with forecast errors is not so much how big they are but how efficient the forecasts are. There is an irreducible uncertainty in the world and forecasting is by its nature error-prone. Can the forecast errors be reduced? The first three rows of Table C.1 set out the autocorrelation coefficients for the forecast errors for 1982–2000 and the subsamples of 1982–91 and 1992–2000; if

Table C.1 Autocorrelation and bias in revenue and expenditure forecast errors

	[(Final–planned)/planned]*100			[(Final–planned)/GDP]*100		
	Revenue	Expenditure	Net balance	Revenue	Expenditure	Net balance
Autocorrelation						
1982–2000	0.35	0.41	0.21	0.33	0.37	0.18
1982–1991	0.38	0.37	0.23	0.35	0.33	0.13
1992–2000	0.21	0.36	0.22	0.26	0.33	0.21
Average forecast error						
1982–2000	−3.122	−3.864	0.741	−0.487	−0.612	0.123
1982–1991	−5.579	−5.180	−0.399	−0.973	−0.826	−0.148
1992–2000	−0.393	−2.402	2.008	0.051	−0.375	0.425

forecasters use all available information, their forecast errors should be uncorrelated. The next set of rows sets out average forecast errors, which are an indication of forecast bias. There are four points of interest.

1. Forecast errors with respect to revenue and expenditure are significantly serially correlated, implying that they make systematic forecast errors. Policy makers could make use of the fact that they make systematic forecast errors to improve the accuracy of their forecasts. The autocorrelation in expenditure forecast errors has not generally changed significantly in the 1990s compared to the 1980s, but it has for revenue forecasts.
2. The serial correlation of net revenue forecast errors is much smaller than for the gross revenue and expenditure components and is only marginally significant. In this sense, forecasting of the net revenue balance is relatively efficient.
3. The revenue and expenditure forecasts are biased, typically with outcomes higher than what was initially planned. The bias in revenue and expenditure forecasts has become substantially smaller over time.
4. The bias in the net revenue balance is much smaller than for the components (which is expected since net numbers are smaller than gross numbers), but it has increased over time. In this sense, forecasting of the net revenue balance has become relatively less efficient. This is consistent with Jun's observation that net revenue forecasts have become less accurate over time (as measured by the average absolute error).

There is something here for everyone. Getting expenditure figures as right as possible is important, for example, in social planning. Getting net revenue figures right is important, for example, in planning bond financing. These additional figures suggest that the fiscal authorities are not doing everything wrong, even if there is room for improvement.

Jun is also concerned about debt sustainability and notes that making people save now for their pensions can reduce the future debt burden. This is right but it is worth noting that compulsory saving can have other, even good, unforeseen effects. Australia, for example, has a compulsory long-term savings scheme to fund future pensions which is operated on market principles: savings are managed in an open private fund management system. This has had an unforeseen effect on financial markets and corporate governance. The big rise in funds under management has created strong market demand for new investment instruments, substantially boosting the corporate bond market and the derivatives markets which are so vital to risk management. It has also created big institutional shareholders who have the clout to monitor the activities of the firms in which they invest. The upshot is that fiscal arrangements can have effects far beyond what they were intended, either positive or negative.

Now to the three questions.

What is the effect of bracket-creep in Korea? Nominal wages tend to increase with inflation which, given a differentiated marginal tax rate structure, will push income earners into higher tax brackets over time. This happens even at low rates of inflation when there is a complex marginal tax rate structure. Bracket-creep helps expand the tax base but it means that workers end up having to pay more tax and it can create disincentives to work. How does this operate in Korea? Is it important?

How successful have specific tax and expenditure measures been in achieving their aim? One of the advantages of fiscal policy as a control tool is that it can be directed to specific problems or issues. Has this worked in Korea?

What is the scope for the government to sell public assets and use the proceeds to pay off debt, thereby easing the debt sustainability problem identified by Jun? Some countries have used the proceeds from public asset sales, especially of utilities and telecommunications firms, to pay down government debt. This can have a radical effect on the estimated sustainability of government debt. What is the debate in Korea on this issue?

SOCIAL POLICY

Lee has written a very interesting chapter and presented research with two new data sets. I cannot help but admire his passion and share his deep apprehension about the social costs of the financial crisis in Korea.

My main reservation[6] with his chapter is that on occasion he tends to interpret changes in income equality and other social indicators during the 1990s as secular or long-term changes. The endpoint of the 1990s is of course a very severe recession, and it surely cannot be right to draw conclusions about longer-term trends when the last observation, at least with the DERI data, is the worst year of the crisis. It is better to couch the analysis in terms of the costs of a crisis. Some of these have been unwound; some cannot be.

I do not want to trivialize the social costs of the crisis, but I do see more grounds for optimism in his analysis than Lee does. Consider two examples. First, he notes that land ownership is highly skewed to people in the top income deciles, and that people in the lower three income deciles in Korea do not own land. But his figures also show that land ownership at the lower fourth, fifth, sixth and seventh deciles increased each year in the 1990s, even during the financial crisis. Second, he notes that people in the lowest income decile moved into debt during the crisis, lowering their net worth. Economists would interpret this as evidence of financial markets functioning by allowing people to smooth their consumption in the face of temporary changes in current income. That said, I agree with him that fiscal transfers may be a more human way of enabling this.

NOTES

1. Comments welcome to gordon.debrouwer@anu.edu.au. These comments are the views of the author and do not necessarily reflect those of any institution with which the author is associated.
2. East Asian demand for Australian goods and services accounts for close to 15 per cent of Australia's GDP: over 60 per cent of Australia's exports go to East Asia and exports account for over 20 per cent of GDP.
3. If inflation is analysed in a Philips curve framework, a primary focus on inflation implicitly means that the central bank also focuses on achieving maximum sustainable output growth since inflation is managed by manipulating the output gap. The controversial issue in this case is how the central bank trades off variability in inflation with variability in output and jobs growth.
4. See, for example, de Brouwer (2001).
5. I am also unsure how to interpret the results because I am uncertain about some of the terminology. Does 'year-on-year' inflation mean the average of the index for a year divided by the average of the index for the previous year (which is what Australians call year-on-year inflation), or is it the index at a given quarter divided by the index at the same quarter in the previous year (which we call 'through-the-year' inflation)? The latter gives a much better sense of the underlying inflationary pulse. Using quarterly annualised figures is not appropriate.
6. Another reservation I have is that Lee talks about the Korean crisis as if it is the fault of the IMF: the crisis 'was largely caused by IMF intervention in the economy and the fiscal and monetary austerity that the IMF required.' I agree that the Fund made some serious mistakes before and during the financial crises in East Asia of 1997 and 1998, some of which remain unacknowledged. But I do not believe that Lee is right to say that the IMF *caused* the crisis, and especially not in the case of Korea where the key vulnerabilities (focus on short-term capital flows, unhedged foreign currency borrowing, and concentration in lending and industrial sectors) were domestic.

8. Financial restructuring[1]

Joon-Ho Hahm

MOTIVATION AND QUESTIONS

There has been a large volume of research seeking to determine the nature and causes of the Korean financial crisis.[2] Despite this, there is still no consensus on how the crisis and its resolution have affected the financial system. This chapter, by focusing on the corporate financing pattern and portfolio structure of financial institutions, endeavors to characterize the ongoing transition in the post-crisis Korean financial system. Based upon this characterization, it then evaluates the progress in financial restructuring and derives implications for further reform. Specifically, the chapter addresses the following questions:

- How can we characterize the pattern of credit allocation during the pre-crisis investment spree that so heightened the vulnerability of the financial system?
- How has the flow of funds changed during the crisis and the post-crisis restructuring period? Specifically, how has restructuring affected the financing behavior of nonfinancial firms and the portfolio allocations of commercial banks?
- What has been the result of the reform measures undertaken following the crisis? From the viewpoint of comparative financial systems, how can we characterize the ongoing structural transformation of the Korean financial system?
- What are the risks associated with the structural shift, and what are the policy implications?

THE FLOW OF FUNDS BEFORE THE CRISIS

In recognition of the problems associated with the tight control exercised by the authorities over the financial system, the Korean government began to liberalize the financial sector in the 1980s. The first step was the reprivatization of the commercial banks. Coincident with their privatization, the government tightened its control over bank credit in an attempt to limit the concentration of economic power among the *chaebols* and to ensure the access of small and medium-sized enterprises to commercial bank credit.[3] As noted by Hahm (2002), the availability of bank credit to the *chaebols* was limited, and small and medium-sized enterprises received increasing shares of commercial bank loans.[4]

In response, the *chaebols* sought alternative sources of finance. One such alternative was direct financing. This alternative was rendered more attractive by the deregulation of the capital markets, which increased the availability of direct financing to the corporate sector. As shown in Figure 8.1, the share of direct financing in total corporate financial liabilities increased substantially through 1996.[5]

Commercial paper and corporate bonds also emerged as important vehicles for direct financing. In particular, the share of commercial paper increased sharply in 1995 and 1996, largely reflecting the response of the *chaebols* to changing regulatory policies.[6] The sharp rise in reliance on commercial paper meant that the maturity structure of the debt shortened substantially in the pre-crisis period (as shown in Figure 8.1).

Faced with tight controls over commercial bank credit, Korea's large industrial conglomerates increasingly turned to nonbank financial institutions (NBFIs) to meet their financial needs.[7] Lending by NBFIs accounted for more than 50 percent of total indirect corporate debt by the early 1990s (see Figure 8.1). An important nonbank financial intermediary in this context was the merchant bank. Merchant banks virtually monopolized the commercial paper underwriting business.[8] Thus the shortening of the maturity structure of corporate debt, noted above, was closely intertwined with the growing market share of NBFIs.

The investment spree of the 1990s and the nature of bank–firm relations had important implications for the financial system, in terms of both systemic risk and economic efficiency. There is some evidence that the efficiency of credit allocation had deteriorated substantially by the first half of the 1990s.[9] As we have seen, two notable features of credit allocation in this period were the rising volume of NBFI intermediated credit (both loans and direct financing via NBFIs) and the increasingly short maturity structure of corporate debt (both domestic and foreign). These developments, in turn, were corollaries of the financial liberalization policies implemented in the late 1980s and early 1990s.

The financial liberalization program pursued by the Korean government was unbalanced and asymmetric. As argued by many authors (including Y. Cho 1999; C. Lee et al., 2000; Choi, D.-Y. 2002), one important asymmetry was unbalanced deregulation across the commercial bank and nonbank finan-

174   *The Korean economy beyond the crisis*

Share of direct financing in total corporate financial liabilities

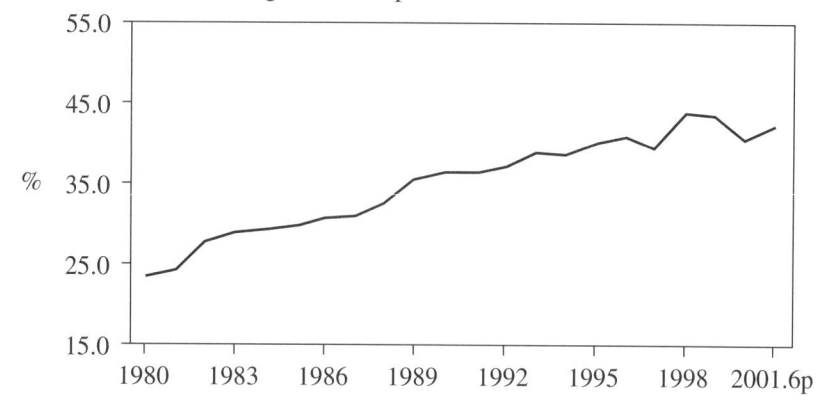

Share of short-term financing in corporate direct financing

Share of NBFI borrowing in direct financing

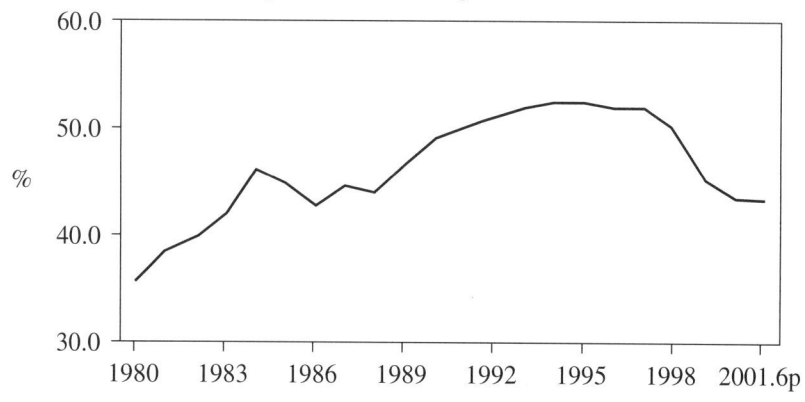

Source: Bank of Korea, *Database on Flow of Funds Account* (various issues).

Figure 8.1   The transition in corporate financing patterns

cial industries. NBFIs were allowed much greater freedom in their management of assets and liabilities and were permitted to offer higher interest rates on their deposits and loans.[10] Large deposit rate differentials between commercial banks and NBFIs persisted throughout the period. The deregulation of interest rates on nonbank financial products such as commercial paper, in the face of continuing control of commercial bank deposit rates, artificially shifted liquidity toward loosely supervised NBFIs and consequently magnified risks for the entire financial system. Not only were NBFIs not adequately supervised, encouraging risk taking made possible by the competition for deposits, but the increasing share of intermediation that took place through NBFIs caused a substantial shortening of corporate debt maturities, exposing both corporations and financial institutions to additional risk.

A second asymmetry came from poorly sequenced deregulation of the capital account, especially after 1992. While foreign borrowing by financial institutions was comprehensively liberalized, foreign borrowing by nonfinancial firms, especially long-term borrowing, was not. This asymmetric treatment of financial and nonfinancial firms was partly due to recognition by the government that free access by the *chaebols* to low-cost foreign capital would cause a further concentration of economic power (D.-Y Choi, 2002). External borrowing through financial institutions was also preferred because the government was concerned about possible destabilizing impacts of volatile capital flows on the securities markets. The gradual deregulation of trade-related short-term corporate borrowing and aggressive short-term borrowing by the NBFIs, most notably the loosely regulated merchant banking corporations, produced a rapid increase in short-term external debt which exposed both the corporate and financial sectors to additional foreign exchange risk.[11]

But the most fundamental factor behind the pattern of corporate financing in the pre-crisis period was the government's implicit guarantee. The perceived risks of the financial products of the NBFIs and of new financing instruments like corporate bonds and commercial paper were no higher than those attached to similar bank products. This reflected the strong influence the *chaebols* had over NBFIs and the implicit government insurance extended to *chaebols*, based on the belief that they were too big to fail (Hahm, 2002). Furthermore, the government implemented policies effectively guaranteeing direct corporate debt in an attempt to foster direct financing and the capital markets. Corporate bonds were guaranteed by commercial banks, which contributed to the formation of the implicit government guarantee as commercial banks were perceived to be almost semi-public entities.

CORPORATE FINANCING IN THE POST-CRISIS PERIOD

Thus, by the mid-1990s Korea's economic system had become increasingly vulnerable to exogenous shocks. When a major terms-of-trade shock hit the economy in 1996–97, therefore, resulting in a steep decline in export prices, the consequent spate of corporate bankruptcies seriously jeopardized the soundness of the financial sector. The currency crisis that then erupted at the end of 1997 quickly widened into a full-fledged financial crisis.[12]

In an effort to overcome an economic crisis of unprecedented severity, the Korean government undertook a range of structural reforms, some new and some accelerated versions of reforms already underway before the crisis. In turn, these reforms affected the financing and asset allocation behavior of corporations and financial institutions. Changes in the pattern of corporate financing in the post-crisis period included those that follow.

An Increasing Share of Internal Financing

Internal financing had accounted for approximately 30 percent of total corporate financing before the crisis (as shown in Table 8.1). In the post-crisis period, that share rose to nearly 50 percent. In part this reflects the temporary decline in corporate investment in the face of heightened uncertainty, but the change also has a long-term structural aspect, reflecting shifts in attitudes in the corporate sector toward the perceived risks and attractiveness of relying on external financing.

Normalization of Direct Debt Financing

The share of direct financing in total corporate financial liabilities (shown in Figure 8.1) indicates a decline in 1997 followed by a sharp rise in 1998 and another fall in 2000. Table 8.1 reveals that the sharp rise in the share of direct financing in 1998 resulted from an increase in the share of corporate bonds. With the collapse of the merchant banking industry, the commercial paper market became paralyzed, and commercial bank and NBFI loans were in net redemption as those institutions adjusted their portfolios in an effort to comply with the BIS (Bank for International Settlements) capital adequacy ratio; hence the growing importance of bonds. Faced with a credit crunch, corporations, especially ailing *chaebols*, issued a large volume of bonds to address their liquidity problems.

Investment trust companies (ITCs) played a central role in intermediating these instruments.[13] In turn, reflationary monetary policy facilitated the rapid expansion of ITC funds.[14] The policy of allowing bond financing through ITCs while restructuring the banking system was intended to prevent a severe credit

Table 8.1 Structure of corporate finance (based upon annual flows)

	1985	1990	1995	1998	1999	2000
Total finance	100.0	100.0	100.0	100.0	100.0	100.0
Internal finance	37.1	28.2	29.2	49.7	49.4	–
External finance	62.9	71.8	70.8	50.3	50.6	–
Total external finance	100.0	100.0	100.0	100.0	100.0	100.0
Indirect finance	46.7	38.3	31.8	−56.6	4.1	17.1
Banks	29.4	15.7	14.9	2.5	29.2	35.2
NBFIs	17.3	22.6	16.9	−59.1	−25.0	−18.0
Direct finance	25.2	42.4	47.9	176.7	46.8	28.6
Stocks	10.8	14.2	17.5	52.5	82.6	35.6
Corporate bonds	13.4	21.5	15.3	163.9	−5.3	−3.2
Government bonds	0.7	2.9	−0.9	2.0	0.0	−2.2
Commercial papers	0.3	3.7	16.1	−41.7	−30.4	−1.7
Foreign borrowing	4.2	6.5	8.6	−33.7	24.1	23.7
Other	23.9	12.8	11.7	13.6	25.0	30.6

Notes:
Amounts in %.
Internal financing includes retained earnings, depreciation and amortization.
'Other' includes borrowings from the government and trade credits among corporate firms.

Source: Bank of Korea, *Understanding the Flow of Funds in Korea* (2002).

crunch and the failure of solvent firms. However, the high degree of control that the *chaebols* exercised over ITCs, combined with the belief that the *chaebols* were still too big to fail, aggravated distortions in the flow of funds. As a result, a large volume of funds flowed through the capital market into insolvent *chaebols* like Daewoo. Thus the authorities' sequential approach to financial restructuring – banks first, ITCs later – not only postponed the resolution of insolvent corporate firms but actually magnified the problem.[15]

With heightened uncertainty in the aftermath of Daewoo's collapse, the flow of funds reversed, shifting away from the ITC industry and toward commercial banks. Marking to market for ITC funds was introduced in July 2000, and the commercial banks discontinued the practice of guaranteeing corporate bond issues. Already in 1999, more than 90 percent of new corporate bond issues did not bear guarantees. As a result of these changes, the share of direct debt financing fell sharply in 1999–2000, reflecting the shrinkage of both the corporate bond and commercial paper markets.

Thus the dramatic fluctuations in the share of direct debt financing observed in the immediate pre- and post-crisis periods should be seen as temporary. The rapid expansion of the corporate bond and commercial paper markets in the pre-crisis period resulted from regulatory asymmetries and implicit government guarantees, neither of which were sustainable. The breakdown of the guarantee system implies that risk must now be fully priced in financial markets, and the recent shrinkage in direct debt financing reflects the prevalence of unusually high levels of credit risk during the restructuring period. Indeed, the share of direct financing in 2001 seems to have returned to a moderate, sustainable long-term path.

Improvements in the Maturity Structure of Direct Financing

The collapse of the merchant banking industry and commercial paper markets meant that corporations could no longer roll over short-term debt. As corporate borrowers redeemed commercial paper by issuing corporate bonds and stocks, the share of short-term debt in total direct financing fell sharply (as shown in Figure 8.1).

The Fall of the NBFIs and Re-emergence of Commercial Banks

As depositors and investors began to perceive risks associated with NBFI financial products and with the resolution of insolvent NBFIs, the share of NBFIs in indirect financing, which had exceeded 50 percent in the 1990s, fell sharply in the post-crisis period (as shown in Figure 8.1). Depositors' preference for safety helped the commercial banks to reclaim their share of the market, especially once they had succeeded in restoring the adequacy of their capital, with the help of the government's bank recapitalization program.

COMMERCIAL BANK PORTFOLIO STRUCTURE IN THE POST-CRISIS PERIOD

The crisis and restructuring also gave rise to important changes in asset allocation by financial institutions. The main features of this transition are summarized below.

Rise in the Share of Securities and Decline in the Share of Loans

A particularly visible change in the portfolios of commercial banks is the sharp rise in the share of securities. With the government's policies to foster the development of Korean capital markets, the share of securities in the bank balance sheet started to rise in the early 1990s (see Figure 8.2). That rise accelerated in the post-1997 period, reflecting the commercial banks' prefer-

Financial restructuring 179

Share of loans vs securities in bank domestic assets

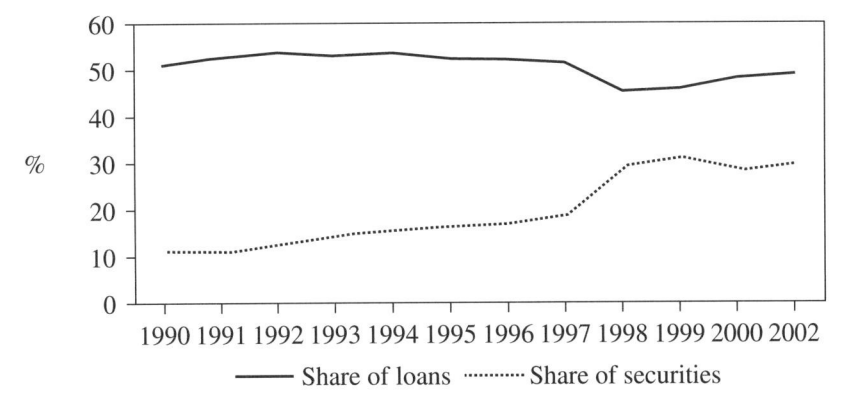

— Share of loans ········ Share of securities

Share of government bonds vs corporate bonds in bank security holdings

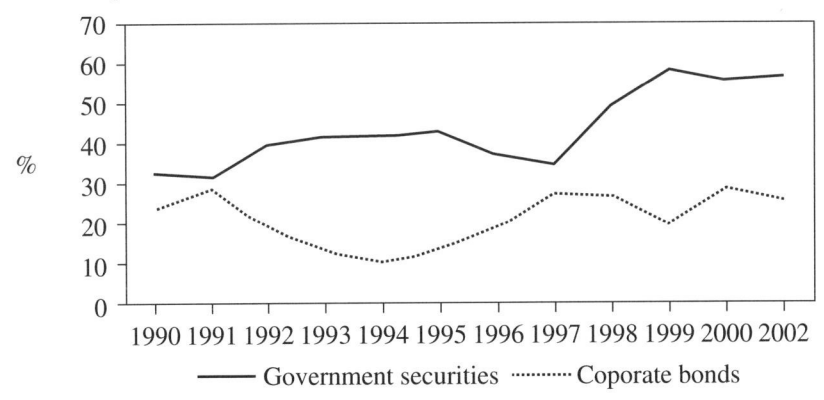

— Government securities ········ Coporate bonds

Share of corporate loans vs computer loans in total bank loans

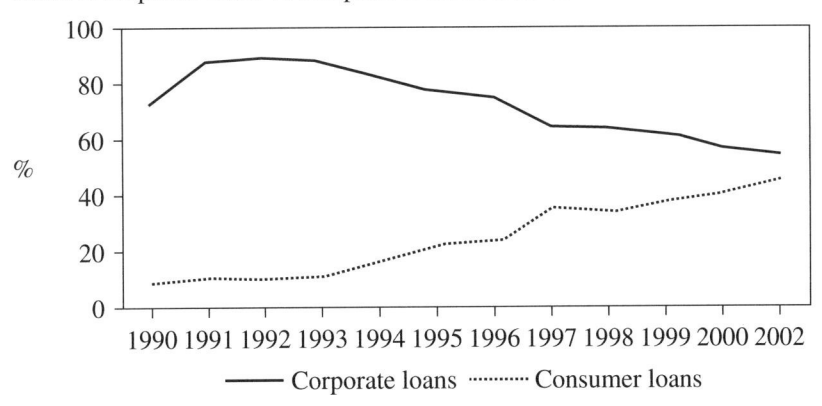

— Corporate loans ········ Consumer loans

Source: Bank of Korea, *Database on Flow of Funds Account* (various issues).

Figure 8.2 The transition in commercial bank portfolio structure

ence for safer and more liquid assets as well as holdings of investment securities generated in the process of corporate restructuring (such as stocks and convertible bonds obtained through debt/equity swaps). The share of loans dropped in 1998 and remained low in 1999, as commercial banks sought to reduce their credit risk by refusing to refinance existing loans. In 2000, however, the share of loans began to recover, along with the economy.

Increase in the Share of Government Securities

Government securities account for most of the increase in the securities holdings of commercial banks in the immediate post-crisis period (Figure 8.2). As noted above, banks preferred safer assets and converted private credits into government securities to prop up their capital ratios. The development of treasury debt markets accelerated once the government began running budget deficits and issuing additional debt. The emergence of the treasury bond market and the adoption of the marking to market valuation system in July 2000 contributed further to the development of a more active and liquid fixed income market. Reflationary monetary policies and the decline in market interest rates also induced banks to invest in government bonds. Finally, in the recapitalization process, commercial banks in which the government intervened received bonds issued by the Korea Deposit Insurance Corporation (KDIC).

Increase in the Share of Consumer Loans and Decrease in Corporate Loans

The share of loans in commercial bank assets gradually recovered to pre-crisis levels, but there was also a shift in underlying composition away from loans to enterprises and toward loans to households. This trend was already evident before the crisis: the share of loans to enterprises had in fact been in decline since 1992, although this movement further accelerated in 1997 (Figure 8.2). As a result, the share of consumer loans – loans to households and loans for housing – doubled from 20 percent in 1996 to 40 percent in 2000.

Two factors underlie this shift. One is the development of the capital markets and increasing availability of direct financing for corporations with good credit. The other is the change in the risk appetite of the commercial banks themselves. As banks recognized the importance of credit risk management, they sought to reduce loan concentrations by introducing exposure limits on corporate loans. This led them increasingly to emphasize more diversified consumer loans.

EVALUATING THE POST-CRISIS TRANSITION

The preceding discussion implies that the Korean financial system had already been experiencing significant structural change even before the crisis. While some of the subsequent changes were temporary responses by financial institutions and corporations to the heightened uncertainties caused by the crisis and restructuring, it cannot be denied that the financial crisis was a catalyst for major institutional reforms and brought about fundamental changes in the behavior of financial market participants.

How, then, should we characterize the transformation? Specifically, has there been a fundamental change in the relationship between providers and users of financial capital following the crisis?

Following the conventional dichotomy that divides financial systems into bank- and market-based or relationship-based and arm's-length systems, it can be argued that the Korean financial system is undergoing a transition from the first to the second of these models.[16] In general, there is no consensus on which model is superior, although there are arguments that the alternatives have comparative advantages at different stages of economic development. Rajan and Zingales (1998) argue that although the relationship-based system may be superior in less developed countries where contracts are hard to enforce and it is relatively easy to find productive investment opportunities, that system becomes increasingly conducive to massive resource misallocation as the economy grows and capital becomes abundant, because that allocation is not based on price signals. In effect, the market-based system has advantages in periods of technological uncertainty when investors need to take bets on competing technologies, while the bank-based system has advantages when technological uncertainty is low and growth depends mainly on the mobilization of savings for investments in known technologies. A bank-based system would perform well when the economy is in the phase of extensive growth where capital accumulation is more important for development, but a transition toward a market-based system is required as the economy increasingly depends upon intensive growth, where innovation, flexibility and technological uncertainty are critical.[17]

From this perspective, it is interesting to note that Korea had a relatively sizable and active capital market before the crisis. According to Demirgüç-Kunt and Levine (1999), pre-crisis Korean financial markets were sufficiently well developed that the country's financial system already deserved to be classified as market based.[18] This is in contrast to other authors, such as Y. Park (1993), who regard the pre-crisis Korean system as bank based. Demirgüç-Kunt and Levine point out that Korea already had a relatively active and efficient equity market, and that the market share of NBFIs exceeded that of commercial banks. However, as emphasized above, the growth of NBFIs and

Size index (stock market capitalization/deposit money bank assets)

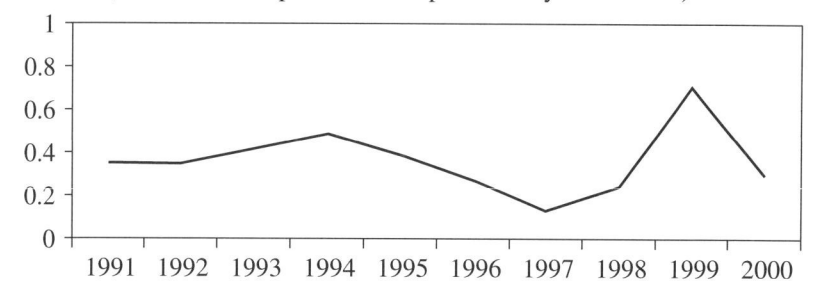

Activity index (stock trading value/DMB private credit)

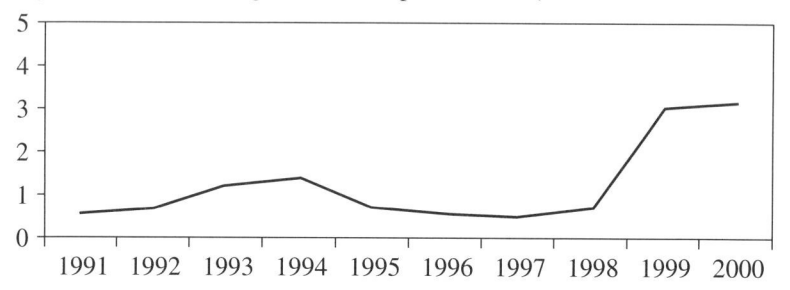

Efficiency index (bank net interest margin × stock trading value/GDP)

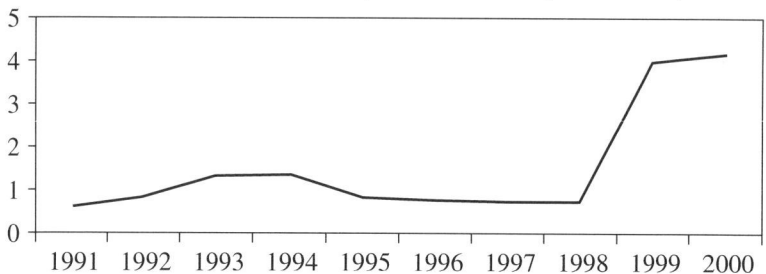

Composite index

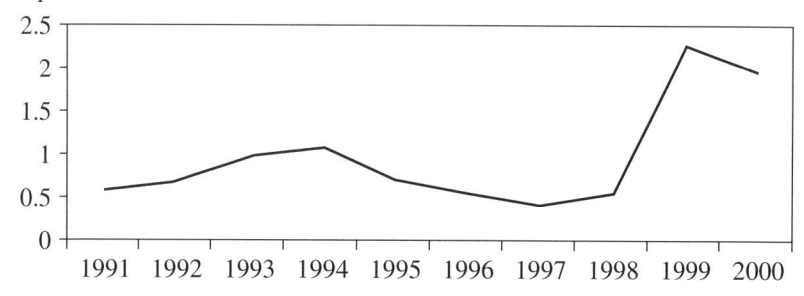

Source: Bank of Korea, *Monthly Bulletin* (various issues).

Figure 8.3 Indicators of the transistion toward a market-based financial system

direct debt financing through such vehicles as corporate bonds and commercial paper during the 1990s was a result of unbalanced financial liberalization and the implicit guarantee extended by the government. Direct debt instruments were often guaranteed by commercial banks, and NBFIs were heavily controlled by the *chaebols* that were regarded as too big to fail. Hence, the importance of direct finance and nonbank financial intermediation was not a normal market development. It may be misleading, therefore, to characterize the Korean system as market based.

Figure 8.3 shows the time-series behavior of the size, activity and efficiency measures developed by Demirgüç-Kunt and Levine as a way of characterizing the development of the Korean financial system over time. Note that the size index fluctuates wildly. While the shares of corporate bonds and commercial paper contracted in the post-crisis period, the share of stocks in corporate financing increased sharply. In contrast, the activity and efficiency indices show a clear transition toward a more market-based system in the post-crisis period. Consequently, the composite index in Figure 8.3 suggests that the Korean system is evolving in the direction of a more market-based system.[19]

BANK CONSOLIDATION AND REMAINING TASKS FOR RESTRUCTURING

Unlike countries where bank consolidation occurred voluntarily as a natural way of reaping economies of scale and scope, bank consolidation in Korea responded to government impetus.[20] The number of commercial banks declined by 42 percent, from 26 in 1997 to 15 as of December 2001 (as shown in Table 8.2), and the number of branches and employees in the commercial banking industry declined by 20 percent and 40 percent, respectively. Note that consolidation has brought about a substantial increase in the average value of commercial bank assets, which has increased by 84 percent from its 1997 base. Consolidation has also solidified the dominance of a few large banks, as evidenced by the increase in the asset shares of the top five banks since 1997.[21]

As a result of the restructuring program, both capital adequacy and profitability have improved (as shown in Table 8.2). The BIS capital adequacy ratio has exceeded 10 percent since 1999, and the share of nonperforming loans (NPLs) classified as substandard or below fell sharply to 3 percent, from more than 13 percent in 1999. To the extent that asset classification criteria have been strengthened during the restructuring period, the rapid fall in NPL ratios since 1999 implies that a substantial number of bad loans have been resolved in the last three years.[22]

Table 8.2 Consolidation and performance of the commercial banking industry

Consolidation indicators (end-of-period values)	1993	1995	1997	1999	2000	2001
Number of commercial banks	24	25	26	17	17	15 (−42.3)
Number of branches	3317	4557	5987	4780	4709	4776 (−20.2)
Number of employees (1000s)	87.7	103.2	113.9	74.7	70.6	68.4 (−39.9)
Total bank assets (trillions)*	232.9	395.6	606.6	562.3	582.6	641.4 (5.7)
Average bank assets (trillions)	9.7	15.8	23.3	33.1	34.3	42.8 (83.7)
Share of top five banks** in assets (%)	44.0	48.4	45.3	57.8	59.6	70.1

Financial indicators (%)	1994	1995	1996	1997	1998	1999	2000	2001
BIS capital ratio	10.6	9.3	9.1	7.0	8.2	10.8	10.8	10.8
NPL ratio***	5.8	5.2	4.1	6.0	7.4	13.6	8.8	3.3
ROA****	0.4	0.3	0.3	−0.9	−3.3	−1.3	−0.6	0.8
ROE****	6.1	4.2	3.8	−14.2	−52.5	−23.1	−11.9	15.9

Notes:
Figures in parentheses denote percentage changes from 1997 values.
   * Including trust accounts.
  ** Kukmin, Hanvit, Chohung, Shinhan, Hana Bank.
 *** Ratio of assets classified as substandard or below.
**** During the period, including trust accounts.

Source: Financial Supervisory Service, *Bank Management Statistics* (various issues).

Figure 8.4 shows the pre-provision profit, provisions, and net profit of commercial banks in the post-crisis period. The total amount of provisions accumulated during the 1998 to 2001 period is 35.6 trillion won, while the pre-provision profits accumulated during the same period is only 20 trillion won. With continuous NPL resolution efforts and the improving bank business environment, pre-provision profit began to exceed provisions in 2001, and commercial banks finally began recording profits.

Notwithstanding these positive developments, the profitability and asset quality of Korean banks remain weak by international standards. As a result, there remain significant risks to the system. Removing them requires pushing ahead with the reforms outlined below.

Figure 8.4 Pre-provision profit, provisioning and net profit of commercial banks

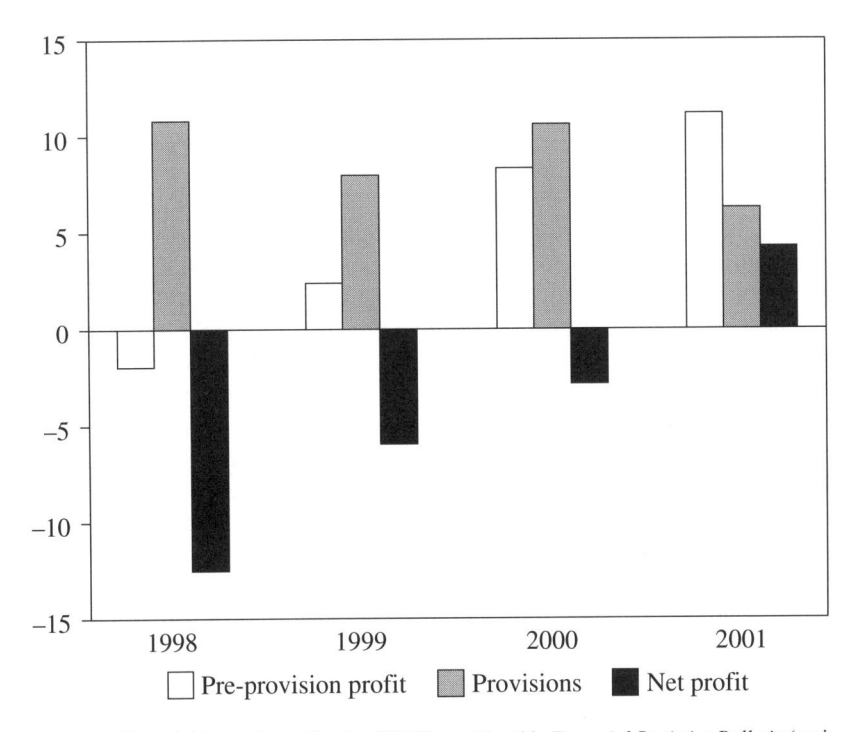

Sources: Financial Supervisory Service (2001) and *Monthly Financial Statistics Bulletin* (various issues).

Improving Borrower Credit Ratings

The debt service capacity of the corporate sector remains weak, although much improved since 1998. Banks have accumulated provisions against credit risks following the forward-looking criteria (FLC) adopted in 2000. But many loans to problem firms are still classified as 'precautionary' – an asset category just above the 'substandard' – which indicates that banks still retain a nontrivial amount of assets that could become problematic if macroeconomic fundamentals were to begin to deteriorate again.[23]

Risk-Based Pricing

It is not easy to reduce loan exposure to problem borrowers, since refusing to refinance can lead to immediate default by those ailing firms and an increase in NPLs for the banks themselves. An alternative is to establish and apply an effective pricing scheme so that the risk premium and expected losses can be appropriately priced when interest rates are renegotiated.

Increasing Profitability

Relatively low loan–deposit spreads and high provision rates have been the main causes of the poor profitability of Korean banks (Ji, 2000; D. Lee and Kim, 2001). The loan–deposit spread increased sharply in 1998, reflecting heightened uncertainty and liquidity preference during the crisis period. Spreads then declined in 1999 and 2000 as market interest rates fell, but widened again in 2001 as a large volume of liquidity flowed into the relatively safe banking sector in the then-prevailing low interest rate environment.

Understanding bank profitability requires considering the cost side as well. The consolidation in the banking sector significantly lowered operating costs, and provisioning requirements fell sharply in 2001.[24] Unfortunately, there now seems to be little room for further improvements in cost efficiency. Nor does there appear to be much scope for increasing the loan–deposit spread, given the growth of competition in the loan market. To maintain profitability in the traditional lines of business, the commercial banks will have to rely on increasing the efficiency of their credit evaluation procedures.

This discussion implies that the scope for further increases in bank profitability will be limited unless the banks restructure their loan portfolios. Traditional loan–deposit business is becoming increasingly competitive as depositors become more interest-rate-sensitive. At the same time, it is becoming more difficult to retain good credit borrowers who have access to a wide range of instruments of direct financing. Banks need to restructure their business portfolios toward higher-value-added businesses and to expand their provision of fee-based services. The share of fee income in gross operating income for Korean commercial banks was under 28 percent 2001, which is much lower than that of the leading international banks, among whom this ratio often reaches 40 percent. Moreover, the fee income of Korean banks includes interest income from credit card loans, while genuine fee-based businesses such as mergers and acquisitions, corporate restructuring, and asset and wealth management still remain at the early stages of development.

Strengthening of Core Capital Adequacy

Capital adequacy plays a pivotal role in the propagation of financial crises (Hahm and Mishkin, 2000). Hence, it is worrisome that the core capital position of Korean banks is still weak by the standards of their major international competitors (D. Lee and Kim, 2001). In an attempt to increase their capital adequacy during the restructuring period, Korean banks issued substantial amounts of subordinated debt, which is counted as Tier 2 capital according to the Basel standards. The share of Tier 1 capital out of total capital for Korean banks was 63 percent in 1999, while the corresponding ratio was well above 70 percent in most other countries (D. Lee and Kim, 2001). Relying on subordinated debt allows depositors and supervisors to make use of the market's evaluation of the risk characteristics of commercial banks. However, excessive dependence by banks on subordinated debt raises the cost of capital and may also have a negative impact on profitability.

Upgrading Risk Management and Credit Allocation Practices

While financial intermediaries have strengthened their risk management capacities, a genuine culture of risk management has yet to be established. It is imperative to establish an internal institutional channel through which risk considerations are systematically linked to key bank portfolio strategies. For this, incentive and reward systems need to be upgraded to reflect risks appropriately.

Notwithstanding efforts to upgrade credit allocation practices, much still remains to be done. Rough and ready BIS capital-based credit management must be replaced with more sophisticated practices based on concepts like capital at risk, and both large exposure limits and limits based on individual debt service capacity must be implemented and monitored. Transparency in the loan approval process must be enhanced, and that process should take into consideration bank-wide credit risks, not only the risk of specific loans.

TOWARD A MARKET-BASED SYSTEM

The ultimate goal of capital market reform is to establish a robust infrastructure for a market-based financial system. Critical to this process is enhancing the transparency and credibility of information so that market participants can efficiently monitor the ultimate users of finance. Accordingly, various reform measures have been implemented to improve the transparency and accountability of corporate governance and to upgrade accounting and disclosure systems. Measures designed to improve corporate governance and the reliability of information include the introduction of outside directors and audit committees, upgrading internal accounting and compliance systems, repeal of M&A (merger and acquisition)-related regulations, strengthening of minority shareholders' rights, and the reform of accounting standard and regulations on external audits.

Additional factors accelerating the transition toward a more market-based system include the growing role of foreign investors in the Korean market, reflecting on ongoing integration of capital markets on a global scale, and the growing frequency of cross-border M&A transactions, which tend to speed the convergence of accounting and governance standards across countries. Indeed, Korean capital markets have expanded substantially since 1997, with the increasing participation of foreign investors.[25] Nevertheless, the corporate governance practices in Korea are still regarded as poor, and the phenomenon of the 'Korea discount' in the stock market is often regarded as reflecting the relatively poor governance practices of Korea's corporate sector (H.-S Chang 2002).

The withdrawal of the government's implicit guarantee for corporate bonds and the breakdown of the too-big-to-fail belief have worked in the other direction, shrinking the share of direct debt finance, at least temporarily.[26] But the impact of these developments was damped when, as emergency measures to support corporate bond refinancing of ailing firms, the government introduced a 'fast underwriting system' for corporate bonds and various asset-backed securities such as primary collateralized bond obligations (CBOs) and secondary CBOs with public guarantees attached.[27] The contraction of the direct debt market has been limited as a result of the operation of these government support schemes.

Given the underdevelopment of bond markets for high-risk, sub-investment-grade borrowers, government support may have been indispensable for preventing additional failures of solvent but illiquid firms. The cost of this support was to delay the exit of insolvent firms. The implication is that government support should be withdrawn as the credit crunch continues to recede. Already, with the reduction in uncertainty, the issuance of BBB grade corporate bonds is increasing rapidly, and a stable risk premium on sub-investment-grade bonds has been established, as if the operation of the corporate bond market is beginning to normalize.[28] Meanwhile, the range of financial products has expanded enormously. Mutual funds and real estate investment trusts (REITs) as well as various asset-backed securities such as collateralized bond (loan) obligations have been introduced, which will further facilitate direct financing and contribute to the deepening of the capital markets.

CONCLUDING REMARKS

Korea is currently in a structural transition toward a more market-based financial system. While this will promote efficiency by endowing the country with a financial system better suited to its current stage of economic development, that transition also brings with it risks and challenges.

The transition implies that further banking sector consolidation will be required. The demand for bank loans will shrink as borrowers acquired easier access to direct financing.[29] Furthermore, increased competition among domestic banks and foreign entrants will raise banks' funding costs and squeeze margins. As observed above, the capital adequacy of Korean banks is not robust, and impaired balance sheets have not yet been fully repaired. Marginal banks will ultimately exit the industry, and it is the task of the regulators to ensure that this process of exit occurs in an orderly way, without negative side effects. Until now, bank consolidation has been driven by the government. Future consolidation, if it is to succeed in enhancing efficiency and profitability, will have to be driven by market forces.

The transition presents new risks for surviving banks. Hoshi and Kashyap (1999) have observed that capital market deregulation in Japan allowed large firms to become increasingly independent of banks in their financing. But because regulation was less favorable to savers, banks continued to receive large inflows of funds and had to search for new places to invest their balances. Increasingly, bank liquidity was channeled into risky investments like real estate and construction loans. This experience holds important lessons for Korea, which already shows signs of developing similar symptoms. Regulators must be vigilant for signs that banks, in response to the loss of their traditional customers, are funneling their liquidity into high-risk markets like construction and real estate. As capital markets develop, their regulators must take care to provide access to savers as well as borrowers, so that funds can be channeled to the capital markets; in turn, this requires the development of appropriate investment vehicles (mutual funds, pension funds, and the like). With the transition toward a market-based system, banks also need to develop their corporate financing and investment banking businesses so that they can continue to provide financing to customers with good credit. Doing so will make it easier for banks to restructure their business portfolios by increasing the share of fee-based businesses. Bank regulators need to facilitate this transition by providing a flexible regulatory environment.

At the same time, prudential supervision of banking activities must be strengthened. Supervisors must keep tabs on the effects, both positive and negative, of the erosion of restrictions on bank funding and lending practices and of the risks that banks are taking in the pursuit of higher earnings. As the banks' own risk management practices become even more important for the stability of the financial system, the focus of the supervision must also be shifted from static capital adequacy to a dynamic form of supervision focusing on the soundness of internal control processes. Supervisory discipline must work hand in hand with market discipline; this means relying more on market-based regulation, by *inter alia* applying differential deposit insurance premiums according to the level of risk perceived by the market, based for instance on the yield on bank subordinated debentures.

There is also the prospect that ongoing consolidation will produce an industry dominated by a small number of large banks. Not only does this create a danger of oligopolistic behavior, but it could also create a situation where banks were regarded as too big and too few to fail; there would be an incentive for regulatory forbearance as the failure of one or more large banks could jeopardize the stability of the entire financial system. Knowledge that this was the case could weaken the incentive for depositors to monitor banks and penalize them for taking excessive risks.

It is urgent, therefore, to devise a regulatory framework capable of preventing excessive risk taking and limiting the other effects of moral hazard on the part of large banks. The authorities must clearly announce and consistently apply the least-cost principle of bank resolution. While they should be concerned with systemic risk and provide official support for banks that are innocent bystanders and at risk of collateral damage, they should not bail out problem banks that are the source of financial problems (Hahm and Mishkin, 2000).

Finally, the transition toward a market-based system also implies the development of other sources of systemic risk. The shift in household assets from insured bank deposits to nonbank institutions and capital markets represents a *de facto* reduction in the safety net, which could render financial markets more fragile. No doubt the growth of collective investment institutions such as investment trusts and mutual funds will encourage the depth and diversification of the financial system. However, there may in fact be less diversification than meets the eye; as shown in the recent failure of investment trust companies related with Daewoo, the collapse of confidence in some of those institutions may precipitate a massive sell-off of securities, causing a financial crisis. The growing use of financial derivatives also has the capacity to destabilize the system.

But extending bank-like regulation and safety nets to nonbank financial institutions is not the answer; doing so would only aggravate moral hazard and distortions in resource allocation (as argued by Edwards, 1996). To cope with the risks presented by the transformation of the Korean financial system, the only effective solution is to strengthen market discipline – that is, to create an environment in which market participants have an incentive to monitor risks. This means that the financial market infrastructure must be strengthened further. Establishing a well-functioning governance system at financial institutions and providing the information needed for that governance system to operate is thus the key step in building a truly robust financial system.

NOTES

1. I thank Hyunwook Park for his excellent research assistance.
2. See, for instance, Borensztein and Lee (1998), Hahn (1999), Claessens et al. (2000) and B.K. Lee (2000) for corporate investment behavior in pre-crisis Korea; Shin and Hahm (1998) and Hahm and Mishkin (2000) for vulnerability of the financial sector and propagation of the crisis; and J.-K. Kim (1999), Y. Cho (1999) and C. Lee et al. (2000) for *chaebols* and financial liberalization policies in the 1990s.
3. The bank credit control system was formally incorporated into the revised Banking Act in 1982. In 1987, the basket credit control system was introduced to limit directly the shares of bank loans to the 30 largest *chaebols*.
4. The share of loans received by the top five *chaebols* in total deposit money bank loans fell from over 12 percent in 1988 to less than 6 percent in 1991.
5. According to the flow-of-funds account, total corporate financial liabilities include equity financing as well as debt financing.
6. D.-Y. Choi (2002) argued that the introduction of quotas in corporate bond issuance in March 1992 and the adoption of the bank credit regulation in April 1995 to directly limit the gross sum of large bank loans below 500 percent of bank capital substantially reduced the availability of corporate bond and bank loan financing for *chaebols*, and that the regulatory shifts led *chaebols* to commercial paper financing, which was not heavily regulated.
7. In contrast to commercial banks, no outright ownership restriction was applied to NBFIs. In the absence of transparent entry requirements, discretionary issuance of licenses resulted in the increasing ownership of NBFIs by *chaebols*. The influence of *chaebols* over NBFIs had been increasing from the 1980s and its dominance culminated at the onset of the financial crisis. For instance, according to J.-K. Kim (1999), the 70 largest *chaebols* owned 114 NBFIs at the end of 1997, which was approximately 23 percent of all NBFIs. However, in terms of asset size, the dominance was much bigger since many of the large NBFIs were owned by *chaebols*. For instance, the top 70 *chaebols* owned 14 merchant banks, 12 securities houses, 10 investment trust companies and 14 life insurance companies at the end of 1997.
8. See Hahm (2002) for more detailed discussions of the evolution of corporate financing and bank credit allocation patterns during the liberalization and pre-crisis periods in Korea.
9. For example, Hahm (2002) reported an increase in the incremental capital–output ratio (ICOR) in Korea in the 1990s relative to the 1980s, which indicates that aggregate investment efficiency was deteriorating in the 1990s. For more direct micro-evidence on the efficiency of credit allocations in pre-crisis Korea, see Borensztein and Lee (1998). Borensztein and Lee (1999) also argued that credits appear to have been reallocated in favor of more efficient firms after the 1997 crisis relative to the pre-crisis episode. As for the *chaebols*' investment behavior in the pre-crisis period, Hahn (1999) reported evidence that the *chaebols* in fact preferred riskier businesses in expectation of loss protection from the government.
10. Throughout the late 1970s and 1980s, the government encouraged the establishment of NBFIs and applied lenient regulations to them in order to absorb informal financial agents into the formal financial system. In the 1980s, the government further liberalized the NBFIs as a second-best strategy for including banks in a more comprehensive liberalization of the financial system. The government continued to control bank credit for policy purposes (Y. Cho and Kim, 1997).
11. The short-term external debt ratio in Korea increased from 58.8 percent in 1992 to 65.8 percent in 1994.
12. See Hahm and Mishkin (2000) for detailed descriptions of the propagation mechanism of the financial crisis in Korea.
13. The balance of ITC funds expanded sharply from 121 trillion won in June 1998 to 258 trillion won in April 1999.

14. The benchmark three-year corporate bond yield decreased from 16 percent in June 1998 to 7 percent in April 1999. While the market interest rate was low, the ITCs were able to offer relatively higher returns on their funds by pooling previously issued higher yield bonds with newly issued lower yield bonds. This practice was possible as the ITC funds were valued according to the book value and not marked to market.
15. Oh and Rhee (2001) found that 43 percent of total corporate bonds issued in 1998 eventually became nonperforming and argued that the 'bank-first, ITC-later' restructuring policy of the government delayed the resolution of nonviable corporate firms and magnified the amount of distressed debt in the financial system. In recognition of the problem, in July 1998 the government imposed a limit on the volume of commercial paper issued by a *chaebol* group that a financial institution could hold. A similar regulation was introduced for corporate bonds in October 1998.
16. While the former is a distinction based on corporate financing behavior, the latter is based on the nature of financial transactions and contracts. The bank-based financial system emphasizes relationship banking as an effective tool of information production and reduction in agency cost. In this relationship-based system, financial contracts are implicit and long term, and the reputation matters as a means of enforcement (Diamond, 1991). Risks are shared intertemporally, which in turn implies less variation in risk premiums across projects of the same borrower over time. Monitoring functions are often housed in a leading bank, which selects and monitors borrowers and intervenes in case of corporate failure. Banks often provide subsidies to younger firms that are subject to severe information asymmetry and to temporarily distressed firms, as banks have some degree of monopoly power to extract compensation later when firms become mature and get out of financial trouble (Allen and Gale, 1997; Rajan and Zingales, 1998). In the market-based system, capital markets play a central role in aggregating and processing diverse information, allocating financial capital and monitoring firms. Institutional investors and information service providers such as credit rating agencies facilitate monitoring functions of the capital market. Transactions are short-term-oriented in nature and prices are determined based on the risk and expected return of the respective project. Risk sharing is intratemporal and providers of capital are protected by explicit contracts where legal enforcement is essential. For the system to work efficiently, diverse and publicly available information is critical, and, naturally, transparency and strong disclosure requirements are emphasized.
17. In a similar vein, C. Chang (2000) argued that while the government-directed credit allocation in a centralized financial system is not likely to significantly misallocate resources in the early development stage when low labor costs are important, a financial system that promotes security trading is more likely to guide efficient resource allocation in the more advanced development stage.
18. Demirgüç-Kunt and Levine (1999) constructed a composite index of financial structure based on measures of size, activity and efficiency to characterize the financial systems of 150 countries. The size index was the ratio of domestic stock market capitalization relative to the domestic assets of deposit money banks, and the activity index was the ratio of the total value of stock transactions on domestic exchanges relative to private credit by deposit money banks. They used two measures of efficiency index: total value of stock transactions/GDP multiplied by bank overhead costs, and total value of stock transactions/GDP multiplied by the bank net interest margin. The composite index was constructed as a demeaned average of the above three measures. Korea obtained 0.89 for the composite structure index compared to overall mean of 0.03. Sweden, the UK, Singapore, the US, Switzerland, Hong Kong and Malaysia were the countries ranked as more market-based than Korea.
19. The evidence must be interpreted with caution in that the activity and efficiency indices will also be affected by the fluctuation in stock prices if transactions value is significantly related with stock prices.
20. From November 1997 to June 2001, the Korean government has mobilized and allocated public funds of 137.5 trillion won (27 percent of the year 2000 nominal GDP), out of which 81.4 trillion won (59.2 percent) was used for recapitalization and NPL resolution in the banking sector.

21. K. Kim (2002) studied the degree of concentration in the Korean banking industry and found that the share of the top five banks in deposit markets increased from 47 percent in 1997 to 70.1 percent after the merger of Kookmin and Housing & Commercial Bank in November 2001. The Herfindahl–Hirschman index also increased during the same period. Kim noted that the degree of concentration in the Korean banking industry is higher than in the US or Japan and similar to the average of European countries, and argued that the increasing degree of concentration may cause potential problems, including unfair pricing, ineffective monetary policy transmission and magnified systemic risk.
22. From November 1997 to June 2001, the government spent 24 trillion won to resolve bad loan problems of commercial banks mainly through the NPL purchase program of the Korea Asset Management Corporation (KAMCO). Commercial banks themselves have also used up most of the operating income generated for loan loss provisioning and NPL write-offs.
23. The precautionary assets accounted for 3 percent to 8 percent of total assets at major commercial banks in Korea as of December 2001.
24. Financial intermediation cost is the total cost related with the deposit and loan-making businesses and is computed as the sum of operating expense, loan loss provision, taxes and other expenses. The ratio of operating expenses to total bank assets decreased to the 1 percent level in 2000 and 2001 from the pre-crisis 2 percent level. The financial intermediation cost ratio fell below the pre-crisis level to 2.1 percent in 2001 as loan loss provisions fell sharply.
25. The combined market capitalization of the Korea stock exchange and KOSDAQ more than doubled from 145.7 trillion won at the end of 1998 to 307.7 trillion won at the end of 2001. The outstanding volume of the bond markets also increased rapidly during the same three-year period, from 336.1 trillion won to 483.1 trillion won. The share of foreign investors in the stock market in terms of market capitalization increased from 18.6 percent at the end of 1998 to 36.6 percent at the end of 2001.
26. The share of guaranteed bonds out of general corporate bonds issued fell sharply from 85.1 percent in 1997 to 3.5 percent in 2001.
27. Under the 'fast underwriting system,' the Korea Development Bank first underwrote 80 percent of maturing corporate bonds and then those bonds were redistributed to creditor banks and primary CBO funds. To qualify for fast underwriting, the applicant was required to obtain agreement from creditor banks and the Credit Guarantee Fund on the viability of the candidate firm.
28. According to the Bank of Korea, the share of BBB grade bonds in total general corporate bonds issued increased rapidly from 21.2 percent in December 2001 to 48.9 percent in January 2002, and to 53 percent in February 2002.
29. Note that corporate bond yields are in general lower than bank loan rates as better credit borrowers have access to the capital markets. However, the rates have traditionally been reversed in Korea, indicating that bank loans have been subsidized. As a result, a significant distortion between direct debt financing and loan financing has persisted. The distortion will be gradually eliminated as banks try to reflect appropriate risk premiums into loan rates, and the correction will further accelerate the shift of good credit borrowers to the capital markets.

9. Corporate restructuring

Sung Wook Joh

INTRODUCTION

Without question, weaknesses in the corporate sector played a major role in the Korean crisis. The low rates of profitability characteristic of Korean corporations in the decade leading up to the crisis, and the financial problems of the country's large conglomerates (or *chaebols*) in particular, are consistent with the argument that problems in the nonfinancial sector were what rendered Korea so susceptible to the contagion from abroad. A weak system of corporate governance had allowed sub-par rates of profitability to persist, uncorrected, for years. Six of the country's 30 largest conglomerates had failed, their meager profits being insufficient to cover their debt servicing costs, even before the crisis broke out in Thailand and spread to the rest of the East Asian countries (Joh, 2001b). The failure of these large firms weakened the position of Korean financial institutions, saddling them with enormous loads of bad debt. Alarmed by these developments, foreign investors sold off their holdings of Korean equities, and foreign banks demanded repayment of the short-term loans they had extended to Korean financial institutions, bringing the crisis of November–December 1997 to a head.

In this chapter, I describe the structural environment that allowed these deep-seated problems to develop. I then examine how Korea's weak system of corporate governance, along with supportive government policies, allowed poorly performing firms to remain afloat for so long. Finally, I summarize the measures taken since the crisis to reform corporate governance and strengthen the performance of the financial sector generally, and offer a preliminary assessment of the effectiveness of those reforms.

CRISIS AND CORPORATE SECTOR PROBLEMS

The conventional wisdom regarding the Korean crisis emphasizes financial factors. Domestically, supervision and regulation of the country's newly liberalized financial sector was inadequate.[1] Internationally, financial markets were disturbed by turmoil in Thailand and Indonesia, which worked to undermine investor confidence in other Asian economies, including Korea.[2]

But while these domestic and international financial factors undoubtedly played a role in the Korean crisis, they were not the entire story, or even the most important part. Korea was particularly susceptible to destabilization by these financial developments because of the weakness and vulnerability of its corporate sector. This weakness and vulnerability explain why the crisis hit Korea harder than Taiwan and certain other East Asian economies.

Both international and intertemporal comparisons highlight problems in the corporate sector. Krueger and Yoo (2001) show that corporate profitability was lower in Korea than in other countries. They provide evidence that corporate profitability had been declining for some time. Joh (2001a,b) shows that the average rate of return on equity was often lower than the borrowing cost of capital. She argues that such poor performance forced some firms to make interest payments only by incurring additional debt. It would appear, by these measures, that much of the capital used in the corporate sector had been spent on unprofitable investment projects.

Some will wonder how Korea grew so rapidly given the poor performance of its corporate sector. Excessive rates of investment that reached the point of severely diminishing returns could, of course, reconcile rapid growth with poor profitability. But it is hard to argue that corporate investment in general had reached the point of diminishing returns. Korea had not yet approached the technological frontier defined by the most advanced industrial countries; in principle, there was still ample scope for profitable investment to close this gap. To be sure, some industries subsidized or otherwise supported by the government may have invested beyond the point where their investments offered normal rates of return on capital; for this reason they may have encountered diminishing returns. The returns on investment in these industries reflected the artificially low cost of capital made available by the government and artificially low corporate income taxes.[3] Investing in response to these incentives may have been rational for the individual firm, but it was not rational for society. In other words, investment in these industries exceeded socially optimal levels and drew resources from other, more socially productive activities.

Korean investment rates rose still further in the 1990s, and the returns, gauged in terms of output, were even more disappointing. Hahm (2002) shows that the incremental capital–output ratio rose still further between the second half of the 1980s and the first half of the 1990s. Inefficient *chaebols* drew more resources from banks and nonbank financial institutions than did the country's independent firms. While the *chaebols* thereby raised their investment rates still further, the returns on that investment, whether measured in terms of output or profits, were disappointing.[4]

Poor Corporate Performance

To analyze the determinants of corporate financial performance, I utilize data compiled by National Information Credit Evaluation, Inc. in the period 1993–97, the five years leading up to the crisis. In the Korean context, accounting data are likely to provide a better measure of performance than stock prices, since stock prices are easily manipulated and only a small, less than representative fraction of Korean firms has had publicly traded shares.[5] Previous studies have shown that accounting measures have information content useful for predicting bankruptcy (Altman, 1968; Takahashi et al., 1984) and financial distress (Hoshi et al., 1991), two important manifestations of the general phenomenon of poor corporate performance.

Once financial institutions and government-controlled firms are eliminated, I have 19 587 observations for manufacturing firms subject to outside auditing. I use these to ask whether the affiliates of *chaebols* outperformed independent firms, or vice versa, and whether concentrated ownership was good or bad for profitability. I also examine the hypothesis that a situation where owners held more control rights than warranted by their ownership rights was bad for the firm's performance. When a controlling shareholder's rights exceed his ownership rights, he has an incentive to expropriate the firm's resources. Expropriation is more likely when the disparity between control and ownership is large and when the position of the controlling shareholder is secure. In turn, firms suffering greater expropriation of resources are likely to display inferior performance.[6]

To anticipate, I find, after controlling for firm size, capital structure, and a variety of firm-and industry-specific characteristics, that firms with high controlling shareholder ownership outperformed those with low controlling shareholder ownership.[7] Likewise, independent firms outperformed the affiliates of large conglomerates. The results are consistent with the argument that large disparities between control and ownership rights allow controlling shareholders to pursue private agendas at the expense of other shareholders and the enterprise as a whole.

The dependent variable in this analysis is the ratio of net income to assets. Explanatory variables include firm size, financial structure and ownership structure. Each regression includes a vector of controls for industry (disaggregated to the four-digit level). Finally, I include a dummy variable for large *chaebols*, which equals 1 when a firm is affiliated with one of the 70 largest business groups.

Table 9.1 reports the estimated coefficients, with *t*-statistics in parentheses. The results suggest that high equity/debt ratios are positively associated with profitability. Concentrated ownership positively affects profitability as well. And firms affiliated with *chaebols* performed less well than other

Table 9.1 Determinants of profitability of Korean firms

	All years Net income to assets	1993 Net income to assets	1994 Net income to assets	1995 Net income to assets	1996 Net income to assets	1997 Net income to assets
Log (asset)	1.0010 (13.38)	0.6569 (3.85)	0.3942 (2.70)	0.8989 (6.20)	1.2722 (8.56)	1.4114 (6.16)
Equity ratio$_{t-1}$	0.0594 (26.54)	0.0034 (0.78)	0.0241 (5.75)	0.0791 (18.04)	0.1028 (20.13)	0.1741 (20.52)
Ownership concentration	0.0153 (6.47)	0.0119 (2.15)	−0.0001 (−0.03)	0.0146 (3.24)	0.0173 (3.65)	0.0456 (6.20)
Large 70 *chaebol* dummy	−2.8973 (−11.09)	−3.0489 (−5.33)	−1.8918 (−3.96)	−2.0098 (−3.98)	−3.0606 (−5.66)	−2.7783 (−3.15)
Industry dummies	Included	Included	Included	Included	Included	Included
No. of observations	19 497	3 953	4 007	4 189	4 456	2 892
R^2	0.1393	0.1098	0.1199	0.2137	0.2344	0.3510

Notes: The above results suggest that three main factors negatively affect firm profitability: high debt-ridden firms (therefore, low equity ratio) show lower profitability; ownership concentration positively affects firm performance; firms with *chaebol* affiliation performed less well than other firms. These results hold not only for pooled data, but also for yearly data.

Source: See text.

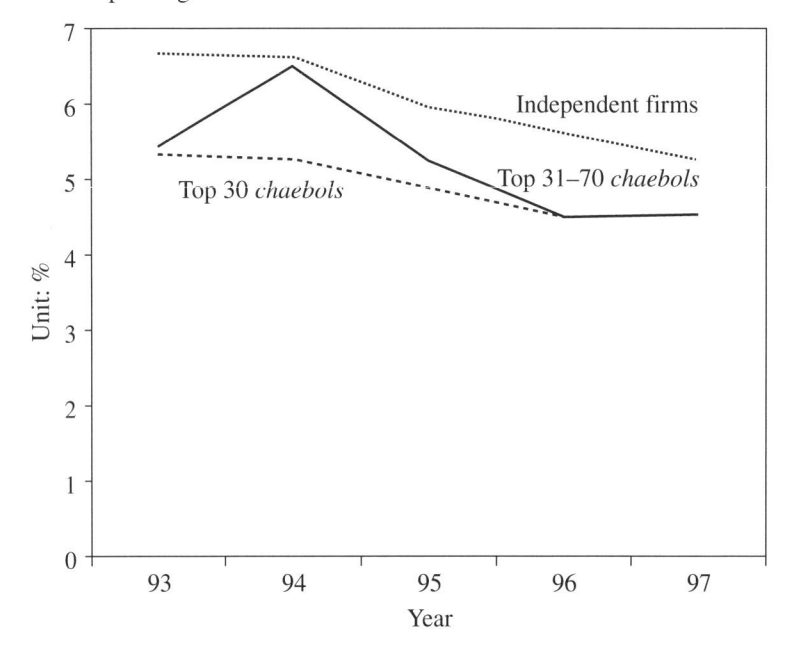

Operating income to sales ratio

Figure 9.1 Accounting performance and capital structure before the crisis

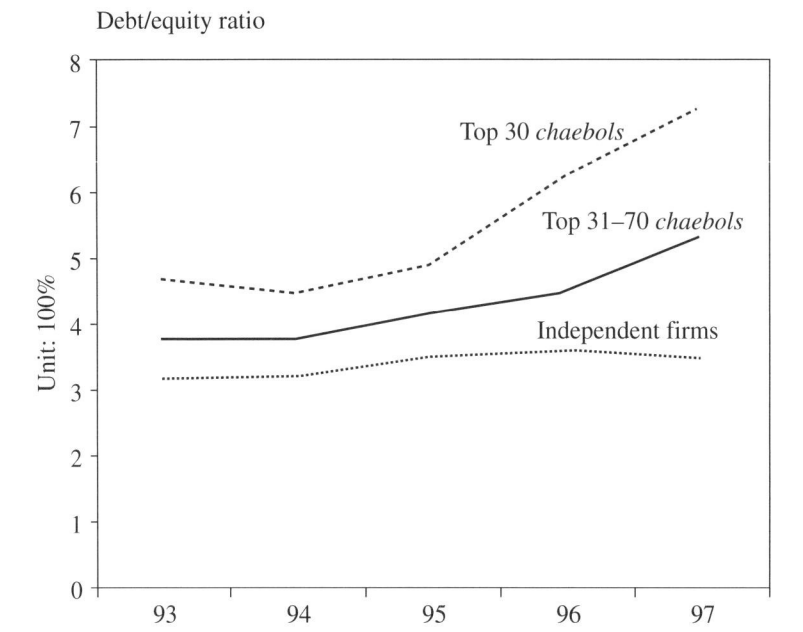

Source: Author's calculations based on financial statement compiled by the NICE.

Interest payment over sales ratio

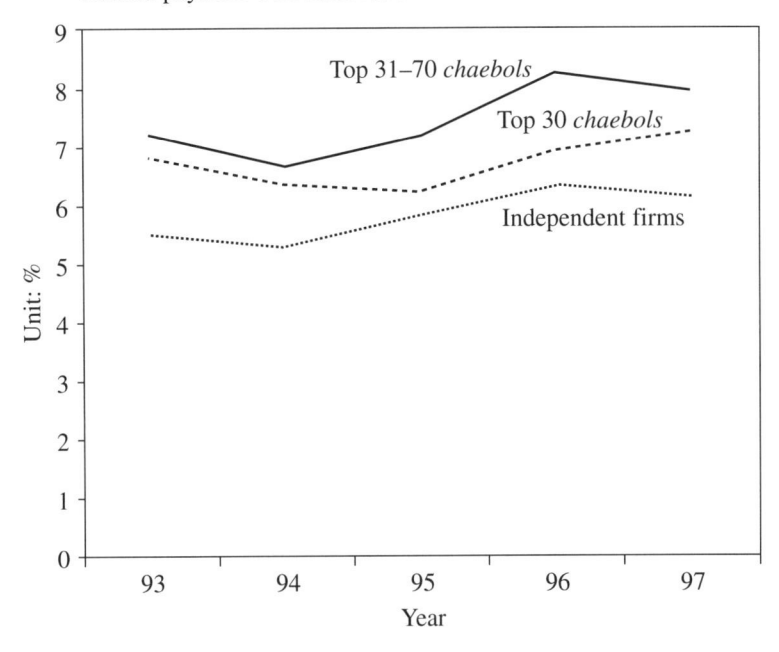

Figure 9.1 continued

firms, consistent with arguments suggesting that disparities between ownership rights and control rights adversely impact firm performance. These results hold not only for pooled data but in annual cross-sections (not reported).[8]

Figure 9.1 shows accounting performance over time for firms that are subject to outside auditing, again controlling for firm size and industry. Firms are divided into three groups: top 30 *chaebol* affiliated firms, top 31–70 *chaebol*-affiliated firms, and independent firms. Clearly, the debt/equity ratios of *chaebol*-affiliated firms were higher. In addition, the operating-income-to-sales ratios of *chaebol*-affiliated firms were lower, while the ratio of interest payments to sales was higher. All these indicators suggest that, after deducting financial expenses, *chaebol*-affiliated firms performed more poorly.

One result of this poor performance was a growing incidence of large corporate failures. Six of the 30 largest *chaebols* went bankrupt even before the onset of the 1997 currency crisis, aggravating the problem of nonperforming loans in Korean financial institutions. This series of *chaebol* defaults, starting with the January 1997 default of the country's fourteenth largest conglomer-

Operating income to sales ratio

Debt/equity ratio

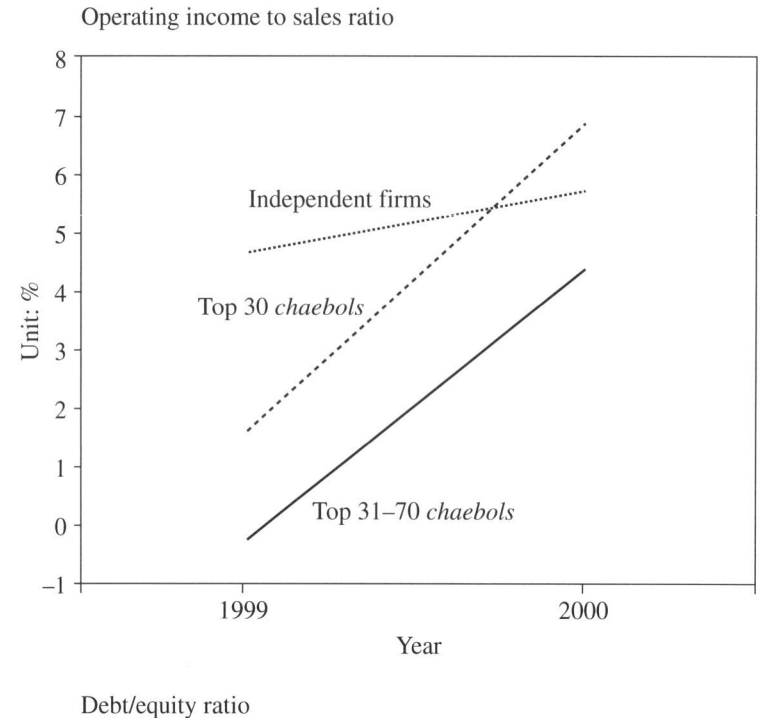

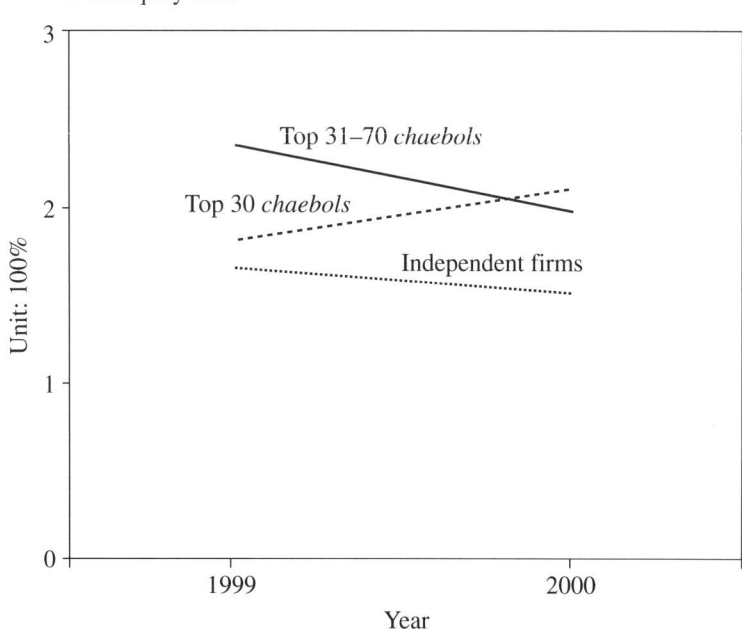

Source: Author's calculations based on financial statements compiled by the NICE.

Figure 9.2 Accounting performance and capital structure after the crisis

Interest payment over sales ratio

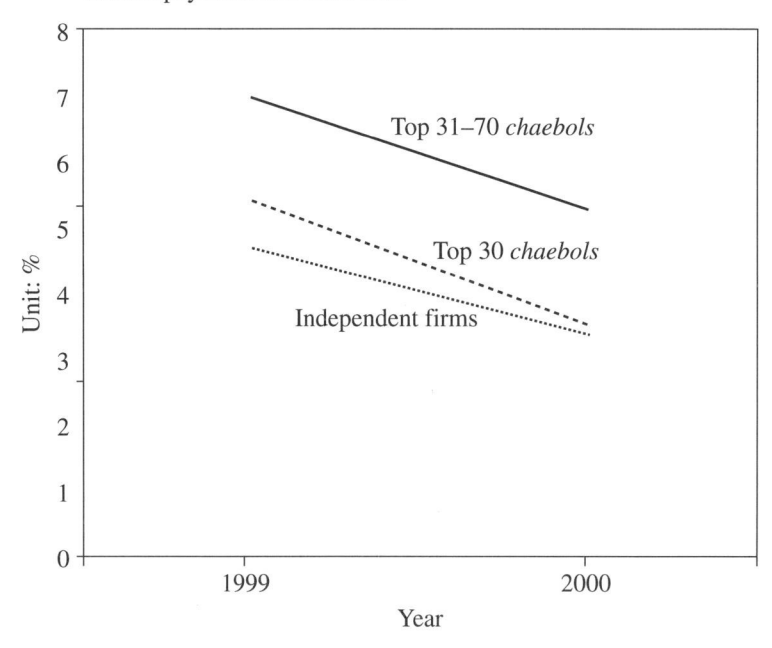

Figure 9.2 continued

ate, Hanbo (ironically, Hanbo means 'Korea's Treasury' in Korean), created doubts about the conglomerates' prospects and about the soundness of the financial sector and the public finances. The total debt of these bankrupt conglomerates was 24.0 trillion won, equivalent to 35.5 percent of the government budget and 5.3 percent of 1997 GNP.

Due to the sheer size of these conglomerates and the dependence of other firms on subcontracting relationships with them, these *chaebol* failures had devastating repercussions.[9] The financial sector's nonperforming loans soared, reaching 6.7 percent of total loans in December 1997, 8.9 percent in March 1998, and 10.2 percent in June 1998. It is no wonder, then, that confidence in the public finances and commercial banks suffered.

Factors Contributing to Sub-par Performance

Table 9.1 identifies high debt, low ownership concentration and *chaebol* affiliation as three factors in Korean firms' disappointing accounting performance. This section asks how firms accumulated so much debt and explains why low levels of ownership concentration and *chaebol* affiliation had such destructive effects.

How did the corporate sector borrow so much money? Firms were encouraged to incur enormous amounts of debt by the government's economic development strategy. The government provided low-cost capital and assumed some of the risk associated with heavy debt burdens. Poor credit evaluation and monitoring by banks and other creditors provided no counterweight to this influence.

In the 1960s and 1970s, Korea was still a capital-poor economy. The government therefore mobilized and allocated scarce capital to firms and industries based on its assessment of their contribution to the nation's industrialization and modernization. Using nationalized banks, it provided cheap capital to targeted firms, thereby guiding their behavior.[10] In effect, the Korean government operated an internal capital market that channeled subsidized credit to targeted firms and industries (C. Lee, 1992). Borrowing from the National Investment Fund or from commercial banks for export was profitable for these firms; only after 1981 were interest rates on bank loans greater than savings interest rates for time deposits (Y. Cho and Kim, 1997). Financial institutions, for their part, simply implemented the government's development strategy, factoring export-oriented firms, and effectively making no independent decisions.

Using these subsidized resources, firms were encouraged to invest in labor-intensive export industries in the 1960s and then in the heavy and chemical industries in the 1970s.[11] Large firms in particular received low-cost capital for ambitious investment projects and implicit guarantees of their returns. This created an incentive for already large firms to expand further, thereby becoming 'too big to fail.' Kook et al. (1997) argue that Korea's major business groups were concerned more with size than profitability when they invested. Between 1973 and 1980, the period of the heavy and chemical industry push, when the government's policy of directed credit really got under way, Korean GNP rose by 655 percent, from 5238 billion won to 34 322 billion won, but the sales of the eight largest *chaebols* rose by an astounding 3520 percent, from 479 billion won to 16 855 billion won (Lee, 1987).[12]

Since the country's large firms incurred huge amounts of debt, they were vulnerable to declines in demand. The 1997 crisis was not the first such disruption; in fact, it had a series of predecessors. Each time one of these disruptions occurred – the 1972 debt crisis, the 1979–83 recession, and 1984 difficulties – the government intervened to rescue troubled firms (Y. Cho and Kim, 1997). It froze their debts, extended bailout loans, provided subsidies, and engineered corporate consolidations to limit competitive pressure.[13] In 1972, the government froze corporate private debts to ease financial distress of many debt-ridden firms. In 1984–88, it provided creditor banks special 3–6 percent interest rate loans (the general bank loan rate having been about 12 percent at the time).[14] It also allowed the banks to write off bad loans, extend loan maturities, and replace existing loans with longer-term loans bearing lower interest rates.[15] In short, the government shared the business risks of the banks.

Financial institutions, for their part, should have done more credit evaluation and credit risk management. Unfortunately, Korean financial institutions did not monitor borrowing firms adequately. Banks had neither the incentive nor the expertise to monitor or discipline firm management. Although commercial banks had been privatized in the 1980s, the legacy of government control remained, in the form of interest rate regulation, directed credit policies and government-appointed executives.

In addition, commercial banks typically required borrowing firms to provide debt payment guarantees to secure their loans instead of developing suitable credit evaluation and risk management techniques to make informed loan decisions. This allowed the *chaebols* to increase their borrowing still further through the use of cross-debt-payment guarantees. Despite theoretical advantages such as lower information costs, the main effect of debt payment guarantees in practice seems to have been to facilitate excessive borrowing by already heavily indebted corporate groups (B. Lee, 1998) and to trigger a chain reaction of bankruptcies of affiliated firms when a subsidiary went broke. Typically, a handful of relatively well-performing firms in the *chaebol* group guaranteed as much as 80 percent of the group's total debt. The total debt payment guarantees of this subset of larger and better-performing firms often exceeded the value of their equity, raising doubts about their viability. Despite such doubts, however, the continuing flow of capital to large conglomerates suggests that financial institutions were not making lending decisions based on the credit risks of *chaebols* or their affiliates.

Close connections between the *chaebols* and nonbank financial institutions (NBFIs) exacerbated the problem. *Chaebols* that owned and operated NBFIs, such as merchant banking corporations, tended to have unusually high debt/equity ratios, while *chaebol*-controlled NBFIs tended to have unusually low returns on assets (J.-K. Kim, 1999). These observations suggest that *chaebols* were using NBFIs over which they had control to transfer resources to themselves.

The result of all this was that the most poorly performing firms had exceptionally high debt/equity ratios. The 30 largest *chaebols* had very high debt/equity ratios, averaging 348 percent in 1995 and 519 percent in 1997. In some cases their debt/equity ratios exceeded 1000 percent, extraordinary by any standard. Moreover, even before the crisis, more than 40 percent of the

30 largest *chaebols* had experienced losses. Thirteen of the 30 largest *chaebols* lost money in 1995. By 1997, the accumulated losses of some *chaebols* had eroded their paid-in capital completely. With nothing left to lose, it is no wonder that they engaged in risky behavior.

In general, shareholders have an incentive to monitor and induce management to maximize shareholder value. However, when a few large shareholders exercise greater control than is warranted by their ownership rights, or when managers are not monitored adequately by shareholders, management will have an incentive to pursue their private interests. As the discrepancy between control rights and ownership rights increases, controlling shareholders will behave in an increasingly opportunistic manner. Clearly, this will not be compatible with maximizing value for shareholders as a class.

Monitoring by individual shareholders has the character of a public good. Any shareholder who decides to monitor management incurs the costs thereof but cannot exclude others from sharing the benefits of his action. Even if he is somehow able to overcome the free-rider problem associated with the public-good nature of monitoring, an individual shareholder is likely to find it difficult to act on his findings because the exercise of shareholder rights typically requires a minimum of 5 percent ownership, which is beyond the financial means of most individual investors. In Korea, shareholders lacking 5 percent ownership could not remove a director, request an injunction, file a derivative suit, demand a convocation, scrutinize the company's books, inspect affairs and company property, or request removal of a receiver if the firm were in liquidation. This means that, in practice, over 97 percent of shareholders lacked these rights. In principle, minority shareholders as a group could be protected by class action suits and by the fiduciary duties required of directors and managers.[16] In practice, however, class actions suits were not allowed. Minority shareholders had few legal rights or investor protections, and they experienced great difficulty in influencing controlling shareholders and firm managers, and in preventing the latter from pursuing their private interest.

In principle, the board of directors was responsible for monitoring and disciplining managers and for mitigating opportunistic behavior by controlling shareholders. In Korea, however, few boards of directors pursued such actions. In the pre-crisis period, over 75 percent of firms reported that they rarely if ever considered the opinions of minority shareholders when selecting directors and auditors (I. Jun and Gong, 1995). In practice, controlling shareholders were able to elect the directors they preferred. Controlling shareholders effectively possessed more than 40 percent of the shares of the 30 largest *chaebols*, because they controlled not only family holdings but also in-group holdings (that is, shareholdings by subsidiaries that belonged to the same *chaebol*). As a consequence, controlling shareholders were able to select the directors they preferred.

Once elected, directors and auditors did not work to maximize the firm's value or advance the general shareholder's interest. The legal responsibilities of directors were based on the principle of 'duty of care.'[17] Under this principle, directors were given the benefit of the doubt when questions of conflicts of interest arose. Their willfulness or negligence had to be legally proven beyond a shadow of a doubt. In practice, board members were accountable only to controlling shareholders, and small shareholders with less than 5 percent of ownership had no capacity to remove them.

Normally, market discipline – that firms that fail to invest productively and to earn normal profits are taken over or forced to exit the market – acts as a check on management's private agenda. In Korea, however, government limitations on mergers and acquisitions (M&As) and ownership structure compromised the operation of this mechanism. Hostile acquisitions were not allowed, and only small firms were permitted to be the targets of even friendly M&As.[18] Any merger or acquisition involving foreigner investors and more than two trillion won in assets required government approval. A mandatory tender offer system required investors who acquired over 25 percent of a firm's shares to publicly purchase over 50 percent of the shares, which was a further financial disincentive for M&As.

In addition, the interlocking ownership of the *chaebols* obstructed takeovers by outside investors. Controlling shareholders with considerably less than 10 percent of direct ownership often possess effective control through their interlocking ownership of other firms in the same *chaebol* group. Therefore, corporate raiders needed to buy the incumbent controlling owners' shares, the interlocking firms' shares, and more in order to obtain effective control.

Lengthy and opaque bankruptcy procedures further weakened exit mechanisms. There exist three types of bankruptcy procedures in Korea: liquidation, composition and corporate reorganization (similar to Chapter 11 of the US bankruptcy code). However, these formal procedures were rarely used for large firms. Lengthy proceedings, often lasting several years, invited strategic debtor behavior, reducing the attractiveness of bankruptcy as an alternative for creditors. Although more than 17 000 cases of insolvency were reported in 1997, only 490 actually went to court.[19] And these produced only 38 liquidations.[20] The law allowed firms that owed less than 250 billion won (a little more than $250 million when converted by the annual average exchange rate for 1997) to use a settlement (composition) procedure in which the court played only a minor role, while debtors retained possession of their estate. Since composition offered few guarantees to creditors, nearly two-thirds of insolvent firms applied for settlement. The remaining firms applied for corporate reorganization, but their financial condition had often deteriorated so greatly that they could not be saved by restructuring.[21]

Before the crisis, the government's implicit guarantee meant that large firms faced virtually no exit threat.[22] As discussed earlier, the government had repeatedly rescued failing *chaebols*. One motivation was that, because of debt payment guarantees, poorly performing subsidiaries could cause financial distress for high-performing subsidiaries, as a result of which the failure of a few subsidiaries of a large conglomerate could cause a chain reaction of failures, with devastating impact on the entire group and the economy. Fearing the impact on employment and on the economy as a whole, the government would typically arrange for the banks to lend more money to these failing firms. This kind of government behavior gave rise to the widespread perception that the *chaebols* were too big to fail.

Using annual census data, S. Joh (2000) showed that the Korean manufacturing sector had a high turnover rate for small plants but not for large plants. Entering and exiting plants accounted for 4.1 percent and 5.4 percent of total output, respectively. Between 1990 and 1998, the output ratio of entering and exiting plants (including switching plants, that is, plants that change their main business from one industry to another), was 12 percent and 17 percent of total output, respectively. The corresponding figures for entering and exiting plants as a share of total plants were even higher, reaching 14.4 percent and 17.7 percent, respectively. When switching plants are included, the ratios jump to 24 percent and 32 percent. Interestingly, these turnover rates are higher than those in most other industrial countries. For example, exit rates (as a percentage of producers) for the US, the UK, Germany and Canada are only 7.0 percent, 11.5 percent, 4.6 percent and 4.8 percent, respectively (S.W. Joh, 2000).

But the turnover rate varies with size of plant. It is significantly lower for large plants than small ones, not mainly because of different entry rates but because small plants exit the market when they fail at a faster rate than large plants. Table 9.2 summarizes the effects of size on turnover. Panel A shows the effects of the number of employees, while Panel B shows the effects of asset size, and Panel C shows the effects of the capital/equipment ratio. All three panels point to similar conclusions. Birth and death rates are lowest in the group of plants with the highest numbers of employees, assets, or capital ratios. Evidently, the exit threat for large firms was not as effective as for small plants. Without a credible threat to firm survival, managers of large firms had less incentive to improve the firm's performance. As a result, uneconomical large firms continued to operate, drawing off resources from smaller, more profitable competitors.

Ideally, the market continuously revolutionizes from within, ridding the economy of old, nonviable firms and creating new ones (Schumpeter, 1952). As weak, old firms fail, they are replaced by newer and stronger ones which provide employment for idle resources. In Korea, this process of 'creative destruction' was so weak as to border on nonexistent.

Table 9.2 *Output ratios by plant turnover status when size is measured by employees, assets and capital equipment, 1990–98 (%)*

	Continuing	New plants	Switch-ins	Dying plants	Switch-outs
Panel A (no. of employees)					
Top 20%	76.9	2.5	7.3	3.3	10.0
21–40%	73.0	5.2	6.7	6.8	8.3
41–60%	67.3	8.3	7.0	8.9	8.5
61–80%	57.5	11.5	8.2	12.6	10.2
81–100%	45.8	17.2	8.2	20.0	8.8
Panel B (asset)					
Top 20%	77.1	2.6	7.3	3.2	9.8
21–40%	72.6	4.8	6.8	6.6	9.2
41–60%	69.2	6.8	6.7	8.8	8.5
61–80%	56.8	10.8	8.7	13.3	10.4
81–100%	46.2	17.9	7.5	18.8	9.6
Panel C (capital equipment ratio)					
Top 20%	76.8	3.1	7.5	3.2	9.4
21–40%	74.6	3.6	7.2	5.0	9.6
41–60%	75.0	3.5	6.5	5.5	9.5
61–80%	70.5	5.0	6.5	7.8	10.2
81–100%	54.5	11.5	8.6	13.3	12.2

Source: Joh (2000).

Inadequate information hinders the ability of investors to evaluate management. In Korea investors lacked accurate and reliable information on firm and management performance due to weak accounting standards, inadequate transparency, and government incentives for firms to exaggerate their size. Because accounting practices did not conform to international standards, poor auditing hindered efforts to monitor and evaluate performance. When firm A guaranteed firm B's debt payment, A did not have to report the guarantee on its balance sheet. Furthermore, with easy access to debt financing, the *chaebols* did not have to maintain financial transparency in order to appeal to equity investors. To the contrary, withholding information from other shareholders served to consolidate control by the dominant shareholder.

It is difficult to quantify the opacity of the financial statements before the crisis or to compare the extent of this problem across different classes of

Table 9.3 Review of special auditing, Daewoo-affiliated firms (trillion won)

Firms	Equity* Books (A)	Equity* Due diligence (B)	Difference * A–B	Improper report**
Daewoo Inc.	2.6	–17.4	20.0	14.6
Daewoo Motors	5.1	–6.1	11.2	3.2
Daewoo Heavy Industry	3.1	1.0	2.1	2.1
Daewoo Electronics	0.7	–3.0	3.7	2.0
Daewoo Communication	0.3	–0.9	1.2	0.6
Subtotal	11.8	–26.4	38.2	22.5
Other affiliated firms	2.5	–2.2	4.7	0.4
Total	14.3	–28.6	42.9	22.9

Notes:
*   As of August 1999.
** As of December 1998.

Source: Financial Supervisory Service, *Press Release* (15 September 2000).

firms. There were, however, some egregious cases. For example, outside auditing of financial statements of Daewoo-affiliated firms revealed many flaws (see Table 9.3). In addition, a recent wide-ranging review of financial statements found that 72 percent of the audits had flaws. Auditing problems ranged from minor errors to outright fraud. It is likely that the less carefully scrutinized financial statements issued in earlier years were more misleading.

EFFECTS OF RECENT REFORM MEASURES

Several measures have been taken to reform the corporate sector, with a focus on creating a more credible exit threat for large firms and strengthening their capital structures. Measures were also introduced to strengthen corporate governance, both internally and externally. These included legalization of mergers and acquisitions, strengthening of minority shareholders' rights, mandating the appointment of outside directors, and increasing the roles of boards of directors.

Major Changes

The general direction for the corporate restructuring measures introduced after the crisis was set by the International Monetary Fund and the World

Bank, which made reform in this area a condition for the extension of financial assistance. These international organizations sought to improve corporate governance and corporate structure, and to enhance the transparency of corporate balance sheets through the adoption of generally accepted international accounting standards and by requiring full disclosure and the provision of consolidated statements for business groups. They wished to encourage the rationalization of corporate finances by reducing debt/equity ratios, promoting the development of securities markets, and altering the system of cross-debt-payment guarantees. They wanted to eliminate government involvement in bank management and lending decisions. And they desired to abolish the extension by the government of subsidies and tax privileges to individual corporations and bailouts to financially distressed firms.

The actions taken subsequently fall into seven areas.[23] The first is to revise accounting standards and require *chaebols* to issue consolidated financial statements. Second is to eliminate cross-debt-payment guarantees. Third is to improve firms' capital structure. To this end, the government set a uniform maximum debt/equity ratio of 200 percent for all firms, to be met by the end of 1999, and did not allow firms to deduct interest expenses on debt exceeding 200 percent of equity from their tax liabilities. Fourth is to identify core businesses and strengthen cooperative relationships with small and medium-sized companies. Fifth is to enhance the accountability of management and controlling shareholders. Sixth is to separate commerce from finance. Seventh is to discourage circular equity investment (a practice in which owners enhance their control rights by investing in one another's firms) and unfair intra-group trading.

Effects of the Reform Effort

In the wake of the crisis, the capital structure and accounting performance of the *chaebols* improved significantly. Debt/equity ratios were reduced, partially because firms better appreciated the risks of high debt, and partly because of the government's 200 percent ceiling on debt/equity ratios. The *chaebols*' profitability improved as well.

As had already become evident before the crisis, debt payment guarantees could trigger a dangerous chain of bankruptcies of affiliated firms when one *chaebol* subsidiary went broke. This realization, driven home by the crisis, generated support for limiting debt payment guarantees. At the same time, the 200 percent ceiling imposed by the government was criticized as too low. It was argued that the debt/equity ceiling did not account for profitability of additional debt issuance by particular firms – that it might restrain the expansion of firms with high growth potential, in high-growth industries in particular. It was also argued that the debt/equity ceiling did not yield the benefits anticipated by policy makers. Firms were expected to reduce their debt/equity ratios by selling off subsidiaries or assets, by issuing new stock, or by closing failing businesses. In practice, however, many *chaebol*-affiliated firms simply issued additional equity, often through the device of cross-holdings (that is, by increasing the equity stake of affiliated firms).

Despite these problems, the lowering of debt ratios almost certainly had positive overall effects. Firms have become less vulnerable to shocks. Lower debt has reduced their interest payment obligations, improving their accounting performance (as shown in Table 9.4).

Table 9.4 Performance of the manufacturing sector, 1990–2000

	1990–1996 avg.	1997	1998	1999	2000
Debt/equity ratio	301.7	396.3	303.0	214.7	210.6
Operating-income-to-sales ratio	7.6	7.4	8.8	7.8	8.6
Financial-expenses-to-sales ratio	5.8	6.2	9.3	7.4	5.1
Ordinary-income-to-sales ratio	2.6	1.4	–0.4	4.2	5.1

Source: W. Lim (2002). Original data from Bank of Korea, *Financial Statement Analysis* (various issues).

Not only has the performance of the manufacturing sector improved in general, but that of the *chaebols* has improved in particular. The surviving largest *chaebols* show substantial improvement in their debt/equity ratios and a remarkable improvement in their operating income. The gap in performance between the surviving *chaebols* and independent firms has narrowed markedly.

Credible Exit Threats

With less debt and fewer cross-debt-payment guarantees, one firm's financial distress is less likely to be transmitted to other firms, reducing the systemic risk in the economy. This has made it less risky to let large firms go bankrupt, finally creating a credible exit threat. Daewoo, the second largest *chaebol*, was ultimately allowed to go bankrupt. The failure of Daewoo and several other large *chaebols* either signals a new readiness by the government to stand aside from corporate sector problems, or else it indicates that failing *chaebols* were losing so much money that the government may have lacked the funds to save them from bankruptcy.[24]

Table 9.5 Large chaebols under insolvency procedures (as of August 1999)

	Daewoo W/O	Donga W/O	Halla R/O	Kohap W/O	Jinro C/O	Anam W/O	Haitai C/O	Kangwon W/O	Shinho W/O
Rank in 1996	2	11	17	18	22	23	24	26	29

Note: W/O denotes workout, R/O reorganization, and C/O composition.

Source: Ministry of Finance and Economy (2001).

Table 9.5 summarizes the position of the most important large conglomerates in bankruptcy proceedings (although it does not include some *chaebols* that emerged from bankruptcy, such as Kia Motors).

There were also institutional arrangements to facilitate exit. The conditions governing mergers and acquisitions, including hostile takeovers and foreign takeovers, were liberalized. Compared to 1997, the number and the volume of M&As, especially by foreign firms, skyrocketed in 1999 from 418 (19 by foreign firms) to 557 (116 by foreign firms). The value of M&As by foreign investors exploded more than ten-fold, from $0.84 billion in 1997 to $8.8 billion in 1999.

The bankruptcy code was also revised. One important change was to introduce an 'economic test' to determine whether a firm filing for bankruptcy is viable and better off reorganized than liquidated. Another major change was the out-of-court workout system. The Corporate Restructuring Agreement, signed by financial institutions in 1998, introduced informal debt workouts as an alternative to formal insolvency proceedings. Informal workouts can be initiated with impetus from the main lending financial institution of a debtor firm.[25] During informal workouts, the firm and its creditors can negotiate rescheduling or restructuring with more flexibility, so the process can be less costly and speedier than formal proceedings.

In a recent study, Y. Lim (2002) finds that the productivity of insolvent firms in 1997 and 1998 had been lower than that of solvent firms long before they declared bankruptcy. This suggests that firms undergoing bankruptcy proceedings had in fact been ailing for some time. Their financial distress was due not merely to the macroeconomic shock of the crisis, but also to their own prolonged weakness. Moreover, Lim shows that firms selected for workouts in 1999 (a group dominated by Daewoo affiliates) had lower productivity than insolvent firms undergoing reorganization. This implies that the selection of firms for workouts was heavily motivated by noneconomic considerations.

Thus, whereas the low productivity of insolvent firms implies that some of them should have been liquidated, the selective application of bankruptcy proceedings indicates that this was not done in an economically rational manner in the early post-crisis years. Subsequently, however, the exit threat to large firms became more credible, as a growing number of failing firms were finally subjected to bankruptcy proceedings. There can be no denying that this is one of the most important changes wrought by the crisis.

Based on the belief that there was widespread excess capacity in certain Korean industries and many conglomerates were vastly overdiversified, the *chaebols* were then encouraged to concentrate on a few core lines of business. To reduce excess capacity and debt/equity ratios, the government proposed a series of business swaps and consolidations. Firms undertaking such swaps enjoyed reduced swap-related taxes, deferred capital gains taxes, deferred corporate taxes and reduced individual taxes. Along with these carrots there was also a stick: the government threatened to cut off the credit of noncomplying firms.[26] In August 1998, the Ministry of Trade, Industry and Energy identified ten industries with excess capacity and requiring restructuring. Debt-ridden and in urgent need of credit from government-directed banks, the top five *chaebols* announced their support for the 'Big Deal' plan in October and December in eight of these industries.

Subsequently, I. Lee (2000) challenged the presumption that all industries encouraged to execute 'Big Deals' suffered excess capacity. In some of these industries, he observed, operating rates had been higher than the economy-wide average throughout the 11-year period ending in 1998. Even where excess capacity was a problem, the efficacy of the 'Big Deal' remains unclear (OECD, 1999). The newly reorganized and consolidated firms will remain in financial distress; simply swapping lines of business will do nothing to improve their balance sheets. Without cost cutting (for example layoffs and plant closures), the problem of excess capacity will remain. Moreover, an undesirable consequence of encouraging each conglomerate to focus on a single industry will be to reduce the level of competition. Reducing the number of firms in each industry facilitates collusive behavior to the detriment of consumers. Most importantly, the 'Big Deal' sets a bad precedent as yet another example of government influence in private business matters.

After the crisis, policy changes were taken to protect investors' rights, shareholders' rights in particular. The government lowered the minimum shareholding requirements such that shareholders holding as little as 0.01 percent of the value of a firm ownership can file a derivative suit.[27] This strengthening of shareholders' rights has given investors in Korean firms the same protection as investors in other countries. La Porta et al. (1998) proposed a set of six indicators to evaluate the extent of protection of minority shareholders against expropriation: whether a country (1) allows proxy voting by mail (making it easier for minority shareholders to exercise their voting rights), (2) blocks the shares for a period before a general shareholders' meeting (making it harder for shareholders to vote), (3) allows cumulative voting (making it easier for a group of minority shareholders to elect at least one director of their choice), (4) gives the minority shareholders who feel oppressed by the board the right to sue or otherwise get relief from the board's decision, (5) gives minority shareholders a pre-emptive right to new issues (protecting them from dilution by the controlling shareholders who could otherwise issue new shares to themselves or to friendly parties), and (6) requires relatively few shares to call an extraordinary shareholder meeting, at which the board can presumably be challenged or even replaced, whereas in other cases a large equity stake is needed for that purpose. An international comparison shows that only 10 percent of the countries in La Porta et al.'s sample scored lower than Korea before 1998. By 1999, however, only 37 percent of the countries in La Porta et al.'s sample achieved the same score or higher than Korea.

In addition, firms are now required to appoint outside directors and are required to impose stronger requirements on the composition of the board's membership: half or more of the members of the boards of large publicly traded firms must be outside directors. Furthermore, changes to the commercial code have strengthened the role of outside directors by requiring the board's approval on all intra-group transactions above a certain minimum size. That said, there are still questions about the independence of outside directors from management and controlling shareholders. In 1999, more than 73 percent of newly selected board members had been recommended by controlling shareholders, and the initiative taken by outside directors was in many respects disappointing. Their agenda approval rates were very high, exceeding 99 percent. Their attendance rate during meetings convened to approve transactions involving controlling shareholders was low, less than 37 percent in 2000.[28] By these measures, the oversight role of boards of directors is still very limited.

While shareholders' rights were strengthened after the crisis, there have been fewer changes in other creditors' rights. This is partly due to the fact that other creditors already enjoyed a relatively favorable position. As Table 9.6 shows, the overall ranking of creditor rights was strikingly high in Korea, compared with other countries, although, as discussed earlier, creditors did not always exercise those rights.

We have already seen evidence that firms with *chaebol* affiliations underperformed independent firms. Moreover, the potential collapse of large *chaebols* threatened the economy at large. K.-J. Yoo (2000) argued that the ultimate goal of the government policy toward the industrial sector was therefore to bring an end to the *chaebol* system. But did the authorities succeed in achieving this goal?

Using a multi-factor model analysis of daily stock market returns for each *chaebol* and its affiliates for the 25 largest *chaebols* between January 1996

Table 9.6 International comparison of creditor rights

	English origin	French origin	German origin	Scandinavian origin	All La Porta et al. sample	Korea
No automatic stay on assets	0.72	0.26	0.67	0.25	0.49	1
Secured creditors first paid	0.89	0.65	1	1	0.81	1
Restrictions for going into reorganization	0.72	0.42	0.33	0.75	0.55	0
Management does not stay in reorganization	0.78	0.26	0.33	0	0.45	1
(Overall) creditor rights*	3.11	1.58	2.33	2	2.3	3
	(78%)**	(14.3%)**	(50%)**	(25%)**	(42.8%)**	
Legal reserve required as % of capital	0.01	0.21	0.41	0.16	0.15	0.5

Notes:
Each column shows the average scores of the countries that have a certain legal origin. There are 18 nations included in English-origin countries, 21 in French-origin, 6 in German-origin and 4 in Scandinavian-origin countries. Altogether, there are 49 countries in the La Porta et al. sample.
* The sum of the scores of the four categories above, where 1 = creditor protection is in the law, and 0 otherwise.
** Figures in parentheses indicate percentage of countries in the subsample whose measure is higher or equal to 3 (Korea's overall measure).

Source: Data compiled from La Porta et al. (1998).

and December 1999, Joh and Ryoo (2000) showed that the prices of equity claims on *chaebol* subsidiaries have varied more independently since the crisis than before, as if investors believe that subsidiaries are now behaving more independently. This result does not hold for the largest *chaebols*, however. Specifically, changes in the stock prices of the five largest *chaebols* are still highly correlated with those of their affiliated firms (a result largely driven by the distressed condition of a few major *chaebols* such as Daewoo and Hyundai, which has similarly affected their subsidiaries).

Joh and Ryoo (2000) also examined the extent of a controlling shareholder's private gains. As a proxy for the latter, they use the proportional voting rights premium, or PVRP, which is the difference between the common stock price and the preferred stock price (as a share of the preferred stock price). The rationale is that the holder of common stock has voting rights but receives lower dividends, while the holder of preferred stock has no voting rights but receives higher dividends. Thus the PVRP should increase in periods when corporate control over a firm is contested (for example M&As) and when control rights are valued, or it should be higher when and where a shareholder can reap private gains as a result of disparities between ownership and control. PVRPs average 5.3 percent, 6.5 percent and 13.3 percent in the US, Sweden and the UK, respectively, which provides a basis for attaching a value to control rights in Korea.

The PVRP in Korea has been very large, but it has also been subject to wide fluctuations. It averaged nearly 95 percent in 1996, before the crisis. Because takeover threats were virtually nonexistent due to legal constraints, the premium before the crisis presumably reflects the private benefits of control. In 1999, after corporate reform, the PVRP was lower, in the order of 81 percent, but still very high by international standards. This suggests that investors still believe that controlling shareholders enjoy extraordinary private gains, notwithstanding the efforts of the authorities to strengthen other creditors' rights.

CONCLUSION

After decades of high growth, the abrupt collapse of the Korean economy in 1997 raised many questions. Why did the crisis occur? Might a similar crisis occur again, or have subsequent reforms averted this danger? More broadly, what have been the consequences of post-crisis reforms? This chapter focuses in particular on problems in the corporate sector and seeks to ascertain whether reform measures have had a significant impact.

While policy toward the corporate sector played an important role in Korea's period of industrialization and modernization, that growth came at a cost. It produced high debt/equity ratios, artificial expansion by firms, and bank lending without proper credit evaluation. Government policy promoted the development of some industries over others and favored large firms over small ones. Firms consequently had an incentive to inflate their size and to create the impression of even greater size through cross-holdings and cross-debt guarantees. Government-directed banks, for their part, lent money to firms with little if any capacity to produce profits, purely on their basis of observed size, which was taken as a sign of official support. As a result, many firms, large firms in particular, ended up with extremely high debt/equity ratios, and corporate profitability declined steadily over time. Ownership-control disparities and the *chaebol* organization were correlated with low profitability, suggesting that controlling shareholders exploited these unprofitable investments for their private gain. Korea's weak system of corporate governance allowed these problems to persist, uncorrected, for the better part of a decade.

Years of low profitability and high debt finally led to massive corporate failures in 1997. That crisis spurred change, including the introduction of new rules on corporate governance, accounting standards, and mergers and acquisitions. Some of the largest *chaebols*, including Daewoo, were allowed to fail. Considerable pressure has been placed on the corporate sector to change. Accounting performance has improved, and debt ratios have been lowered. As a result, Korean firms appear to have become stronger and less vulnerable. There is also some evidence that the influence of controlling shareholders has diminished, reducing the danger of expropriation of minority shareholders. Together, these changes make it more likely that the corporate sector will make a positive contribution to the further growth and development of the Korean economy.

NOTES

1. Hahm (2002), Park and Rhee (1998), Shin (1998), Shin and Hahm (1998), Y. Park (1998)
2. Cho and Hong (2000).
3. C.-Y. Kim (1997) reports that President Park Chung Hee held monthly Cabinet meetings in which policy measures were formulated to promote exports. Exporting firms received credits at lower interest rates and were subject to only half the standard corporate income tax rate.
4. Joh (2002) showed that the performance of the *chaebols* was inferior to that of independent firms. Lee and Lee (1999) showed that the debt/equity ratio of the *chaebols* was higher than that of independent firms.
5. In Korea, the stock market might be inefficient and easily manipulated. There were only 687 publicly listed firms in 1993 and 776 in 1997. The KOSDAQ (the Korean counterpart of the NASDAQ) was of negligible importance before 1998.
6. For further discussion, see Jensen and Meckling (1976) and Joh (2002).
7. See Martin (1993) for a brief summary of how these variables affect firm performance.

Corporate restructuring 217

8. The poor performance of *chaebol*-affiliated firms has been confirmed by other studies. Using a longer time-series of firm and business-group-level data, Hwang (2001) and K. Lee et al. (2002) have shown that any efficiency and profitability advantage that may have once been enjoyed by the *chaebols* had largely disappeared by the early 1990s. Similarly, using firm data from 1975 to 1982, Chang and Choi (1988) showed that *chaebols* performed better than independent firms only when tax and financial costs were considered.
9. Chung and Yang (1992) report that the shares of the top five and top 30 *chaebols* of GNP were 9.2 percent and 16.3 percent, respectively. The Korea Economic Research Institute reports that in 1995 the shares of the top four and top 30 were 9.2 percent and 16.2 percent, respectively.
10. Jones and SaKong (1980).
11. These industries include power-generating equipment, automobiles, engines, heavy electric equipment, telephone-switching systems, refined copper, and so on.
12. Figures in this sentence are in nominal terms. The eight *chaebols* were Hyundai, LG, Samsung, SK, Daewoo, Ssangyong, Hyosung and Kukje.
13. For more discussion on how the government dealt with each recession, see Joh (2001).
14. The Bank of Korea provided six commercial banks with 1.7 trillion won between December 1985 and May 1987 and recovered only 0.37 trillion won by September 1990. See S. Lee (1995) and Kim (1991).
15. See Y. Cho and Kim (1997) and Kim (1991). Acquiring firms and consolidating firms received 7.28 trillion won in subsidies. Source: Ministry of Finance document submitted to the National Assembly (1988).
16. See Johnson et al. (2000) for more discussion on fiduciary duty and the duty of care for managers and directors.
17. See Johnson et al. (2000) for more discussion on fiduciary duty and duty of care for managers and directors.
18. In May 1998, six months after the 1997 crisis, the Korean government removed all restrictions on M&A activities.
19. Bank of Korea.
20. OECD (1998).
21. Koo (1998) showed that the average debt/equity ratio of these firms was a remarkable 1200 percent.
22. Kukjae's failure in 1984 was a politically motivated exception.
23. The government announced an eighth principle: blocking unlawful bequests. However, it is not included in the discussion because it is not directly relevant to corporate reform.
24. Policy toward Hyundai was more consistent with the second interpretation. Policy in this case was in conflict with the stated principle of non-intervention, since the authorities assisted the firm through the agency of the Korea Development Bank.
25. After conducting due diligence, the main bank proposed a restructuring plan. If the creditors representing more than 75 percent of the firm's debt agree, it is binding on all the institutions. If the creditors fail to reach an agreement after two attempts, the case will be referred to the Corporate Restructuring Coordination Committee (CRCC), whose decision will become binding. The CRCC is responsible for arbitrating differences among creditors and modifying workout plans.
26. The *Wall Street Journal* (8 October 1998) reported, 'Korea threatens to halt credit to five *chaebols* after talks stall.' *Maeil Economic Daily* also reported that the government wanted banks to cut off new loans and even call back old loans from the top five *chaebols* if corporate restructuring proposals were not satisfactory.
27. For specific information on how minority shareholders' rights have been legally strengthened, see Joh (1999).
28. See C. Chang (2000) for more discussion on the directors' attendance rates by agenda category.

10. Changes in the labor markets and industrial relations[1]

Young-Ki Choi and Dae Il Kim

INTRODUCTION

This chapter documents changes in labor markets and industrial relations in Korea since 1997. The crisis and ensuing restructuring have had a dramatic impact on the labor market. The workforce contracted by five percentage points in 1998 and did not recover to pre-crisis levels for an additional two years. The shift in labor demand toward skilled workers in the course of restructuring has manifested itself in higher unemployment, widening wage inequality, and a serious deterioration in job quality for unskilled workers.

Given unfavorable market conditions, firms attempted to reduce their payrolls, and to make this possible, the government sought to amend the country's labor laws to allow the layoff of redundant workers. These changes meant that only higher labor productivity would ensure job security. Maintaining and enhancing labor productivity in turn requires smooth and efficient labor–management relations, something that the government sought to achieve by promoting workplace partnership.

Achieving such a partnership entails breaking away from the confrontational labor–management relationship that prevailed in the past. Following the outbreak of the crisis, however, workers and unions continued to use confrontation to protect their jobs. Because unions had succeeded in blocking legislation legalizing layoffs of redundant workers as recently as 1996, they had reason to believe that they could do so again in 1998 (despite the fact that deterioration in economic conditions wrought by the crisis was far more severe). Moreover, the history of government intervention in labor disputes fostered the expectation of additional such intervention among firms and unions alike, encouraging opportunistic behavior on the part of both social partners. Thus, for example, the unions sought to reach a political bargain with the government, attempting to commit the latter to the maintenance of job security, something that the government resisted as incompatible with its vision of restructuring. Above all, deep-seated distrust between management and unions made it difficult to break away from the confrontational approach.

Without mutual trust, the workplace partnership for higher productivity that the government emphasized could not be achieved.

This chapter makes these points as follows. The next two sections discuss the government's attempts to develop a social consensus on reforming the economy and restructuring the labor market. In this context, the Tripartite Commission that was the authorities' vehicle for pursuing these objectives receives special attention. A further section documents and evaluates subsequent changes in the labor market, while the next does the same for industrial relations. The concluding section emphasizes the need for workplace partnership and efficient supply responses to changing market conditions and the role that the government might play in bringing these about.

THE NEED FOR SOCIAL CONSENSUS AND THE TRIPARTITE COMMISSION

The early stages of economic growth in Korea were based on low-wage industries such as textiles and apparel, and a strong labor movement was seen as threatening the international competitiveness of these industries. The 1980s were essentially a continuation of past practice, as the military government sought to suppress the labor movement and limit wage growth.

Partly in reaction to this past, union activity then soared when the union movement was liberalized in 1987. That year saw 3749 strikes, a fourteenfold increase from 1986. The number of workers participating in these strikes rose from 46 941 to 1.26 million, while days lost increased from 72 025 to 6.95 million. Time lost to strikes was still more than 1.4 million man-days in the mid-1990s.

This history of confrontation was not a propitious context for the far-reaching restructuring needed to resolve the crisis. The IMF therefore pointed the government toward the example of the social pact negotiated following the crisis in Mexico in 1994–95. Mexico's social pact was an agreement among labor, business, government and farmers on sharing the costs of restructuring, restoring financial stability and pursuing job creation policies. Specific actions included floating the peso, expanding training programs, attempting to limit inflation to 20 percent, and restraining wage growth (Y.-K. Choi et al., 2001). Revealingly, a delegation of members of the new Korean ruling party paid a visit to Mexico early in 1998 to study that country's experience.

The result was the Tripartite Commission, composed of representatives of business, labor and government, established in order to develop a social consensus in favor of the government's approach to economic restructuring. Both national unions, the Federation of Korean Trade Unions (FKTU) and the Korean Confederation of Trade Unions (KCTU), participated in the Commission at the beginning. Unlike the FKTU, which had existed since the 1970s, the KCTU, established in the late 1980s, was not recognized as a legal entity in principle until 1998, since multiple unions were banned at the national level.[2] The need to build a social consensus during the crisis, however, finally led the government to recognize the KCTU as a legal entity.

Reaching a consensus with labor on policies for enhancing flexibility was essential for a successful response to the crisis. The opposition of the unions could have jeopardized not just the restructuring process but also the political survival of the government itself. The ruling party therefore promised to liberalize the political activities of unions and the organization of teachers and public employees, as well as to grant more generous unemployment benefits, in exchange for the unions' consent to the legalization of mass layoffs of redundant workers.

There had been a few instances of experimentation with social dialogue before the Tripartite Commission: the Bilateral Wage Moderation Pact was one, and the Industrial Relations Reform Committee of the mid-1990s was another. These initiatives were temporary, however, and the role of the unions was mostly limited to consultation on specific labor issues. The Tripartite Commission was more ambitious: its role was to develop a social pact in favor of restructuring and to monitor implementation of restructuring policies.

Some argue that the social pact was essential to the success of the restructuring program and that the Tripartite Commission was an indispensable venue for discussions between the social partners. In particular, the primary goal of the Commission, demobilization of the nascent anti-restructuring campaign of organized labor, was successfully achieved, as the unions were persuaded to agree to the social pact. Others criticize the Commission for failing to transform industrial and labor relations or to create an effective workplace partnership. They point to the political entanglements of the unions and to the resurgence of labor disputes in the second half of 1998. They observe how, when the Ministry of Justice delayed the legalization of teachers' right to organize and of the right of unemployed workers to join non-enterprise level unions, the KCTU withdrew from the Commission. Left as labor's sole representative, the FKTU then attempted to exert more political influence, which only politicized the Commission further.[3]

That the Tripartite Commission was dominated by politics is hardly surprising. The Commission had been established by President-elect Kim Dae Jung and was chaired by members of the ruling party. The public interest frequently took a back seat to the private interests of its members.[4] The government's attempt to use the Commission to consult with union and business leaders on a wide range of issues was problematic given that the participating unions represented only a fraction of their putative constituents, and that their views were not always representative of the broader labor movement.[5]

LABOR MARKET RESTRUCTURING

The labor market policies agreed to by the Commission addressed three issues: improvements in flexibility, policies toward unemployment, and the promotion of workplace partnership.

Labor Market Flexibility

The urgent need to restructure Korean industry led the government to legalize redundancy layoffs and temporary work. This reflected the perception that flexible employment was important for corporate restructuring and attracting foreign investors alike. Implementation was not smooth, however. Workers opposed layoffs, while union leaders accepted them only in return for a commitment to extend large-scale unemployment benefits.[6]

There was also criticism that the new law and its administration did not in practice make it easier to adjust employment. Redundancy layoffs had not been prohibited before passage of the new law; the Supreme Court had already acknowledged management's authority to utilize them. The real change lay in the new procedures, some of which were quite restrictive. Firms were required to first exhaust all efforts to avoid redundancy.[7] They were then required to engage in good-faith consultations with union leaders before proceeding with actual layoffs. It was always possible to challenge whether a firm had exhausted all efforts to avoid layoffs or whether it had consulted in good faith.[8] Union leaders, for their part, were reluctant to consult with employers regarding layoffs, given the predictable reaction of their rank and file.

These requirements imposed non-trivial costs on firms. The case of Hyundai Motor Co. is exemplary. The company had only a 40 percent utilization rate in March 1998, leading it to propose the layoff of some 8000 workers. It offered severance pay to those offering to leave voluntarily before giving pink slips to 2678 employees. The union then called a strike, which lasted a month and half. The case finally closed with the layoff of 277 employees, 10 percent of management's initial target.[9]

Despite having limited layoffs to 277 workers, union leadership was subjected to a vote of confidence, which it survived by a narrow margin. Again this illustrates how vehemently the rank and file opposed the idea of layoffs.

The Hyundai affair can be seen as giving birth to new route of employment adjustment, namely honorary retirement. Firms offered generous severance compensation packages while pressuring workers with the threat of layoff. This approach was repeatedly used in the ensuing restructuring of the financial sector and public enterprises. Thus, while the new law was not very effective in facilitating redundancy layoffs, it did open an alternative, albeit higher-cost, avenue of employment adjustment.

Two other changes were made in addition to redundancy layoffs. First, restrictions on temporary work were relaxed.[10] Although outsourcing of temporary workers was legally permitted only in a few occupations, it contributed to the growth of non-regular employment during the period of the crisis. Second, firms were allowed to temporarily replace striking workers in order to maintain production.[11] In practice, the impact of this last innovation was not large, since replacement was allowed only within the establishment concerned – that is, replacement workers could not be hired from outside the firm. While firms could reallocate workers not on strike to the production site vacated by their striking colleagues, in fact strikers were rarely replaced, as picket-line crossing was almost unheard of.

Unemployment Policy

Unemployment policy had various components. The government attempted to limit job loss by extending subsidies for job sharing and rehiring laid-off workers. A subsidized loan program for new businesses, principally so-called venture businesses, was established to encourage new hires. Training and placement services were expanded: whereas training programs covered 301 244 jobless persons in 1998, their number increased to 324 623 persons in 1999.[12]

Each of these initiatives came in for considerable criticism. Although the full effects of subsidies for rehiring laid-off workers are difficult to measure, they are unlikely to have been large, since temporary layoffs were not the major reason for job losses; most job losses in practice were due to bankruptcies.[13] There were at least three problems with the program extending subsidies to venture firms: the overly narrow definition of a venture business as one using sophisticated computer technology; that the labor demand induced in such businesses, if any, did not match the supply made available by unskilled workers who had lost their jobs, so that encouraging the inflow of capital into the venture sector led to excessive competition for very high-skilled workers, raising their wages and the wage gap between the skilled and unskilled; and that administration of the program was inefficient, given the inability of bureaucrats and politicians to evaluate the future profitability of highly technical projects.[14] Finally, the government's training schemes were mostly ramped-up versions of initiatives that had already proven not to be very effective. Publicly subsidized training was linked not to final demand but to the training capabilities of the provider. Placement services were ineffectual: as of 1999, only 6.7 percent of job searchers relied on job placement services, public or private.[15]

Unemployment policy also targeted females and youths. Starting in October 1998, the government subsidized one-third to one-half of the wages paid to newly hired female heads of households who had recently lost their jobs. This resulted in additional short-term job opportunities, mostly in social service and childcare, for low-income women. The policy also targeted recent college graduates: approximately 45 000 jobless graduates were awarded six-month internships in the public sector in 1998.

The large sums of money allocated to such programs (over 10 trillion won in 1998 alone) loosened spending discipline, and as a result much money was spent on schemes that in practice provided few economic benefits. Although the expansion of short-term public employment provided temporary relief to those adversely affected by the crisis, it did not offer permanent solutions. Nor did it create new jobs or generate additional human capital.

Unemployment insurance, previously limited to firms with 30 or more employees, was expanded to firms with ten or more employees in January 1998, to firms with five or more employees in March 1998, and to all firms in October 1998. The impact was delayed, however, since eligibility was limited to those who had paid in premiums for at least six months at the time of separation. Only 11 percent of job losers, and an even smaller fraction of the unemployed, were eligible for benefits in 1998.

Thus poverty had to be addressed by other means. In 1998 public assistance programs were expanded to cover an additional 310 000 persons.[16] A subsidized loan program supported new business start-ups and provided living expenses.[17] In addition, the government spent 1.4 trillion won in 1998 on public work programs involving some 400 000 individuals, and some 2.3 trillion won in 1999 on programs involving 380 000 persons.[18] It introduced a Basic Livelihood Protection Program which pays up to 930 000 won per month – compared with the minimum wage of 421 490 won – to a four-person household.

Finally, a Wage Claim Guarantee Fund was established to compensate workers in bankrupt firms for unpaid wages. And, in 2000, the government also extended the coverage of minimum wages, work accident insurance, and labor standard law to all firms from firms with five or more employees.

The effectiveness of these programs depends on administrative acuity, since many of them will be wasteful or ineffective in the absence of tight monitoring of eligibility. Unfortunately, the government did not have accurate income data on self-employed workers and non-working households. It similarly lacked the means to monitor small firms.[19]

Workplace Partnership

President Kim proposed workplace partnership as an alternative to confrontational labor and industrial relations. However attractive the vision, implementation was imperfect. The campaign for workplace partnership was government led, not a voluntary movement of workers and employers. Although the social partners understood that confrontation was inefficient, distrust was deeply rooted. And, because the government failed to provide a mechanism that might dissolve such distrust, workplace partnership became little more than a political slogan.[20]

Voluntary cooperation could be achieved only when employers and workers identified common interests. But the government failed to provide an environment conducive to the identification of such interests. It could have offered the evolution of industrial and labor relations in the UK during the 1980s and the 1990s as a benchmark but instead relied mainly on discussion of, *inter alia*, high-performance workplace innovation while failing to devote much attention to how effective pressure for such innovation might be applied.[21]

MAJOR CHANGES IN THE LABOR MARKET

The most obvious effect of the crisis on the labor market was the sharp drop in employment and the rapid rise in unemployment.[22] This was the period of massive bankruptcies among small firms caught in the vice of sky-high interest rates and credit rationing. Manufacturing and construction jointly lost one million jobs in 1998, reflecting heavy debt loads in these sectors. In contrast, employment in agriculture and fisheries and in public administration, which had been following a declining trend, recorded substantial growth in 1998, as these sectors helped to buffer the shock to workers and households.

The 1999 recovery was generally a mirror image of the 1998 job losses, as manufacturing employment rose by 115 000, and agriculture lost 117 000 jobs, offsetting the previous year's growth. There were a few exceptional sectors: construction lost jobs in 1999 for the second year in a row, although the number of additional losses (110 000) was smaller than in the preceding year. And the public sector showed strong job growth for the second year running.

Not surprisingly, job losses affected unskilled workers disproportionately.[23] Despite the generally strong employment growth in the latter part of 1998, jobs for less educated workers recovered only slowly, and jobs for the 20- to 29-year-old population declined further. An exception is the increase in the

Labor markets and industrial relations 225

employment of unskilled laborers in 1999, which rose more than seven times as fast as in 1996–97. This pattern suggests occupational downgrading during the recovery, as does the fact that newly created jobs were relatively low-paying and required longer hours.[24]

There has been extensive job creation and destruction in the post-crisis period (see Figure 10.1). As noted above, many newly created jobs are low paying, while many high-wage jobs were destroyed. The public sector was responsible for many new jobs, most of which were unskilled.[25]

The increase in unemployment was unprecedented in Korea's history.[26] Unemployment was still much higher at the end of 1999 than at the end of 1996, despite the fact that the level of employment was basically unchanged.[27] D. Kim (2000a) shows that the entry of nonparticipants and job losers into unemployment rose substantially during the crisis. The fraction of nonparticipants entering unemployment (that is, starting job search) rose from

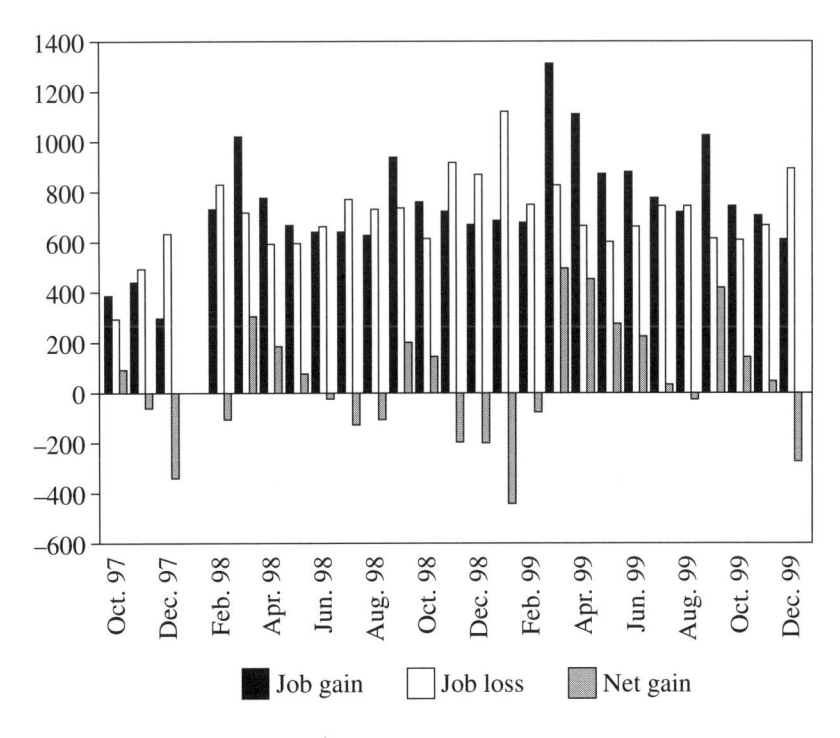

Note: All bars are measured in 1000 persons.

Source: D. Kim (2001a).

Figure 10.1 Job gains, job losses and net job gains during the crisis

0.5 percent in September 1997 to 2.5 percent in September 1998. The share of job losers entering unemployment instead of exiting the labor force also doubled, from 20 to 40 percent, in this period. Evidently, the jobless population became more inclined to stay in the market during the crisis.

This tendency to remain in the market reflects two factors. First, job losses had left many households poorer, and previously nonparticipating members of such households might have been induced to enter the market to supplement household income.[28] In addition, the value of search may have risen relative to the value of nonparticipation due to government policy. While unemployment insurance was one potential cause of such changes, only a fraction of job losers was covered. Other dimensions of government policy, including additional employment of unskilled workers in the public sector, are more likely to have had widespread effects.[29] Although this pattern is often taken to indicate the effectiveness of the public work program in offering jobs to unemployed workers, it may have also created an incentive for jobless persons to register as unemployed in order to gain eligibility for public work. This eligibility condition is one example of how policy increased the value of unemployment relative to nonparticipation.[30]

As a result, unemployment data surely understate the deterioration in labor market conditions. High-wage jobs in manufacturing have been replaced with low-wage jobs in trade, agriculture and fisheries. Clearly, the share of temporary and daily employees has risen since the crisis (see Table 10.1). (Note that regular employees are those on one-year or longer labor contracts or with contracts of unspecified length.[31] Workers who have had their short-term contracts renewed repeatedly are also counted as regular workers if they are eligible for statutory benefits such as retirement allowances. Temporary employees are those on contracts of one to 12 months' length who are also ineligible for statutory benefits, as well as daily employees. Non-employees are employers, the self-employed, and unpaid family workers working at least 18 hours per week.[32]) Self-employment also rose during the crisis, as did the number of unpaid family workers (after falling in 1997). It is possible that many small businesses were converted to family businesses in order to cut labor costs, and that many job losers may also have become unpaid family workers.

Non-regular jobs offer organizational flexibility.[33] And if flexibility renders the organization more productive, this may increase the security of primary workers.[34] The pattern of job growth during the crisis, however, is not consistent with the organizational flexibility hypothesis. Non-regular job growth was more prevalent in firms with fewer than ten employees, while the need for greater organizational flexibility presumably would have been greatest among large firms (Figure 10.2). Further, the increase in the use of non-regular workers was *positively*, not negatively, associated with the job

Table 10.1   Distribution of employment (1000 persons)*

	1996	1997	1998	1999
Employees				
Regular**	7326.6	7084.1	6402.7	6011.2
	(36.9)	(35.4)	(33.7)	(31.3)
Temporary***	3787.8	4097.2	3914.9	4081.3
	(19.1)	(20.5)	(20.6)	(21.2)
Daily***	1690.2	1783.9	1654.8	2172.2
	(8.5)	(8.9)	(8.7)	(11.3)
Non-employees****				
Employer	1585.9	1612.4	1405.1	1351.6
	(8.0)	(8.1)	(7.4)	(7.0)
Self-employed	3692.0	3757.9	3797.4	3886.0
	(18.6)	(18.8)	(20.0)	(20.2)
Unpaid FW	1749.3	1687.0	1808.4	1724.7
	(8.8)	(8.4)	(9.5)	(9.0)

Notes:
*   Figures in parentheses are percentage of total.
**   Regular employees are those on one-year or longer labor contracts or those with contracts of unspecified lengths. Workers who have repeatedly renewed shorter-term contracts are also counted as regular workers if they are eligible for statutory benefits such as retirement allowances.
*** Temporary employees are those on contracts of between one month and one year and are ineligible for statutory benefits, and daily employees are those employed on a daily basis.
**** Non-employees are employers (hiring employees), self-employed (on own account), and unpaid family workers working no fewer than 18 hours a week. Unpaid family workers working fewer than 18 hours a week are classified as jobless.

Source: Author's calculations based on data from the National Statistical Office, *Survey of Economically Active Population* (1996–99).

separation rate of regular workers (D. Kim, 2001b).[35] If it reflected greater organizational flexibility, the increased use of non-regular workers should have improved the job security of regular workers. That non-regular job growth and job loss among regular workers occurred together indicates that firms were trying to cut labor costs rather than to increase organizational flexibility.

As mentioned above, public work programs were an important source of non-regular job growth in the late 1990s. However, the government probably also induced a portion of this non-regular job growth by enacting the law

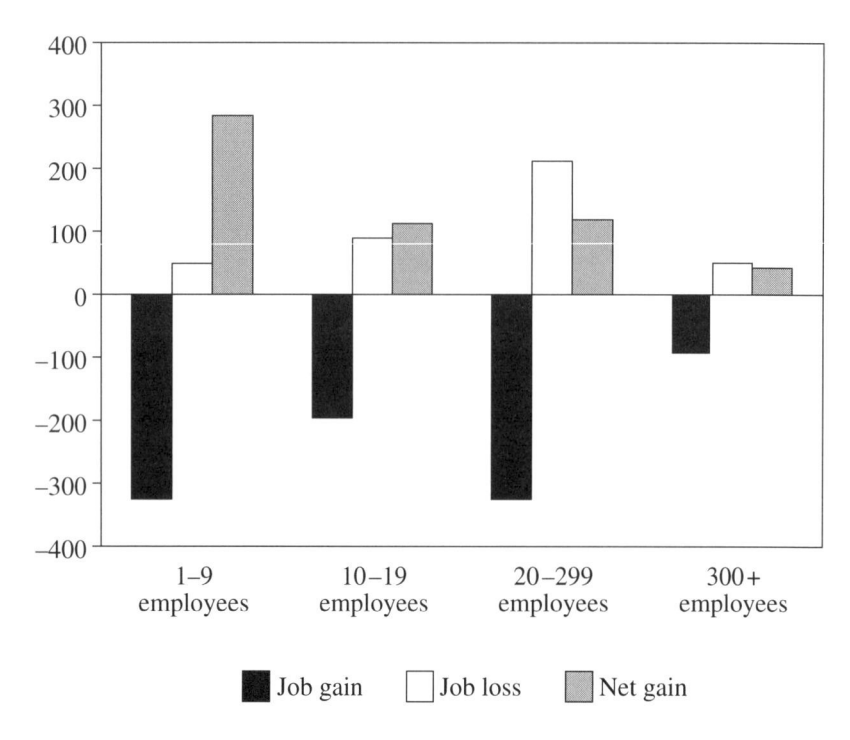

Source: D. Kim (2001a).

Figure 10.2 Changes in employment type by firm size, 1997–2000 (1000 persons)

authorizing redundancy layoffs. But the Hyundai case gave firms a clear signal that employment adjustment was still costly. Consequently, they preferred short-term contracts to regular contracts.[36]

Workers in large firms (who were often unionized) appear to have used the recovery as an opportunity to raise their wages. While jobs tended to grow more among smaller firms, wages tended to increase faster among larger firms. Given that the economy was recovering, it is likely that jobs would have grown among the large firms as well had it not been for the rapid wage growth. Those who would have obtained a job among large firms were thus pushed into smaller firms, where lower wages and non-regular jobs prevailed. Evidently, unionized workers in large firms protected their interests at the expense of potential new hires, reflecting the 'insider/outsider' problem characteristic of Korea's industrial and labor relations.

Wages had grown strongly for most of the 1980s and 1990s, which some have regarded as a contributing factor in the crisis.[37] But labor productivity also grew robustly, essentially keeping pace with the rise in labor costs. Moreover, the steep increase in wages stopped in 1998; nominal wages fell by 5.9 percent between July 1997 and July 1998. This amounted to a 12.5 percent decline in the real wage, given the acceleration in the inflation rate in 1998.

During the period of wage growth, inequality had been shrinking (as shown in Figure 10.4). The Gini coefficient measuring wage inequality had been falling since the late 1970s (with the sole exception of 1994). Male–female differentials, the age premium and the college premium all contributed to the decline in inequality.[38] Wage inequality then appears to have risen, or at least its decline slowed, during the crisis. Both the age and college premia widened in 1998 (see Table 10.2).[39]

Table 10.2 Employment in sectors with strong unions (1000 persons)

	1995	1996	1997	1998	1999	2000
30 largest chaebols	893	940	937	808	763	741
Public enterprises	250	255	260	253	237	232
Financial sectors	418	441	450	411	392	388

Note: All employment figures are October figures for each year.

Source: Korea Labor Institute, Employment Insurance Data Base (1995–2000).

These non-neutralities suggest that income inequality widened during the crisis. Figure 10.3, which plots changes in nominal wages by wage decile from 1997 through 1999, confirms this supposition. Between 1997 and 1998, the bottom 20 percent lost in nominal terms, while the top 40 percent gained an additional 1 to 2 per cent. Rising wage inequality was most evident in 1998, when the crisis was most intense.[40]

In 1998–99, nominal wage gains were still greatest among the top 10 percent, causing wage inequality to widen further. An important difference now, however, was that the middle groups now gained more than the seventh through ninth deciles. The strong gains in the middle groups appear to have reflected fast wage growth among organized production workers in large firms. Figure 10.4 plots wage growth and the share of unionized workers by wage decile; it shows that wage growth closely resembles the share of unionized workers (the exceptional top decile notwithstanding).[41] Given that workers in small firms not covered in the data were likely to have lost ground in terms of wages, this union effect probably increased the wage gap between the middle and the bottom. Furthermore, faster wage growth among large unionized

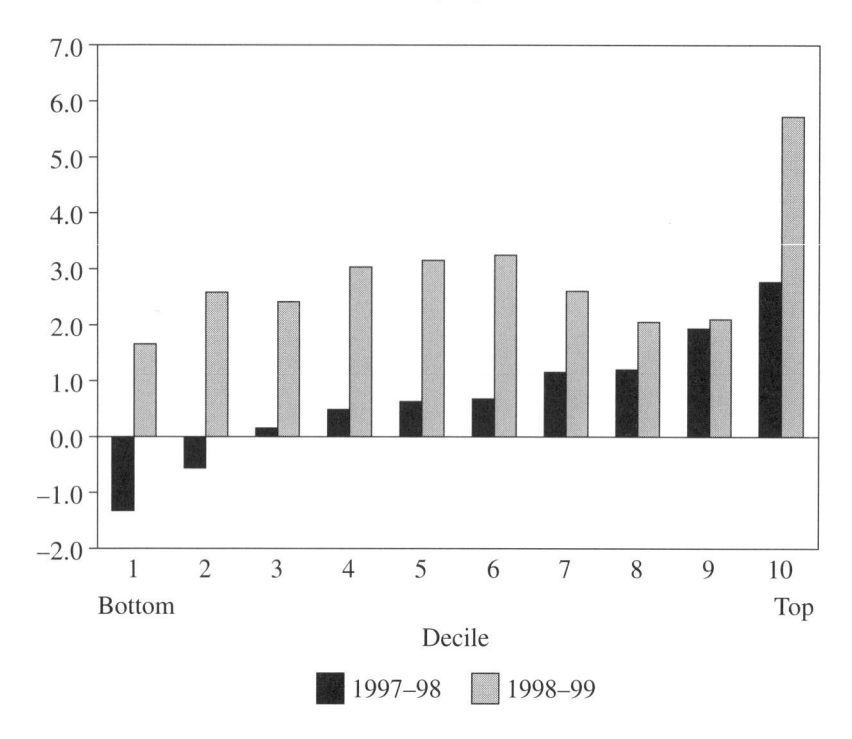

Source: Authors' calculation based on data from Ministry of Labor, *Wage Structure Survey* (1978–99).

Figure 10.3 Percentage changes in wages, by decile, 1997–99

firms contributed to the growth of non-regular jobs in smaller firms, which further widened wage inequality toward the bottom of the distribution.[42]

INDUSTRIAL RELATIONS SINCE THE CRISIS

Job security had not been a major issue before the crisis, as unions were concentrated among the *chaebols* and large firms, which enjoyed product market power that insulated them from pressure to lay off workers in downturns. The crisis, however, exposed these large firms to increased market pressure: employment in highly organized sectors declined in 1998 (Table 10.2), despite an unprecedented concession by labor of a 2.7 percent nominal wage cut.

Facing continued downward pressure on employment, unions have placed greater emphasis in bargaining on job security and on the monitoring of

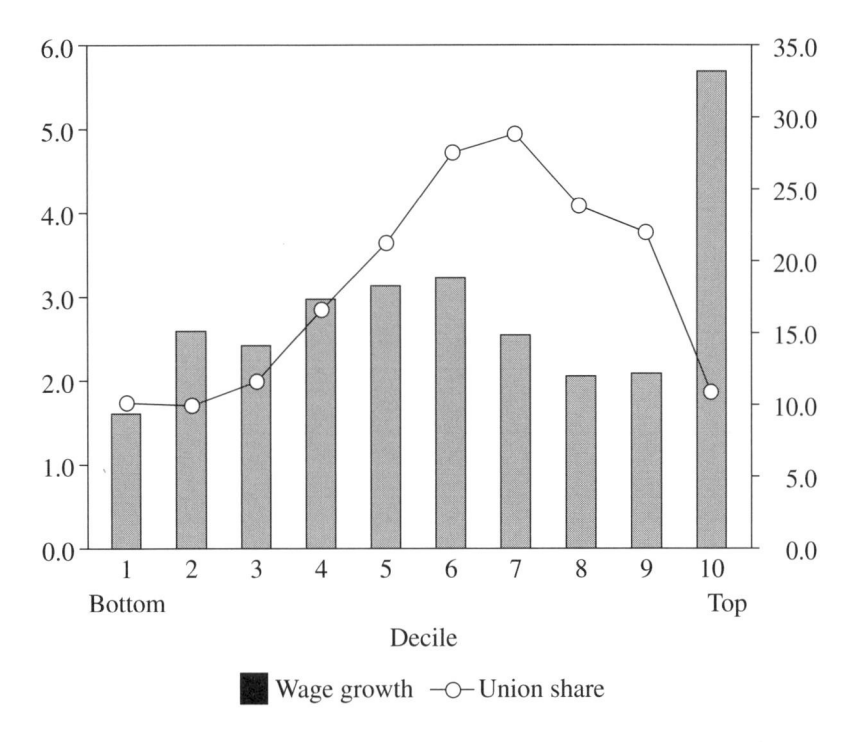

Note: Union share is calculated as the share of production workers in unionized firms as a fraction of all workers in each decile.

Source: Authors' calculations based on data from Ministry of Labor, *Wage Structure Survey* (1978–99).

Figure 10.4 Wage growth vs union share, 1998–99 (%)

agreements. They have requested input into managerial decisions on employment issues, sometimes actively through management–union agreements, at other times through more passive mechanisms such as information sharing.[43] These efforts by unions to maintain job security showed up in an increased number of strikes over employment issues, as shown in Panel A of Table 10.3.

In contrast, there was little sign of cooperation between unions and firms designed to improve productivity with the goal of enhancing job security. The KCTU, for example, focused on efforts to obtain a no-layoff pledge from employers; the result was an increase in strikes and workdays lost (see Panel B of Table 10.3).[44] Meanwhile, politically oriented unions, again led by the KCTU, engaged in an anti-redundancy campaign against the government.

Table 10.3 Indicators of union activity

A. Strikes by issue in the 1990s

	1991	1993	1995	1997	1998	1999	2000
Wage raise	132	66	33	18	28	40	27
Unpaid wages/layoffs	12	12	1	3	26	22	9
Collective agreement	90	66	54	57	67	136	194
Employment issues*	34	14	5	6	10	47	27

B. Union Activity, 1995–2000

	1995	1996	1997	1998	1999	2000
Number of unions	6605	6424	5733	5560	5637	5698
Union membership**	1615	1599	1484	1402	1481	1527
Strikes	88	85	78	129	198	250
Strike participants**	50	79	44	146	92	178
Workdays lost***	393	893	445	1452	1366	1894

Notes:
* Includes issues on work condition, workloads, redundancy layoff, layoff in M&As, contract buyout, M&A, work assignment and promotion.
** 1000 persons.
*** 1000 man-days.

Source: Ministry of Labor (1987–2000).

They continued to argue to their members that political arrangements could negate the basic market principle that job security cannot be ensured unless firms remain productive and competitive.[45]

There was also a movement toward industrial unions, again orchestrated by the KCTU and motivated by the belief that workers would have more power if organized into large industrial unions rather than a multitude of independent establishment-level unions.[46] This movement met with some success, as industry-level unions were formed among teachers, nurses, bank employees, taxi-cab drivers and metal-manufacturing workers. A substantial fraction of the membership of the KCTU (approximately 40 percent) belonged to industry-level unions by 2001.

Industry-level union organization may have two opposing effects on the Korean economy. To the extent that industrial unions provide an institutionalized communication channel exclusively for discussion of social and political agendas, bargaining on enterprise-level issues such as wages and employment can be facilitated.[47] In the past, social and political agendas were often intermingled with wage and employment issues in enterprise-level negotiations, complicating the conclusion of agreements. The increased political influence of industrial unions, if focused on social issues and pursued through channels outside the workplace, thus promises greater workplace harmony and efficiency.

However, it is also possible that the growth of industrial unions will increase the economic leverage of the unions, weakening their incentive to participate in a cooperative partnership. Moreover, industrial unions may make insider/outsider problems more serious if they devote their monopoly power mainly to enhancing their incumbent members' interests.[48] More frequent strikes and faster wage growth in unionized sectors during the crisis suggest that this negative outcome is a real danger in Korea.[49]

THE ROLE OF GOVERNMENT

The 1997–98 financial crisis and the subsequent process of restructuring have created a Korean economy more exposed to competitive pressure. The *chaebols* and large firms have become more subject to market discipline, as their monopoly rents have disappeared and the latitude for government intervention has declined. Union jobs are no longer protected from downsizing, and the shift in industrial structure in directions that strengthen the demand for skilled workers makes it more difficult to protect the high-wage union jobs of unskilled workers. The quality of jobs has already deteriorated among less-skilled workers, and wage inequality has increased.

Workers and unions in Korea have responded to the deterioration in their economic situation through collective action to protect their wages and job security. However, collective action to defend existing prerogatives is not a sufficient response to the far-reaching changes in the structure of the Korean economy. Skill-biased technological progress and capital mobility will continue to place less-skilled workers at a disadvantage, and only higher labor productivity will effectively secure jobs and wages. Neither collective action nor government intervention will be an effective means of protecting jobs and wages unless they contribute to the enhancement of productivity.

Consequently, the role of government should be to promote workplace partnership and investment in human capital with the aim of raising labor productivity. The government should retain a posture of neutrality toward industrial relations and refrain from politically motivated interventions. The more government intervention is expected, the less effort will be expended by the social partners in forging a cooperative partnership.[50] At the same time, the government needs to promote competition in the market to reduce non-competitive rents that would weaken market discipline in industrial relations.

Labor market policy should focus on job creation, education and training to ensure efficient supply responses to the shift in demand toward more skilled workers. That shift is certain to continue due to a combination of technological progress, increased international trade and increased capital mobility. Human capital investment, in particular, should be a high priority, especially in so far as the crisis interrupted such investment.[51] Training, so long as it is efficiently provided, benefits both firms and workers. It offers yet another context in which workplace partnership can be promoted. Finally, given the widening wage and income inequality experienced since the crisis, there is a need for redistribution policies, such as a progressive income tax, earned income tax credit, effective placement service and a stronger social safety net.

If these policies are pursued together, they will create the possibility that Korea can finally put behind it the atmosphere of confrontation that has long characterized its industrial relations and develop a truly productive workplace partnership.

NOTES

1. The authors gratefully acknowledge the financial support for this research from the Research Center for International Finance (RCIF) at Seoul National University. The views expressed in this chapter are the authors' own and do not necessarily reflect the views of the RCIF. Any remaining errors are the authors' own.
2. Although the KCTU had been influential because it organized most unions at the *chaebols* and large firms, its lack of legal status had been used to exclude it from talks between labor and the government and also for repressing its militant strikes.
3. The KCTU also gained politically from both the anti-redundancy campaign and withdrawal from the Tripartite Commission as many workers took sides in response to the decision. The membership of the KCTU kept increasing during the crisis, from 400 000 in 1997 to 615 000 in 2000, while that of the FKTU declined.
4. The FKTU, which supported the ruling party during the presidential election, attempted to pressure that party through the Commission to protect its interests. However, the small labor party formed by the KCTU in the election failed to attract sufficient attention from voters.
5. The agreement between the FKTU and the business leaders to postpone the ban on employers' payments to full-time union officials and the introduction of multi-unionism within establishments in February 2001 was an example of such collusion. A further problem was that the participating unions were concentrated among large firms and represented only 13 percent of all wage and salary workers. Estimated from data in Ministry of Labor (1987–2000).
6. The Commission was called upon by President Kim Dae Jung to shape labor market policies during the crisis. It consisted of union representatives, business representatives, and a neutral party of government officials and professionals. The major issues discussed in the Commission included the introduction of redundancy layoff and temporary work agency, and unemployment policies.

7. As a result, many firms tried wage reductions, work sharing, not filling vacancies arising from quits or retirement, no new hires, and contract buyout with a bonus before executing redundancy layoffs.
8. If a firm executed a layoff before going through all these steps, the employer would be subject to a fine and possible imprisonment. However, imprisonment was rare, and the court had ruled for restoration of the previous employment relationship in most unlawful layoff cases. Still, lengthy strikes and costly lawsuits were frequent until final rulings.
9. Ultimately, the company shed additional workers, but only through 'honorary retirement,' a type of contract buyout that included generous severance pay. But, more than anything, this case illustrated how difficult it remained for a company to adjust its workforce even under the newly introduced layoff law. See below.
10. Previously, a temporary employment contract exceeding a year was illegal in Korea, but the restriction was loosened to improve labor market flexibility, allowing employers to outsource workers from employment agencies on longer-term contracts.
11. It was allowed in the labor law amendment in 1997, a year earlier than the redundancy layoff bill.
12. The job placement rate among trainees was 21.2 percent in 1998, and 35.3 percent in 1999.
13. For example, among those who involuntarily lost their job in 1998, only 18 percent was through semi-voluntary retirement or layoff from surviving firms.
14. Not surprisingly, many instances of fraud have been reported, and the program created little employment in the aggregate.
15. And most of them were older individuals.
16. The program classifies the beneficiaries into three groups – home care, institutional care, and self-support. Those under home care received 162 000 won per month in 1998 (22 percent higher than in 1997), and those under institutional care received 125 000 won per month (16 percent higher). Those in the self-support program were eligible for in-kind transfers and subsidized loans, but not for cash benefits as they were considered to be able to work. Among the additional 310 000 people covered, 233 000 were classified in the self-support program as most were job losers able to work (Ministry of Labor, 1988, 1999).
17. These programs had only a limited impact for two reasons. First, the government intended to finance the program by issuing bonds, but sales of the bonds were far below the target as yields were set below the market interest rate. Second, the loan windows were set up in commercial banks, and the banks applied a set of restrictive conditions on loan approval. For example, applicants for loans were requested to provide some collateral or co-signers, neither of which was easy for a jobless person.
18. The public work program also had some side effects. First, a major portion of the participants in the program was previously nonparticipating population, not job losers. Second, the compensation level was too generous at 500 000 won per month, which was approximately 50 percent higher than the legal minimum wage. As a result, workers who would have sought employment in small, low-wage businesses tended to prefer public work programs.
19. Even unemployment insurance, which covered relatively large firms, was not fully functional, in that only 11 percent of the eligible actually received the benefits, as noted above. See Ministry of Labor (2001).
20. See Y. Choi (2002) for a detailed discussion on workplace partnership.
21. More detailed discussion on the UK case will be given in a later section. See Aoki (1988), Atkinson (1984), Kalleberg (1997), Ouchi (1981) and Thompson (1967) for the literature on the high-performance workplace. Abraham (1990) and a more recent study by Cappelli and Neumark (2001) find little evidence for correlation between job security and organizational flexibility.
22. In addition, the share of households with no earners rose from 6.3 percent to 6.8 percent between 1997 and 1998.
23. High school dropouts lost more than a million jobs, while 20- to 29-year-olds lost 710 000.

23. See D. Kim and Yoo (2001) for the detailed sectoral and demographic pattern of employment changes.
24. See D. Kim (2001a). Newly created jobs would have paid 6 percent lower wages than destroyed jobs even in the absence of downward pressure from the economic crisis as most new jobs were retail/service and unskilled jobs while destroyed jobs were high-wage manufacturing jobs. Weekly work hours tended to be longer by 3.7 hours. Such wage and hours gaps between destroyed and created jobs tended to be greater among high-skilled workers, suggesting the possibility of occupational downgrading.
25. In 1998, for example, more than half (51.2 percent) of newly created daily-work positions were in the government sector, an enormous increase from 2.8 percent in 1997. Employment in agriculture and fisheries and public administration, which had following a declining trend, recorded substantial net growth in 1998. Evidently, the traditional and public sectors have helped to buffer the shock to hard-hit workers and households.
26. G.-J. Yoo (1999a) estimates that the natural rate of unemployment may have risen to 6.7 percent in 1998, while K.-H. Shin (1999) estimates it at 5–6 percent in 1998. Yang (1999) argues that unemployment has had a tendency to persist. Unemployment rose from 452 000 in October 1997 to 1.65 million in July 1998, with three-fourths of the increase in a five-month period between October 1997 and March 1998. For the detailed demographic pattern of unemployment changes, see D. Kim and Yoo (2001).
27. This permanent increase appears to reflect changes in search behavior. Unemployment increased 'too fast,' given the magnitude of demand shock. The demand shock placed on the economy by the crisis is roughly comparable to the shock that took place in 1979–80 following the second oil shock. Between 1979 and 1980, real GDP growth fell by 9.8 percentage points and the unemployment rate rose by 1.4 percentage points. Real GDP growth fell by 10.8 percentage points between 1997 and 1998, which was reasonably comparable to the 1979–80 changes, but the unemployment rate increased by 4.2 percentage points. Although the two shocks were almost 20 years apart and the level of industrialization differed, the differences in unemployment responses appear too large. Other studies also point out that unemployment rose too fast in 1998. G.-J. Yoo (1999b) shows that the unemployment rate in 1998 should have been 4.4 percent based on the Okun coefficient from the past three decades.
28. Indeed, middle-aged women accounted for a majority of the increase in the numbers initiating job search from nonparticipation, at least a part of which is the added worker effect (D. Kim, 2000a).
29. See D. Kim (2001a).
30. It is still unclear whether the public work program has absorbed more unemployed workers than nonparticipants drawn into unemployment by the program. D. Kim (2000b) shows that labor supply increased most among the population traditionally detached from the market: women, old and less educated. He concludes that they might have remained idle had it not been for the unemployment benefits offered by the government.
31. Labor standard law in Korea did not allow a fixed-term contract exceeding a year in most cases. As a result, most permanent employees have contracts with an unspecified term length.
32. Unpaid family workers working fewer than 18 hours a week are classified as jobless.
33. A part of the sharp increase in non-regular workers represents the public work program offered to the unemployed. D. Kim (2001a) shows that the government sector accounted for 51.2 percent of the net increase in daily employment in 1998, which increased from a mere 2.8 percent in 1997.
34. Similar implications flow from the literature on high-performance organizations.
35. D. Kim (2001b) considered the high-performance organization and core–periphery worker arguments against the cost-reduction hypothesis to explain the increase in non-regular workers. K.-S. Choi (2001) also reports a similar result.
36. An OECD report indicates that worker protection tends to increase the size of non-regular employment (OECD, 1999).
37. Real wages (nominal wages adjusted for producer prices) grew by 14.9 percent and 12.2 percent per year during the two subperiods referred to in the previous footnote.

38. The decline in the gender wage gap reflected a relative increase in demand for women. The declines in age and college premiums appeared to have reflected the growing number of older workers and college-educated workers in the economy.
39. In addition, wage changes were not the same in all sectors. Nominal wages fell by 6–10 percent in manufacturing, construction, retail and wholesale trades, and financial, insurance, and real estate (FIRE) between July 1997 and July 1998, while changing little in transportation, communication and services, and even rising in public utilities. Utilities, of course, are heavily unionized public enterprises.
40. One should bear in mind that the increase in income inequality is quite likely to be greater than reported in the figure because the results are obtained from 'wages of employees' without considering non-employees. The share of households with no labor earnings increased from 6.8 percent in 1998 to 7.9 percent in 1999, suggesting that the employment effect could be a major factor in inequality.
41. Whether a worker is a union member or not is not identified in the data; only whether a union exists in the firm in which the worker is employed is identified. For this reason, we classify production workers in unionized firms as unionized workers. Of course, some clerical and sales workers can belong to a union, but we exclude them because they tend to be less represented by a union than production workers. Thus readers must not interpret the numbers in Figure 10.4 as the actual 'penetration' rate, but as a proxy for unionization.
42. Non-regular jobs are not covered in the survey on which Figure 10.2 is based. Non-regular jobs paid an estimated 10–20 percent less in wages than regular jobs (Bae, 2001). Note also that, as mentioned before, subsidized loans to high-tech 'venture' businesses may have also contributed to widening wage inequality.
43. The managerial issues in which unions participated varied across industries. In manufacturing, subcontracts were the main issues, while continued employment in M&As was the main issue in construction. In the financial sector, non-regular employment was the main issue. These cases indicate the various sources of job insecurity. After the crisis, collective agreements often included a job security clause. In 2000, 15.9 percent of all agreements included such a clause, and so did 24.7 percent of agreements in firms with 1000 or more workers. However, job security clauses were only symbolic in half of them (or 49.6 percent) and were not actually practical (J.-K. Kim et al., 2001).
44. Such a strategy was not altogether successful. The strike by subway workers in Seoul in 1999, the strike by financial sector workers in 2000, and the strike of Daewoo workers in 2001 all failed to achieve job security.
45. Lack of understanding of market discipline appears to be more serious in public enterprises such as railways and gas and electricity utilities. For example, in 1999, the subway workers' union in Seoul voted out the leadership that had emphasized partnerships and no strikes.
46. There were a few driving forces for the movement toward industry-level organization. First, the ban on employers paying full-time union officials was scheduled to go into effect in 2002, although it was postponed until 2007 in an agreement in the Tripartite Commission without the KCTU's presence. Industrial unions would make it easier to maintain unions in small firms which otherwise would not be financially self-sufficient under the ban. Second, the legal constraints on industrial-level unions were relaxed through the amendment of the Trade Union Act in 1997, which allowed conversion of existing enterprise-level unions into industrial unions. Before the amendment, enterprise-level unions had to be dissolved before setting up a branch of an industrial union.
47. Such social and political agendas may include social insurance, taxation and labor regulations, and bargaining costs can be reduced at least at the enterprise level.
48. Industry-level unionism has often shown poorer economic performance than enterprise-level unionism (Calmfors and Driffill, 1988; IMF, 1999).
49. Log wage differentials between organized and unorganized firms rose from 0.234 in 1998 to 0.333 in 2000 among men, and from 0.280 to 0.360 among men in manufacturing sectors during the same period. See also E.-J. Shin (2001) for the increase in the union wage effect and polarization between organized and unorganized sectors during the crisis.
50. See Pencavel (1996) for the importance of government neutrality in industrial relations.

One may also refer to Tony Blair's 'New Labour' in the UK, which is differentiated from the past Labour government by non-interventionist government and emphasis on partnership. In particular, Mr Blair made clear that the government places strong emphasis on 'free' business and would not support unions hindering it (McIlroy, 1998).

51. The fraction of 15- to 17-year-olds enrolled in school declined by 0.4 percentage points between 1997 and 1999, and the fraction searching for jobs increased by 0.2 percentage points during the same period (National Statistical Office, 1987–99). In addition, many households reduced educational expenditures during the crisis quite substantially. Educational expenditures declined by 8.7 percent among urban working households in 1998. The decline was greater among low-income households: it declined by 13.0 percent among the households in the bottom 40 percent of the income distribution, while it declined only by 4.4 percent among the top 40 percent. If this continues, intergenerational earnings mobility will be seriously impaired in the Korean labor market.

Comment on Chapters 8, 9 and 10

Stijn Claessens

OVERALL COMMENTS

This is a very nice set of chapters on three closely related areas written by excellent scholars in their respective fields. Financial and corporate sector behavior and restructuring and labor policies relate closely in any circumstance, but especially around crises. This is even more so in Korea where, as the chapters show, the three aspects have had long-lasting and mostly symbiotic relationships. The chapters are also related as they have a common theme, which is the role of the state. Before the 1997 crisis, the state had a large role in triggering some of the problems. During the crisis, the government had to take a large role in the restructuring. The issues and the lessons in all three areas are on how to phase out the state after the crisis.

There are also common weak points in the chapters, however. In particular, none of the chapters does much in the way of cross-country comparisons. This makes it hard to benchmark how far Korea has come with its restructuring and structural reform. One can have one's own opinion on whether the glass is half-full or half-empty; my view is that it is more half-empty. Preferably, however, one would like to see some numerical measures and qualitative benchmarks which can help guide policy makers as to what still needs to be done and what is most urgent. This also relates to the other common weak point, which is that there is very limited quantification of specific issues and questions. For example, the degree of restructuring and possibly nonperforming loans or the corporate governance issues are not analyzed with any new data. This is probably unavoidable in these overview chapters, but perhaps more evidence from other papers could be cited. I now provide some specific comments on each of the three chapters.

Financial Sector Chapter

The chapter shows very clearly how an unbalanced (or, perhaps better, what turned out *ex post* to be 'ill-designed') financial liberalization and too much government control, with extensive guarantees and moral hazard, both *ex ante* and *ex post*, can lead to many risks and abuses, and finally a financial crisis in 1997. The chapter also shows the weakness of a 'finger-in-the-dyke' approach. It is impossible to stem problems in one segment of the financial system with some makeshift or special regulations, as problems will spill over from one market to another. The chapter shows clearly how many times this has happened in Korea. Before the crisis, external borrowings became the escape valve. During the crisis, problems moved from the banking system to the NBFIs as *chaebols* issued large amounts of bonds, and then back, as the banks had to provide financing to the NBFIs. The lesson is that as long as the system is not fully reformed, that is, the deeper structure is not changed, any changes to the regulations at the margin may be immaterial. And, most importantly, the government is likely to absorb the costs.

The chapter also shows Korea was undertaking reforms before the crisis, but not rapidly enough. The crisis was a catalyst in that sense and led to an improvement in the overall regulatory and supervisory framework, recapitalization and consolidation of the banking system, and so on. The crisis may thus have been a good thing, and the glass would not be as full, or would be more empty, had it not been for the crisis.

I have some comments on the restructuring section. The chapter shows that the restructuring involved a large role of government, as in most systemic bank restructuring cases. The chapter highlights the various measures the government undertook in the restructuring phase, some of which were new to me. It also stresses the implications and complications. Although stability has returned, it has required a government guarantee that remains partly in force, at least in terms of perception. The chapter is also less sure to what extent nonperforming loans have been reduced or whether most of the restructuring has been cosmetic. I would be skeptical of the official figures, as these have proven time and time again to be overly optimistic, in most countries and also in Korea.

The chapter downplays the still very large government stake in the Korean banking system, insurance, nonbank financial institutions, and so on. It could have highlighted the limited ownership changes that have taken place and the few 'good' strategic owners that have been introduced following the crisis. This lack of good owners is all the more important as the chapter shows that profitability in the banking system is still slim. Combined with the weak corporate governance, this raises questions about whether banks are now overextending in real estate and consumer finance, leading to new risks.

In terms of the chapter's analysis of the more structural dimensions of financial reforms, I have a few comments. I find too much stress is given to the label 'market-based' financial system that has been attached to Korea at some point. It probably does not fit, as Korea is much more bank-based, but the data just ended up assigning the label. More relevant is that the latest findings suggest that the functions performed by different financial services matter most, rather than the 'institutions' that house the various services. In turn, this means that the basic foundations for a financial system are key necessities – good laws, proper accounting, adequate disclosure, good incentives, and so on – rather than a certain specific mix of banks and securities markets.

I also consider the chapter too strong on the issues of concentration in the banking system. The Korean banking system may seem concentrated, but the system was overcompetitive before the crisis, as margins were very slim and there were too many banks and nonbank financial institutions competing with banks. Further consolidation in the banking system may still be necessary. The real issue, as economic theory tells us, is contestability, that is, a clear entry and exit regime. One weak link is entry, as few domestic parties are qualified and few foreign investors have shown interest. But the policy issue in Korea is more exit; that is, there needs to be an adequate closure regime for weak financial institutions. This exit regime was surely weak before the crisis, but I am not sure how much better it is now. Even with some structural changes, the government still has a bias in favour of bail out.

In my mind the lesson of financial sector reform in Korea is that improved credit evaluation (risk management) is a key factor. Capital adequacy, often used as a measure of progress, may not be the relevant measure. First, it is hard to measure capitalization, but also the implicit government guarantee is still large, making capital adequacy less relevant. The question rather needs to be: do owners have their own capital at risk and, thus, are the incentives right? Here more attention could have been devoted to the corporate governance dimension. The lack of good owners in Korean banks was a problem before the crisis. As noted, even today there are few strategic owners. This puts a heavier burden on corporate governance and the chapter could have reported more what is being done in relation to disclosure, requiring subordinated debt, enhancing minority rights, and the like. Lastly, the chapter needs to comment on whether there was a missed opportunity to privatize more of the banking system to foreigners. Other country examples suggest that this can be very effective in changing the mindset of bank managers.

I have a few minor questions on this chapter as well. It argues that risk-based pricing helps to resolve nonperforming loans. I think this should not be called 'risk-based pricing' but rather the need for regulations that require banks to provision in accordance with risks and penalties to create incentives for creditors to accept write-offs. I was also puzzled by the comment on high interest rates leading to higher margins. This need not be the case. Yes, deposit rates typically will go up faster than lending rates and *ex ante* the spread may thus go up. But, *ex post*, the real margin earned is rather likely to decline as the quality of loans worsens due to the economic crisis and as interest rates go up.

Corporate Sector Chapter

The chapter outlines succinctly the history of government direction and associated corporate sector bailouts in Korea. In earlier decades, these bailouts were at the industry level. More recently and in the crisis period, the bailouts have been at the firm (*chaebol*) level. The chapter also makes clear that the corporate sector is the mirror image of the financial sector. Finally, the chapter demonstrates that the corporate governance framework in Korea did not keep up with the diminished role of the state. No alternative outsider emerged to fill the gap left by the state. This weak oversight led, before the crisis, to poorer corporate sector performance and a build-up of financial and real risks. Following some smaller bankruptcies, the problems accelerated in 1997 and then the *chaebols* became 'too large to ignore' in the crisis. Many corporations were *de facto* bailed out, most notably Daewoo, through government assumption of nonperforming loans. The crisis did trigger some major restructuring in the corporate sector, however, and started rounds of structural reforms.

I have some comments on the analysis of the problems before the crisis. The chapter could have tried to pull the facts before the crisis closer together in a single unified framework. Korean corporations were not necessarily badly run, but they engaged in a set of related risky activities. They took many real risks through excessive diversification. Part of this risk-taking was allowed by passive debt holders (banks and bonds), but banks and to some extent bond-holders had the benefit of moral hazard and *ex post* bailouts. Not all of the rewards of the corporations' activities went to outside investors. For the profitable firms, insiders took many returns privately and minority shareholders faced expropriation. This led to a set of related outcomes. One was risky financial structures, as shown in the high financial leverage, and much short-term and foreign exchange borrowing. The second outcome was low measured rates of return, low valuation for corporations with worse ownership structures and a high control premium. These issues are related and the chapter could have quantified and linked these issues more closely together.

In terms of my comments on the crisis and restructuring sections, it is clear that compared to other (East Asian) countries, restructuring in Korea was reasonably well executed. The bankruptcy system worked quite well, and some large *chaebols* even went bankrupt. Complemented with a relatively tight out-of-court framework (the London rules), corporate sector restructuring was fairly efficient. Labor restructuring (layoffs, wage cuts) were relatively large, asset spin-offs considerable, and in the end the corporate sector recovery was quite quick. The situation today also looks fairly good. Financial leverage is much lower, interest coverage is better, and accounting rates of return have improved. Firms' market valuations have recovered and economic growth is up, although still below pre-crisis levels. Moreover, group-affiliated firms are now acting more independently, showing that the hold of the *chaebol* structure has declined. Various structural reforms have also accompanied restructuring, although one can debate their depth. Overall, the restructuring was well executed. My main criticism is that the restructuring was probably more government directed than necessary and at high fiscal costs.

I have more comments on the (post-) restructuring, structural reform agenda. Here the chapter may be too positive. Questions remain among many observers on the depth of reforms and the sustainability of the recovery. A few specific doubts can be mentioned. The restructuring early on was very cosmetic in nature and it took several rounds to get the problems to the surface. Who is to say that the last round has been reached? Another point is that leverage has often been lowered due to some questionable accounting measures. Also the improvement in interest coverage may be mostly due to lower interest rates. There may still be many firms that risk illiquidity or even insolvency if (international) growth slows down or if (domestic) interest rates go up. Finally, firm valuation is still below international levels: does this reflect minority shareholders' concern about expropriation, poor performance, bad firm management, or all three?

Restructuring typically takes time and these questions are common when evaluating restructuring successes. Yet one can question the success of Korea on two counts. Across countries, it has become clear that any final success will require both ownership changes and deep structural reforms. On both counts, Korea is somewhat behind. Let me analyze both.

The large government role in restructuring was inevitable, but maybe an opportunity was missed, as the government did not actively seek new owners. Several options could have been pursued or pursued more aggressively. One would have been to get more foreign owners to buy distressed assets and corporations, especially in the financial sector. Another option to change ownership would have been to endow new private pension funds with the (nonperforming) assets from banks, instead of transferring the nonperforming loans to KAMCO and then having KAMCO sell them. Over time, these assets could have been converted into equity. With proper private sector governance of such funds, this could have created a new class of owners. A third option would have been using mixed private–public corporate restructuring vehicles where (foreign) managers take on the role of managing, on a performance basis, nonperforming assets. Another option would have been to sell stakes on an industry or firm basis to employees, as happened in Chile.

Such ownership changes are important as corporate governance changes, while on paper better, still lack enforcement and are not deep enough. Intra-group transactions, for example, seem to worsen again in transparency.

The other areas where Korea is behind are the structural reforms. Many deeper reforms are still necessary, in my assessment. While progress to date is hard to assess, in part because cross-country comparisons are missing from the chapter, many indicators raise questions about the reforms' depth. Facts such as the large premium for control, low firm valuation, the lack of a market for corporate control, the limited influence of minority directors, and so on suggest to me incomplete corporate governance reform. Also, the quality of financial information and disclosure is still insufficient, as daily news reports make clear. And there is still a lack of a credible exit threat for large firms. This combines with the role of creditors, which is limited, as the financial sector is still weak and weakly governed. Although creditor rights have improved, creditors' incentives are thus still not sufficient. I would thus be more cautious about progress.

Labor Markets Chapter

This is not my area of research, but the chapter shows that problems in the labor sector are similar to those in other sectors. It makes clear that Korea has had difficult relationships between corporations and labor. Many reforms have been undertaken, but mistrust remains. My main comment here is that Korea may have missed an opportunity to make labor part of the restructuring by letting it share in new ownership structures. During the crisis, the government nationalized many corporate sector assets. Vehicles could have been created to provide more incentives for labor to participate in positive restructuring by giving labor an explicit ownership stake. The models could have been some of those mentioned above in my discussion of the corporate sector restructuring chapter. An ownership stake for labor could have reduced the tensions post-crisis. It could also have created a new class of owners, important for corporate governance in the longer run. More generally, it could have made voters more interested in the success of reforms, which, as some of the other chapters in this book show, is a long-term weak point in the Korean reforms to date.

Comment on Chapters 8, 9 and 10

Mitsuhiro Fukao

After reading these three chapters, I am especially impressed by the extent of the changes in the economic structure of the Korean economy since 1997: the resolution of the NPL (nonperforming loan) problem, the liberalization of financial markets including the elimination of exchange controls on international capital transactions, and the deep reform in corporate governance structures. These reforms that were recommended by the IMF after the crisis were resisted by Korean people at the time of implementation. However, the prescribed bitter medicine has started to work, and the intervention by the IMF was a disguised blessing after all.

The Japanese economy is still suffering from deflation and an extremely fragile financial system. Japan's GDP deflator has fallen by about 8 percent since 1994 (adjusted for the increase in consumption tax in 1997) and it is still falling at about 1.5 percent per annum at the time of writing. As a result, the corporate sector has been suffering from the increasing real value of its liabilities. The banking sector has been losing money ever since 1993 and its net cash flow is not enough to write off new loan losses even in financial year 2001. The Japanese corporate governance structure is suffering from lack of shareholder discipline. In particular, Japanese banks face little pressure form shareholders even though they have been losing money for a long period of time. This is because about half of the largest five shareholders of major Japanese banks are mutual life insurance companies that have a weak governance structure. Since the management of mutual life insurance companies can effectively choose the participants of the representative policy-holders' meeting, they can self-perpetuate without shareholder discipline. Moreover, many life insurance companies do not have enough capital and ask banks to provide equity. This effective cross-shareholding between banks and life insurance companies significantly weakened the market discipline felt by major financial institutions.

The chapter by Hahm is a very well written overview of the changing Korean financial system and I learned a great deal about this important subject. I felt that the Korean crisis was yet more evidence of the difficulty of managing the financial liberalization process. When an economy tries to liberalize its financial system, the sectors that had faced credit constraints suddenly find that they can raise money fairly freely. In the Korean case, in the early 1990s *chaebols* found that they were no longer facing credit allocation by the government and started to invest freely with short-term funds from NBFIs. Most Nordic countries and Japan had a similar experience in the late 1980s (see Shigemi, 1995).

Regarding the following description of the Japanese financial system 'savers continued to supply funds to banks, and banks, with increasingly abundant liquidity, had no choice but to increase their lending on risky projects, including real estate, as they were not allowed to engage in new businesses,' I have a different interpretation.

Since banks could easily reduce the size of intermediation by increasing the spread between lending interest rate and deposit interest rate, we should interpret their aggressive lending behavior as a conscious decision. In my opinion, banks tried to maintain profits in the face of increasing defection of traditional customers, big companies, to the newly liberalized capital market in the early 1980s. In order to keep asset size and profit, they went into a new line of business, the 'middle market.' In fact, the middle market was lending for real estate development. Thanks to the very loose monetary policy in the mid-1980s and gradually rising real estate prices, banks could easily increase loans secured by real estate. Until the end of the 1980s, real estate lending was the safest business, with almost no loan losses. Thus, this process created a huge real estate bubble that will be remembered by historians as a successor to the tulip bubble in the Netherlands.

Regarding the issue of market discipline on banks, I do not expect that depositors provide strong discipline because they are protected by deposit insurance system. I believe it is important to wipe out the equity capital and the subordinated debts of a failed bank. By making sure that the government never protects the capital of a bank, stock prices and the yields on subordinated debt will function as good indicators of the financial health of the bank. In the Japanese case, the government did wipe out the equity capital of the Long-Term Credit Bank of Japan and Japan Credit Bank but protected the investors of their subordinated debt, that is, life insurance companies. In future, the government should wipe out the subordinated debts of failed banks.

I learned a great deal from the Joh and Choi–Kim chapters about the changes in the Korean corporate sector and labor market. One missing issue in these two chapters is discussion on the compatibility of the new liberal financial structure and the still rigid employment structure.

Japanese firms have been trying to maintain a long-term employment system with upward-sloping age–wage structure and a large severance payment at the very end of employment. This employment structure needs a fairly stable management that can honor this long-term commitment. Because of the weakening capital base of banks, talented and ambitious young workers are deserting Japanese banks and joining foreign financial institutions. Moreover, I speculate that the seniority-based compensation structure would not work in most companies in the long run. This is because most senior managers of such companies would receive over-generous compensation compared with their true value in the job market. As a result, these managers would become yes men because they would try to stay with the generous company as long as possible. A CEO surround by yes men cannot make good decisions and his company will lose competitiveness in the long run.

Because of the recent liberalization of mergers and acquisitions of Korean companies, employees cannot count on long-term stability of management. This is probably the background of the changing tactics of labor unions that are counting on the government as a guarantor of long-term employment. However, government cannot guarantee long-term employment in a single firm when the Korean economy is facing stiff competition from other fast-growing economies, including China. Given the difficulty of outright layoff of redundant workers, one possible way to go is to introduce a more flexible compensation system. If a company is allowed by law to cut wages and salaries of a redundant worker by 20 percent per year, for example, it can adjust employment with prices rather than with quantities. Certainly, this is also a very tough way for any politician to go. In any event, the rigid structure of the labor system might become the Achilles' heel of the Korean economy.

11. Transparency and social capital

Jaeyeol Yee

INTRODUCTION

Five years have passed since the outbreak of the Korean crisis. Painful changes have taken place in the economy, and continue to this day. The country's shattered financial system has been rebuilt.[1] The standard IMF policy package of stabilization, financial restructuring and structural reform has been applied with only slight modification. Reform politics have replaced growth-driven government initiatives. There has been a systematic effort to restructure the economy so as to render Korea more competitive in an increasingly interdependent and open global economy. Five sets of initiatives dominate the reform agenda: raising corporate transparency, strengthening the financial sector, revamping the public sector, introducing labor market flexibility and amicable labor relations, and creating a viable social welfare system.

Compared to other South East Asian countries experiencing financial crises, Korea has successfully reduced its debt overhang in a relatively short period of time by following the IMF's prescriptions. Even before his inauguration, President-elect Kim Dae Jung played a key role in persuading the IMF to become involved in Korea. Market prescriptions have indeed contributed to the subsequent recovery of the economy.[2]

But while the objective of reform has been to strengthen market competition, the result after five years is not fully consistent with the goal. Whereas reform was equated with the elimination of excessive government intervention in the private sector, government agencies have continued to exert a strong influence over the operation of the Korean economy. Rule by law was the motto of the reformers, but personal networks remain central to Korean business. And, in the areas of finance and corporate governance, Korea still lags global standards of transparency.

This gap between aspirations and achievement cannot be explained without considering the institutional and cultural context for reform. Whereas the central intent of the reform agenda was to alter Korea's institutions, the reform effort was itself embedded in that same institutional matrix; it was inevitably compromised as a result. Notwithstanding the apparent triumph of the market, the acclimatization of domestic culture and social institutions to the imperatives of economic and financial liberalization remains incomplete. This is evident in the social turmoil and the clash of conflicting ideas and interests so evident in recent years.

This chapter aims to extend simple economic explanations of the course of post-crisis reform by analyzing its social dimensions. I start by introducing a framework that can be used to classify the different social systems in which the market economy is embedded. I then contrast the Korean and Anglo-American versions of market capitalism and draw implications regarding the causes of the crisis and the course of reform.

ANALYTICAL FRAMEWORK

Three Aspects of a Comparative Typology

A market economy exists in a cultural and social context, which I refer to as the social system. In this chapter I focus on the contrast between the Korean system and the Anglo-American system (the *K-type* and *A-type*, respectively). I distinguish three different dimensions of these systems, as shown in Table 11.1.

Table 11.1 Relational elements of the social system

	K-type	A-type
Power distribution	Unequal, hierarchical	Equal, democratic
Actor	Personalist and obligational collectivism	Opportunistic and self-interested individualism
Contractability	Opaque and private	Transparent and public

Source: See text.

The first dimension is the distribution of power, which can be measured in terms of 'power distance.' At one extreme, power distance is short, and equally endowed agents interact with one another on an equal basis, through what may be referred to as horizontal coordination. At the other extreme, power distribution is long, and agents interact through more hierarchical forms of coordination (forms that typically distinguish principal from agent or leader from follower). In a hierarchical society, people in lower ranks have difficulty registering their opinions, reflecting this long power distance. Hierarchy is often seen as reflecting innate ability. For example, teachers are seen not simply as experts who convey knowledge but rather as masters who teach the wisdom of life. Students are therefore expected to respect their teachers and elders and to receive their instruction passively.[3]

In more individualistic societies characterized by short power distance and horizontal coordination, in contrast, hierarchy is understood as purely instrumental inequality. Teachers and students are regarded as equal human beings who simply have different backgrounds and play different economic and social roles. This has important implications for social interactions; in individualistic societies students are more likely to challenge their teachers' instructions.

The second dimension contrasts the economist's vision of the ego-centered agent with the sociologist's vision of the social being for whom obligation and compliance are the principles shaping human action. This dimension reflects the cultural contrast between individualism and collectivism (Hollingsworth and Boyer, 1997: 9–12).[4] Traditionally, the Western view of human nature was based on individualism. It was derived from a radical interpretation of the concept of freedom, from a divine concept of self as a basis of morality, and from the existence of an absolute standard consisting of self-identity and a sense of right and wrong.[5] Hofstede (1995: 106) offers an interesting formulation of the contrast between collectivism and individualism. As he puts it, in a collectivist environment individuals focus on their extended family or inner group, while in an individualist environment they focus on the nuclear family or themselves. Under collectivism, the social network is of overriding importance, whereas under individualism the individual is the ultimate source of identity. Under collectivism, education begins by learning about 'us' and about the importance of harmony among group members, while education under individualism emphasizes 'me' and honesty. The context for communication also differs in these two settings. In collectivist cultures, individuals convey meaning in contextual terms, while in an individualist culture they tend to be more direct in their communication. Finally, in a collectivist culture, those who violate the rules suffer shame and loss of face but are not considered to be guilty in the same definitive sense as in an individualist culture. These differences find reflection in different management styles: in collectivist societies, employers and employees resemble a family, whereas in individualist societies employment is more of a contractual relationship.

The third dimension according to which social systems can be characterized is the transparency or opacity of the rules governing social relationships. Transparency means that there exists a set of universal rules that are both publicly documented and respected by social actors. Violators can then be punished, in principle, without exception. Opacity means that there is no universal set of rules governing social relationships; rather, the rules are constantly under negotiation by the participants.

Combining these three dimensions, we can distinguish eight types of system, as shown in Table 11.2.[6] While this typology is too simple to capture all the subtleties and complexities of social reality, it is still useful for conceptualizing the questions raised at the beginning of this chapter.

Table 11.2 Typology of social systems

	Power distance	Individualism	Transparency	Labeling
1	Low	Low	Low	Community
2	Low	Low	High	Tocqueville's democracy
3	Low	High	Low	Hobbesian society
4	Low	High	High	Market (A-type)
5	High	Low	Low	Patrimonial Office (K-type)
6	High	Low	High	Rule of the Right
7	High	High	Low	Social Darwinism
8	High	High	High	Bureaucracy

Source: See text.

The first of these eight social systems is *community*, a setting where individuals with equal rights live in interpersonal trust. Cooperatives, credit unions and traditional villages can be thought of as examples of this ideal type. Under community there exist no universal rules applicable to larger society, but individuals have high levels of trust and respect reciprocal ethics *vis-à-vis* other members of their group. The community is an 'island of trust' in the sense that the scope of trust is limited to face-to-face relationships. Thus ties of blood, regional background and religion tend to be vital to the operation of communal systems.

The second system is *patrimonial office*, which involves the exchange of loyalty and patronage within hierarchically organized groupings. Although communal order is often idealized, in practice community often tends to be coupled with hierarchy, in which patron–client relationships play an important role.[7] It is this coupling that distinguishes patrimonial office from community. Korean society is close to this type.

Hobbesian society is a situation where individuals with equal rights compete with each other under neither legitimate rules nor personal trust.

Social Darwinism combines self-interest with hierarchical coordination in the absence of consistent and universal rules. In this system there exists neither interpersonal trust nor institutionalized rule. Because power and authority are distributed unequally, this type of system is sometimes referred to as the law of the jungle or the survival of the fittest. The Machiavellian view of politics and the realist approach to international politics reflect this image of the social system.

The *market* is a system in which equal agents make exchanges to maximize their individual utility subject to a clear set of institutionalized rules. Economists emphasize that the voluntary participation of independent actors is crucial for the existence of an equilibrium consistent with the interests of diverse market participants. But the market requires not only the voluntary participation of independent individuals but also transparent rules for the enforcement of transactions and contracts. According to neo-institutional economists such as North (1990), the rise of the market in Western Europe was crucially conditioned by the development of such rules. In this view, clearly defined and enforced property rights are essential for the development of the market economy because they enable transparent exchange among individuals.[8] In a capitalist market economy, actors are assumed to behave opportunistically when possible; in the absence of clearly defined property rights, that opportunistic behavior may be corrosive to the operation of the market.[9]

Although the Western ideal is equality oriented, there is also the view that it is impossible to have a humane society on the basis of procedural justice and arm's-length contracts alone. The additional element that is required for the smooth functioning of such a system is procedural democracy. Under procedural democracy, citizens actively participate in voluntary associations in both the private and public spheres, giving rise to civic norms that regulate their behavior. We call this *Tocquevillian democracy*.[10]

When unequal hierarchy is combined with transparency, we have *bureaucracy*. As formulated by Weber, this refers to the organizational setting where a concrete document defines the role of participants and a clear assignment of responsibilities and ranks, for which personal and informal trust cannot substitute. Bureaucracy is a system whose efficiency depends on excluding all roles for personal influence and attributes. Predefined rules and procedures enable the organization to operate efficiently regardless of the specific individuals who occupy bureaucratic positions at a point in time.

While communities in the Asian tradition tend to be islands of trust, they have sometimes become efficient organizations when combined with powerful leadership. The efficiency of such systems derives from the leadership's very strong authority. In Confucian culture this is idealized as the *rule of right* (a notion not dissimilar from Plato's concept of the philosopher–king). The source of authority is the charisma or honorable demeanor of the leader. Traditional Korean society under the Confucian order idealized the hegemonic leadership of the *literati* and the voluntary participation and obedience of farmers and lower class, as for example in the case of the *hyangyak*, the traditional Korean community code of ethics (Y. Chang, 1991). The Japanese model of production, known as *Toyotaism*, is a contemporary economic version of the rule of right, in which hierarchy is strong but the moral example of management is combined with significant empowerment of the workers, thereby maintaining flexible structure and enhancing efficiency by eliciting a moral commitment from employees.

Empirical Mapping

To locate the Korean economy in this matrix, I employ data for a range of countries. I measure the individualism and collectivism of different societies using Hofstede's (1995) data. I also draw my measure of power distance from this source.[11] Finally, I measure transparency using the index published annually by Transparency International (TI).[12] All three measures are available for a total of 47 countries. Figure 11.1 shows the mapping of selected countries.

This mapping suggests that the Anglo-American system (*A-type*) and East Asian system (*K-type*) are polar opposites. Korea and Taiwan share a large power distance and strong collectivist or personalist culture combined with high opacity. The Anglo-American system is distinguished by low power distance and high individualism, coupled with relatively high transparency. The East Asian cases have many of the characteristics of patrimonial office, while the Anglo-American cases are closer to the ideal market type or procedural democracy.[13] Note that Singapore is an exception among the East Asian cases. It shares the high power distance and strong collectivism of other Asian countries but also shows exceptional transparency. Although Singapore, Taiwan and Korea are all pointed to in the literature as examples of societies that display so-called 'Asian values,' the findings here suggest that there are important differences in these different manifestations of the Asian model: while Singapore resembles the 'rule of right,' Taiwan and Korea are closer to the traditional patrimonial system. Note also that Japan shares high power distance with Korea but displays less opacity and collectivism.

The competitiveness of an economy is correlated with all three of these dimensions of the social system, but most strongly with transparency (Table 11.3). I measure competitiveness using the index in the *World Competitiveness Yearbook* (2001) published by the Institute for Management Development.[14] This measure is negatively correlated with power distance (the simple correlation is –0.58), and positively correlated with individualism (here the correlation is 0.58). But it shows the strongest correlation with opacity (the simple correlation with competitiveness is –0.82). While cultural inheritances like strong

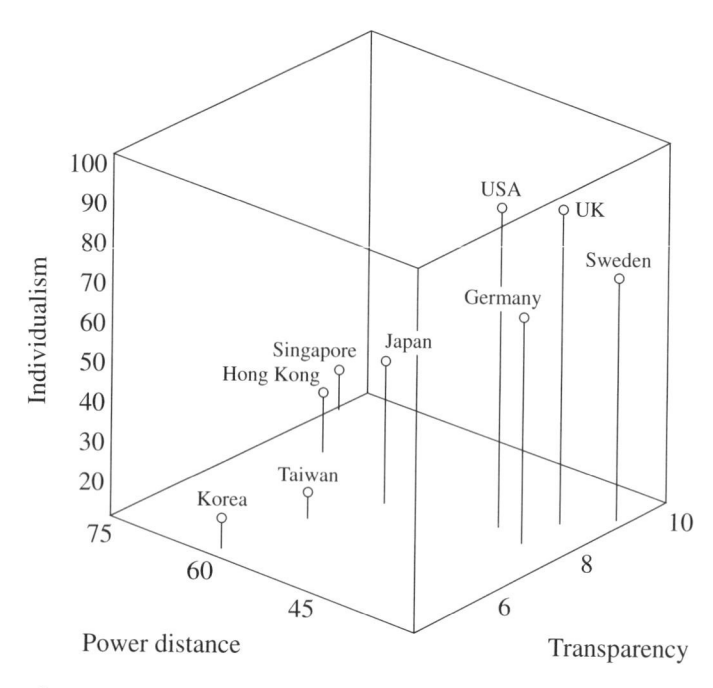

Figure 11.1 International comparison based on social typology

Table 11.3 Correlation of characteristics of social systems

	Competitiveness	PDI	INV	Opacity
Competitiveness	1.000			
PDI	−0.581**	1.000		
INV	0.577**	−0.680**	1.000	
Opacity	−0.822**	−0.694**	−0.715**	1.000

Note: ** p < 0.01.

Source: See text.

power distance and lack of individualism can be negatively related to competitiveness, inadequate transparency is evidently a particular obstacle to enhancing the international competitiveness of an economy.

Comparison of K-type and A-type

The ideal Anglo-Saxon economy, or *A-type*, relies on arm's-length contract relationships among equal actors. Bureaucracy is important for specifying tasks, evaluation procedures and differential rewards for differential effort. The *K-type*, in contrast, is characterized by longer power distance and less individualism. It displays strong collectivist attitudes, whereas the *A-type* attaches high value to individual choice and responsibility.

Such differences are illustrated by the organization of automobile production according what is called *Fordism* in the United States and *Toyotaism* in Japan. Fordism illustrates some of the disadvantages of the low levels of trust characteristic of the *A-type*. It admits a minimal role for input by workers and allows maximum discretion for the manager of the system. To integrate immigrant workers into the modern mass production system, Henry Ford assumed that workers could not read or speak English and organized his factories accordingly. This mode of organization was critical to the success of Fordism in the first half of the twentieth century, when the automobile industry in the United States relied on unskilled and semi-skilled workers. The need for coordination on the shop floor was relatively slight (aside from that automatically provided by the assembly line), and the value of reverse flows of information from the factory floor to the management suite was limited. To put it another way, Fordism thrived because it drew a sharp distinction between development and execution that was well suited to the technological and organizational imperatives of the time.

In contrast, Toyotaism can be understood as a trust-based system. Toyota introduced lifetime employment and encouraged the participation of line workers, allowing them more discretionary power. This facilitated coordination on the shop floor and the reverse flow of information from lower to higher up the managerial hierarchy. Under the market and technological conditions of the late twentieth century, this system facilitated quality manufacturing and encouraged cost-reducing organizational innovations.

The *K-type* shares many similarities with the Toyota system. And to all appearances it was very efficient before the outbreak of the economic crisis in 1997. After the crisis, however, the *K-type* system became a target of criticism; it was disparaged as a hotbed of 'crony capitalism' and cited as the source of Korea's system failure. The question, then, is how a system that had been a source of Korea's strength for many years could suddenly become a source of weakness.

One answer runs as follows. The efficiency of the *K-type* system was maximized when a well-ordered workforce was managed by charismatic leadership, as for example in the President Park era and the period of rapid growth of *chaebol* groups under the charismatic leadership represented by

Chung Joo Young of Hyundai. The cold war facilitated the operation of this system by providing an additional basis of support for Korea's charismatic leaders, in so far as the leadership promised to secure the country from threats emanating from outside.[15] The *K-type* system, characterized by the guiding role of government, strong political leadership and authoritarian mobilization of traditional values, was a highly successful basis for economic growth in the early period.

The economic crisis occurred when the *K-type* system became incompatible with the increasingly global and interconnected world economy. With the collapse of the Eastern bloc and the end of the cold war, economic development as an end in itself was no longer as compelling an imperative as before. Moreover, the world began to work as an open, interconnected market for the first time in nearly a century. Adapting to this new environment required modifying the national economic system. When Korea failed to adapt its system with sufficient speed, it succumbed to the crisis (Castells, 2000).

Which aspect of the *K-type* system was primarily responsible for the country's vulnerability? While the charismatic leadership characteristic of the *K-type* was efficient in promoting the large-scale mobilization of resources, it failed to accommodate diverse interests. The relaxation of government guidance revealed the depth of the cleavages separating interest groups. This episode also revealed that the *K-model*, when coupled with a strong hierarchical structure, has a high potential for system failure. A case in point is the *chaebols*. The scale and complexity of *chaebol* groups constitute a challenge to the family-firm style of management. Yet it was not uncommon for the owners of *chaebol* groups to appoint their offspring as their successors. The second-generation owner, inexperienced at the task of managing a huge modern enterprise, often lacked the requisite expertise.

This problem was compounded to the extent that the distinction between the public and the private is blurred in the *K-type* system. In Korean business culture, loyalty to the supreme chief is synonymous with commitment to the organization. The result is far from the ideal of rational bureaucracy imagined by Weber. Rigid hierarchy and personal loyalty endow the owner with monopoly power and place the entire organization at the whim of a single individual. The result was that Korean firms often assumed higher risks than their Western counterparts. The decisions of one top owner might therefore result in the disastrous bankruptcy of an entire *chaebol* group. Compared to Western corporations, whose ownership is more widely dispersed and whose CEOs are responsible to shareholders, Korean firms therefore tended to be high-risk systems prone to system failure.[16]

Relation-based systems are problematic when combined with strong centralized political power. A clientelist political process can then result, severely distorting the allocation of resources as political parties are run like traditional patrimonial offices instead of like modern democratic organizations. In Korea, because the boss and not the electorate nominated candidates for national and local election, politicians were more concerned about their relationship to the party boss than with representing their constituents and passing effective laws.

Moreover, the dependence of the *K-model* on personal relationships makes it difficult to establish transparency. While transparency is often equated with freedom from corruption, more fundamentally it means the free and unbiased distribution of information. A relational system tends to limit the circulation of information to trusted group members. The result is opacity that promotes clientelism and erodes the effectiveness of public rules. If legal processes are transparent, individuals will depend less on patron–client relationships. If the law is negotiable and arbitrarily applied according to the intimacy of relationships, on the other hand, individuals may rely more on clientelistic mobilization of resources.

As a result, the transparency of public institutions, especially of the legislature, the administration and the judiciary, plays a crucial role in transforming societal trust into social capital. Arguably, the most serious obstacle to Korea's social development has been lack of trust in these public institutions.

LOGIC OF TRANSITION AND ECONOMIC RESTRUCTURING

An economic crisis can be understood as a clash between a *K-type* system and an *A-type* environment. The *K-type* system being based on relationships, finance is relational. The financier possesses implicit or explicit ownership rights in the firm. Under this system, he attempts to secure returns on his investment by retaining some kind of market power over the firm. The basis for this market power is proprietary information; this explains the opacity of such a system.

Given the imperfect nature of the information environment and the supportive role of legal institutions, the *K-type* system was very effective at the early stage of Korean economic development. However, a financial crisis occurs when *K-type* agents borrow a large amount of capital from *A-type* financiers in response to market pressures which create the need to access more funding than can be easily mobilized via existing relationships. The result in the Korean case was a tidal wave of foreign capital pouring into a *K-type* system unprepared to manage the consequences. Or, as Rajan and Zingales (1998) put it, there was a mismatch between long-term need and short-term supply of capital. Denied information on the deployment of their funds and deprived of institutional safeguards to protect their investments, foreign lenders relied for protection on liquidity – on the short-term nature of their loans and investments, which allowed them to close out their position at any time.

So long as the Asian economies continued to grow, all of the parties to this transaction were happy. But growing worries on the part of investors, whether prompted by the realization that capital was poorly invested as the first *chaebols* began to fail in 1996, or by the 'wake-up call' transmitted by the Thai devaluation in 1997, transformed the situation. Arm's-length capital began to flee, precipitating the collapse of the economy.

Centralization or Decentralization?

Greater decentralization was needed to reduce the risk of failure of this social system. Following the agreement with the IMF, the Korean government reached an understanding with the five big *chaebols* and leading creditor banks on the reform of corporate governance. Up to that point, the fusion of ownership and control and control by the founding family of the entire corporate group had left even strong subsidiaries vulnerable to poor performance by their weak siblings. The government's first action was therefore to dismantle the system of cross-payment guarantees among subsidiaries. It prohibited the office of the secretary of the CEO from organizing financing and promotion decisions *chaebol* wide, transferring these functions to the so-called Group Restructuring Coordination Headquarters (GRCH), even though the GRCH in fact possessed no legal authority in these areas. Some *chaebols*, responding to pressure from both the market and government, broke themselves up. The Hyundai Group, once Korea's largest *chaebol*, split into five smaller groups.[17] Sixteen other *chaebols* were forced out of the market. Daewoo Group, once Korea's second biggest conglomerate, was dismantled.

The only guarantee of sound corporate governance is accountability. Until the economic crisis in 1997, the chairmen of the *chaebols* were able to make decisions free of checks and balances. These prerogatives are now widely seen as one of the central causes of the crisis. As a first step toward rectifying this situation, the *chaebols* are being made more accountable internally through the creation of more active and independent boards of directors and externally through the expansion of rights for minority shareholders. However, some question the effectiveness of these reforms on the grounds that the role of minority shareholders and outside directors remains largely symbolic.

In response to the crisis and in a further attempt to create a more decentralized Korean economy, the government took steps to relax its monopoly over economic policy. Authority over budgeting was removed from the Ministry of Finance and Economy and transferred to the Planning and Budget Ministry; the independence of the Bank of Korea was also strengthened. Many of the powers of the Finance Ministry were transferred to the Financial Supervisory

Commission (FSC), then the Financial Supervisory Service (FSS). To promote consumer rights and limit the concentration of economic power among the *chaebols*, the Fair Trade Commission was strengthened.

However, economic reform in Korea has not entailed a wholesale retreat by the government from the market. To the contrary, the authorities have continued to intervene in the economy using the same methods as in the past, notably industrial deals and mergers brokered from above. The irony, then, is that the Korean government was forced to rely on the old model of government intervention to restore the strength of bank and nonbank financial institutions so that the latter could assume the supervisory role of the government. To be sure, a certain degree of decentralization has occurred in the course of economic reform. The newly formed Financial Supervisory Commission (FSC) has exerted tremendous power in regulating business, especially the *chaebol* groups.[18] But, by and large, personal networks remain more important than rule by law.

In particular, there is the problem of personal networks linking financial institutions with their regulators. Since government intervention had been largely responsible for the subsequent problems of illiquidity and insolvency in the financial sector, the operation of these personal networks, which have allowed former FSS officials to find new jobs in private financial institutions, is clearly undesirable.[19] Until recently, former employees of the supervisory organs dominated positions as auditors in banks, securities companies and investment trust firms. For example, 11 high-ranking officials of the FSS found new jobs at financial institutions immediately before the new Public Service Ethics Act took effect.[20] This raises obvious questions of whether officials of the supervisory agencies are carrying out their duties with one eye toward their prospects for subsequent employment in the private sector.

The most vivid example of government intervention is the so-called 'Big Deal' – the large-scale exchange of lines of business by leading *chaebols* – and mergers of financial institutions for the purpose of creating mega-banks. The government had a direct hand in the exchange of businesses by the *chaebols* and acted as minister for the marriage of a number of larger and smaller banks. Of the seven Big Deals, only the merger of a shipbuilder and an engine manufacturer has succeeded in the sense of recording a profit. Most other Big Deals are criticized as failures. The biggest failure of all has been the government-initiated agreement by the rolling-stock sectors of Hyundai, Daewoo and Hanjin to set up the Korea Railroad Rolling Stock Company in September 1999.[21] The purpose of this deal was to alleviate oversupply, avoid cross-investments and facilitate restructuring. However, doing so by forming a mega-enterprise created perverse incentives for the government's supposedly hands-off approach to the private sector. The OECD criticized government pressure for Hyundai, Daewoo and Hanjin to agree to this deal as inconsistent with the basic principles of a market economy. It noted further that reducing the number of corporations in a sector to a handful increases the risk of monopolistic or collusive behavior.

Thus, although the aim of reform has been to decentralize the economy and enhance the autonomy of minor players, the unintended result has been to concentrate yet additional resources into a small number of firms and banks and to encourage continued government intervention.

Is the Personalist Ethic Declining?

Another important change is greater reliance on arm's-length contracts. This is often equated with the introduction of market competition. For example, the government has declared that a certain proportion of higher-ranking positions of the government bureaucracy should be open to outside specialists. For it to open senior positions in its own internal labor market to outside specialists would be revolutionary. Predictably, however, a revolution in public recruitment has not occurred in practice.[22]

The government established a Civil Service Commission in May 1999 to ensure that the civil service system would become more open while maintaining fairness and neutrality in government appointments. After three years, its founding chairman, Kim Kwang-woong, was forced to confess that 'regional, school, and blood ties in the civil bureaucracy were still a barrier to merit-based recruitment and promotion.'[23]

A more drastic experiment was carried out in the private sector. Measures were introduced to facilitate layoffs and create more flexibility in labor markets. Originally, the government had promised to spread the pain of the IMF bailout throughout society, not excluding the *chaebols* and the public sector. However, restructuring led to a constant string of layoffs and to the perception that less was being done for workers than for many others. The perception of inequities has given rise, understandably, to protests by labor, amplified by the fact that for the first time in Korean history, labor was allowed a strong voice at the bargaining table. While this has kept labor from instigating major strikes and disruptions, it has also encouraged political responses rather than economic solutions to ongoing restructuring problems. The result is that organized labor has been well protected while non-union workers have suffered very high job insecurity.

It is especially hard for workers to cope in this turbulent age of restructuring when there is no adequate social safety net. Restructuring led to a sharp rise in unemployment and to heavy strains for existing training and retraining programs. In this sense, workers have borne the brunt of the shift from *K-type* to *A-type* employment (a shift that is sometimes more charitably described as from the 'lifetime workplace' to the 'lifetime job'). Meanwhile, Korea's organizational culture, which traditionally emphasized harmony and networking skills, is slowly being replaced by a more competitive system that emphasizes individual achievement and ability.

While this is obviously a change from personalism, it is not yet clear whether it implies the advent of full-fledged individualism in the workspace. Rather, the main thing that may be happening is de-personalization – that is, the removal of interpersonal trust from the workplace. And, absent the establishment of transparent legitimate rule, destruction of the old system may lead not to the development of a viable market system but to a Hobbesian society characterized by the survival of the fittest.

More Transparency?

The reform agenda attached priority to greater transparency in the marketplace and stronger accountability of economic agents. In order to raise accounting standards to international levels, Korean commercial law was revised. The government strengthened disclosure requirements to ensure that investment information was more widely distributed and shared. In fiscal year 1999 consolidated financial statements were required for the first time. In principle, this was an important step in allowing investors to ascertain the true financial condition of a company or group, for without this information it is impossible for investors and lenders to get a clear picture of the *chaebols'* financial structures. Oversight has been strengthened with the goal of preventing window-dressing and accounting fraud. Companies that fabricate financial statements are fined, and management is now subject to harsh civil and criminal punishments. The Outside Director System has been strengthened by organizing and providing pools of outside directors. The government recently introduced several additional measures to improve accounting, auditing and disclosure. It now prohibits certified public accountants from auditing businesses in which they have interests. Peer review was introduced within the Association of Certified Accountants, and quarterly financial statements are now required for companies listed on the KSE and KOSDAQ.

However, the government's repeated insistence that these reforms have succeeded in enhancing transparency has been greeted somewhat skeptically. Figure 11.2 is consistent with the skeptical view: it suggests that Korea is still far behind many of the countries with which it competes when it comes to corruption. Singapore has the highest score on the anti-corruption scale, followed closely by the United States and Japan. While Taiwan's score has improved markedly since 1996, Korea's has barely recovered to pre-crisis levels.

Another recent survey conducted by PricewaterhouseCoopers comes to similar conclusions, in particular that Korea is still less transparent than Taiwan and

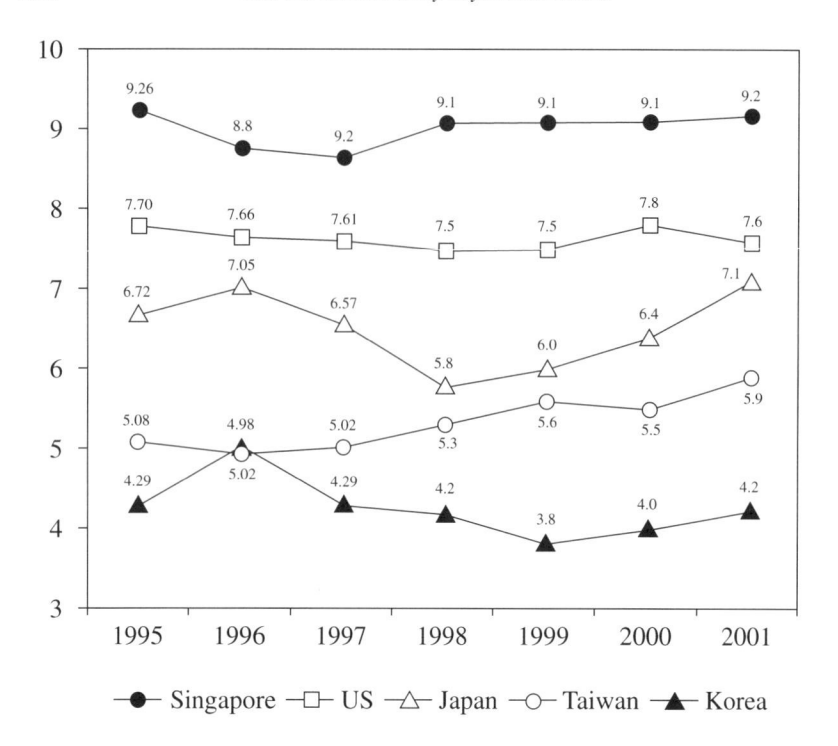

Figure 11.2 Corruption index, selected countries, 1995–2001

Source: Transparency International.

Japan. Opacity does not necessarily mean corruption, of course; in addition it can reflect uncertainties about the operation of the legal system, lack of consistency between macroeconomic and financial policies, inadequate standards and practices in the areas of auditing and accounting, and an opaque regulatory system. Korea has the highest levels of opacity in accounting and corporate governance of any of these countries, and it does not do much better in the areas of legal uncertainty and economic policy consistency. This indicates that relational elements rather than corruption are the more fundamental cause of opacity in economic transactions. For example, there is a relationship between cultural values and the accuracy of consolidated financial disclosure in annual corporate reports (Gray, 1988; Fechner and Kilgore, 1994; Baydoun and Willett, 1995). According to these studies, the extent of disclosure varies directly with the individualism of the national system and indirectly with power distance, uncertainty avoidance and long-term orientation.

Contrary to the original aim, Korea is still below global standards with regard to corruption and bribery. One recent survey ranks Korea as one of the most corrupt of the 15 economically emerging countries surveyed (when corruption is measured by the propensity to pay bribes).[24] This is remarkable in light of the passage of the Anti-Corruption Act of July 2001 and the creation of an agency expressly charged with rooting out corruption (the Korea Independent Commission Against Corruption, or KICAC).[25] It shows that the country still has a way to go in transforming its economic system.

CONCLUSION

One way of characterizing post-crisis reform in Korea is that progress has been fastest where international involvement is greatest. Korea has opened the financial market and introduced a wide range of measures and laws to properly accommodate the demands of outside financiers. Reforming the structure of the *chaebols* and providing an extensive social safety net could hardly have been imagined without IMF involvement. To be sure, in some cases the government itself requested the inclusion of tough policy measures in the IMF package, such as the legalization of layoffs; in this way, the Korean government could circumvent resistance from the working class. But this only reinforces the point.

Skeptics continue to worry that these reforms have had too little impact on day-to-day business practice – that they amount to simply putting new clothes on an old body. The internal dynamics of the Korean economy, they argue, are still based on traditional modes of behavior. As a result, there are inconsistencies between economic policy and corporate culture. From the beginning, President Kim Dae Jung made clear that he was committed to making market competition the guiding principle of economic reform. The problem, as this chapter has shown, was that long-time bureaucrats accustomed to the model of government-led economic development were responsible for implementing this neoliberal policy.

In addition, to appease the working class, a Tripartite Commission was hastily created, following the corporatist model developed in Europe. However, attempting to transplant the European model to the Korean context has created continuing conflict. The Federation of Korean Trade Unions (FKTU) and the Korean Confederation of Trade Unions (KCTU), the two leading union organizations in Korea, first compromised with the business sector and the government on a pact for economic reform. But soon after the inauguration of the Commission, each party began to accuse the other of not living up to their promises. The result was a chaotic reform process driven by conflicting interests and incompatible philosophies.

The most serious problem in Korea is the lack of institutionalized trust and legitimate social rule. Rules-based systems are difficult to develop in a society with weak political institutions (Noland, 2001). Even President Kim's credibility was thrown into doubt by a series of corruption scandals, accusations of nepotism and failed political projects. For Korean society to enter a new era, public trust must be built upon consistent and predictable social rules formulated and upheld by legitimate public authorities. The role of the legislature is to produce the social rules which the executive executes and the courts enforce. With egoistic behavior thereby sanctioned, citizens will develop public trust instead of continuing to rely on personal relationships.

Rules-based systems are difficult to develop in a political environment endowed with little social capital and a weak civic culture. The solution to these problems is to build trust in public institutions. The absence of clear social rules grounded in trust in public institutions has disrupted public life, as each individual and group has struggled to pursue its interests by negotiating over the rules. The collective outcome has been a 'tragedy of the commons,' that is, an erosion of the public space. Changing rules coupled with group egoism tends to increase group conflict and coordination costs. Lack of transparency also imposes a penalty on financial transactions, preventing good firms from obtaining access to capital. After repeated campaigns for transparency, Korea is still regarded as 'semi-transparent' by outside evaluators, and it is assigned a significant transparency risk premium when foreigners consider whether to invest in the Korean economy.

Without transparency, the result of the government's withdrawal from the economy will be not market competition but unbridled interest conflict. The lack of transparency has thus become the Achilles' heel of the Korean economy.

NOTES

1. By July 1999 only 11 of the 30 original merchant banks survived, while an extensive program of closures and mergers consolidated 26 commercial banks into 12 and eight investment trusts into four. Tight control over the financial market and high interest rates froze the cash flows of already fragile firms and eventually led to an unprecedented bankruptcy rate (B.-K. Kim, 2001).
2. For example, Korea's foreign reserves had risen to US$101.7 billion as of 30 November 2001 from virtually zero around the end of 1997. As reserves swelled, the Korean government fully repaid its IMF loan (US$19.5 billion) three years ahead of the schedule. Now, Korea is a net creditor nation in the international financial market, in contrast to its position as a net debtor at the end of 1997 (Ministry of Finance and Economy, 2001c).
3. Authoritarianism thus tends to be a feature of hierarchical systems.
4. This is sometimes interpreted in terms of the difference between arm's-length and relational systems.
5. The Asian view of human beings is somewhat more collectivist and relational. In collectivist society, personalism regulates relationships among people. As a result, individuals in a collectivist culture are more accustomed to long-term relationships and reciprocity than immediate and egoistic calculation. People in collectivism are under higher pressure to internalize the social norms and values of their groups and society. As a result, the effect of trust seems quite different in the two cultures. Trust under individualism is a result of

investment and calculation, while trust in collectivism is treated as a desirable virtue and moral exemplar (Hall and Ames, 1999).
6. For a more detailed explanation about this typology and its meaning, refer to Yee (1998).
7. The Confucian ethic takes for granted that social hierarchy is functional for the whole of society.
8. In the political realm, *formal or procedural democracy* is defined as a situation where equally endowed individuals, without resort to personal relationships, create a political system following the unambiguous rules structured in the public sphere.
9. While the experiment in high-trust systems such as socialism turned out to be a failure, the high-distrust system of the market turned out to be sustainable so long as it was subject to clear rules of the game. The secret underlying the success of democracy and capitalism is the irreversibility of trust building. In other words, building trust is very difficult; it is much easier to destroy. The success of the high-distrust system is accounted for by the institutional structure that imposes high opportunity costs and risks on the betrayer of the trust. In a democratic and capitalist system, people could build trust from a baseline of distrust. The addition of trust to this high-distrust system could be a source of efficiency for the whole system.
10. The Emilian model of production, found in the Third Italy, is an economic version of this type where small firms create rich and horizontal ties based on kinship, religious beliefs and political ideology.
11. Hofstede's data are based on a survey collected by IBM on their employees scattered in about 50 countries. They include a number of different indices, such as power distance, individualism, masculinity, uncertainty avoidance, and so on. For the purpose of this study, I recoded the power distance and individualism indices for certain countries. As the data were collected in 1985–87, there may be an issue of anachronism when we combine this with more recent data on transparency and competitiveness. This is a defensible procedure, since cultural traits do not change rapidly.
12. Transparency is a multidimensional concept measured by several different indicators. First, it is measured by corruption, or the degree of malfeasance or abuse of public authority measures for the private benefit in case of taxation, licensing, and export and import licensing. Second is legal transparency, implying legal impartiality and predictability in the definition and protection of property rights. In addition, there is informational transparency, measuring easy accessibility of corporate accounting and financing data (Transparency International, 2001).
13. It is noteworthy that European social-democratic countries such as Sweden and Germany share small PDI and high transparency with the Anglo-American model, but show stronger collectivism. This reflects the strong egalitarian attitude in these countries.
14. The competitiveness of a country is a composed index of more than 300 criteria covering macroeconomic performance, government efficiency, business efficiency, and technological and human resources infrastructure.
15. In addition, rivalry between capitalism and socialism might have provided a semi-periphery country such as Korea a chance for 'development by invitation.'
16. In terms of corporate governance, Korean capitalism is dubbed 'familial capitalism,' where the ownership and management are not separated and the firm is run by an owner family. 'Shareholder capitalism,' typically found in the US, has separated management from ownership, but corporate instability is high because the CEO is responsible for the short-term performance and it the firm is vulnerable to hostile takeover. 'Stakeholder capitalism,' which is another name for Japanese and German capitalism, is characterized by a more stable corporate structure due to the significant role of institutional investors, but it does not readily adapt to a changing environment.
17. In a sense, however, this was more like cell segmentation in the process of conceiving minor children following the death of the father than a separation at birth; there was no real dismantling of the interlocking structure.
18. Like the Ministry of Finance (MOF) and Economic Planning Board (EPB) before it, the FSC tried to trigger corporate restructuring through regulations on cross-shareholding, insider trading, cross-loan guarantees, as well as debt/equity ratios, but much more ac-

tively by setting tough quantified target goals and specifying a tight timetable, which in turn justified the FSC's extracting detailed plans for divestitures and asset sales from the *chaebols*. The continuity is not only in policy ideas, but also in personnel. Lee Kyu Seong, with long career experience in the MOF, which included service as a vice minister, headed the MOFE. Lee Hon Jae chaired the FSC for his 1974 experience in managing financial crisis as an MOF bureaucrat. The former EPB officials similarly made major advances under Kim Dae Jung, with Jin Nyum heading the Planning and Budget Commission (PBC) and Kang Bong Kyun serving as Senior Presidential Secretary. See B.-K. Kim (2001).

19. The most common example of government intervention is an order to banks demanding that insolvent companies receive aid. Banks must make commercial loans to companies based on independent evaluations. However, when the government intervenes in the process, both companies and banks become vulnerable.
20. *Joongangilbo* (25 June 2001).
21. The petrochemical Big Deal between Hyundai and Samsung Petrochemical failed to consolidate their factories and induce foreign investment. Moreover, the Korea Railroad Rolling Stock Company, which was created by consolidating the rolling-stock division of Hyundai, Daewoo and Hanjin, has come to the point where it needs to split up into separate entities. In addition, creditors and major shareholders of Hyundai, Daewoo and Samsung's consolidated Korea Aerospace recently voted to provide additional support funds of 530 billion won after it failed to induce investments from Boeing in the US. The Big Deal of Hyundai Oil and Hanwha Energy remains unsettled as Hyundai Electronics is still struggling with the side effects of the acquisition of LG semiconductor (*Chosunilbo*, 20 December 2000).
22. The result has been not been the opening of positions but a disguised extension of tenure for early-retiring bureaucrats.
23. 'A government cannot be healthy if those who campaigned for the president during the election linger on within the administration like blood clots.' The chairman acknowledged that there has been a shift from a pyramid-style bureaucracy toward a network style. 'But it is not a network formed by task and function, but by personal ties.' He added, 'The civil service system is like that of the military. The mentality of civil servants, from young starting civil servants to secretaries at the Blue House, is ossified.' (Joongangilbo, 22 May 2002).
24. Transparency International (TI), the global anti-corruption organization, released its Bribe Payers Index (BPI) 2002, showing very high levels of bribery in developing countries by corporations from Russia, China, Taiwan and South Korea, as well as numerous leading industrial nations, all of which now have laws making bribery of foreign officials a crime. A total of 835 business experts in 15 leading emerging market countries were asked: 'In the business sectors with which you are most familiar, please indicate how likely it is for companies from the following countries to pay or offer bribes to win or retain business in this country.' A perfect score, and a perceived propensity to pay bribes, is 10.0. The rankings below start with companies from countries that are seen to have a low propensity for offering bribes. Korea's score is 3.9, followed by Taiwan, China and Russia.
25. According to one study, the economic costs associated with this level of opacity were the equivalent of an additional tax rate of 35 percent. By comparison, the tax equivalents associated with the levels of corruption even in Japan and Taiwan were 25 percent each, while that for the US was 5 percent, and that for Singapore was zero (PricewaterhouseCoopers, 2001). Such opacity has also compromised the credibility of the country and led to higher interest rates on external borrowing.

12. Social realignment, coalition change and political transformation

Hyun-Chin Lim and Joon Han

INTRODUCTION

'History repeats itself.' When it comes to Korea, this Western proverb is telling. As past politics become history, history presents past politics. As the five-year term of President Kim Dae Jung draws to a close, political cleavages are deepening. Conservatives discontented at the lopsided North–South dialogue label President Kim a 'Communist', while radicals frustrated by the slow pace of restructuring call him a 'reformist in disguise.' Some would say that the conservative–progressive conflict now visible in Korea is almost as heated as the one that led to the Korean War more than half a century ago. Added to regional antagonism and class division, the result is a divisive social and ideological rift. It is ironic that the Kim Dae Jung regime, the beneficiary of the first instance of horizontal power transfer through election in Korea, has seen social conflicts worsening instead of improving.

Why is social conflict so prevalent? How are the reform measures aimed at by the Kim Dae Jung regime related to and affected by the growth of this phenomenon? What changes have occurred in the ruling coalition among key social and political players since the crisis of 1997–98? This chapter attempts to answer these questions.

The literature on structural adjustment tells us that economic restructuring brings with it social realignment and political change (see Coak et al., 1994; Veltmeyer et al., 1997; Smith and Korzeniewicz, 1997; Smith et al., 1994a, 1994b).[1] Korea is no exception. Since the crisis, the country has undergone a profound social and political transformation as a result of the International Monetary Fund's (IMF) program of liberalization, privatization and deregulation. This chapter investigates the resulting structural realignment and the associated power shift, social conflicts and coalition change. Specifically, we consider the changing nature of political power within the ruling coalition and examine the dynamics of power relationships among social classes and interest groups. A close examination of the relationship among economic restructuring, social realignment and political change will help us to identify development alternatives in the twenty-first century.

Our starting point is the belief that the stability of a regime depends not only on economic performance but also on social and political performance. The current Korean situation might even be taken to suggest that social and political factors are more important than economic performance in evaluating structural adjustment programs.

ANATOMY OF REFORM

Revealingly, in the 'Third Wave' of democracy (Huntington, 1991), only three countries – Spain , Portugal and Greece – have succeeded in consolidating democracy.[2] Since its transition from authoritarianism, Korea has been struggling to do the same.[3]

The history of modern Korea has been plagued by student revolts, worker protests, military *coups* and civil uprisings. After the Roh Tae Woo regime (1988–93), which was the last to be headed by a former military leader and which was democratic only to a limited extent, Korea embarked on a full-scale drive for democratization. Civilian governments under Kim Young Sam (1993–98) and Kim Dae Jung (1998–2003) enacted policy measures to root out authoritarian legacies in the name of democratic reform. Kim Young Sam sent former presidents to jail, and Kim Dae Jung recognized and rewarded the victims of authoritarian rule. Both governments tried to limit the power of the *chaebols* and to render the economy more transparent and open.

However, the heads of both of these governments had made wide use of reform rhetoric while still opposition leaders in order to differentiate themselves from their predecessors, military officers who had become presidents. They continued to use that rhetoric to advance their own ends upon assuming office. Despite their attempts to display a sense of historical mission in rebuilding Korea out of the authoritarian debris, both leaders in some sense degraded democratic reform by relying on political rhetoric and failing to develop any feasible blueprint or concrete strategy for the future.[4] Both failed to recognize the difficulty of reform, naïvely believing that they could complete the process during their terms.

Before the onset of the financial crisis, Kim Young Sam had enacted a series of sweeping reform measures under the political slogan of building 'a new Korea.' Kim Dae Jung took society-wide reform measures in the name of 'government for the people.' However, both administrations fell prey to policy confusion, administrative incompetence and rampant corruption. Both leaders acted like Machiavellian princes, taking advantage of reform politics by espousing the rhetoric of change in order to disguise their real purpose, which was to advance their own power regardless of the consequences (B.-K. Kim and Suh, 1999: 23).[5]

The Kim Dae Jung regime is an outgrowth of the so-called Kim Dae Jung and Kim Jong Pil (DJP) coalition formed between the progressive National Congress for New Politics (NCNP)[6] and the conservative United Liberal Democrats (ULD)[7] in late 1997. The DJP was a political collaboration of two ideologically and regionally different political forces linked by a proposed constitutional amendment that would create a parliamentary cabinet system.[8] A minority party in the National Assembly, the NCNP had difficulty submitting and passing reform bills, not to mention overcoming its policy differences with the ULD, the heir of the authoritarian past.

No sooner did this coalition form than the sense of crisis began to fade, allowing partisan, regional and group differences to reassert themselves. These groups refused to accept the fact that reform is painstaking and inconvenient, that it requires compromises and sacrifices, and that compromises and sacrifices will only have political support when they are decided by an inclusive coalition. Reform entails a shift in power and wealth distribution: the privileged few have to share power and prerogatives with the underprivileged majority (Hirshman, 1973: 251). It is, thus, crucial to build a broad coalition among diverse social classes in order to overcome resistance.

Faced with this dilemma, a government has four options: 'decretism,' 'mandatism,' 'parlimentarism' and 'corporatism' (Pereira et al., 1994: 196). The Kim Dae Jung government chose a combination of corporatism and mandatism, attempting to secure the cooperation of business and labor while using statist means to pursue reform from above. Even while announcing that it would cooperate with business and unions, it pursued its policy goals by issuing administrative mandates. Kim Dae Jung's overconfidence about his popular support kept him from building the kind of broad and cohesive political coalition, achieved through a process of extensive consultation and compromise, required for successful reform. As a result, the restructuring package presented by the IMF and embraced by the government lacked popular support.

The government therefore employed a strategy of appeasement and containment. On one hand, it looked to unions and business associations for support by way of a neo-corporatist social partnership. On the other hand, it attempted to undermine counterforces, such as opposition parties and the media, through the pursuit of neo-statist reform.

Thus, in January 1998, the Kim Dae Jung government established a Tripartite Commission composed of labor, management and government. It was hoped that this commission would manage conflict through compromise.[9] Notwithstanding some initial successes, the Commission ultimately failed, for at least two reasons. First, business associations and labor unions signed a social agreement to work through the Commission under intense government pressure at a time of crisis. Business came to regret its hasty concession to accept labor participation in the policy-making process, and unions felt that they had been betrayed by a government that was prepared to accept massive layoffs. Second, the structure of the Commission proved ineffectual; it was a loose consultative body of representatives from the government, business community and labor unions lacking any real legal and administrative power. It provided only recommendations which could be ignored by the government, business associations and labor unions. To avoid conflicts with the affected parties, the National Assembly simply discarded the Commission's proposals without giving them serious consideration. As a result, the Tripartite Commission did not live up to the spirit of social agreement.

Under the political banner of 'democracy, market economy, and productive welfare,'[10] Kim Dae Jung's reforms addressed a wide range of areas, including politics, labor, finance, business, media, education, and law and health care, among others. The outcome, however, was disappointing. From the outset, Kim Dae Jung appeared to confuse reform with restructuring.[11] While he envisaged broad structural reform, the IMF called for narrow structural adjustment. The president pursued two seemingly contradictory objectives simultaneously: establishing market discipline, and transforming the structure of the economy to conform to the authorities' own vision. These goals were less than compatible. This tension is familiar to many new democracies undergoing structural adjustment programs (see Gamarra, 1994), and is also evident in the Kim Dae Jung regime's vacillation between restructuring and structural reform.

Devoid of public participation, the Kim Dae Jung regime has lost sight of its original goal of structural reform. The regime is one of many newly democratized civilian governments that favor structural adjustment programs (see Stallings and Kaufman, 1989: 216). The choice appears inevitable, since Keynesian policies are already on the wane and the ideology of neo-liberalism is gaining global acceptance. Accordingly, Korea is becoming more involved than ever before in the capitalist world system.

CHANGING STATE–SOCIETY RELATIONS

Over the course of its modern history, Korea has seen considerable change in the organization of political power.[12] The Kim Dae Jung regime represented hope for further change. That regime was only Korea's second civilian government, tasked with democratic consolidation in the aftermath of authoritarianism. Its political responsibility was to advance reform measures after the Kim Young Sam regime's efforts toward eradicating the legacies of authoritarianism. In addition, the Kim Dae Jung regime differed from the Kim Young Sam regime in that Cholla rather than Kyungsang was its regional power base. Although the Kim Young Sam regime was Korea's first civilian government, it was essentially a continuation of the Kyungsang power that had dominated Korean politics for almost half a century. (All previous Korean presidents had come from the Kyungsang region.)

The Kim Dae Jung regime has not lived up to hopes that it would transform the political landscape. As mentioned previously, born out of the DJP coalition, the Kim Dae Jung regime did not have much choice but to accept the *status quo*. The president's weak power base forced him to ally with elites from the authoritarian regimes such as Chon Doo Hwan and Roh Tae Woo. Many political elites from the old establishment participated in the cabinet, and long-time bureaucrats remained responsible for policy decisions. Rather than building a cohesive political coalition for reform, Kim Dae Jung compromised with the old establishment.[13] Rather than a fundamental change in the social organization of political power, there was only the replacement of old elites from Kyungsang with new elites from Cholla. Previously, the people of Cholla had been excluded from key posts in both the public and private sectors. They now assumed key positions in the government apparatus in the National Intelligence Service, the National Revenue Service, the Prosecutor's Office, the Presidential Secretariat Office and the Ministry of Defense. Table 12.1 shows the rise of Cholla power in major government agencies.

Furthermore, the process of market-oriented restructuring was initiated at a time when changes in the organization of political power were widely anticipated. Restructuring entails changes in the relations between the state and society. In contrast to the development state model of the previous four decades, the neoliberal market-oriented restructuring envisaged by the IMF would heighten the influence of transnational agencies like multinational corporations (MNCs) over the economy, in turn weakening the autonomy of the state. As some would put it, the government becomes subordinated to the logic of multinational capital (Hoogvelt, 1997: 168–9). Under the IMF's influence, the government pursued a market-driven structural adjustment program. But, in serving the immediate interests of multinational capital, the government is losing its capacity to adjust national industrial and financial policies.

In spite of its strong administrative power, the government's 'embedded autonomy' is shrinking.[14] The government no longer enjoys much control over social groups and classes. This is an apparent retreat from 'organic statism,' in which the government intervenes both directly and indirectly in society and the economy. Neoliberal restructuring in turn creates a new social and political matrix in which the government gradually loses its centripetal ability to pursue its own interests.

Table 12.1 Regional background of Cabinet ministers and vice-ministers, 1963–2000

Period	Kyongsang	Cholla	Seoul-Inchon	Chungchong/Kyunggi	Other	Total
3rd and 4th Republics (1963–80)	30.1	13.2	14.1	13.9	28.7	100 (N=432)
5th Republic (1981–88)	43.6	9.6	18.0	13.5	15.3	100 (N=156)
6th Republic RTW (1988–93)*	37.0	14.8	22.2	11.1	14.9	99.9 (N=27)
KYS Civilian Government (1993–94)	36.0	17.4	19.8	16.3	10.5	100 (N=86)
KDJ People's Government (February 2000)**	21.4	35.7	14.3	10.7	17.9	100 (N=28)

Notes:
* The first Cabinet of the Roh Tae Woo Administration.
** The Monthly Chosun (February 2002).

Sources: M. Kim (1988) and Dong (1994).

Deepening Class Divides

During the last four years, the restructuring of the economy along neoliberal lines has coincided with attempts to strengthen economic democracy. This has resulted in a new social structure more open to the outside world but more fragmented internally. Before the crisis, Korea's growing middle and working classes were gaining political, economic and social power. Now both the middle and working classes are losing ground due to massive layoffs and unemployment.

Due to insolvencies, shutdowns and downsizing, unemployment rates more than quadrupled following the crisis. Including those working fewer than 15 hours per week, the number of unemployed reached 2 million, or 10 percent of the labor force, in 1998. Thanks to government-initiated public works programs and the economic recovery since 1999,[15] the number of unemployed has since declined (to 3.6 percent in 2002). However, restructuring has also created increased labor market segmentation and produced a large number of contingent workers. Temporary and daily workers now account for 52.9 percent of the total workforce, surpassing regular workers (who account for the remaining 47.1 percent).

The widening disparity in incomes is evident in Figure 12.1. The income share of the wealthiest 20 percent climbed from 37.5 percent in 1995 to 40.3 percent in 2001, while the income share of the poorest 20 percent declined from 8.5 percent to 7.5 percent during the same period. As a result, the income share of the wealthiest 20 percent increased from 4.4 to 5.4 times the income share of the poorest 20 percent. The Gini coefficient for the distribution of income rose from 0.283 in 1997, to 0.315 in 1998, and to 0.319 in 2001.

Some of the implications for class structure can be seen in Table 12.2. The upper and lower classes have increased in size while the middle class has shrunk, in effect leading to the emergence of a three-tier society. The bottom 15 percent of economically inactive workers are unemployed or marginalized, the lower-middle 15 percent of workers have little job security, the upper-middle 50 percent of workers are secure in their jobs, and the top 20 percent hold tenured jobs.

Alarmed by growing poverty, rising inequality and deepening class divides, the Kim Dae Jung government tried to cope with these problems by enacting various social policies. (The IMF and World Bank also pushed for the creation of a social safety net.) The social welfare policies of the Kim Dae Jung government are based on the idea of 'productive welfare,' which combines self-support and public services. However, the government failed to implement the original idea of productive welfare, which encourages the unemployed to get more training and thereby enhance their employability.

Ratio (5th/1st)   Gini index

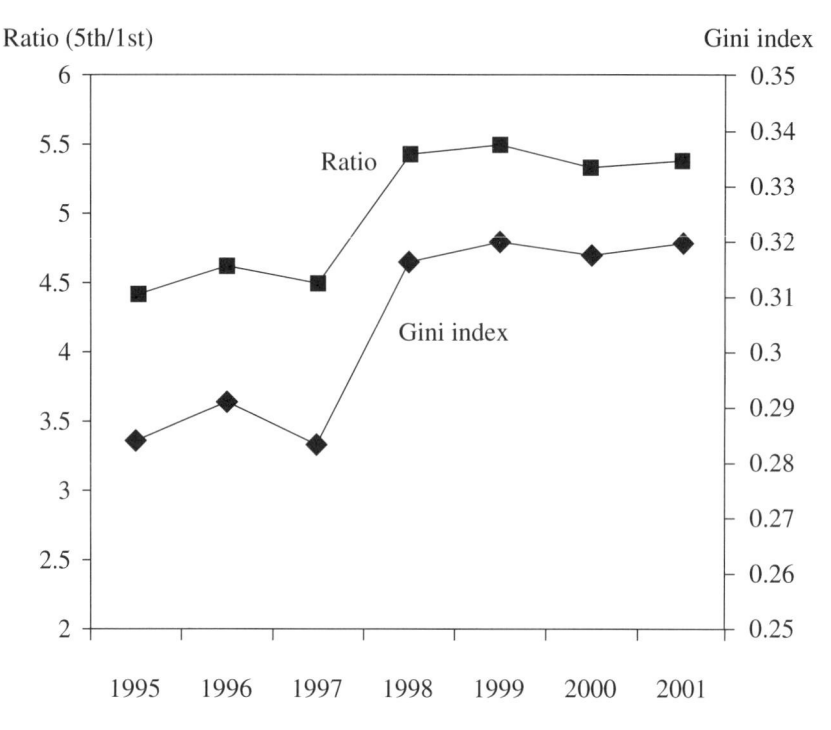

Source: National statistics Office, *Kosis Database* (various isues).

Figure 12.1 Trends in Gini coefficient and ratio of high- and low-income quintile

Table 12.2 Class structure in terms of income (%)

	1997	1998	1999 (1st half)
High income	21.8	22.9	22.9
Middle income	68.5	65.4	65.1
Upper	54.8	51.6	51.4
Lower	13.7	13.8	13.7
Low income	9.7	11.7	12.0

Note: Income classes are defined as follows: people earning more than 150% of median income belong to the high-income class while those earning less than 50% belong to the low-income class. Middle-income class is further divided into upper-middle and lower-middle classes, with 70%–150% and 50%–70% of median income respectively.

Source: K.-J. Yoo (2000).

Instead, the rise of unemployment was so rapid that the government had to take emergency measures to create temporary jobs.

The Kim Dae Jung government's efforts to strengthen the social safety net resulted in the establishment of the National Basic Livelihood Security System, effective October 2000. This system secures a basic livelihood for individuals earning less than the minimum cost of living by covering the living expenses for those households regardless of the recipients' age or ability to work. Critics question the sustainability of the government's welfare policy because it is a huge burden on the budget.

Coalition Change and Social Conflict

Korea is well known for a partnership between government and business that essentially excludes labor (H. Koo, 1995). In part, this arrangement reflects the internal structure of the respective sectors: business leadership is centralized and unified, while labor is internally divided into many disparate organizations with competing ideologies. Under these circumstances, the government tends to bargain more with capital than labor (see P. Hall, 1986: 269–70). This goes some way toward explaining why the country's post-crisis restructuring policy has been designed more to increase productivity rather than to achieve equality.

During the Kim Dae Jung regime, the power of capital was challenged by the state. But, despite the challenge to the power of the *chaebols*, the latter are likely to benefit from corporate restructuring in the long run. They have reduced their debt-to-equity ratios to less than 200 percent, strengthening their financial position. And, despite this financial consolidation, the top 50 *chaebols* still control almost half of all business assets and liabilities nationwide.

This is not to deny that economic crisis has brought about significant change in Korea's development alliance. Four years of restructuring replaced or at least supplemented the old alliance between the state and local capitalists with a new alliance between transnational agencies and the state. That the outcome is a hybrid is hardly surprising, since both Korea's economic boom and economic crisis are products of 'dependent development' in which factors of success and factors of failure are intermixed. Dependent development in Korea has relied upon the double alliance of the state and local capitalists (Lim, 1985).[16] This is different from the experiences of Latin American countries, where the state, local capitalists and transnational capital constituted a triple alliance.[17] In South Korea , the state's nationalist logic of capital accumulation has prevented transnational capital from participating in the process of dependent development. Thus dependent development has given rise to class confrontation between local capitalists, workers and farmers.

With progress in restructuring, the traditional alliance between state and local capital is likely to evolve toward a new alliance between transnational capital and state, with local capital in a more peripheral position and the working class and farmers largely excluded. The opening of the market following neoliberal logic has increased inflows of foreign capital. Foreign investment funds and financial institutions now hold more than 30 percent of the capitalization of the South Korean stock market.[18] In 1999 and 2000, foreign direct investment (FDI) in South Korea amounted to more than $15 billion, which is more than a third of annual GDP. The total volume of FDI during those two years is nearly equal to all FDI from 1962 to 1997. As a consequence of such massive flows, the number of firms with more than 10 percent foreign participation increased from 3877 in 1996 to 9423 by the end of 2000.

Growing labor disputes provide evidence of labor's dissatisfaction with the situation of labor market and industrial relations. While the frequency and severity of labor disputes fell in the period preceding the crisis, they soared subsequently (as shown in Table 12.3). Labor has not welcomed the new law allowing for temporary workers with flexible working hours. Having witnessed massive layoffs and the resulting unemployment, workers have a sense of foreboding about the process of restructuring. The weakening of labor is also evident in the decline in union membership (again, see Table 12.3). Currently, union membership is estimated at a little over 10 percent of the wage labor force. Ideological division among workers and enterprise unionism are major contributors to the decline in unionization since the early 1990s. However, changes in the labor laws after the economic crisis, which have made the labor market more flexible by legalizing temporary help services, are also responsible for lower union participation. Although the right to organize has been extended to public workers, including teachers in primary and secondary schools, and civil servants, this has not stimulated much growth of union membership.

While reform measures have worked to shape the behavior of social and political actors, resulting in the relative empowerment and disempowerment of some groups and classes, virtually all social groups and classes feel cut off from the process of reform. It is not a matter of who are the major beneficiaries and the disadvantaged. Rather, it is that no group feels that it has had adequate input into the process.

Most reform efforts in the area of finance, enterprise, labor, education, medicine, pharmacy, law and media are far from success stories. A good example is the division of labor between physician care and the provision of prescription drugs. The government's attempt to separate the two functions caused physicians to strike, resulting in considerable social turmoil. Medical reform thus ended up raising insurance fees and worsening the financial deficit of the National Health System.

Table 12.3 Unionization and labor disputes

Year	Wage-earners × (1000 men)	Union members × (1000 men)	Unionized rate* (%)	Number of cases	No. of participants × (1000 men)	Work-days lost × (1000 work-days)
1970	3746	473	12.6	4	1	9
1975	4751	750	15.8	52	10	14
1980	6464	948	14.7	206	49	61
1985	8104	1004	12.4	265	29	64
1986	8433	1036	12.3	276	47	72
1987	9191	1267	13.8	3749	1262	6947
1988	9610	1707	17.8	1873	293	5407
1989	10389	1932	18.6	1616	409	6351
1990	10950	1887	17.2	322	134	4487
1991	11349	1803	15.9	234	175	3271
1992	11568	1735	15.0	235	105	1528
1993	11751	1667	14.2	144	109	1308
1994	12297	1659	13.5	121	104	1484
1995	12736	1615	12.7	88	50	393
1996	13043	1599	12.2	85	79	893
1997	13228	1484	11.2	78	44	445
1998	12191	1402	11.5	129	146	1452
1999	12522	1481	12.6	198	92	1366
2000	13142	1527	11.6	250	178	1894

Note: * The rate of union members among all the employed workers.

Source: National Statistical Office, *KOSIS* (www.nso.go.kr).

The comparative study of restructuring in newly democratized societies does not lead to the conclusion that worsening economic circumstances in the course of the transition must necessarily result in increased social and political conflict (Haggard and Kaufman, 1992). Social and political conflict is only likely when economic performance is poor and political and social institutions are weak. This is one interpretation of the intense conflict that has characterized the process of post-crisis restructuring in Korea.

EMERGENCE OF THE 'DUAL DEMOCRATIC REGIME'

Democratic consolidation has a long way to go in Korea. Neither 'horizontal accountability,' on the basis of separation of powers among the executive, the legislature and the judiciary, nor the government's 'vertical accountability' to civil society (O'Donnell, 1992, 1994) is fully established and consolidated. Not until the late 1980s did civil society really begin to grow.[19] Despite two successive civilian governments' accession to power through democratic elections, democracy is only 'partially institutionalized.' In this sense, what Korea enjoys at present is 'electoral democracy' rather than 'liberal democracy.'[20]

It has been argued that the mode of democratic transition influences the structure and performance of the resulting democracy (Karl and Schmitter, 1991). Korea had a 'transition by transaction' (Mainwaring, 1992: 320), in which the ruling elites made a political pact with opposition groups. This allowed part of the old establishment to survive, since the old elites held some power in the newly formed democratic government. More significantly, the political pact was not accompanied by a social pact in the process of democratization. Citizens, students and workers acquired a voice in the resulting democracy, but their role was not acknowledged by the political elites. Consequently, the new democracy was incomplete because it had only precarious support from the various social classes and groups.

Korea has a presidential system modeled after the United States, in which the three branches – executive, legislature and judiciary – share power, at least in theory. Unlike the American prototype, however, the Korean version is characterized by weak checks and balances. The judiciary does not have real autonomy, since the president intervenes in its decisions; the legislative branch does not exercise autonomous law-making power either, since the executive branch controls the governing party. The ideal of power sharing among the three branches has been threatened even under civilian government, given the dominance of the executive over the other two branches. Policies are made primarily through executive-controlled channels without sufficient input from the political parties.

Why this is the case is not hard to see. Korea's presidential system tends to be autocratic, thereby undermining party politics. The country's president serves as president of the ruling party. He dominates the legislature, marginalizing the national assembly, not to mention the parties. Political parties are leader-oriented rather than program-oriented (Kim, 1998: 138). Political parties cannot function as the central articulators of interests in civil society. The linkages between parties and citizens are not strong, and the majority of citizens question the legitimacy of parties and elections.[21]

Political parties do not direct national policies. Again, why this is so is no mystery. The lack of clear policy lines, combined with opportunism, has hindered the development of a stable party system. Party politics are still fluid and volatile. Given this fluid and unarticulated party system, it is unrealistic to expect democracy to work smoothly. Even electoral participation has become a tool of political gaming. The procedures of democratic governance have only been partially established because elections do not reflect differing policy preferences (see Valenzuela, 1992: 71–3).

The major parties, the NMDP (New Millennium Democratic Party), GKP (Grand Korea Party) and ULD (United Liberal Democrats), are not mass parties but remain at the disposal of individual political leaders. The 'three Kims' and their successors have continuously reorganized them.[22] The NMDP, GKP and ULD are all led by region-based cadres built upon the founder's personal charisma.[23] Table 12.4 illustrates the extent of regional cleavages in Korea. The 1987, 1992 and 1997 presidential elections show almost the same pattern of regional voting behavior. The Cholla region was the NMPD's stronghold, Kyungsang was the GKP's, and Chungchong was the ULD's. While party membership among the electorate is low, voters continue to vote in blocs on the basis of regional favoritism. A clear indication of this is the seat distribution of the sixteenth National Assembly, where the NMDP dominates Cholla (25 out of 29), the GKP nearly sweeps Kyungsang (64 out of 65), and the ULD controls a large block in Chungchong (11 out of 24).

Ironically, a strong presidency is as much intact under the civilian presidents' democratic rule as under the military presidents' authoritarian rule. One might say that a strong presidency is necessary if reform is to succeed in eradicating the authoritarian past. Yet behind the phenomenon of the so-called 'imperial presidency' are civilian presidents who have utilized profoundly undemocratic tactics in their struggle against authoritarianism. These civilian presidents are accustomed to authority, hierarchy and obedience. Familiar with a political culture in which personalized authority outweighs institutionized power, they have tended to pursue supreme power as executive leaders. The outcome of the personalization of power embedded in the Confucian hierarchical political culture is an imperial presidency.

As O'Donnell (2001) anticipated in his observations on new democracies in developing countries, Korea's civilian leaders have cultivated a form of delegative rule. Delegative rule refers to the ability of the executive to do whatever it sees fit for the country, as if it has been deputized to do so by the populace. Executive authority is thus hostile to the strengthening of political institutions, resulting in weak horizontal and vertical accountability. Korea's civilian leaders have pursued clientelism and nepotism even while paying lip-service to the formal rules and institutions of polyarchy. Power remains concentrated in the executive, resulting in a deep gulf between the government and the public.

It is not particularly illuminating to argue that both the Kim Young Sam and Kim Dae Jung regimes appeared strong but remained weak in substance, since this weakness was not their fault. Because of the delegative nature of political power in Korea, both regimes were limited in their ability to create a

Table 12.4 Votes by region, three presidential elections

	1987 PE				1992 PE				1997 PE			
	RTW	KYS	KDJ	KJP	KYS	KDJ	CJY	PCJ	KDJ	LHC	RIJ	KYG
Total	36.6	28.0	27.1	8.1	42.0	33.8	16.3	6.4	39.7	38.2	18.9	1.2
Seoul	30.0	29.1	32.6	8.2	36.4	37.7	18.0	6.4	44.9	40.9	12.8	1.1
Inchon	39.4	30.0	21.3	9.2	37.3	31.7	21.4	7.9	38.5	36.4	23.0	1.6
Kyung-ki	41.4	27.5	22.3	8.5	36.3	32.0	23.1	6.9	39.3	35.5	23.6	1.0
Kang-won	59.3	26.1	8.8	5.4	41.5	15.5	34.1	6.9	23.8	43.2	30.9	1.0
Taejon					35.2	28.7	23.3	11.2	45.0	29.2	24.1	1.2
N. Chungchong	46.9	28.2	11.0	13.5	38.3	26.0	23.9	9.4	37.4	30.8	29.4	1.3
S. Chungchong	26.2	16.1	12.4	45.0	36.9	28.5	25.2	6.7	48.3	23.5	26.1	1.0
Taeku	70.7	24.3	2.6	2.1	59.6	7.8	19.4	11.7	12.5	72.7	13.1	1.2
Ulsan									15.4	51.4	26.7	6.1
N. Kyungsang	66.4	28.2	2.4	2.6	64.7	9.6	15.7	8.2	13.7	61.9	21.8	1.5
Pusan	32.1	56.0	9.1	2.6	73.3	12.5	6.3	6.6	15.3	55.3	29.8	1.2
S. Kyungsang	41.2	51.3	4.5	2.7	72.3	9.2	11.5	5.5	11.0	55.1	31.3	1.7
Kwang-ju	4.8	0.5	94.4	0.2	2.1	95.8	1.2	0.4	97.3	1.7	0.7	0.2
N. Cholla	14.1	1.5	83.5	0.8	5.7	89.1	3.2	0.8	92.3	4.5	2.1	0.4
S. Cholla	8.2	1.2	90.3	0.3	4.2	92.2	2.1	0.6	94.6	3.2	1.4	0.2
Cheju	49.8	26.8	18.6	4.5	40.0	32.9	16.1	8.8	40.6	36.6	20.5	1.4

Notes:

Taejon votes were included in South Chungchong Province in 1987, before it became a 'special city' with an independent local government of its own. The votes of Ulsan City residents were counted separately only in 1997. Before it became a 'special city', its votes were counted as a part of North Kyungsang Province's votes. 1987 PE: RTW: Rho Tae Woo, Democratic Justice Party; KYS: Kim Young Sam, Unification Democratic Party; KDJ: Kim Dae Jung, Peace Democratic Party; KJP: Kim Jong Pil, New Democratic Republican Party. 1992 PE: KYS: Kim Young Sam, Democratic Liberal Party; KDJ: Kim Dae Jung, Peace Democratic Party; CJY: Chung Joo Young, National Party; PCJ Park Chan Jong, New Party. 1997 PE: KDJ: Kim Dae Jung, National Congress for New Politics; LHC: Lee Hoi Chang, Grand Korea Party; RIJ: Rhee In Jae, New Party for the People; KYG: Kwon Young Gil, The People's Construction Triumph 21 (Labor Candidate).

Source: Central Election Management (drawn from B.-K. Kim, 2001, p. 182).

consensus in civil society. They were incapable of managing social conflicts and political cleavages because of their weak power bases.

In Korea, competing visions of the political system reflect a wide gulf between maximalist and minimalist concepts of democracy. As in many new democracies, popular debate has been dominated by feuds between reactionaries who believe the achievement of social and economic democracy will lead to socialism and that radicals who suppose they can achieve social and economic democracy without resorting to political democracy. This ideological disagreement can only be resolved by a democratic compromise that allows both the right and the left to compete in national policy making. It is a truism that Korea is not ready for class compromise. In order for a democratic compromise to succeed, the major social and political actors should be granted power to represent their diverse interests in civil society. Yet in Korea, where political parties do not play a central role in interest representation, the major social and political actors do not have any institutional mechanism to influence policy formulation and implementation.

Given the absence of such a mechanism, the failure of the Kim Dae Jung regime's effort to create a neo-corporatist arrangement is self-evident.[24] The country does not have a tradition of political negotiation, and government, labor and capital do not yet trust each another. The Government–Management–Labor Tripartite Commission has been incapable of creating a true social partnership. This setback has led the Kim Dae Jung regime to seek an alliance with a strategic segment of political and civil society. Such an alliance would exclude the majority of social and political actors by neutralizing their capacity for collective action.[25] The inclusion of a strategic minority and the exclusion of the majority is what Acuna and Smith (1994) refer to as a 'dual democratic regime,' in which political stability is secured by 'a dual logic of government power (respect for the allied minority and disarticulation of the rest) and unequal distribution of resources (benefits are extended only to allied sectors of business and organized labor)' (Acuna and Smith, 1994: 47).

The aggravation of political cleavages and growing social conflicts are then corollaries of the dual logic of power and unequal distribution of resources that results from the process of exclusionary neoliberal reform. Elections are losing importance because of the dual nature of power and distribution. As Putnam (1997: 59) has observed in another context, 'While democracy is spreading globally, it is also eroding locally.' Globalization and restructuring have made Korea a place of inchoate procedural democracy and have delayed democratic consolidation.

CONCLUSION

Korea is in the midst of rapid and drastic change. The 1997 economic crisis was the watershed event responsible for this societal transformation. Neoliberal restructuring has paved the way for radical changes in state–society relations. The state no longer assumes a leading role in organizing society and managing the economy. Structural adjustment has resulted in social and political arrangements focused on the process of market-oriented accumulation. The Kim Dae Jung regime's achievement of the first horizontal transfer of power has also brought on coalition change, as Cholla has replaced Kyungsang as the center of the ruling coalition, even though substantive change in technocratic and administrative arrangements in fact remains quite limited.

The Kim Dae Jung regime's inability to implement systematic, coherent reform measures can be explained by its failure to fundamentally reconstruct political power. The regime has tried to maintain stability by a dual logic of political power and unequal distribution. However, reform without democratic consensus will inevitably be characterized by sociopolitical tensions. Reform efforts that lack clear vision, strategies and policies will naturally lead to social conflict and political cleavage. All this renders the attempt to promote both political democracy and market-oriented reform a tall order.

With benefit of hindsight, we can say that Korea should have taken full advantage of the need to restructure in the wake of the crisis to remedy the inefficiencies in its economy, to limit political corruption, and to reduce the fragmentation of society. But the steps taken have not succeeded in healing the economic system. And the reform efforts of the Kim Dae Jung regime have only exacerbated the existing social conflicts and political cleavages.

History teaches us that a crisis can provide the opportunity for a radical reorientation of economy, politics and society. The UK pioneered the welfare state in the economic downturn of the 1930s; the United States created a New Deal society in the Great Depression; and Germany developed the social market economy after its defeat in World War II. In Korea, in contrast, the opportunity was missed. The construction of a stronger economic system remains a task for the next administration. Unfortunately, the failures of the last two civilian governments suggest the next regime may also have difficulty pushing ahead with structural reform.

In order to face the challenge of globalization, Korea is in urgent need of remaking the nation. Instead, the Kim Dae Jung regime has used reform politics to curry favor with the electorate and secure re-election. All Koreans have a calling to reorient their history in order not to repeat it.

NOTES

1. In this chapter, restructuring and structural adjustment are used interchangeably. Following Nelson (1990: 3–4), however, we distinguish between structural adjustment programs designed for one or two years of short-run stabilization and three to five years of medium-term structural change. Note that most existing studies deal with Latin American countries. There is a paucity of literature on Korea addressing social and political consequences of economic restructuring (Lim and Hwang, 2000).
2. According to Samuel Huntington (1991), the first wave of democratization occurred between 1828 and 1926, and mostly European and Northern American countries turned to democracy. In the second wave, between 1942 and 1962, former fascist countries and colonies joined the democracies. During the latest wave of democratization, which started around 1974, many former authoritarian countries in Latin America and Asia entered the long process of democratization.
3. In the existing literature, there has been much controversy about the utility of democratic transition and consolidation. For analytical purposes, however, by democratic transition we mean the installment of civilian government to replace an authoritarian regime (including both military and non-military in nature). We can say that democracy is consolidated when its institutions, norms and procedures become 'the only game in the town.' See Diamond (2001: xii–xvi) for a detailed exposition.
4. In coming into power, both Kim Young Sam and Kim Dae Jung used a kind of 'transformism,' that is, a mechanism whereby authoritarian and democratic forces coexist. The former applied a strategy of party merger between three regional leaders, and the latter used a strategy of party coalition between two regional leaders. They are determined politicians who believe that the ends justify the means.
5. They differ, of course, in policy lines or outcomes of reform. We are, however, more interested in their latent rather than manifest purpose or function of reform here.
6. The NCNP has no distinctive ideology, little organizational linkage, and weak policy orientation. Kim Dae Jung, the virtual owner of the party, has frequently disbanded it and merged it with other parties in pursuit of the presidency. The NCNP reveals a general characteristic of political parties in Korea – they are managed by money, politics and regional connections. It was later renamed the New Millennium Democratic Party (NMDP).
7. Kim Young Sam, Kim Dae Jung and Kim Jong Pil were notorious for their endless pursuit of the presidency. Among the so-called 'three Kims', Kim Jong Pil is the least popular, because of his career as a maker of *coup d'états* and as prime minister under the Park Jung Hee regime. His unpopularity is the reason he made a deal with Kim Dae Jung to change the constitution toward a parliamentary system. He thought that he had little chance to win election in a presidential system. He still favors a parliamentary system, as he tried to use it as a political bargaining chip for the 2002 presidential election.
8. In September 2001, the governing NMDP and its coalitional partner ULD ended their three-and-a-half years of cohabitation over the dispute of the 'Sunshine Policy' towards North Korea. There have been deep gulfs between the two parties, since the leader of ULD, Kim Jong Pil, thought Kim Dae Jung betrayed him by not pursuing the constitutional amendment.
9. It was the first official attempt by the country to create a neocorporatist mechanism of interests intermediation. It clearly contrasts with the former government's policy of excluding representatives of workers from the negotiation process and only deal with them when there is trouble. For a different view on the Korean government's attitude toward workers, see Campos and Root (1996). At first, the Tripartite Commission reached a dramatic compromise on ten major reforms including 90 specific items. They are as follows: government and employers would construct nationwide organizations and prepare a policy package for employment; all parties in the Tripartite Commission would make an effort to improve job security by introducing work-sharing; all parties would try to minimize layoffs and revive financially troubled firms; all parties would make progress in eliminating unfair labor practices and would establish bodies to monitor compliance;

the policy-making process would be open to labor unions; unions would participate in both the making and implementation of important policies affecting wage-earners' standard of living; all parties would input in the restructuring of *chaebol* firms; reform of public enterprises would occur through agreements between labor and management; the teachers' union would be legalized; all parties would make an effort to improve worker participation in management (see Song, 2001: 12–13).

10. One of the Kim Dae Jung regime's theoreticians proposed a 'democratic market economy' in which the government intervenes in the economy to achieve fairness while following a market mechanism for efficiency (cf. J. Choe, 1998). As an imitation of the German social market economy, however, the democratic market economy did not survive the Kim Dae Jung regime, due to its emphasis on the logic of competitiveness.

11. After the crisis, Koreans tend to take restructuring as introducing a neoliberalist market system, and reform as promoting democracy in various sectors.

12. Acuna and Smith (1994: 19) define the social organization of political power as an institutional ensemble of all the interacting social and political actors seeking to serve their respective interests and objectives, with different resources and capacities.

13. One might say that the political will to drive reform was stronger for Kim Young Sam than for Kim Dae Jung, since Kim Young Sam was valiant enough to put Chon Doo Hwan and Roh Tae Woo and their associates on trial for treason, corruption and murder. Immediately after his inauguration, Kim Dae Jung pardoned all of them.

14. A good example is the series of recent resistances to reform measures by the affected interest groups, such as school teachers, entrepreneurs, physicians, pharmacists, journalists and lawyers.

15. In pursuing neoliberal restructuring, the Kim Dae Jung regime has tried to build a social safety net. Korea's emphasis on social policy is quite different from most Latin American countries, where a social safety net is largely neglected.

16. Dependency theory has argued that economic dependency results in lack of development or underdevelopment. However, some Latin American economies such as Brazil and East Asian economies such as South Korea have experienced economic growth despite a high level of dependence on a foreign economy. Dependent development refers to the fact that economic growth did happen under dependency in these economies and the fact that economic growth failed to reduce the level of economic dependency.

17. See Evans's seminal work on the case study of Brazilian dependent development (Evans, 1976).

18. Most of the foreign investment is private, short-term, liquid and volatile. This supports talk about the possibility of another economic crisis in Korea.

19. Leading this trend are the Citizens' Coalition for Economic Justice, the Korea Federation of Environment Movement, and the People's Solidarity for Participatory Politics, the key social movement organizations.

20. Following Schedler (2001: 151), we add two subtypes of democracy between authoritarianism and advanced democracy. Electoral democracy is a 'diminished subtype of democracy' that holds 'inclusive, clean, and competitive elections but fails to uphold the political and civil freedoms essential for liberal democracy.'

21. This is well evidenced by the low voting rates shown in the recent local elections. In the local election of June 2002, voter turnout was 48.8 percent. Only 16.9 million of the 34.7 million in the electorate voted in this election, and this rate is the lowest in Korean election history.

22. Korea has three major parties, of which the Grand Korea Party (GKP) as an opposition party has a majority in the National Assembly . The GKP was originally formed by Kim Young Sam and is currently headed by Lee Hoi Chang. Other parties are Kim Dae Jung's NMDP and Kim Jong Pil's ULD. All three Kims are now in their late 70s; among them, only Kim Young Sam has formally retired from politics.

23. It should be remembered that these regional cleavages did not originate at the society level, but were imposed upon civil society by the political elites.

24. The efficacy of corporatism decreases due to shrinking labor power and increased capital mobility in the throes of globalization. As a pioneer theoretician of corporatism, Schmitter

(1989: 72) observed long ago that: 'I have become less and less concerned that corporatism ... will survive, much less be as much an imperative for the future of capitalism.'
25. Based on the Latin American experience of neoliberal reform, Acuna and Smith (1994: 41–9) add three politico-economic scenarios to 'double democracy'. First, 'organic crisis': unleashing a tug-of-war among social classes and groups amid increasing sociopolitical tensions as a result of failed restructuring. Second, 'fragmented and exclusionary democracy': the fragmentation of the social classes and groups and the exclusionary design of social and economic policies in order to achieve neoliberal reform. Third, 'inclusionary democracy': the incorporation of social classes and groups in the process of policy design based on sociopolitical pacts.

Comment on Chapters 11 and 12

Dwight Perkins

Both of these chapters attempt to understand the nature of the reform process in Korea not so much by analyzing the effectiveness of particular measures introduced by the government as by looking at the underlying political and social forces at work. Yee attempts to do this by first developing a typology of Korean style and Anglo-American style systems. Lim and Han mainly employ a framework based on social conflict between different groups or classes. I find the Yee framework more helpful but feel that this framework could be put into more of a historical context. The Lim–Han framework, as presented here, argues that there is a growing social conflict, but it isn't entirely clear just who the groups in conflict are or what they want. I will start with the Yee chapter.

Starting with the three components that Yee uses to place societies in space: (1) political equality versus hierarchy, (2) group values versus individualism, and (3) transparency versus opaqueness, there is little doubt that the Korean system, like the economic systems of most of East and Southeast Asia, is far removed from the Anglo-American system. There is also no question, as the author argues, that these differences have had a profound impact on the performance of these economies and societies more broadly. The question I would like to address is: how did societies evolve in such apparently different ways and what are the implications of that evolution for reform in Korea and the rest of Asia?

If one looks at late nineteenth- and early twentieth-century America and Europe, the characteristics attributed to year 2000 America and Europe are much less apparent. Most companies in the earlier period, for example, were family businesses, minority shareholders where they existed had few rights, and there was little transparency when it came to the inner workings of these firms. American culture was more individualistic although there were strong social norms in small-town America and these norms were rigorously enforced, unlike today. And in Europe the system was still quite hierarchical even where democracy existed. The rules that governed these societies evolved slowly as a natural organic response to the needs of these evolving societies. The beginnings of rule of law emerged in societies that were still primarily rural and where businesses were small. Reining in authoritarian discretionary power took centuries in the case of England, and America was able to build on that heritage.

The contrast with Asia begins with the fact that much of East Asia went from being poor peasant societies to relatively rich industrial societies in the course of little more than three decades. In addition, institutions such as the legal system did not grow naturally in response to evolving social needs in the region; these institutions were often adopted wholesale from Europe either voluntarily as in the case of Japan or imposed as in the case of all countries that were colonies of either a European power or Japan. Given the alien nature of these Western institutional transplants, particularly the formal legal systems, it is not surprising that they did not take firm root in Asian soil. Even in Hong Kong and Singapore, the two societies that are considered to have the strongest legal systems today, rule of law was not widely used in the commercial world until the last two decades of the twentieth century. In China or Indonesia, at the other end of the spectrum, there was almost no use of the rule of law and the courts in economic affairs. Japan, Korea and Taiwan fall somewhere in between these two extremes. Until very recently, the formal legal systems of these latter three economies, while highly developed in areas like criminal law, have been too small to take on a major role in the governance of these economies.

The rapid East Asian economic expansion that began in the second half of the twentieth century, therefore, had to be built on institutions that had deep roots in these societies. The key relationship for establishing the trust that is necessary in so many business transactions was obtained through family ties and through associations based on regional origin that had some of the same characteristics as family ties. But these ties could only provide part of what was needed. The development of modern industry also required support and rules that could not be readily supplied by ties based on personal relationships. Lacking much of a legal system, the government stepped in to provide guidance and rules. By 1997 these methods of doing business came to be referred to in the popular press as 'crony capitalism,' but for most of the latter half of the twentieth century these relationships were essential to the kind of growth that occurred. Someone had to sweep away the many bureaucratic obstacles to investment with which these economies were riddled, someone had to determine who would be forced into bankruptcy and who would not, or which firm would be taken over by another, and so on. The legal system was not remotely up to the task but the executive branch of the government was.

The remarkable thing is that these pre-modern institutions of family-like ties and authoritarian governments had so much success for so long without creating the institutions found in the modern economies of the West. But these traditional institutions became increasingly inadequate as these economies became more complex and the political systems became increasingly democratic. Building modern institutions based on the rule of law, however, is a difficult and long-term task, not something that can be created in a few years or even a decade or two.

When Korea and other East Asian countries faced the need to restructure their economies, therefore, the government could not simply get out of the way and let market forces take their course. The breakup of the *chaebols* in Korea, or the opposite movement in China to form individual enterprises into business groups, for example, could not be left to the decisions of individual firms guided by market forces. There must be rules guiding these market forces, rules that are enforced either by the courts or by independent regulatory agencies. But the courts and regulatory agencies in most of Asia either did not exist or were not up to the task. If the society wanted quick action, therefore, the only choice was to turn to the executive branch of the government. But the more one turns to the executive branch of government to provide the required guidance, the longer one will wait before institutions develop that can make this discretionary government intervention unnecessary. That is the dilemma that Korea faced in 1998 and, like much of the rest of Asia, still faces today. Korea has a big advantage over countries like China in this regard, however, in that it at least has a solid foundation on which to build the kind of legal system that will make it possible for the government to get out of the activist industrial policy business.

Professor Yee, in my opinion, is generally correct in the way he analyzes the current nature of the system and why it is no easy task to transform that system to meet the needs of today. I have tried to put the current situation in its historical context with the hope that this will provide a clearer sense of the road ahead that will turn Korea into a true modern market economy.

I find myself in less agreement with the arguments of Professors Lim and Han. Part of my problem is that I have never found the social or class conflict framework to provide an effective tool for understanding the evolution of Korean society, which is not to say it can't be useful in other contexts. I find it even harder to use this framework when the social groupings or classes are not defined in a precise way. The task is made even more difficult when terms like reform are used without making clear what constitutes reform. Early on in this chapter, for example, it is stated that reform requires power to shift from reactionary classes to diverse social groups or classes, but just who are these people? And is the term reactionary class really appropriate in social science analysis, or should it be left to political activists? A couple of pages later the chapter states that President Kim Dae Jung confused reform with restructuring, but what do these terms mean? There is the statement that President Kim did not live up to the expectation that he would completely reshuffle power, but what exactly does this mean? There are hints in the chapter that what the authors have in mind when they talk about reform and completely reshuffling power would have been a government dominated by labor and unions pushing for some kind of socialism. If this is correct, then it seems hardly surprising that Korean citizens did not vote for this outcome and that President Kim did not provide it.

Lim and Han argue more clearly that they see power shifting toward multinational corporations (MNCs) and that this constrains the power of the government to seek its own interests. In a similar vein later, it is stated that the government is allied with 'transnational agencies.' At a certain level these statements are no doubt correct. The globalization of the world economy with MNCs operating across borders has greatly restricted what governments can do in all advanced economies, including those of North America and Europe. It is also true that when a country's government and business sector gets into so much trouble that it requires an IMF bailout, transnational agencies are going to have a good deal of influence at least in the short run. If the argument is that Korea has an unusual degree of MNC and transnational influence over its economic affairs, a degree not found in many other countries, then I would disagree. Korea, like Japan, has had a very nationalistic economic policy when it comes to policies toward the MNCs, and this has resulted in Korea having an unusually low level of foreign direct investment relative to most advanced and most successful developing economies. The current policies, in my opinion, are designed to move Korea a bit closer to the more normal global pattern, but Korea is still a long way from that pattern. If Korea is going to be a full and leading member of the global economy, and I suspect that is what the government and much of the population wants, it will have to move further in this direction. As for Korea's involvement with transnational agencies such as the IMF, it will have no need for the IMF if in the future it avoids the kind of macroeconomic mismanagement that prevailed in 1997—I think a repeat of 1997 any time soon is highly unlikely.

The final part of the chapter makes the point that civil society in Korea is weak and that means that democracy in Korea in not yet on a firm foundation. This statement is clearly valid although one could argue at length over how weak civil society may or may not be. My main comment about this part of the chapter is that this issue, like the issue discussed above about missing modern economic institutions, needs to be seen in its historical context. It is hardly surprising that Korea, after four decades of colonial rule and four decades of authoritarian rule, has yet to fully develop a complete pluralistic society of the kind found in, say, North America. That said, however, Korea, in my opinion, has made much more rapid progress in this direction than many of the societies of Latin America. I have much more confidence about the future of democracy in Korea than I do for this other important part of the globe.

13. Recurrence of financial crises: cross-country patterns and implications for Korea[1]

Kiseok Hong, Jong-Wha Lee and Changyong Rhee

INTRODUCTION

While some economies have been ravaged repeatedly by financial crises in recent years, others have remained virtually unscathed. Table 13.1 shows the marked variation in the frequency of crises across countries. While some of the 110 developing countries listed there experienced no crises in recent decades, others experienced as many as five. The conclusion holds whether we measure recurrence by the number of currency crises, the number of banking crises, or the number of times a country went to the International Monetary Fund (IMF) for financial assistance.[2] Korea is a member of the first category: it had never experienced a serious crisis until the one that broke out in late 1997.

To be sure, the frequency of crises may vary across countries even when the *ex ante* probability of crisis is constant; some countries may simply be unlucky. But the differences in Table 13.1 seem to be too great to be ascribed to luck of the draw. One possible explanation is that the probability of a crisis depends on history. The likelihood of a crisis in the future may be higher in countries where crises have occurred in the past. In this chapter, we investigate this hypothesis using a large panel of developing countries and draw out the implications for the risk of further crises in Korea. The goal is to determine whether recent policy actions have eliminated the danger of further financial instability or if there remains a significant danger that events like those of late 1998 might recur.

Existing studies of the causes of crises find that crisis incidence is related to economic fundamentals in systematic ways. Some countries experience recurring crises, these studies suggest, because they have weak fundamentals. Note, however, that this finding is not necessarily inconsistent with the view that the probability of crises is history-dependent. If an initial crisis has lingering adverse effects on the fundamentals, then a crisis-hit country will

Table 13.1 Recurrence of crises by country (110 countries)

Currency crisis indicator (1960–97)

Number of crises	Number of countries	Conditional ratio
5	6	42.9% (6/14)
4 and above	14	58.3% (14/24)
3 and above	24	58.5% (24/41)
2 and above (recurrence)	41	48.2% (41/85)
1 and above	85	78.7% (85/108)

Banking crisis indicator (1970–97)

Number of crises	Number of countries	Conditional ratio
5 and above	4	26.7% (4/15)
4 and above	15	55.6% (15/27)
3 and above	27	60.0% (27/45)
2 and above (recurrence)	45	68.2% (45/66)
1 and above	66	61.1% (66/108)

IMF financial assistance indicator (1975–97)

Number of crises	Number of countries	Conditional ratio
5 and above	18	52.9% (18/34)
4 and above	34	61.8% (34/55)
3 and above	55	83.3% (55/66)
2 and above (recurrence)	66	82.5% (66/80)
1 and above	80	74.1% (80/108)

Source: See text.

be more likely to develop another crisis in the future. Studies of post-crisis adjustment confirm that the shocks precipitating crises and, even more, the consequences tend to be persistent. For example, Hong and Tornell (2000) show that while the GDP growth rate recovers to its pre-crisis level fairly quickly (within two or three years) after a crisis, the associated credit crunch and problem of nonperforming loans can last for at least five years. Because crises can result in protracted financial sector difficulties, a country suffering a crisis may remain vulnerable long after the initial shock has passed.

Several studies have examined the linkage between past crises and current crisis probabilities. Glick and Hutchison (1999) and Kaminsky and Reinhart (1999) report that countries hit by a banking crisis are more likely to experience a currency crisis subsequently. In contrast, this chapter is interested in whether past crises increase the likelihood of future crises of the same kind (whether past currency crises increase the likelihood of future currency crises, or whether past banking crises increase the probability of future banking crises); we refer to this phenomenon as 'recurrence.' We not only examine the existence of a relationship between past and current crises but also attempt to identify the channels through which past crises create a possibility of recurrence.

Korea recovered rapidly from its 1997 financial crisis on the back of substantial macroeconomic and structural improvements. We compare Korea's post-crisis adjustment with previous crisis episodes, analyzing both the speed of recovery and the nature of macroeconomic and structural improvements.

The remainder of the chapter is organized as follows. The next section describes the data and variables used in our analysis, paying special attention to the definition of our crisis indicators, after which a section analyzes the problem of recurrence. The following section then discusses the implications for crisis in Korea, and a final section concludes.

DEFINITION AND DATA OF FINANCIAL CRISES

To examine the causes and nature of financial crises, we first need to define a financial crisis.

Defining Currency Crises, Banking Crises and IMF Financial Assistance

A crisis, being a complex event, can be defined in various ways. Several alternative indicators have been used in the literature. A currency crisis is typically defined as occurring when an index of exchange market pressure exceeds a critical threshold. This method was pioneered by Eichengreen et al. (1995). The advantage of this measure is that it captures instances of speculative pressure that do not lead to large depreciations; specifically, it should capture episodes when the authorities successfully defend the currency by intervening in the foreign exchange market or adjusting domestic monetary policy. Hence Eichengreen et al. (1995), Kaminsky and Reinhart (1999), and Glick and Hutchison (1999) all measure exchange market pressure as a weighted average of nominal depreciation, the change in international reserves, and the change in the domestic interest rate. A currency crisis is considered to have occurred if the composite indicator increased above a threshold defined in terms of the country-specific moments.

This approach is subject to a number of problems. In particular, an orderly change in foreign reserves or domestic interest rates can occur even in the absence of a speculative attack. Moreover, since we lack reliable data on interest rates and foreign reserves in many developing countries, implementation of this approach for a large sample of such countries is impractical.

Alternatively, Frankel and Rose (1996), Milesi-Ferreti and Razin (1998), and J.-W. Lee et al. (2001) focus on the nominal rate of currency depreciation and define crisis periods as those in which the index increases sharply relative to a threshold rate of depreciation that is assumed to be common to all countries. This approach has the advantage of not requiring data on interest rates and international reserves for all countries in the sample. Frankel and Rose, for example, deemed a country to experience a crisis if its currency depreciated by at least 25 percent in a quarter and the current rate of depreciation exceeded that in the previous quarter by at least 10 percentage points.[3] Our indicator of currency crises follows this approach.

Indicators of banking crises are also widely used, although identifying the incidence of banking insolvency or other forms of banking sector distress is not straightforward. While bank runs and large-scale government intervention in the banking system are readily observed, other corollaries of banking crises are not so easily identified. Financial distress can be protracted; that it can last for many years makes it hard to pinpoint a crisis. Moreover, bank asset quality is not easily measured; a deterioration in the quality of bank assets is not easily detected. Typically, analysts rely on subjective judgments of the severity of banking sector problems, basing their assessments on loan losses, the erosion of bank capital, or the extension of large-scale government assistance. In this study, we base our indicators of banking crises on subjective measures developed by Caprio and Klingebiel (1996), Demirgüç-Kunt and Detragiache (1998), and Glick and Hutchison (1999), who have documented episodes of large-scale bank insolvency using both quantitative and qualitative criteria.

Countries experiencing financial difficulties often seek IMF financial arrangements. As an alternative to the above, we therefore identify the incidence of financial crises by the dates when countries agree with the IMF on the terms of a stabilization program. An IMF program can come in the form of a Stand-by Arrangement (SBA) or through the Fund's Extended Fund Facility (EFF), its Structural Adjustment Facility (SAF), or its Enhanced Structural Adjustment Facility (ESAF). Among these, SBAs and EFF loans are the main types of programs designed to provide short-term balance of payments assistance to IMF member countries. (The SAF and the ESAF were introduced in the late 1980s to aid structural adjustment in low-income countries, mostly

Sub-Saharan African countries and former centrally planned economies.) In this chapter, our third measure of financial crises is based on whether a country has agreed to either an SBA or an EFF program with the Fund. To be sure, countries approach the IMF for a variety of reasons, not all related to financial distress. We use the IMF indicator here despite this limitation, because the issue of what countries negotiate IMF programs is of independent interest, and because one reason that some countries approach the Fund is precisely in order to head off future crises.[4]

In order to identify a financial crisis (whether a currency crisis, a banking crisis, or IMF financial assistance), we construct an exclusion window of two years around the event. That is, further such events occurring within three years of the initial one are considered a continuation of the same crisis rather than a new episode.

Data

We developed a measure of the incidence of crises for 110 developing countries spanning the period 1960–97. Countries that joined the OECD before 1990 are not included in the sample; we assume that the likelihood of crisis recurrence in these countries was lower and that, in any case, the underlying structure was different. We identify 154 currency crises in our 110 countries in this period.[5] Information on banking crises is available only for the period starting in 1970. Over the 28 years from 1970 through 1997, we identify 165 banking crises.

We then compiled data on IMF financial assistance for the period 1975 to 1997. Because information on IMF programs and other macroeconomic variables used in the regression analysis is more broadly available after 1974, we limit the sample for our empirical work to the period from 1975 to 1995. In these two decades there were 119 currency crises, 134 banking crises and 152 cases of IMF financial assistance.

The appendix table shows the types, number and dates of these various financial crises for each of the 110 countries in the sample. Obviously, some countries experienced multiple crises at the same time. About one-third of all currency crises were 'twin' crises in which a currency crisis was accompanied by a banking crisis in either the current or immediately successive year. That said, there is considerable evidence that different types of crises occur independently. The bivariate correlations among the three types of crises, even when we include further crises occurring in the year immediately following the initial event, are less than 0.3. Evidently, a financial crisis can manifest itself in any of the three ways considered in this chapter but need not take the form of all three simultaneously. In particular, about two-thirds of our crisis observations selected on the basis of IMF program participation are not also identified as currency or banking crises.[6]

Table 13.2 *Macroeconomic variables during the crisis period*

	No. obs.	Mean	Rank	St. dev.	Median
GDP growth					
All observations	2107	3.22		6.07	3.73
Currency crises	244	1.34	1	5.53	1.91
Banking crisis	272	2.18	3	6.32	3.23
IMF arrangements	395	1.91	2	5.78	2.57
Inflation					
All observations	1863	18.45		28.54	10.53
Currency crises	202	31.25	1	33.95	21.91
Banking crisis	243	23.59	2	35.43	11.63
IMF arrangements	359	22.51	3	32.28	12.52
Current account/GDP					
All observations	1901	−4.65		8.59	−4.19
Currency crises	224	−5.71	2	8.39	−4.82
Banking crisis	264	−4.81	3	9.24	−4.11
IMF arrangements	357	−6.03	1	7.10	−5.22
Export growth					
All observations	1881	4.37		15.58	4.75
Currency crises	239	1.07	1	19.78	3.34
Banking crisis	271	5.01	3	16.73	4.96
IMF arrangements	385	3.22	2	14.45	3.90
Import growth					
All observations	1881	3.60		16.21	3.50
Currency crises	238	−0.38	1	19.85	0.80
Banking crisis	271	2.58	3	16.76	2.36
IMF arrangements	384	0.57	2	16.77	1.22
Fixed investment/GDP					
All observations	1933	21.58		8.70	20.84
Currency crises	232	18.80	1	7.57	18.70
Banking crisis	267	19.61	2	7.61	19.28
IMF arrangements	366	20.09	3	8.92	18.83
Unemployment					
All observations	473	8.86		5.88	7.20
Currency crises	54	10.99	1	6.74	8.45
Banking crisis	79	8.38	3	4.68	6.90
IMF arrangements	107	9.74	2	6.79	7.90

Table 13.2 continued

	No. obs.	Mean	Rank	St. dev.	Median
Manufacturing employment growth					
All observations	924	2.25		8.73	2.09
Currency crises	89	–0.12	2	7.98	0.60
Banking crisis	120	–0.79	1	8.46	0.00
IMF arrangements	182	1.66	3	9.54	2.05
Real wage growth					
All observations	949	3.51		12.16	2.29
Currency crises	92	1.65	1	12.88	0.98
Banking crisis	126	2.22	2	16.71	0.30
IMF arrangements	190	3.81	3	15.01	2.37

Notes:
Crisis period includes the crisis year and one year before the crisis.
Rank is by the order of the worst performance in terms of the mean of each macroeconomic variable during the crisis period.

Source: See text.

In Table 13.2 we report the means of key macroeconomic variables in crisis periods.[7] For the purposes of this table, a crisis period is now defined as the year in which the crisis erupted and the immediately preceding year. The preceding year is included because in some cases our indicators may detect a crisis with a lag. For example, a country could have been hit by currency and banking problems at the end of one year, but only experienced large reserve outflows, large increases in nonperforming loans, or IMF financial assistance at the beginning of the next.

Table 13.2 shows the mean of each macroeconomic variable in both crisis and non-crisis years. As expected, indicators like GDP growth, inflation, export growth and the rate of unemployment show that macroeconomic conditions deteriorate in a crisis. However, these macroeconomic variables paint a different picture depending on the particular crisis indicator utilized in the analysis. For instance, the average per capita growth rate of GDP was 1.34 percent per annum in crisis periods when the latter is measured by our indicator of currency crises but 1.91 percent per annum when we measure crises by the IMF program indicator and 2.18 percent per annum when we base the measure on the banking crisis indicator.

Table 13.2 compares the behavior of each macroeconomic variable in currency crises, banking crises and IMF programs. Rank 1 denotes the type of crisis in which the performance of the particular macroeconomic variable is worst. For most variables, the length of the currency crisis has rank 1, implying that currency crises typically have a more severe impact on that variable than banking crises and instances when a country negotiates a program with the fund. However, IMF assistance has rank 1 for the current account balance, indicating that IMF financial assistance tends to be extended to countries experiencing balance of payment difficulties.

RECURRENCE OF CRISES

In this section, we turn to the issue of recurrence, asking whether the probability of a crisis differs depending on whether or not a country experienced a crisis previously. Determining whether such a pattern exists can be useful for predicting crises.

In addition, we ask whether, within the group of countries experiencing crises, we can determine why some countries are significantly more prone to recurrence. In addition, we ask whether it is possible to identify the determinants of the length of time before recurrence. Answers to these questions may be useful for identifying policies that limit recurrence risk.

To answer the first question, we need to contrast countries that have experienced crises previously with those that have not. To answer the second question, in contrast, we limit our attention to countries that have previously experienced crises.

Defining Recurrence

Since there is no single definition of a crisis, defining recurrence is not straightforward. For present purposes, we define recurrence as a second crisis occurring within seven years of a previous crisis in the same country. A variant is to define recurrence as a crisis that is preceded by one or more crises in the preceding seven years. For both variants we restrict our definition of the recurrence to cases in which a crisis is followed by another crisis of the same kind (for example, a currency crisis that is followed by another currency crisis).

We chose seven years as the time span relevant for recurrence for practical reasons. Many studies of crises, including our own, use a two- or a three-year window in defining crises in order to avoid double counting the same event.[8] The underlying assumption is that the impact of the initial crisis is felt for two to three years. Needless to say, the length of the time span used in defining recurrence must be greater than the length of the window. At the same time, that time span should be reasonably short to avoid counting widely spaced crises occurring for entirely unrelated reasons as instances of recurrence. Crises that are separated from one another by ten years or more are unlikely to be closely related; it is not useful to categorize them as instances of recurrence.[9]

The choice between the two definitions of recurrence (a crisis followed by another within the following seven years, and a crisis preceded by another within the previous seven years) will differ depending on the questions under consideration.[10] When analyzing recurrence, it is natural to distinguish between crises that have been preceded by other crises during the previous seven years, versus those that have not.[11] If the group of observations associated with past crises has a higher probability of experiencing current crises, then we can conclude that crises have a tendency to recur. As will be seen below, this distinction facilitates direct comparisons between our analysis and previous studies.

In answering the question of what determines recurrence, on the other hand, it may make more sense to start with the observations that are currently classified as crises and to group them as a function of whether another crisis followed in the succeeding seven years. Since our hypothesis is that what happens after an initial crisis is important for determining recurrence, it makes sense to consider each crisis episode (and macroeconomic adjustment in succeeding years) as a single observation.[12]

Do Crises Recur?

Table 13.1 shows that, in the period from 1960 through 1997, 85 of our 110 developing countries experienced at least one currency crisis, while 41 countries experienced at least two currency crises, and 24 countries at least three currency crises. This means that some 79 percent of countries experienced at least one currency crisis and that some 37 percent experienced more than one crisis. For banking crises, the corresponding percentages are 61 and 42 percent, respectively. The average number of years between the initial crisis and its recurrence is 3.9 years for currency crises, 3.3 years for banking crises, and 4.0 years for IMF financial assistance.

Table 13.1 also reports a series of conditional probabilities denoting the percentage of countries with more than n crises within the total group of countries with at least n crises. For instance, the figure of 48.2 percent for countries with two or more currency crises indicates that out of 85 countries with at least one crisis, 41 countries had two or more crises during the sample period. Once a country was hit by a crisis during the sample period, in other words, the probability that it would experience another was nearly 50 percent. A particularly interesting finding is that these ratios do not decline as the number of crises considered rises from two or more to four or more. For currency crises, the conditional probabilities are 48.2 percent for two or more (as noted above), 58.5 percent for three or more, and 58.5 percent for four or more. In other words, the probability of two or more crises conditional on one or more crises is roughly the same as the probability of three or more crises conditional on the occurrence of two or more; the same is true of the probability of four crises conditional on the occurrence of three or more. Similar persistence is evident for banking crises (the conditional probability is 68.2 percent for two or more, 60.0 percent for three or more, and 55.6 percent for four or more) and IMF financial assistance (where the conditional probability is 82.5 percent for two or more, 83.3 percent for three or more, and 61.8 percent for four or more). This pattern suggests that the probability of a crisis in the underlying population is not equal across countries. Were crisis probabilities constant in the underlying population, the conditional probabilities should fall with increases in the number of crises. If the probability of crisis is 7 percent and each country has 30 years of annual observations (this assumption is broadly consistent with our sample), conditional ratios for the resulting binomial distribution would be 71 percent for one or more crises, 56 percent for two or more, and 44 percent for three or more. Compared with this example, the data suggest that cross-country differences in the frequency of crises are not purely random – to the contrary, the probability of crisis is systematically higher in countries where more than one crisis has already occurred.

We can marshal additional evidence on the existence of recurrence by comparing the unconditional probability of a crisis with its conditional probability. The unconditional probability is obtained by dividing the number of crisis episodes by the total number of observations. Table 13.3 reports the results. For currency crises, the conditional probability is about 11 percent, much higher than the unconditional probability of 4 percent. Similar results obtain for banking crises: here the conditional probability is 17 percent, while unconditional probability is 10 percent. A z-test shows that the difference between the two probabilities is statistically significant for both indices.

Table 13.3 Conditional vs unconditional probabilities of crises

	Unconditional probability	Conditional probability	z-statistic
Currency crisis	0.04	0.11	6.41
Banking crisis	0.10	0.17	3.08
IMF assistance	0.17	0.15	−1.22

Source: See text.

This clearly suggests that crises recur and that certain countries tend to experience a higher incidence of financial crises.

Interestingly, for the IMF index the two probabilities (a conditional probability of 17 percent and the unconditional probability of 15) are not significantly different from each other. It is often said that the same countries return to the IMF for financial assistance again and again. Our analysis suggests that the reality is more complicated. We will have more to say about this below.

The preceding analysis is univariate; that is, it does not control for other factors that influence the persistence of financial problems. Also, the conditional probability does not ask whether many past crises increase the probability of an additional crisis more than just one past crisis. Analyzing these possibilities requires a multivariate analysis that controls for additional potential determinants of the probability of a crisis and takes into account the precise number of crises experienced by the country in the past.

We therefore estimate a probit model, taking the crisis index as the dependent variable and including measures of past crises and various other controls as explanatory variables. The key explanatory variable, the number of crisis episodes during the previous seven years, not only distinguishes the presence and absence of crises in the past but also captures the frequency of past crises. We also consider other crises (in other words, when analyzing the recurrence of currency crises, we consider past banking crises and IMF programs in addition to past currency crises).[13] Some observers have argued that the occurrence of a banking crisis or the implementation of an IMF financial program in previous years has predictive power for a currency crisis the current year (see for example Kaminsky and Reinhart, 1999 and Glick and Hutchison, 1999). To test this hypothesis, we define a dummy variable that takes the value of one if there was a crisis in the preceding two years for banking crises and again for IMF programs. These two dummies are then included as additional explanatory variables in the probit regressions for currency crises. This same procedure is applied symmetrically to the other crisis cases.

The control variables include standard macroeconomic variables like the debt/GDP ratio, short-term debt as a share of GDP and per capita GDP growth.[14] To attenuate simultaneity bias, all of these variables are lagged by a year. Probit estimation of this type has been widely used in previous studies, starting with Eichengreen et al. (1995). The difference here is the introduction of explanatory variables reflective of past crisis experience. This allows our findings to be easily compared with previous studies.

The results of estimating our probit equations can be found in Table 13.4. Column 1 of Table 13.4 shows that, for both currency and banking crises, our indicator of past crises enters with a positive sign that is significantly differ-

Table 13.4 Probit estimates

	Coefficient	p-value	Coefficient	p-value
Currency crisis				
Currency crisis dummy (past 7 years)	**0.0572**	0.000		
Banking crisis dummy (past 2 years)	−0.0098	0.583		
IMF program dummy (past 2 years)	−0.0160	0.338		
Total debt/GDP	0.0002	0.133	**0.000**	0.006
Short-term debt/GDP	0.0009	0.115	0.001	0.402
Private debt/total debt	0.0005	0.567	0.000	0.794
Net FDI/total debt	**−0.0060**	0.003	**−0.006**	0.005
Growth of real GDP per capita	**−0.0042**	0.000	**−0.004**	0.001
Foreign reserve/import	**−0.0054**	0.075	**−0.006**	0.061
Growth of domestic credit	0.0003	0.414	**0.001**	0.015
Current account surplus/GDP	0.0006	0.570	0.002	0.186
Number of observations		989		989
Number of crises		81		81
Log likelihood		−246.8		−256.2
Banking crisis				
Banking crisis dummy (past 7 years)	**0.0602**	0.000		
Currency crisis dummy (past 2 years)	0.0282	0.415		
IMF program dummy (past 2 years)	−0.0081	0.754		
Total debt/GDP	0.0002	0.274	**0.000**	0.031
Short-term debt/GDP	−0.0006	0.560	−0.001	0.562
Private debt/total debt	0.0002	0.910	0.001	0.705
Net FDI/total debt	**−0.0089**	0.003	**−0.009**	0.004
Growth of real GDP per capita	0.0014	0.432	0.001	0.466
Foreign reserve/import	0.0018	0.686	0.005	0.267
Growth of domestic credit	**−0.0011**	0.049	**−0.001**	0.075
Current account surplus/GDP	−0.0008	0.644	0.000	0.927
Number of observations		721		721
Number of crises		83		83
Log likelihood		−223.9		−246.2
IMF financial assistance				
IMF program dummy (past 7 years)	**0.1088**	0.000		
Currency crisis dummy (past 2 years)	0.0690	0.117		
Banking crisis dummy (past 2 years)	0.0020	0.941		
Total debt/GDP	**−0.0006**	0.011	**0.000**	0.047
Short-term debt/GDP	**0.0019**	0.049	**0.001**	0.303
Private debt/total debt	**0.0027**	0.042	**0.003**	0.043
Net FDI/total debt	**−0.0109**	0.000	**−0.013**	0.000
Growth of real GDP per capita	**−0.0052**	0.006	**−0.004**	0.022
Foreign reserve/import	**−0.0224**	0.000	**−0.028**	0.000
Growth of domestic credit	−0.0001	0.935	0.000	0.662
Current account surplus/GDP	−0.0029	0.123	−0.002	0.411
Number of observations		820		820
Number of crises		133		133
Log likelihood		−306.6		−326.3

Source: See text.

ent from zero at standard confidence levels. This result is consistent with the univariate analysis in Table 13.3. However, whereas Table 13.3 indicated no significant difference between conditional and unconditional probabilities in the case of IMF assistance, Table 13.4 shows that once the limitations of the univariate analysis are relaxed, past crises become important for the IMF assistance index as well.

The coefficients on the indicators of past crises are economically as well as statistically significant. In the probit estimates for currency and banking crises, the coefficients on past crises are both on the order of 0.06. This indicates that the probability of a crisis increases by about six percentage points as the number of past crises increases one by one. Since the average value of the fitted probability for crisis observations is about 20 percent in our sample, this increase is quite substantial.[15] For the IMF program indicator, the effect of past crises is even greater, at 0.11. This supports the view that there is a considerable problem of recidivism with respect to IMF programs. Overall, these results suggest that the tendency of recurrence of crises is of practical importance and thus needs to be taken into account in predicting future crises.

Our estimates suggest that twin crises do not significantly explain current or future crises; their explanatory power is particularly weak in the case of currency crises. This contrasts with the finding of Kaminsky and Reinhart (1999) and Glick and Hutchison (1999) that banking crises have predictive power for currency crises. We suspect that the discrepancy stems from the different control variables used by these authors. While our specification includes a comprehensive set of macroeconomic controls, Glick and Hutchison's specification for currency crises includes only export growth and the reserve-to-M2 ratio. For its part, Kaminsky and Reinhart's (1999) analysis was bivariate; that is, it included no controls. Since past banking crises or past IMF financial assistance tend to be correlated with lagged macroeconomic indicators, omitting the latter will cause their effect to be spuriously correlated by the former. Thus it is not surprising that these earlier authors found stronger effects of previous crises than reported here.

The coefficients on the other explanatory variables are broadly consistent with previous findings. Although many of the controls are insignificant individually, they are highly correlated with one another, creating problems of multicollinearity. In any case, previous studies have reported the same finding. And, when the controls are significant individually, their coefficients enter with plausible signs. For example, a high percentage of short-term debt, a low level of foreign direct investment, a low GDP growth rate, and a low level of foreign reserves all increase the probability of a currency crisis. Also, as we can see from column 2 of each table, the coefficients are reasonably stable, regardless of our treatment of past crises.

What Determines Recurrence?

While the previous subsection established that crises have a tendency to recur, and that this tendency is of substantial importance, it did not identify the channels through which past crises affect the probability of recurrence. One conceivable explanation, of course, is that country-specific effects underlie this pattern of recurrence. Some countries may experience chronic political instability, for example, that is not captured by standard macroeconomic variables. The implication of this view is that adjustments in macroeconomic policy alone will not be sufficient to eliminate the problem. Another view, however, is that post-crisis macroeconomic adjustments and policy responses can systematically affect the likelihood of recurrence. If, for example, the proportion of short-term debt is reduced after a crisis, the probability of another may be reduced significantly. In this subsection, we take this second view and examine which macroeconomic variables are useful for explaining – and presumably preventing – crisis recurrence.

For these purposes, we limit our attention to country–year observations that are classified as crises, dividing these into two groups depending on subsequent events. Adopting our second definition of recurrence, crises that were followed by one or more crises within the succeeding seven years are classified as 'recurring' and therefore as members of Group I, while other cases are classified as 'not recurring' and therefore as members of Group II. Using this classification, we can identify determinants of recurrence by comparing the values of various macroeconomic variables in the two groups of countries during post-crisis periods. We focus on the post-crisis periods because we are interested in the relationship between post-crisis adjustment and the probability of recurrence.

Note that the length of the post-crisis periods cannot be given uniquely, since another crisis may recur at any time after the initial crisis, and we want to exclude the years of recurrence from our post-crisis periods.[16] Intuitively, we are interested in whether inadequate macroeconomic adjustment during post-crisis periods tends to be associated with an increased probability of another crisis. For this reason, the time span relevant for defining post-crisis periods differs for each crisis: it covers the years between the initial crisis and its recurrence. For countries in Group II, the length of post-crisis periods is set at four years, which is the average for Group I.

Table 13.5 compares the sample means of various macroeconomic variables during post-crisis periods for Groups I and II, where differences that are statistically significant at the 10 percent level or better are in bold type. Column 1 of Table 13.5 indicates that Group I countries experiencing currency crises have lower GDP growth, higher inflation, higher current account deficits, greater reliance on short-term debt, lower net inward FDI and larger

Table 13.5 Determinants of recurrence

	(1) Currency crisis		(2) Banking crisis		(3) IMF assistance	
	Mean	p-value	Mean	p-value	Mean	p-value
Real GDP growth						
Group I	1.60	**0.004**	2.05	**0.021**	2.48	0.112
Group II	3.37		3.71		3.11	
Inflation rate (CPI)						
Group I	40.51	**0.012**	24.54	0.172	25.35	**0.076**
Group II	28.99		19.11		20.25	
Current account/GDP						
Group I	−7.42	**0.001**	−4.37	0.347	−5.54	0.369
Group II	−4.14		−3.51		−4.99	
Real export growth rate						
Group I	−0.73	**0.000**	4.49	0.282	3.60	0.857
Group II	7.33		6.28		3.79	
Real import growth rate						
Group I	0.36	**0.014**	2.77	0.287	2.62	0.373
Group II	5.54		5.30		3.84	
Gross fixed investment/GDP						
Group I	18.09	**0.004**	19.00	0.346	18.84	0.636
Group II	20.63		20.00		19.11	
Unemployment rate						
Group I	11.44	0.387	8.29	0.623	9.10	0.898
Group II	9.96		8.78		9.23	

Total debt/GDP					
Group I	113.54	0.338	85.68	0.676	68.08	**0.007**
Group II	101.88		81.97		82.09	
Short-term debt/total debt					
Group I	13.46	**0.006**	13.32	0.729	13.21	**0.000**
Group II	10.69		13.79		10.20	
Private debt/total debt					
Group I	3.89	0.246	5.16	0.288	5.31	**0.000**
Group II	3.12		6.67		3.21	
Net FDI/total debt					
Group I	0.91	**0.003**	1.77	0.159	1.51	0.838
Group II	3.18		3.65		1.56	
Foreign reserve/import					
Group I	2.26	**0.002**	3.33	0.699	2.70	0.646
Group II	3.05		3.46		2.61	
Budget deficit/GDP					
Group I	-7.00	**0.001**	-3.87	**0.047**	-4.51	0.249
Group II	-3.81		-2.38		-5.14	

Notes:

Group I indicates the episodes of recurrence crises, when an initial crisis is followed by one or more crises within the following seven years.

Group II is the episodes of non-recurrent crises, when a crisis is not followed by another crisis within the following seven years.

The *p*-value indicates the significance level associated with the test of the hypothesis that the sample means of each macroeconomic variable between Group I and Group II during the post-crisis period are equal.

Source: See text.

budget deficits. Evidently, countries in which currency crises recur have weaker domestic economies and weaker international accounts. We consider these patterns to be consistent with common perceptions regarding the causes of recurrence. They suggest that country-specific effects are not the only source of recurrence: crisis-hit economies perhaps can reduce the risk of recurrence by improving their macroeconomic fundamentals.

For banking crises and IMF assistance, the differences between Group I and Group II are not as apparent. Column 2 of Table 13.5 shows that the only significant differences for banking crises are in the GDP growth rate and budget deficit. For IMF programs (in column 3), the inflation rate, total external debt, and the shares of short-term debt and private debt are all significant. We suspect this finding is partly attributable to the way that our banking crisis and IMF assistance indicators are defined. In the original series, banking crises and IMF assistance programs are typically indicated for several consecutive years. In Colombia, for example, the years from 1982 through 1987 are all classified as banking crises. Although some may consider this as representing one long banking crisis, our use of a two-year window divides this period into two banking crises. This means that our indicators may place some cases into Group I where they are more appropriately classified as members of Group II. One way of avoiding this problem is to count all consecutive crisis years as a single crisis. But the number of crisis observations then becomes too small for statistical analysis.

POST-CRISIS ADJUSTMENT AND RISKS OF RECURRENCE IN KOREA

The Korean financial crisis of 1997 resulted in a recession of unprecedented magnitude. The rate of GDP growth plunged from the pre-crisis average of 7.0 percent to –6.7 percent in 1998. Thankfully, Korea managed an impressive recovery starting in 1999. That recovery was steeper and more robust than most observers expected: the growth rate rebounded to 10.9 percent in 1999 and 9.3 percent in 2000 (Table 13.6).

Korea's V-shaped recovery is similar to the stylized pattern observed in previous crisis episodes, although it is a particularly impressive example of the genre (J.-W. Lee et al., 2001, and J.-W. Lee and Rhee, 2002). Its adjustment contrasts with the typical pattern in that the initial contraction was sharper and the subsequent recovery was even stronger than elsewhere.

The contraction of GDP in 1998 was largely associated with the collapse in investment. The level of domestic capital formation plunged by 38 percent, and the investment rate dropped from 33 percent in 1997 to 22 percent in 1998 (Table 13.6). Private consumption fell less steeply than investment,

Table 13.6 Principal macroeconomic indicators (%)

	1990–95 Average	1996	1997	1998	1999	2000	2001
GDP growth rate	7.47	6.75	5.01	-6.69	10.89	9.32	3.02
Inflation rate	6.21	4.92	4.43	7.52	0.81	2.26	4.31
Current account /GDP	-1.22	-4.42	-1.71	12.6	6.02	2.65	2.04
Budget deficit/GDP	-0.02	0.26	-1.53	-4.22	-2.71	1.25	1.33
Unemployment rate	2.40	1.99	2.58	6.79	6.28	4.06	3.71
Expenditure on GDP							
Private consumption growth	9.6	7.1	3.5	-11.7	11.0	7.9	4.2
(share in GDP)	(54.7)	(54.9)	(54.1)	(51.1)	(51.2)	(50.4)	(–)
Government consumption growth	0.8	8.2	1.5	-0.4	1.3	0.1	0.2
(share in GDP)	(9.7)	(9.8)	(9.5)	(10.1)	(9.2)	(8.6)	(–)
Gross domestic investment growth	11.4	8.7	-7.5	-38.4	29.5	11.2	-1.9
(share in GDP)	(37.2)	(37.9)	(33.4)	(22.0)	(25.7)	(25.5)	(–)
Export growth	24.6	11.2	21.4	14.1	15.8	20.5	1.0
(share in GDP)	(30.2)	(31.5)	(36.4)	(44.5)	(46.5)	(51.9)	(–)
Import growth	22.4	14.2	3.2	-22.1	28.8	20.0	-2.8
(share in GDP)	(31.7)	(33.9)	(33.3)	(27.8)	(32.3)	(35.7)	(–)

Source: Asian Development Bank (ADB), *Asia Recovery Information Center Indicators* (http://www.aric.adb.org/pre_defined_indicators.asp) and Bank of Korea (http://www.bok.or.kr/).

contracting by 12 percent; as a result the consumption/GDP ratio declined from 54 per cent in 1997 to 51 percent in 1998. This large fall in investment in the crisis period reflects the major role of banking and corporate sector distress in the recession. Clearly, the weakness of corporate and bank balance sheets was a major factor magnifying the impact of foreign disturbances on the Korean economy.

Although Korea's economic fundamentals and macroeconomic policies in the pre-crisis period were regarded as sound and credible, many foreign investors fled Korean financial market when they feared that Korea would suffer macroeconomic and structural problems similar to those that had driven Thailand and Indonesia to the brink of default. Table 13.7 shows that private capital flows reversed from a net inflow of 4.8 percent of GDP in 1996 to an outflow of 3.4 percent in 1997. Net bank lending outflows amounted to 8.3 percent of GDP. Korea first experienced a severe liquidity crisis with the withdrawal of foreign lending and balance-sheet problems with the subsequent currency depreciation. The balance sheets of financial institutions were vulnerable to these events because Korean banks had incurred extensive currency and maturity mismatches.[17]

Table 13.7 External balance (% of GDP)

	1990–95	1996	1997	1998	1999	2000	2001
Current account	−1.22	−4.42	−1.71	12.6	6.02	2.65	2.04
Current account (US$, billion)	−4.27	−23.00	−8.16	40.36	24.47	12.24	8.61
Financial flows	2.1	4.8	−3.4	−2.2	3.0	3.1	−0.7
Direct investment	−0.2	−0.4	−0.6	0.2	1.2	1.0	0.1
Portfolio investment	1.6	3.0	5.4	−0.3	2.1	2.9	1.5
Other investment	0.7	2.2	−8.2	−2.1	−0.3	−0.9	−2.4
Changes in reserves	−0.6	−0.2	4.4	−8.3	−5.4	−5.8	−1.8
Use of IMF fund credit	0.0	0.0	4.1	1.3	−2.4	0.0	0.0

Source: International Monetary Fund, *International Financial Statistics* (March 2002) and Bank of Korea (http://www.bok.or.kr/).

Once the financial sector experienced serious liquidity problems, banks and nonbank financial institutions curtailed their lending. Highly leveraged firms burdened with large amounts of short-term liabilities faced financing difficulties and were unable to service their debts. Bankruptcies soared, exacerbating the downturn in investment. In 1999, investment started to recover, but the rate remained below pre-crisis levels (reaching 25.5 percent in 2000).

While domestic demand remained sluggish, a large increase in exports paved the way for the recovery of the Korean economy. Real exports grew by 14 percent in 1998, by 16 percent in 1999 and by 21 percent in 2000. The export/GDP ratio reached 52 percent in 2000, a marked improvement from 36 percent in 1997. It is one of the stylized facts of previous crisis episodes that the external sector has led the recovery and the turnaround in GDP growth (Y. Park and Lee, 2001). Typically, real exchange rate depreciation following a currency crisis has a strong stimulative impact on export growth. In the Korean case, that export growth was even stronger and the economic turnaround was even quicker than was typical of previous crises. One reason for this may have been that Korean exports in 1998–2000 were supported by favorable external developments: the global economy, especially the United States, was growing strongly. The deterioration of the terms of trade that had helped to set the stage for the crisis was reversed in 1999. And, as argued by J.-W. Lee and Rhee (2002), exports could play an unusually large role in stimulating recovery from the crisis because the Korean economy was so open and export oriented. It follows that when export growth stalled in 2001 due to the deterioration of the global environment associated with the US recession, the decline in semiconductor prices, and depreciation of the Japanese yen, sustaining Korea's recovery from the crisis required that demand then rotate toward domestic consumption.

This strong export growth and rapid accumulation of international reserves helped to reduce the external vulnerability of the Korean economy. The level of usable gross reserves rose impressively from $9.1 billion at the end of 1997 to $48.5 billion in 1998 and $96.1 billion in 2000. The large amount of short-term external debt that had created liquidity problems in 1997 was transformed into liabilities of long-term maturity. The ratio of short-term to total external debt declined from 41 percent in 1997 to 29 percent in 1998, and increased a little back to 35 percent in 2000. Table 13.8 shows that the ratio of short-term external debt to foreign reserves similarly fell from 326 percent in 1997 to 44 percent in 2000.

These improvements in external liquidity have helped to reduce the vulnerability of the Korean economy and thus limit the likelihood that a crisis might recur in the future. The analysis in the previous section showed that currency crises are less likely to recur if a crisis-hit economy has reduced its short-term external debt and augmented its foreign reserves. Similarly, a country is less likely to have to resort to the IMF for financial assistance when external debt, especially short-term private external debt, has been substantially reduced.

In addition, Korea has gone a long way in improving the soundness and profitability of financial institutions and in alleviating corporate financial distress. The government has been actively involved in resolving insolvencies

Table 13.8 External, financial and corporate sector indicators (%)

	1994	1995	1996	1997	1998	1999	2000	2001
External sector								
Usable gross reserves (billion $)	21.5	28.5	29.4	9.1	48.5	74.1	96.1	–
Total debt/GDP	20.8	22.1	27.6	33.5	45.4	32.1	26.8	–
Short-term debt/total debt	52.7	55.4	52.3	41.4	29.3	34.2	34.8	–
Short-term debt/foreign reserve	172	184	219	326	80	60	44	–
Financial sector								
ROE in banking sector	–	4.59	4.21	–21.61	–78.40	–27.69	–12.87	–
Gross foreign liabilities/gross foreign assets	1.01	1.13	1.27	0.85	0.86	0.79	0.73	0.76
Share of NPLs, including those transferred to AMCs	–	–	–	–	–	19.7	20.3	19.3
Capital adequacy ratios of commercial banks	–	–	–	–	8.23	10.83	10.52	10.81
Corporate sector								
Debt/equity ratio	–	470	470	600	470	280	210	–
Return on equity	–	11.4	2.6	–1.6	–1.0	7.3	5.5	–
Percentage of companies with negative returns	–	7.1	23.2	30.0	27.6	11.0	20.5	–

Source: Asian Development Bank, *Asia Recovery Information Center Indicators* (http://www.aric.adb.org/pre_defined_indicators.asp).

of financial institutions and recapitalizing weak but viable intermediaries. Public funds have been provided in the form of equity capital injections, through the purchase of bad loans by the Korea Deposit Insurance Corporation (KDIC). The Korean Asset Management Corporation (KAMCO) has also purchased NPLs from financial institutions. Most banks, including those that had been restructured, have seen a substantial improvement in the quality of their assets and the profitability of their operations. Their lending capacity has also increased, supporting the recovery of the economy.

Korea has also made considerable progress in corporate debt workouts and operational restructuring. Corporate debt/equity ratios have dropped dramatically from 600 percent in 1997 to 210 percent in 2000 (see Table 13.8). Corporate profitability, as measured by the return on equity, has rebounded from −1.6 percent in 1997 to 5.5 percent in 2000.

Korea's achievements are indeed impressive. However, much remains to be accomplished to ensure that the Korean economy will avoid another crisis. Maintaining strong GDP growth, the preceding section has shown, limits the the risk of recurrence. Further progress in corporate and financial sector restructuring and reform are therefore imperative not only in order to minimize structural vulnerability to external shocks but also to maintain Korea's long-term capacity for growth.

In addition, foreign direct investment can play a role in strengthening the international accounts and also in recapitalizing financial institutions and improving corporate governance. As shown earlier, an increase in FDI inflows significantly reduces the probability of crisis recurrence. In the Korean case, however, FDI inflows have not yet reached significant levels; they amounted to just 1.2 percent of GDP in 1999, 1.0 percent in 2000 and 0.1 percent in 2001 (Table 13.7). Since 1998, most foreign capital inflows have come in the form of portfolio investment rather than FDI. A greater flow of foreign direct investment will render the Korean economy less vulnerable to future crises.

CONCLUDING REMARKS

In this chapter, we investigated the question of why financial crises recur. An analysis of a large panel of developing countries indicates that once a country is hit by a crisis it is more likely to experience another in the future. We also find that the macroeconomic adjustments following the crisis influence the probability of recurrence. Post-crisis policy initiatives that improve the current account, strengthen fiscal balance, attract foreign direct investment inflows, and reduce the ratios of short-term and private debt to total foreign debt can significantly reduce the risk of recurrence.

In its recovery since 1998, Korea has managed to improve substantially the macroeconomic and structural condition of its economy. According to our analysis, these improvements significantly reduce the risk of recurrence. Compared to other countries, however, Korea still receives little foreign direct investment and continues to incur substantial short-term debt. Further improvements in these areas will better ensure that Korea will not experience another crisis.

NOTES

1. This work is supported by the Research Center for International Finance, Seoul National University. We thank Barry Eichengreen for his helpful suggestions and Sungmo Choi for his excellent research assistance.
2. The definitions of the crises and the data used in these tabulations will be explained below.
3. This is also the measure used in Lee et al. (2001).
4. One therefore needs to exercise special care when interpreting the results with respect to IMF assistance.
5. Recall that we are excluding from this tabulation crises that erupt within three years of the initial event.
6. This, of course, is simply a manifestation of our earlier observation that countries approach the IMF for a variety of reasons.
7. We exclude some extreme observations such as annual GDP growth rates above 50 percent or below –50 percent, inflation rates above 300 percent or below –300 percent, current accounts/GDP above 40 percent or below –40 per cent, export growth rates above 100 percent or below –100 percent, import growth rates above 100 percent or below –100 percent, unemployment rates above 50 percent, and real wage growth rates above 200 percent or below –200 percent.
8. Frankel and Rose (1996), for example, use a three-year window. Our own window length is two years, as mentioned above.
9. We find that our results are robust to reasonable variations in the time span used for tabulating instances of recurrence.
10. If the time span for recurrence was instead taken as one year the two definitions of recurrence would be exactly the same.
11. In principle, the two definitions of recurrence can be equally relevant for the issue of the existence of recurrence. The first definition suggests a comparison between $P(I_t = 1 | I_{t-1,t-7} = 1)$ and $P(I_t = 1)$, while the second definition suggests a comparison between $P(I_{t+1,t+7} = 1 | I_t = 1)$ and $P(I_{t+1,t+7} = 1)$. Note, however, that questions addressed by the two definitions are not the same. Roughly speaking, one is about the effects of past few years on the next year, while the other is about the effects of past one year on the next few years.
12. If we instead use observations that have been preceded by a crisis during the previous seven years and group them according to what happens currently, we may be comparing observations that are not independent. Thus we start with the question of whether having experienced a crisis in the previous seven years increases the probability that a country will experience a crisis currently. We then ask, in addition, why some crisis countries experience further crises in the seven years following the event, while others do not.
13. We thus capture the incidence and determinants of twin crises. A twin crisis is defined as when two or more kinds of crisis take place in a short interval of time. Thus we are considering only the past two (instead of seven) years for these indicators. Among previous studies on twin crises, Kaminsky and Reinhart (1999) considered the past one year and Glick and Hutchison (1999) considered the past two years.
14. The real effective exchange rate, which is examined in Tables 13.2 and 13.5, is not used

here because of incomplete data. When real exchange rate depreciation is included, the number of observations for the regression is reduced almost by half, and the coefficient on this variable turns out to be insignificant. The results are available from us upon request. Also, we do not consider structural variables (such as indicators of capital controls) because of limited data availability. For the linkage between capital controls and the probability of a crisis, see Bordo et al. (2001).

15. The fitted probability for crisis observations is 0.14 for currency crises, 0.2 for banking crises and 0.27 for cases of IMF financial assistance.
16. Technically, there cannot be a recurrence during the two years immediately after an initial crisis because we use a two-year window in defining crises. This suggests that one may alternatively define the post-crisis periods as the two years that immediately follow a crisis and check whether macroeconomic performance during these two years is correlated with the probability of currency crises in subsequent periods. With this alternative time span, however, we find that differences in post-crisis adjustment between Group I and Group II are not clear.
17. By the middle of June 1997, the foreign liabilities of the banking sector exceeded its foreign assets, and short-term foreign liabilities were more than twice as large as short-term foreign assets (Park and Lee, 2001).

APPENDIX   CUMULATED NUMBERS OF CURRENCY CRISES, BANKING CRISES AND IMF FINANCIAL ASSISTANCE FOR EACH COUNTRY (1975–95)

Country name	Currency crisis	Banking crisis	IMF financial assistance
Afghanistan	1 (94)	0	0
Algeria	2 (90/94)	0	2 (89/94)
Angola	2 (91/94)	0	0
Argentina	1 (91)	3 (80/89/95)	4 (76/83/87/91)
Bahamas, The	0	0	0
Bahrain	0	0	0
Bangladesh	1 (75)	3 (87/90/93)	2 (79/83)
Barbados	0	0	2 (82/92)
Benin	1 (94)	1 (88)	0
Bolivia	1 (85)	2 (86/94)	2 (80/86)
Botswana	1 (75)	1 (94)	0
Brazil	2 (79/93)	2 (90/94)	3 (83/88/92)
Burkina Faso	1 (94)	1 (88)	0
Burundi	1 (83)	1 (94)	2 (76/86)
Cameroon	1 (94)	3 (87/90/93)	3 (88/91/94)
Cape Verde	0	0	0
Central African Republic	1 (94)	5 (80/83/86/89/94)	4 (80/83/87/94)
Chad	1 (94)	6 (80/83/86/89/92/95)	1 (94)
Chile	1 (85)	2 (76/81)	2 (83/89)
Colombia	0	2 (82/85)	0
Comoros	1 (94)	0	0
Congo, Dem. Rep. (Zaire)	1 (92)	1 (91)	5 (76/79/83/86/89)
Congo, Rep.	1 (94)	4 (80/83/86/89)	4 (77/86/90/94)
Costa Rica	1 (81)	2 (87/94)	5 (76/80/85/89/93)
Cote d'Ivoire	1 (94)	2 (88/91)	4 (81/84/88/91)
Cyprus	0	0	1 (80)
Dominica	0	0	2 (81/84)
Dominican Republic	2 (85/88)	0	2 (83/91)
Ecuador	4 (82/85/88/92)	1 (80)	4 (83/86/89/94)
Egypt, Arab Rep.	2 (79/89)	4 (80/83/91/94)	3 (77/87/91)
El Salvador	2 (86/90)	1 (89)	3 (80/90/93)
Ethiopia	1 (92)	1 (94)	1 (81)
Fiji	0	0	0
Gabon	1 (94)	0	4 (78/86/89/94)
Gambia, The	1 (84)	0	3 (77/82/86)
Ghana	3 (78/83/86)	3 (82/85/88)	3 (79/83/86)
Grenada	0	0	3 (75/79/83)
Guatemala	2 (86/89)	1 (91)	3 (81/88/92)
Guinea	1 (86)	2 (85/93)	2 (82/86)
Guinea-Bissau	3 (83/87/91)	1 (95)	0
Guyana	3 (84/87/90)	1 (93)	3 (76/79/90)

Country name	Currency crisis	Banking crisis	IMF financial assistance
Haiti	1 (91)	0	4 (76/82/89/95)
Honduras	1 (90)	0	3 (79/82/90)
India	0	1 (93)	1 (81)
Indonesia	3 (78/83/86)	1 (94)	0
Iran, Islamic Rep.	1 (93)	0	0
Iraq	0	0	0
Israel	1 (81)	3 (77/80/83)	0
Jamaica	3 (78/83/91)	1 (94)	5 (77/81/84/87/90)
Jordan	1 (88)	1 (89)	2 (89/92)
Kenya	1 (93)	4 (85/88/92/95)	5 (75/78/81/85/88)
Korea, Rep.	0	0	3 (77/80/83)
Kuwait	0	4 (80/83/86/89)	0
Lesotho	2 (75/84)	0	1 (94)
Liberia	0	0	3 (76/79/82)
Madagascar	3 (87/91/94)	1 (88)	4 (77/80/84/88)
Malawi	1 (92)	0	4 (79/82/88/94)
Malaysia	0	2 (85/88)	0
Mali	1 (94)	1 (87)	3 (82/85/88)
Malta	1 (92)	0	0
Mauritania	1 (92)	4 (83/86/89/92)	3 (77/80/85)
Mauritius	1 (79)	0	3 (78/81/85)
Mexico	4 (76/81/85/94)	5 (81/84/87/90/95)	5 (77/83/86/89/95)
Morocco	0	0	4 (80/83/86/90)
Mozambique	2 (87/91)	3 (87/90/93)	0
Myanmar	1 (75)	0	2 (77/81)
Nepal	0	3 (88/91/94)	2 (76/85)
Nicaragua	1 (90)	3 (88/91/94)	2 (79/91)
Niger	1 (94)	0	3 (83/86/94)
Nigeria	3 (86/89/92)	1 (93)	2 (87/91)
Oman	0	0	0
Pakistan	0	0	4 (75/80/88/93)
Panama	0	1 (88)	5 (77/80/83/92/95)
Papua New Guinea	0	0	2 (90/95)
Paraguay	2 (84/89)	1 (95)	0
Peru	1 (90)	3 (83/86/89)	3 (77/82/93)
Philippines	1 (83)	3 (81/84/87)	6 (76/79/83/86/89/94)
Rwanda	2 (90/94)	0	1 (79)
Samoa	3 (75/79/83)	0	3 (75/78/83)
Saudi Arabia	0	0	0
Senegal	1 (94)	2 (88/91)	4 (79/82/85/94)
Seychelles	0	0	0
Sierra Leone	3 (83/86/89)	2 (90/93)	3 (77/81/84)
Singapore	0	1 (82)	0
Solomon Islands	0	0	1 (81)
Somalia	3 (82/86/89)	0	2 (80/85)
South Africa	2 (75/84)	3 (77/85/89)	1 (82)
Sri Lanka	1 (77)	2 (89/92)	2 (77/83)
St Lucia	0	2 (75/84)	0

Country name	Currency crisis	Banking crisis	IMF financial assistance
St Vincent and the Grenadines	0	0	0
Sudan	5 (79/82/85/91/94)	0	2 (79/82)
Suriname	1 (94)	0	0
Swaziland	2 (75/84)	1 (95)	0
Syrian Arab Republic	1 (88)	0	0
Tanzania	4 (83/86/89/92)	2 (87/95)	3 (75/80/86)
Thailand	0	2 (83/86)	3 (78/81/85)
Togo	1 (94)	1 (93)	3 (79/83/86)
Tonga	0	0	0
Trinidad and Tobago	2 (85/93)	4 (82/85/88/91)	1 (89)
Tunisia	0	2 (91/94)	1 (86)
Uganda	4 (81/84/87/92)	1 (94)	2 (80/83)
United Arab Emirates	0	0	0
Uruguay	1 (82)	2 (81/84)	4 (75/79/83/90)
Vanuatu	0	0	0
Venezuela	3 (84/89/94)	4 (78/81/84/94)	1 (89)
Yemen, Rep.	1 (95)	0	0
Zambia	4 (76/83/86/92)	1 (95)	3 (76/81/84)
Zimbabwe	1 (91)	1 (95)	1 (81)

14. Reform and the risk of recurrence of crisis

In June Kim, Baekin Cha and Chi-Young Song

INTRODUCTION

A large number of studies have sought to determine the roles of domestic and international factors in the currency and banking crises experienced in East Asian countries, including Korea, in 1997. These studies can be usefully classified into three groups. The first one stresses structural weaknesses in the corporate and financial sectors, misguided economic policies, and deteriorating macroeconomic fundamentals (see for example Corsetti et al., 1998b; Fischer, 1998b; Lane et al., 1999). The second emphasizes the instability of international capital markets, as panicked creditors withdrew their short-term loans to East Asian borrowers (see Radelet and Sachs, 1998; Feldstein, 1998; Stiglitz, 1999). A final group of studies emphasizes the contagious nature of the crisis as it spread from Southeast Asia to Korea (Kaminsky and Schmukler, 1999; Park and Song, 2001b). More analysis is needed to determine the explanatory power of these competing views, but many observers will agree that all three sets of factors played some role in Korea's crisis.

The Korean government approached the International Monetary Fund (IMF) for assistance in November 1997 when it was unable to stem the outflow of capital and the depreciation of the won. Since the IMF considered structural weaknesses to be at the root of the country's crisis, it made the provision of assistance conditional on structural reform. In concert with the Fund, the Korean government implemented a wide range of reforms, including financial and corporate restructuring and further deregulation of the capital account of the balance of payments. The immediate priority was to restore confidence among investors and to stabilize domestic financial markets; to this end, the government closed nonviable financial institutions, began cleaning up the problem of nonperforming loans (NPLs), took steps to reduce the level of corporate debt, and enhanced the access of foreign financial institutions to domestic financial markets, including bond and short-term money markets. After financial markets were stabilized and recovery set in, the main impetus for continuing reform became the prevention of any recurrence of the crisis.

Since 1997–98, the Korean economy has mounted an impressive recovery. Growth has been strong despite the 2001–2 slowdown, while unemployment has declined and inflation has stabilized. The rating agencies have upgraded Korea's sovereign credit. These changes naturally lead us to ask what is driving the recovery, to what extent reform of the banking and corporate sectors has contributed to the country's impressive macroeconomic performance, and whether those reforms together with the recovery have significantly reduced the risk of further crises. More fundamentally, the question is whether and to what extent reforms undertaken in recent years have enhanced the efficiency and stability of the financial and corporate sectors.

In this chapter we seek answers to these questions. The next section discusses financial sector reform in Korea since the crisis, while the following one discusses corporate restructuring. A further section analyzes the impact of the reform on the profitability and cost structure of the banking and corporate sectors and investigates the factors behind the post-crisis recovery. Then we discuss Korea's vulnerability to another crisis, focusing on the effects of economic reform, capital account liberalization, instability in international financial markets, and contagion from other countries. A final section concludes.

FINANCIAL SECTOR REFORM

Aims and Principles

Financial fragility and the insolvency of financial institutions were at the heart of the crisis. As a result of lax supervision and regulation and flawed lending practices, the financial system developed serious structural weaknesses. In particular, balance-sheet risks greatly heightened Korean financial institutions' vulnerability to external shocks. Immediately after the crisis, the Korean government therefore set about designing and applying stronger prudential regulations, and recapitalizing and restructuring the financial sector in order to regain the confidence of foreign investors, while the IMF and World Bank, for their part, emphasized that only quick and decisive structural reform could halt capital flight and restore the prospects for sustainable growth (Fischer, 1999; Lane et al., 1999; Lindgrin et al., 1999).

Financial sector restructuring was implemented in two stages. The first stage was government led and focused on the quick restoration of confidence through the closure of troubled financial institutions and disposal of nonperforming loans. The Ministry of Finance and Economy (MOFE) and the Financial Supervisory Commission (FSC) orchestrated this stage in the restructuring process. These agencies set out both detailed objectives and procedural principles.

Whereas the first stage focused on the immediate task of restoring confidence, in the second stage, which commenced in September 2000, the authorities turned to longer-term efforts to put in place the prerequisites for financial stability and to thereby prevent future financial crises. Their goals at this stage are to remove unrealized NPLs from the balance sheets of both bank and nonbank financial institutions, to close insolvent enterprises, and to enhance efficiency by intensifying competition in the financial sector. In contrast to the first stage, when the authorities had orchestrated reform, the role of the government in the second stage is limited to attempting to create an institutional environment in which the more robust and less crisis-prone markets that are the goal of reform can be developed through the self-motivated actions of market participants themselves. Although the first stage was broadly successful, on the efficacy of the second stage the jury remains out. In particular, questions have been raised about the continued vulnerability of the Korean financial system to large domestic and foreign shocks, as demonstrated by the Daewoo collapse in July 1999.

Banking Sector Restructuring

The profitability of Korea's banks was already low before the crisis, reflecting controlled interest rates, intense competition for deposits, and poor asset-liability management. After the events of 1997, the banks then found themselves with two serious problems: poor asset quality and inadequate capitalization. The bankruptcies of a series of large nonbank corporations, triggered by overinvestment and highly leveraged financial operations, severely damaged loan portfolios. The knowledge that the banks' balance sheets contained substantial numbers of NPLs raised the specter of bank failures, leading depositors to flee low-quality banks for their high-quality competitors.

Soon after the crisis, the Korean financial authorities implemented a prompt corrective action (PCA) system. In this system, the most important indicator of the need for PCA is the capital adequacy ratio.[1] After an evaluation in June 1998, the authorities decided to close five banks at which BIS capital adequacy ratios had already been below 8 percent at the end of 1997.[2] It was decided that these banks would be acquired by five other strong banks through purchase and assumption (P&A), which allows selective acquisition of assets and assumption of liabilities. P&A was preferred to liquidation and to merger and acquisition on the grounds that the adverse effects on related depositors, borrowers and the government, not to mention the acquirers, would be smaller and that the process could be completed in a shorter period of time. According to Kang (1998), in Korea it takes more than three years to complete liquidation on average but no more than two months for a P&A.

Seven other Korean banks were able to avoid closure even though their BIS capital adequacy ratios were also below 8 percent. In fact, the differences between banks that were closed and those that survived were not at all evident, and the financial authorities did not disclose the grounds on which they had based their decision. It was asserted that these banks displayed better asset quality and long-term earning prospects than the five closed banks, but it has also been suspected that political considerations influenced the decision. (Shareholders in some surviving banks were known to be supporters of the ruling party.) Although Bongini et al. (2000) conclude that the bank closure process in Korea, Malaysia, the Philippines and Thailand is now relatively transparent, doubts can be raised about their findings in the Korean case.[3]

The FSC, for its part, approved rehabilitation plans for only 13 commercial banks out of the 20 banks submitting plans. Two commercial banks in distress, Korea First and Seoul Bank, had been nationalized even before the financial crisis, and their initial capital was written down. In an effort to expedite restructuring of the banking sector, the Korean authorities attempted to sell their stakes of these banks to foreign investors. At the end of 1998, following almost a year of negotiation, Korea First Bank was finally sold to the Newbridge Capital consortium, subject to a blanket commitment by the Korean government to assume responsibility for all current and future NPLs. However, the negotiations with the Hong Kong and Shanghai Banking Corporation for selling government shares of Seoul Bank broke down due to a large gap between bid and ask prices. As of August 2002, Hana Bank, another Korean institution, was still negotiating with the government to buy Seoul Bank.

In addition the Korean authorities have tried to strengthen prudential supervision and regulation. Inadequate disclosure and opaque decision making have often been cited as reasons for the Korean financial system's low credibility (see for example, Chopra et al., 2001). Thus, in April 1998, the FSC introduced new disclosure requirements, including mandatory disclosure of information on the value of NPLs, on credit and risk management systems, and on audit results. Six months later it established unified disclosure standards for financial institutions, stipulating that balance-sheet information should be reported twice annually, and it established stronger penalties for false or dishonest disclosures.[4]

The FSC also attempted to bring loan classification standards and provisioning requirements up to international standards.[5] Its new standards are stricter in distinguishing nonperforming assets and require more provisioning for precautionary loans.[6] While the imposition of these new criteria may reduce short-term profitability, the FSC's reforms are expected to reduce banks' balance sheet risks and therefore their vulnerability to internal and external shocks. In addition, the Korean government amended the deposit insurance system to reduce the amount of guaranteed principal. This change should render depositors and investors more concerned about the potential risks and performance of individual banks, mitigating moral hazard. Heightened attention from depositors and investors should in turn strengthen market discipline and expedite market-based restructuring.

All this has resulted in substantial change in the banking sector. The number of commercial banks declined from 33 in December 1997 to 20 in May 2002, and only one new bank entered in the interim. Thus, a third of all banks exited the market in less than five years. The contraction of the banking sector can be also seen in the fall of employment by 40 percent and in the number of branches by 20 percent.

The result appears to be a significant improvement in management performance and asset quality. Table 14.1 shows that per capita operating income rose by a factor of six from 1997 to 2001, and that the share of NPLs fell from 6.0 percent to 2.9 percent in the same period.

Table 14.1 Selected indicators for commercial banks (100 million won, %, person)

Year	No. of employees	No. of branches	NPLs	NPL ratio	Operating income*
1996	103 913	5 105	118 739	4.1	0.33
1997	113 994	5 987	226 521	6.0	0.21
1998	75 677	5 056	212 160	7.4	−0.62
1999	74 744	4 780	273 938	8.3	0.26
2000	70 559	4 709	238 912	6.6	1.07
2001	68 360	4 776	109 760	2.9	1.35

Note: * Operating income per employee.

Source: Financial Supervisory Service, *Monthly Financial Statistics Bulletin* (various issues).

Nonbank Financial Institution Restructuring

When the Hanbo group declared bankruptcy in March 1997, merchant banks, which were engaged in a wide range of business activities with large companies (involving *inter alia* deposits and credits, trusts, securities, international financing and leasing), found themselves saddled with a crushing burden of nonperforming loans. The subsequent bankruptcy of major corporate groups such as Sammi and Jinro in 1997 further eroded confidence on the part of international financial institutions, exacerbating the difficulties faced by merchant banks attempting to fund themselves abroad. In December 1997, the government suspended 14 merchant banks which had recorded enormous losses in the first financial sector restructuring ever attempted in Korea. The licenses of 18 merchant banks were then revoked, and the assets and liabilities of all closed merchant banks were transferred to a bridge bank. The number of merchants banks was reduced from 30 at the end of 1997 to three in May 2002 as a result of the subsequent restructuring.

The authorities were quicker and more determined in closing merchant banks than commercial banks; presumably they anticipated fewer negative repercussions on the financial system and the economy. The impact on employment was trivial, and protests from depositors were few since many merchant banks did not take deposits.

Investment trust companies (ITCs), which serve as fund managers, investment advisers and distributors of beneficiary certificates, suffered substantial capital losses in the crisis. Initially the authorities sought to delay the resolution of ITCs until the rest of the financial restructuring effort had been completed on the grounds that earlier action would lead to more investor redemptions and adversely affect securities markets. (The bearish stock market and high level of interest rates following the outbreak of the crisis had already led many investors to redeem their beneficiary certificates.) Thus, instead of comprehensively reforming the operation of the ITCs, from the beginning the authorities delayed restructuring, relying instead on liquidity injections and restrictions on the withdrawal of funds. While their efforts succeeded in stabilizing the market temporarily, the authorities soon realized that, without radical reform, the sector would continue to be vulnerable to shocks. Hence they moved more quickly to close nonviable ITCs. By May 2002, six ITCs had their licenses revoked, and one was merged.

Even before the crisis, securities companies had already recorded net losses for three consecutive fiscal years, reflecting the lackluster performance of the stock market and rising operational and financial expenses. Investments in establishing new branch offices had resulted in higher operating costs and lower net profits, and increased short-term borrowing had generated a sharp increase in the cost of funding.

While the authorities attempted to restore the credibility of this sector by revoking the licenses of nonviable securities companies, they also attempted to facilitate competition by removing entry barriers. As a result of entry, the number of securities companies increased from 36 at the end of 1997 to 44 by May 2002, despite license revocation, mergers and dissolutions.

Public Funds

Chopra et al. (2001) argue that the large-scale injection of public funds has been necessary in Korea because the institutional investors and small shareholders who held the majority of commercial banks' shares could not be relied on to provide the funds needed to recapitalize the financial sector, since the former were themselves in financial distress while the latter had a collective action problem. Potential new investors, for their part, were reluctant to step in without government backing. Knowing this, the government injected huge amounts of public funds, amounting to 156.3 trillion won by May 2002 (equivalent to nearly 30 percent of Korean GDP circa 2001). It had initially planned to spend a total of 64 trillion won on financial sector restructuring, but when the second stage of the restructuring program was launched in September 2000, this amount was acknowledged as wholly inadequate.

Funds were injected into troubled financial institutions for the payment of insured deposits and purposes of recapitalization mainly by the Korea Deposit Insurance Corporation, and for the purchase of NPLs by the Korea Asset Management Corporation. About 50 percent of public funds were used for recapitalizing distressed financial institutions, and about 25 percent were used for purchasing NPLs. The government has recovered only a small portion of this commitment.

The majority of the funds used for financial sector restructuring (some 65 percent) were raised by issuing bonds, reflecting the government's decision to pass some of the burden to future generations. However, this in turn has generated concern over the deterioration of the government's own financial position.

In order to mitigate moral hazard, the authorities made assistance conditional on efforts by distressed financial institutions to reduce costs, recapitalize themselves by soliciting foreign investments, and write down the capital of existing shareholders. However, the government has been criticized for supporting nonviable institutions, for injecting excessive liquidity in some cases, and for doing too little to recover funds. Responding to this critique, in February 2001 it established a Public Fund Oversight Committee to enhance the transparency and efficiency of fund management and expedite the recovery of funds.

CORPORATE SECTOR REFORM

Goals and Strategies

During Korea's high-growth period, the corporate sector focused on quantitative expansion rather than efficiency improvements and innovation. Overinvestment and overcapitalization were pervasive, undermining productivity and competitiveness. Since Korean companies, especially the *chaebols*, were highly indebted, the crisis, superimposed on this already poor performance, resulted in the rapid increase of NPLs.

In response, the Korean government moved to restructure the corporate sector. It started by classifying companies into three groups, the five largest *chaebols*, the sixth to sixty-fourth largest *chaebols* and other large corporations, and small and medium-sized companies, implementing different restructuring measures for each group. The five largest *chaebols* (Hyundai, Samsung, LG, SK and Daewoo) were charged with restructuring themselves under the terms of the Capital Structure Improvement Plan (CSIP), accepted by the creditor banks. In practice, the banks rarely intervened in the process, leaving the controlling shareholders of each *chaebol* fully responsible for it.

Corporate workouts, which are a means of rehabilitating companies that are currently experiencing managerial difficulties or are expected to experience them in the future, were the main method of restructuring the sixth to sixty-fourth largest *chaebols* and other large corporations. This out-of-court approach to restructuring, often referred to as the London approach, was chosen on the grounds that it was likely to prove more cost- and time-efficient than court-supervised reorganization or receivership (given that Korean commercial courts were already overloaded by the crisis). Insolvent but viable companies were subject to workouts, and they were directed to follow the workout plan as agreed with their creditors.

The Korean government has paid little attention to the restructuring of small and medium-sized enterprises (SMEs), partly because SMEs account for only a fraction of the banks' outstanding loans. Instead of attempting to induce structural change, the authorities have relied on injections of emergency liquidity to prevent SMEs from falling into bankruptcy and having to lay off workers. This policy of benign neglect reflects the belief that the resolution of large corporations' problems will automatically lead to the resolution of SMEs' problems, given that the business performance of SMEs in Korea is largely dependent on that of *chaebols* and other large corporations.

Implementation and Results

Their CSIPs required the five largest *chaebols* to reduce their debt/equity ratios from 352 percent at the end of 1998 to below 200 percent by the end of 1999, to eliminate cross-debt guarantees between their affiliates, and to concentrate on core lines of business by selling off their noncore businesses or exchanging them with other *chaebols* (the so-called 'Big Deals'). The five largest *chaebols*, with the exception of Daewoo, have sold off assets, attracted foreign funds, and separated and disposed of their affiliates in an effort to reduce their debt/equity ratios. Even though they experienced difficulties, particularly in attracting foreign capital, they were able to satisfy the criteria set by the CSIPs. The debt/equity ratios of all four leading *chaebols* were all brought down below 200 percent by the end of 1999.[7]

These large *chaebols* were also successful in eliminating cross-debt guarantees. Initially, they planned to reduce cross-debt guarantees by 2.7 trillion won in 1999, but they in fact managed to eliminate 3.1 trillion won worth. By comparison, the restructuring of their businesses was slow, mainly due to the delays involved in completing the Big Deals. Economic recovery, the bullish stock market and low interest rates allowed the large *chaebols* to engage in asset-valuation disputes and to backtrack on earlier business-swap proposals (Park, 2001). The five largest *chaebols* achieved more, in terms of focusing on their core competencies, through sales and spin-offs of affiliates than through government-engineered swaps of business lines.[8]

Workouts of the sixth through sixty-fourth largest *chaebols* have been implemented under the Corporate Restructuring Agreement (CRA) and the Corporate Restructuring Coordination Committee (CRCC). The CRA, which 210 financial institutions signed, was created in June 1998 to mediate among financial institutions by designating a lead creditor and determining overall implementation procedures. The CRCC provides guidelines for workouts, revises proposals in the event that voluntary negotiations fail, and imposes penalties for violations of the CRA.

By June 2002, a total of 83 corporations had been targeted for workouts. Forty-seven completed the program early, 15 dropped out, and 21 remain on the workout list at the time of writing. Most workouts began when the banks received applications from troubled corporations or directly identified target corporations. For selected corporations, however, workout programs were set up and implemented by the CRA.

Daewoo was very slow in restructuring itself compared to the other large *chaebols*, and its financing difficulties became more severe as it suffered repeated credit rating downgrades. In order to prevent its collapse, creditors renewed Daewoo's debt in June 1999 on the condition that the corporation would reliably implement the Acceleration of Restructuring and Concrete Practice Plan submitted to the creditor group. In addition, Daewoo and its creditors agreed that the creditors were entitled to dispose of their shares if the corporation again failed to abide by the plan. But this initiative again failed to solve Daewoo's short-term liquidity crisis. Consequently, Daewoo was targeted for a workout program on 26 August 1999. On 3 November 2000, creditor financial institutions concluded that ten of Daewoo's affiliates should be sold off.

It should be noted that the creditors were sometimes unable to effectively pursue workout programs because they were obsessed with fear of losses from the liquidation of distressed companies.[9] Neglecting their due diligence, they kept on the workout list some companies that should have been liquidated immediately. Often they tried to revive nonviable companies for fear that their liquidation would impair their own balance sheets and necessitate more provisioning. For example, creditors initially decided to liquidate Hyundai Engineering & Construction and Ssangyong Cement Industries, but they then reversed those decisions. Mako (2001) argues that the creditors' November 2001 exit list included only 52 companies, even though World Bank analysis showed that there were at least 64 companies (excluding Daewoo companies) with negative cash flow.[10]

This suggests that creditors may not have properly assessed the risks when they decided whether or not to liquidate a company. Political concerns and pressures may have played a role in their decisions, especially in the case of creditors that were themselves being restructured by the government. In addition, some managers and controlling shareholders strongly resisted the dissolution of their companies, and employees resisted for fear of losing their jobs. Ultimately, these factors impaired the equity and efficiency of the workout process in Korea.

The government implemented several measures to improve corporate governance and the transparency of management, and amended the legal and tax systems to expedite restructuring. Traditionally, heads of companies had been able to extend their control to affiliates through complicated investments and cross-transactions even when they in fact own only a small portion of the total shares. Corporate governance reform therefore required strengthening the rights of minority shareholders (Gobat, 1998).[11] Listed companies were required to introduce the outside director system and to have an internal auditor or to establish an audit committee, depending on the amount of their capital.[12] In addition, shareholders' proposal rights and cumulative voting were introduced. Finally, the government revised corporate accounting standards to conform with international best practice and introduced consolidated financial reporting, electronic disclosure systems, and penalties for false and unfaithful disclosures.

Table 14.2 provides a glimpse of how restructuring affected the *chaebols*. The debt/equity ratios of the top 30 *chaebols* were significantly reduced from

Table 14.2 Selected indicators of top 30 chaebols (%)

Year	Debt/equity ratio	Output[a]	Employment[b]
1992	402.6	13.14	4.15
1993	349.7	12.97	4.12
1994	355.7	13.35	4.20
1995	347.5	14.98	4.40
1996	386.5	13.61	4.56
1997	518.8	11.97	4.14
1998	379.8	11.94	3.66
1999	218.7	10.21	2.89
2000	171.2	12.86	2.99

Notes:
[a] Shares in GNP.
[b] Shares in national employment.

Source: Center for Free Enterprise (1997–2001).

519 percent at the end of 1997 to 171 percent by the end of 2000. Their shares of economy-wide employment and output are lower at the time of writing than in the pre-crisis period.

REFORM, RECOVERY AND THE SUSTAINABILITY OF GROWTH

Impact of Reform

Have the financial and corporate reforms of the last several years significantly enhanced the efficiency and stability of the financial and industrial sectors? It may still be too early for a definitive answer to this question. Some tentative observations are none the less in order.

We can gauge the efficiency of the financial sector by considering the cost structure and profitability of banks. Table 14.1 showed that employment and the number of commercial bank branches had been reduced significantly in the reform process. This is evidence that reform has pressured the banks to minimize costs. As indicators of profitability, we examine return on assets and return on equity. By both measures, commercial banks continued to record negative profits between 1997 and 2000; they did not return to profitability until 2001 (Table 14.3). However, both measures have continued to

Table 14.3 Selected indicators for commercial banks (billion won, %)

Year	ROA	ROE	BIS Ratio	Assets	Loans
1996	0.3	3.8	9.1	4 726 013	2 896 488
1997	−0.9	−14.2	7.0	6 065 529	3 758 317
1998	−3.3	−52.5	8.2	5 650 802	2 885 048
1999	−1.3	−23.1	10.8	5 623 262	3 282 945
2000	−0.6	−11.9	10.8	5 825 706	3 616 086
2001	0.8	15.9	10.8	6 414 198	3 790 924

Notes: Figures at the end of year. ROA includes trust accounts.

Source: Financial Supervisory Service, *Monthly Financial Statistics Bulletin* (various issues).

improve since 1999, and the 2001 figures exceed pre-crisis levels. This suggests that bank profitability has improved over the last three years.

To measure the stability of the commercial banking system, we use the BIS capital adequacy ratio, as supplemented by the various measures of market structure and business environment in Table 14.3. The BIS capital adequacy ratio rose from 7.0 percent in 1997 to 10.8 in 2001, indicating that the banking sector became less susceptible to shocks. We measure market structure by the ratio of the top three banks' assets to the total assets of all banks (CR3): an increase suggests that concentration has increased, in turn enhancing profitability and net interest margins. CR3 exhibited a big jump in 1998, and remained relatively stable thereafter. In addition, the value of assets and loans has trended upward in the most recent two or three years, suggesting improved stability and favorable changes in the business environment.

Turning to the corporate sector, there is some sign that cost structure and profitability have improved. The fall in employment and debt in the top 30 *chaebols*, already discussed in the previous section, is one sign of these cost improvements. Table 14.4, which presents profitability indicators for Korean manufacturing, shows that the interest coverage ratio has risen since the crisis and that there has been a rebound in the ratio of ordinary income to total assets.

To summarize, our analysis indicates that the Korean banking sector has been rendered more profitable, more concentrated and more dynamic, relative to the pre-crisis *status quo*. This suggests that banking sector efficiency and stability have been improved, although questions can be raised about the compatibility of concentration with cost efficiency, and about whether observed improvements are sustainable in the long run. In addition, we observe

Table 14.4   Profitability of manufacturing sector (%)

Year	1996	1997	1998	1999	2000	2001
Ordinary income to total assets	0.93	−0.3	−1.52	1.38	1.24	0.35
Interest coverage ratio	112.13	129.09	68.28	96.06	157.22	132.55

Source: Bank of Korea, *Financial Statement Analysis* (various years).

weak evidence of improvements in the cost and profitability structures of the corporate sector. It is, however, hard to argue that the changes in profitability, costs and market structures of the banking and corporate sectors are solely attributed to the reforms. In particular, the improvement in profitability may be due largely to the rapid recovery of the Korean economy, which itself is a result of improvements in the external environment. At this point, it is hard to evaluate the effects of reform on the efficiency and stability of the banking and corporate sectors, since much of the expected improvement will be realized only in the medium and long run.

Economic Recovery and Sustainable Growth

The Korean economy has recovered impressively from its crisis. The recovery began approximately one year after the crisis broke out and accelerated through 2000. Following negative growth in 1998, Korea maintained high growth rates for two consecutive years, while keeping inflation under control (Table 14.5). Although Korea experienced a deceleration in GDP growth from 9.3 percent in 2000 to 3.0 percent in 2001, it has recently been showing signs of a rebound. (According to the IMF (2002), real GDP grew by 6.3 percent in 2002.)

Since 1999, all of the major credit rating agencies, including S&P and Moody's, have upgraded Korea's sovereign rating, despite evidence of increased credit risk in other emerging economies, although Korea's rating still remains below its pre-crisis level. Reflecting this reduction in country risk, the sovereign spread on five-year Korean bonds has fallen from 513 basis points in 1998 to 135 basis points in December 2001. Foreign investors have responded by returning to Korea. As can be seen in Table 14.5, the net inflow of foreign portfolio investment in 2000 again reached pre-crisis levels, while the net inflow of FDI is far greater than before.

Korea's recovery has been faster and broader than is typical of the experience of other crisis countries (J.-W. Lee and Rhee, 2002; Chopra et al., 2001; Park and Lee, 2001). The cross-country analysis of Rhee, Lee and Hong

Table 14.5 Selected macroeconomic indicators

Indicators	1995	1996	1997	1998	1999	2000	2001
GDP growth (%)	8.9	6.7	5.0	−6.7	10.9	9.3	3.0
Inflation (%)	4.5	4.9	4.4	7.5	0.8	2.3	4.3
Real export growth (%)	24.6	11.2	21.4	14.1	15.8	20.5	1.0
Current account/GDP (%)	−1.7	−4.4	−1.7	12.7	6.0	2.7	2.0
Net FDI inflows/GDP (%)	−0.4	−0.5	−0.3	0.2	1.3	0.9	0.1
Net portfolio inflows/GDP (%)	2.4	2.9	3.0	−0.4	2.3	2.7	1.5
Unemployment rate (%)	2.0	2.0	2.6	6.8	6.3	4.1	3.7
International reserves (US$ bn)	31.9	33.2	19.7	51.9	73.1	95.9	102.5

Sources: Bank of Korea, *internet homepage* and IMF, *International Financial Statistics* (2002).

(Chapter 13, this volume) shows that while the Korean economy, like others, showed a V-shaped response to the crisis, both the contraction and the rebound were sharper. Chopra et al. (2001) estimate the potential growth rate and the output gap of the Korean economy after the crisis and find some sign of even overheating in 2000. This naturally leads us to ask whether structural factors are responsible for these unusual features of the Korean experience.

Corporate and financial restructuring promotes efficiency and competition, thereby enhancing the efficiency of resource allocation and boosting productivity. In turn, faster productivity growth should improve the long-term growth prospects of the economy and help to restore investor confidence. The problem is that it is hard to know whether observed improvements in productivity and growth in Korea, not to mention the return of foreign investors, are mainly the result of reform efforts. Y. Park (2001) argues that expansionary fiscal and monetary policies and improvements in export competitiveness resulting from the substantial depreciation of the won were mainly responsible for the speed of the recovery.[13] Chopra et al. (2001) conclude that a favorable external environment – not just a weak won but also increases in the external demand for information technology and electronics products – was the main factor responsible for the speed of the recovery.

Even though our earlier analysis shows an improvement in cost competitiveness and profitability in the financial and corporate sectors, many structural problems considered instrumental in causing the crisis have not been resolved. Resolving them may take a long time. Accordingly, it is still premature to assert that extensive efficiency gains have been attained through restructuring, and inappropriate to give much credit to restructuring for the impressive recovery in the economy. Although many NPLs once held by financial institutions have largely been resolved, many additional ones remain; the share of NPLs is still high by global standards. What is more, there is still widespread moral hazard in the financial and corporate sectors, as illustrated in the case of the Hynix resolution process. Hoping to stop losses, creditors have tried to sell the Hynix semiconductor, the world's largest DRAM (Dynamic Random Access Memory) producer. However, the company has not been cooperative in the sales deal, and without strong efforts of highly intensified restructuring it has rather insisted on additional loan extensions for independent survival. Hynix seems to speculate that creditors are not able to liquidate the company since they do not have enough provisions for the expected losses, and the adverse effects of the liquidation on the Korean economy are expected to be enormous.

Indeed, there are reasons to worry that the vigor of the recovery may sap the authorities' commitment to restructuring. As the economy bounces back, the earnings prospects of banks and corporations tend to improve, even when much remains to be done to secure efficiency gains. The structural weaknesses of the financial and corporate sectors can be disguised by favorable macroeconomic performance, in other words. Kawai (2000) also worries that an impressive pace of recovery may slow the progress of reform and, as a result, that 'the remaining structural problems of the financial and corporate sectors may not be adequately addressed.' As mentioned previously, creditors have been reluctant to liquidate insolvent firms for a number of reasons; but whatever their reason, that reluctance has probably been reinforced by the vigor of the recovery, which creates grounds for hope that some of their NPLs would begin performing again.

Our earlier argument about the relationship between reforms and recovery does not necessarily negate a positive link between reforms and long-run economic growth. If reforms accelerate financial development, then growth prospects will be significantly improved. Empirical studies based on both national and international data show that growth responds to the development of the financial system in the long run.[14] A well-developed financial system both helps to mobilize capital for investment and enhances the efficiency of resource allocation.[15]

Productivity improvement is crucial if Korea is to regain the momentum needed for high growth. It is often argued that the Korean economy has already entered into a development phase in which technical innovation and greater flexibility of the economic structure are necessary for sustained growth. Thus the long-term growth prospects of Korea largely depend on the degree to which the financial system develops and how efficiently it allocates financial resources to projects with high rates of return.

Ongoing reforms will promote financial development if they succeed in intensifying competition in the financial markets. However, financial restructuring has left the government holding controlling shares in several major banks, which is not obviously compatible with the desire to intensify competition.[16] In the past, government-owned or -controlled financial institutions often allocated resources inefficiently. In addition, financial institutions have shown only slight improvement in their ability to distinguish promising investments from poor ones; for example, most banks are now focusing heavily on consumer loans even though there are again promising projects in the corporate sector. Efficiency will suffer unless the government substantially reduces its shareholding in banks and unless the financial institutions themselves make a strong effort to enhance their capacity to evaluate investment projects.

VULNERABILITY TO CRISIS

If one believes in the intrinsic instability of international financial markets, then improvements in economic fundamentals are not sufficient for reducing the risk for another crisis. Radelet and Sachs (1998), Feldstein (1998), and Stiglitz (1999) argue that the sudden shift in market expectations and confidence was primarily responsible for the outbreak and spillover of the Asian crisis. They argue that any weakness of economic fundamentals and difficulties in the corporate and banking sectors do not suffice to explain the sudden shift in market expectations. As for Korea, journalistic accounts and statements by market participants suggest that foreign investors were still optimistic about the future development of the Korean economy as late as the beginning of November 1997, indicating that their expectations and confidence in the Korean economy changed abruptly.[17]

The analysis of financial crises suggests that the possibility of sudden shifts in market sentiment exists even in economies which appear to be sound, and that market fundamentals and credit rating are poor predictors of when such a shift may occur. Herd behavior by international investors and traders may then create further instability. Such behavior may be entirely rational if information is asymmetric (leading investors to react to the actions of others, presumably better-informed investors) or fund managers have an incentive not to be outliers in terms of the distribution of returns (Calvo and Mendoza, 2000; Montes, 1998; Scharfstein and Stein, 1990).[18] Therefore herd behavior has often been observed in the midst of financial market turbulence, and it has been cited as one of the main causes of the East Asian crisis.[19] Estimating the index suggested by Lakonishok et al. (1992), W. Kim and Wei (1999) and Choe et al. (1998) found considerable evidence of herd behavior in the Korean stock market during the crisis period.

Contagion also contributes to the risk of a currency crisis. There has been a growing body of literature that investigates contagion effects and their causes in the case of the Asian crisis (Baig and Goldfajn, 1999; Goldstein et al.,

2000, Kaminsky and Reinhart, 2000; Kaminsky and Schmukler, 1999; Park and Song, 2001a, 2001b). The main findings of this work are that contagion in equity and foreign exchange markets was present during the Asian crisis, and that trade and financial linkages, herding and cross-market hedging all played a role in its spread.

The financial linkage interpretation stresses that Japanese banks with exposure to East Asian countries suffered from the Thai crisis; when they withdrew their loans to other East Asian countries to raise liquidity, they thereby spread the crisis to other countries. The trade linkage interpretation emphasizes the extent of intra-regional trade and East Asian countries' intense competition in third markets. The cross-market hedging interpretation emphasizes the tendency for investors to rebalance their portfolios in response to the crisis in order to limit risks.

Since Japanese commercial banks withdrew huge amounts of loans from East Asia since the crisis, and the need of East Asian countries for additional foreign loans has been reduced by their shift to current account surplus, the importance of the financial linkage channel would appear to have diminished since 1997.[20] However, other channels for contagion still exist, and there may be still other channels that are yet to be identified.

Notwithstanding these additional complications, there is no question that ongoing reform has at least partly contributed to the vigor of recovery and the reduction of country risk. Nor do the intrinsic instability of international financial markets and the fact of contagion negate the need for structural reform. However, if current reforms are to truly succeed in reducing crisis risk to low levels, they will have to extend to reforms at the global level that also address problems in international financial markets.

To a large extent, this is a task for the international community. But for Korean policy makers it poses a specific challenge, namely, how to manage the country's liberalized capital account. When the government sought emergency IMF financing in November 1997, among the conditions to which it agreed was the further liberalization of the capital account. Capital transactions, including short-term financing, were widely and immediately liberalized with the goal of stabilizing the domestic financial markets by inducing foreign capital inflows.[21] After the financial markets were stabilized, the government then embarked on the further liberalization of the foreign exchange system. This process extended over a three-year period and divided into two phases, the first of which began in April 1999 with the further liberalization of capital transactions.[22]

Fischer (2001a) notes that all developed countries have open capital accounts. However, recent empirical evidence has rendered some developing countries skeptical of the benefits of embracing the policy at this stage. Rodrik (1998b) fails to find any evidence that capital account liberalization leads to a higher ratio of investment to GDP in a cross-section study, and Edwards (2001) and Arteta et al. (2001) also find no strong causal effects of capital account liberalization on economic growth in developing economies.

As for Korea, we cannot deny that further capital account liberalization was helpful in inducing capital inflows through sales of domestic firms to foreigners, introducing more competition into the financial and corporate sectors, and enhancing transparency of management, strengthening shareholders' rights, and upgrading risk management. However, it would be premature to conclude that capital account liberalization has produced substantial efficiency gains or significantly accelerated the recovery of the Korean economy. In general it takes a long period of time before capital account liberalization affects investment and growth and yields efficiency gains. And the economic performance of Malaysia, which imposed strict controls on capital transactions after the outbreak of the financial crisis, has been nearly as impressive as that of Korea. Haggard and Low (2001) and Hood (2001) argue that Malaysia's controls were effective in revitalizing the stock market, lowering domestic interest rates, and building foreign exchange reserves, which in turn initiated and sustained the country's recovery. Kaplan and Rodrik (2001) also find that the Malaysian controls helped to stabilize the financial markets and the economy as a whole. Even though some also argue that the effects of capital control in Malaysia have been exaggerated, it remains unclear whether and to what extent the deregulation of capital account transactions contributed to the improvement in macroeconomic performance in Korea.[23]

Skeptics may insist that capital account opening leaves the Korean economy more exposed to unstable capital flows, international investors' herd behavior, and contagion effects. As more foreign capital, short-term capital in particular, flows in, the economy will again become vulnerable to swings in market expectations and confidence. In addition, freer capital mobility limits monetary independence, unless the Korean authorities are prepared to adopt a freely floating exchange rate system.

In order to reduce the risk of future crises, Korea must expedite both financial and corporate restructuring. This will strengthen the health of the Korean economy and help it to sustain its growth momentum. Given a higher degree of capital account liberalization, however, reforms must also focus on reducing its exposures to risks related to the unstable international financial markets. One of the lessons of the 1997 crisis is that such risks are a function of the currency and maturity mismatches on balance sheets. Dollarization and currency unification are two options for reducing these risks (currency risk in particular), but they are not feasible in Korea, other than conceivably in the very long run. An immediate alternative would be to monitor more closely financial institutions' foreign exchange positions. The current system, which merely regulates changes in net foreign exchange positions, should be changed to one in which positions are controlled more flexibly, depending on the foreign liability and asset management capacity of the institution and the maturity structure of those liabilities and assets. In addition, a more comprehensive index of such positions, which considers not just foreign liabilities but also liquidity ratios, contingent liabilities, and the maturity structure of foreign assets and liabilities, could be usefully developed in order to measure the relevant risks in a more precise and timely way.

It is also important to promote long-term foreign investments, foreign direct investments in particular, in order to reduce Korea's exposure to external shocks. In this respect, Korea should establish a detailed plan that promotes direct investment. The plan should include the removal of laws and regulations that discriminate against foreigners, the provision of additional tax incentives, improvements in labor productivity to meet global standards, and streamlining of the investment approval and reporting process.

CONCLUDING REMARKS

Since the onset of the crisis, Korea has implemented a wide range of reforms, including restructuring the financial and corporate sectors and further liberalizing the capital account. Our analysis suggests that the banking and corporate sectors have become more cost-efficient and profitable as a result, although more time will be required to gauge the lasting effects.

The Korean economy has recovered impressively from the crisis – more impressively than macroeconomic models estimated on the experience of other crisis countries would have led one to predict. However, it is not clear whether and to what extent the government's financial and corporate reforms are responsible for the exceptional nature of the recovery. Credit for the recovery may be due to the strongly expansionary stance of fiscal and monetary policies, the global economic upturn, and the lower value of the Korean won, rather than to any efficiency gains resulting from the process of reform. More analysis and experience will be needed to determine the exact relationship between reform and economic performance.

The economic recovery and the upgrading of Korea's sovereign credit rating provide no guarantee that there will be no crisis in Korea. The Korean economy is and will continue to be exposed to the instability intrinsic to the international financial markets. Herd behavior by international investors and contagion from other countries will continue to pose risks, regardless of reform or credit rating. In fact, Korea's exposure to this risk has arguably been increased by the further opening of the capital account and of domestic financial markets.

To reduce the probability of a crisis, Korea must take further steps to strengthen the health of its economy. Given the liberalization of the capital account, an appropriate focus for reform efforts would be to reduce exposures to risks related to volatility in international financial markets, herd behavior and contagion. In addition to continuing to pursue economic reforms, Korea should establish an early warning system that would signal emerging crisis risks, thereby giving the authorities the time needed to head them off. Given that we cannot eliminate the risk of additional crises, the least we can do is to invest in the ability to predict when and where they are likely to occur.

NOTES

1. Information about capital adequacy was provided more reliably as the authorities instituted improvements in asset classification standards.
2. The five banks were Daedong, Dongnam, Dongwha, Choongchung and Kyunggi Bank.
3. Bongini et al. (2000) investigated the performance of 186 banks and 97 nonbank financial institutions in Korea, Malaysia, the Philippines and Thailand from July 1997 to July 1999, and found that political connections and influences made closure more, not less, likely.
4. Actually, the new disclosure system applies to all financial institutions, not only banks.
5. For example, it includes the introduction of new asset quality classification standards with forward-looking criteria which incorporate the expected future performance.
6. The provision requirement for precautionary loans has been raised from 1 percent to 2 percent.
7. The average level for these four was 175 percent. The individual ratios were Hyundai: 181 percent, Samsung: 166 percent, LG: 184.2 percent, and SK: 161 percent.
8. Samsung focuses on electronics, financial services and international trade; Hyundai on heavy industry, construction and automobiles; LG on energy, chemicals, telecommunications and financial services; SK on energy, chemicals, telecommunications and construction.
9. A similar argument can be also found in Park (2001) and Mako (2001).
10. In other words, the interest coverage ratios of these companies are less than zero.
11. According to the empirical results of Johnson et al. (2000), the extent of the exchange rate depreciation and decline of stock prices during the 1997–98 East Asian crisis is more related to the corporate governance structure, in particular the effectiveness of the protection for minority shareholders.
12. Since April 1998, at least one-fourth of the board of directors of a listed corporation had to comprise outside directors (minimum one). Since January 2000, listed corporations whose capital assets total over two trillion won have been required to appoint at least half of all directors (minimum three) from outside.
13. The empirical results of Park and Lee (2001) support this view. Their cross-country comparison suggests that the fast recovery of the Korean economy is mainly attributed to the export-oriented economic structure and the swift adjustment of macroeconomic policies.
14. See Levine (1996) for a survey of this issue.
15. See Leahy et al. (2001) for more discussion on the link between the financial system and economic growth.
16. As of November 2001, the Korean government holds controlling shares of four large banks (Seoul Bank, Cheju Bank and Woori Financial Group: 100 percent, CHB: 80.5 percent).
17. See Park (1998).

18. More details on the causes of economic agents' herd behavior can be found in Banerjee (1992), and Shiller (1995).
19. See, for example, Kaminsky and Schmukler (1999).
20. According to data from Bank for International Settlements, Asian countries accounted for only 5.4 percent of total international bank lending from Japan at the end of June 2001, while the corresponding figure was 69.3 percent at the end of June 1996.
21. Measures include the elimination of ceilings on foreign equity ownership, opening of bond and short-term money markets and liberalization of M&A by foreigners.
22. For example, controls on capital account transactions were converted into a negative system.
23. See, for example, Jomo (2001).

Comment on Chapters 13 and 14[1]

Masahiro Kawai

CAUSES OF THE CRISIS AND APPROPRIATE RESPONSES

Soon after the outbreak of the international liquidity crisis of 1997, the Korean government turned to the IMF for financial rescue. Though the economy contracted sharply in 1998, it rebounded strongly in 1999 and 2000 with a V-shaped recovery. Successful macroeconomic adjustment has allowed the economy to reduce external vulnerabilities and risks of another currency crisis by creating large current account surpluses, reducing short-term external debt, and accumulating foreign exchange reserves. Among the crisis-affected economies in East Asia, Korea is clearly the best performer.

Furthermore, Korea has diligently pursued difficult structural reforms prescribed by the IMF and the World Bank, covering the financial and corporate sectors, the labor market and social policy. Reform efforts are bearing fruit in the form of resumption of bank intermediation, improvements in the regulatory and supervisory framework, strengthening of corporate governance, and upgrading of social sector protection measures. In this sense Korea has something to offer to the rest of the world as to how a crisis-affected economy should cope with massive capital outflows, respond to systemic crisis in the banking and corporate sectors, and pursue structural reforms to lay the foundations for economic recovery. Many emerging market economies can learn lessons from the Korean experience because some of them will inevitably face a capital account crisis in the future.

Needless to say, there remain many unfinished tasks. By pursuing further structural reform, Korea will be able to make its economic system not only resilient to future adverse shocks but also more competitive and efficient in the knowledge-intensive global economic environment. It is hoped that Japan will also learn lessons from Korea, complete its financial and corporate sector restructuring quickly and resume its dynamic growth path in the very near future.

THE HONG–LEE–RHEE PAPER

The chapter by Kiseok Hong, Jong-Wha Lee and Changyong Rhee is one of the most interesting chapters collected here. Using a sample of 110 developing countries and mainly focusing on the period 1975–95 – during which there were 119 currency crises, 134 banking crises and 152 cases of IMF financial assistance – and conducting a series of statistical and econometric analyses, the authors reach the following conclusions:

- Once a country is hit by a financial crisis – defined as a currency crisis, a banking crisis, or an event of seeking IMF financial assistance – it is more likely to face another financial crisis of the same kind in the future. In other words, the probability of a crisis is a non-random event and is systematically correlated with the past history of crises. But there is not much evidence of twin crises.
- If a crisis-hit country successfully improves its macroeconomic conditions – the current account, fiscal balance, short-term debt and FDI inflows – then it is less likely to face another crisis in the future (within the next seven years).
- Since 1998, Korea has improved macroeconomic and structural conditions and has thereby reduced the risk of recurring crises. But more efforts are needed to promote structural reforms so as to further reduce vulnerabilities, particularly by opening the economy to FDI.

The chapter conducts statistical analyses in a competent way and draws clear conclusions. I have several comments. First, it is widely claimed that the recent emerging market economy crises have been caused by a combination of imperfections of the international financial markets (capital account crises), domestic structural weaknesses (banking sector vulnerabilities) and regional contagion (see below). But the chapter uses a mixed sample of both emerging market economies and low-income economies, relies mainly on current account crises because of the sample period chosen, and attempts to obtain implications for Korea. From these perspectives, it would be more interesting to: (1) divide the total sample into emerging market economies and non-emerging market economies, and focus on the capital account crisis experiences by extending the sample period until 2002; (2) examine the role played by domestic structural weaknesses, like the adequacy of financial sector regulation and supervision, the soundness of corporate governance and the measure of public sector governance; and (3) explore the role of contagion by entering a dummy variable that indicates the presence or absence of a crisis economy in the same geographical region. In addition, the probit equation may include proxy variables for capital account liberalization and financial sector liberalization to see if financial crises are accompanied by liberalization measures.

Second, policy implications of the statistical analyses should be clearly stated. The prediction that good macroeconomic conditions reduce the probability of crisis recurrence is too general to be operational for policy making. This begs the question of the operational usefulness of the kind of model developed in the chapter, particularly because the model does not predict the timing of crisis recurrence. The finding that IMF financial assistance tends to be repeated poses a very serious problem for the IMF, which needs to carefully monitor the post-crisis developments in a crisis-hit country so as not to have to repeat the financial assistance within a short period of time. Discussions on the implications for Korea are too descriptive. It would be more interesting to estimate the probability of crisis recurrence for Korea, particularly based on a model of capital account crises for emerging market economies, and to examine which variables are important in affecting the probability. The authority can act on these variables to reduce the probability of crisis recurrence.

Third, the role of total debt/GDP is sometimes hard to interpret. In the probit equation for IMF financial assistance (Table 13.4), total debt/GDP has a negative impact on the probability of crisis recurrence. This is counterintuitive. In the grouping analysis for IMF financial assistance (Table 13.5), total debt/GDP is lower for a country group which faces another crisis in the future than for a country group which does not. This result is again counterintuitive because it implies that it is better to have higher total debt/GDP to reduce the probability of crisis recurrence.

THE KIM–CHA–SONG CHAPTER

Relying on qualitative assessments concerning the role of banking and corporate sector reforms in economic recovery, In-June Kim, Baekin Cha and Chi-Young Song reach the following conclusions:

- The rapid recovery of the Korean economy is a result mainly of (1) the expansionary monetary and fiscal policy and (2) export expansion due to favorable external environments in 1999–2000 and won depreciation, rather than the result of restructuring and reforms, though the importance of the latter cannot be completely ignored.
- While it is hard to deny the contribution made by reform efforts over the past several years to reducing vulnerabilities, Korea must expedite the ongoing reform of the financial and corporate sectors to reduce the probability of crisis recurrence.

- Though it is too early to draw definitive conclusions, there is weak evidence for improvement in the banking sector's efficiency and stability and for improvements in the corporate sector's cost and profitability structures.

I believe the authors could give more credit to the role played by financial and corporate sector restructuring and structural reforms in setting the foundations for Korea's subsequent strong economic recovery. Without restructuring and reforms, I believe it would have been hard for Korea to grow at the rates of 11 and 9 percent in 1999 and 2000, respectively. The growth rates of Thailand and Malaysia were much lower, and Indonesia barely grew in 1999.

Korea was able to reach external debt restructuring agreements with international creditor banks and thereby stabilized the financial and currency markets in early 1998. The government then took a decisive, forceful approach to financial and corporate sector restructuring, including recapitalization of nonviable commercial banks through massive public fund injection, establishment of a public asset management company (KAMCO) to carve out NPLs from banks, concluding a restructuring agreement with five big *chaebols* under the Capital Structure Improvement Plans (CSIPs), and stabilizing the financial market at the time of Daewoo collapse in 1999. All these actions were backed by strong political commitments, 'ownership' of reforms, and the strong public sector capacity to carry out the needed restructuring and reform programs. Essentially Korea achieved a good balance between government intervention in the financial and corporate sectors in immediate systemic crisis situations and adopting a market-based approach to medium-term reforms.

The chapter may wish to present important lessons that the Korean case may provide with regard to financial and corporate sector restructuring and reform. Some of the critical requirements for successful financial and corporate sector restructuring may be summarized as follows (see Kawai, 2000; Kawai et al., 2001):

- macroeconomic stabilization and restoration of confidence in the financial and currency markets, which can be ensured by external debt restructuring agreements;
- political leadership, program 'ownership,' and institutional and bureaucratic capacity to carry out the needed restructuring and reforms;
- establishment of a consistent framework to resolve bank NPLs and banking sector restructuring and consolidation, including (1) acknowledgement of the magnitude of NPL problems and of the need for disposal of NPLs, (2) improved classification of loans and requirements for adequate loan loss provisions, (3) use of a public AMC

(Asset Management Corporation) as a possible catalyst for NPL resolution, (4) closure, merger and temporary nationalization of nonviable banks, (5) injection of public funds to recapitalize potentially viable banks, and (6) strong regulatory and supervisory oversight;
- establishment of a framework to accelerate corporate debt and operational restructuring, including (1) inter-creditor coordination, information sharing and mechanisms to resolve inter-creditor disputes, (2) out-of-court negotiation mechanisms backed by a credible threat of legal insolvency procedures such as court-supervised seizure of assets, foreclosure, liquidation, receivership and reorganization, (3) enabling environments through elimination of tax and legal impediments to corporate restructuring, and (4) measures to strengthen corporate governance.

GLOBAL, NATIONAL AND REGIONAL APPROACHES TO CRISIS PREVENTION, MANAGEMENT AND RESOLUTION

There is a growing consensus as to the cause of the Korean – and more generally East Asian or recent emerging market – crisis. It is a combination of:

- instability or imperfections of the international financial markets, including herd behavior, investor panic and multiple equilibria;
- structural weaknesses in the domestic financial and corporate sectors, including moral hazard and distorted incentives on the part of banks and corporations, inadequate regulatory and supervisory frameworks, and weak corporate governance; and
- contagion, particularly within a geographically concentrated region.

Each of these problems would require different, but mutually complementary, approaches to resolve them. In addressing the issue of the imperfections of international financial markets, reforms of the international financial system are necessary to reduce the risk of currency crises and respond to crises effectively once they occur. Some progress has been made in this area, including the introduction of the IMF's Supplementary Reserve Facility, the Contingent Credit Line (CCL), streamlining IMF conditionality, information disclosure of highly leveraged institutions (HLIs), and private sector involvement (PSI). To address the issue of domestic structural weaknesses, reforms of the domestic policy and institutional underpinnings are required. Some progress has been made in this area too, including the introduction of Reports of Standards and Codes (ROSCs), particularly the IMF–World Bank's joint Financial Sector Assessment Program. Persistent structural reform in Korea is highly commendable because it makes Korea less likely to face another financial crisis and makes the country more resilient to a currency crisis and contagion once it occurs. To address the issue of regional contagion, establishing a stronger regional financial architecture is logical.

Despite some progress, reforms of the international financial system are slow and still inadequate – no visible progress on the CCL or the HLIs, and slow progress on PSI. It requires a long time for any emerging market economy to strengthen domestic policy and institutional underpinnings, and even if ROSCs are put in place crises can still take place. Therefore it is increasingly necessary to explore the regional approach to complement the global and national approaches to crisis prevention, management and resolution. East Asia has developed the ASEAN +3 Economic Review and Policy Dialogue Process and is in the process of forming a network of bilateral swap arrangements under the Chiang Mai Initiative. It is desirable to make further progress in this area. But this topic is beyond the scope of the current comment.

NOTE

1. The views expressed in this comment are those of the author and do not necessarily represent the views of the Japanese government.

References

Abraham, Katherine G. (1990), 'Restructuring the Employment Relationship: The Growth of Market-Mediated Work Arrangements,' in Katherine Abraham and R. McKersie (eds), *New Developments in the Labor Market: Toward a New Institutional Paradigm*, Cambridge, MA: MIT Press, pp. 85–119.

Acemoglu, Daron, Philippe Aghion and Fabrizio Zlibotti (2002), 'Distance to Frontier, Selection, and Economic Growth,' NBER Working Paper 9066.

Acuna, Carlos H. and William C. Smith (1994), 'The Political Economy of Structural Adjustment: The Logic of Support and Opposition to Neoliberal Reform,' in William Smith, Carlos H. Acuna and Eduardo A. Gamarra (eds), *Latin American Political Economy in the Age of Neoliberal Reform: Theoretical and Comparative Perspectives for the 1990s*, New Brunswick and London: Transaction Publishers, pp. 17–66.

Aghion, Philippe, P. Bacchetta and A. Banerjee (2000), 'Currency Crises and Monetary Policy in an Economy with Credit Constraints,' CEPR Working Paper 2529.

Ahn, Byung-Chul (1999), 'Economic Crisis and Family Relationships,' paper presented at the Annual Conference of the Korean Sociological Association.

Allen, Franklin and Douglas Gale (1997), 'Financial Markets, Intermediaries, and Intertemporal Smoothing,' *Journal of Political Economy*, **105**, pp. 523–46.

Altman, Edward (1968), 'Financial Ratios, Discriminant Analysis and the Prediction of Corporate Bankruptcy,' *Journal of Finance*, **4**, pp. 589–609.

Aoki, Masahiko (1988), *Information, Incentives and Bargaining*, New York: Cambridge University Press.

Arteta, Carlos, Barry Eichengreen and Charles Wyplosz (2001), 'When Does Capital Account Liberalization Help More Than It Hurts?' NBER Working Paper 8414.

Atkinson, Anthony B., Lee Rainwater and Timothy M. Smeeding (1995), *Income Distribution in OECD Countries: Evidence from the Luxembourg Income Study*, Washington, DC: OECD.

Atkinson, James (1984), 'Manpower Strategies for Flexible Firms,' *Personnel Management*, **16**, pp. 28–31.

Bae, Jin-Han (2001), 'Causes of Non-Regular Job Growth and the Prospects' (in Korean), *Korean Journal of Labor Economics*, **25**, pp. 125–62.

References

Baig, Taimur and Ilan Goldfajn (1999), 'Financial Market Contagion in the Asian Crisis,' IMF Working Paper 98/155.
Ball, Lawrence (1999), 'Policy Rules for Open Economies,' in John Taylor (ed.), *Monetary Policy Rules*, Chicago: University of Chicago Press, pp. 127–44.
Banerjee, Abhijit (1992), 'A Simple Model of Herd Behavior,' *Quarterly Journal of Economics*, **107**, pp. 797–817.
Bank of Korea (1994–97), *Monthly Bulletin*, Seoul: Bank of Korea.
Bank of Korea (1996–98), 'Total NPLs at Korean Banks,' press release of the Bank Supervisory Service, Seoul: Bank of Korea.
Bank of Korea (1996–2001), *Financial Statement of Analysis*, Seoul: Bank of Korea.
Bank of Korea (1999), *Foreign Exchange Statistical Yearbook*, Seoul: Bank of Korea.
Bank of Korea (2001), *National Income Accounts*, Seoul: Bank of Korea.
Bank of Korea (2002), *Understanding the Flow of Funds in Korea*, Seoul: Bank of Korea.
Bank of Korea (various years), *Database on Flow of Funds Account*, Seoul: Bank of Korea.
Bank of Korea (various years), *Management Statistics*, Seoul: Bank of Korea.
Barberis, Nicholas, Andrei Shleifer and Robert W. Vishny (1998), 'A Model of Investment Sentiment,' *Journal of Financial Economics*, **49**, pp. 307–43.
Bark, Sun-Il, Nung-Hoo Park and Sung-Ho Kang (1999), 'The Status and Characteristics of the Poor after the Economic Crisis,' mimeo.
Barsurto, Gabriela and Atish Ghosh (2000), 'The Interest Rate–Exchange Rate Nexus in Currency Crises,' IMF Working Paper 00/19.
Baydoun, Nabil and Roger Willett (1995), 'Cultural Relevance of Western Accounting Systems to Developing Countries,' *Abacus*, **31**, pp. 67–92.
Bayoumi, Tamim and Barry Eichengreen (1995), 'Restraining Yourself: The Implications of Fiscal Rules for Economic Stabilization,' *IMF Staff Papers*, **42**, pp. 32–48.
Berg, Andrew (1999), 'The Asia Crisis – Causes, Policy Responses and Outcomes,' IMF Working Paper 99/138.
Berg, Andrew and Catherine Pattillo (1999), 'Are Currency Crisis Predictable? A Test,' *IMF Staff Papers*, **46**, pp. 107–38.
Bergsten, C.F. (1997), 'The Asian Monetary Crisis: Proposed Remedies,' statement before the Committee on Banking and Financial Services, US House of Representatives.
Blanchard, Olivier J. and Danny Quah (1989), 'The Dynamic Effects of Aggregate Demand and Supply Disturbances,' *American Economic Review*, **79**, pp. 655–73.

Blustein, Paul (2001), *The Chastening: Inside the Crisis that Rocked the Global Financial System and Humbled the IMF*, New York: Public Affairs.

Blustein, Paul and Clay Chandler (1997), 'Behind the South Korea Bailout: Speed, Stealth, Consensus,' *The Washington Post*, 28 December, p. A1.

Bongini, Paola B., Stijn Claessens and Giovanni Ferri (2000), 'The Political Economy of Distress in East Asian Financial Institutions,' World Bank Working Paper 2265.

Bordo, Michael, Barry Eichengreen, Daniela Klingebiel and Maria Soledad Martinez-Peria (2001), 'Is the Crisis Problem Growing More Severe?' *Economic Policy*, **16** (32) pp. 51–82.

Borensztein, Eduardo and Jong-Wha Lee (1998), 'Credit Allocation and Financial Crisis in Korea,' IMF Working Paper 99/20.

Borensztein, Eduardo and Jong-Wha Lee (1999), 'Was There a Credit Crunch or Credit Reallocation? Chaebols and Non-Chaebols in the Korean Financial Crisis,' mimeo.

Calmfors, Lars (1993), 'Centralisation of Wage Bargaining and Macroeconomic Performance: A Survey,' *OECD Economic Studies*, **21**, pp. 161–91.

Calmfors, Lars and John Driffill (1988), 'Bargaining Structure, Corporatism, and Macroeconomic Performance,' *The Economics of Unemployment*, **3**, pp. 165–98.

Calvo, Guillermo A. (1999), 'Fixed vs. Flexible Exchange Rates: Preliminaries of a Turn-of-Millennium Rematch,' mimeo, University of Maryland.

Calvo, Guillermo A. and Enrique Mendoza (2000), 'Rational Contagion and the Globalization of Securities Markets,' *Journal of International Economics*, **51**, pp. 79–113.

Campos, Jose Edgardo and Hilton L. Root (1996), *The Key to the Asian Miracle: Making Shared Growth Credible*, Washington, DC: Brookings Institution Press.

Cappelli, Peter and David Neumark (2001), 'External Job Churning and Internal Job Flexibility,' NBER Working Paper 8111.

Caprio, Gerald and Daniela Klingebiel (1996), 'Bank Insolvencies: Cross-Country Experiences,' World Bank Policy Research Paper 1620.

Castells, Manuel (2000), *The Rise of Network Society*, Oxford: Blackwell.

Center for Free Enterprise (1997–2001), *The Korean Big Business Groups*.

Cespedes, Luis F., R. Chang and A. Velasco (2000), 'Balance Sheets and Exchange Rate Policy,' NBER Working Paper 7840.

Chalk, Nigel and Richard Hemming (2000), 'Assessing Fiscal Sustainability in Theory in Practice,' IMF Working Paper 00/81.

Chang, Chun (2000), 'Stages of Economic Development: The Case of South Korea,' mimeo, University of Minnesota.

Chang, Ha-Sung (2002), 'Korea Discount and Corporate Governance', *Cor-*

porate Governance Studies, vol. 1, pp. 56–71, Centre for Good Corporate Governance.

Chang, Hye-Kyung and Young-Ran Kim (1999), 'IMF Crisis and the Family Issue: Family Life and Family Stability after the Job Loss' (in Korean), *Korean Society*, **2**, pp. 81–116.

Chang, Roberto and Andres Velasco (1998), 'The Asian Liquidity Crisis,' NBER Working Paper 6796.

Chang, Sea Jin and Choi, Ungwhan (1988), 'Strategy, Structures and Performance of Korean Business Groups: The Transactions Cost Approach,' *Journal of Industrial Economics*, **47**, pp. 141–158.

Chang, Seong-Ok (1999), 'The Identity Crisis of the Unemployed' (in Korean), *Studies in Social Development*, **5**, pp. 47–74.

Chang, Yunshik (1991), 'The Personal Ethic and the Market in Korea,' *Comparative Studies in Society and History*, **33**, pp. 106–29.

Chen, Shaohua and Martin Ravallion (2000), 'How Did the World's Poorest Fare in the 1990s?' Policy Research Working Paper 2049, World Bank.

Cheong, Kwang Soo (2001), 'Economic Crisis and Income Inequality in Korea,' *Asian Economic Journal*, **15**, pp. 39–60.

Cho, Dongchul (2002), 'Post-Crisis Structural Changes and Monetary Policy Scheme in Korea,' manuscript, Korea Development Institute.

Cho, Dongchul and Youngsun Koh (1996), 'Liberalization of Capital Flows in Korea: Big-Bang or Gradualism?' NBER Working Paper 5824.

Cho, Dongchul and Kenneth D. West (2001), 'The Effect of Monetary Policy in Exchange Rate Stabilization in Post-Crisis Korea,' in Inseok Shin (ed.), *The Korean Crisis: Before and After*, Korea Development Institute, pp. 257–86.

Cho, Dongchul and Kenneth D. West (2003), 'Interest Rates and Exchange Rates in the Korean, Phillippine, and Thai Exchange Rate Crisis,' in Michael Dooley and Jeffrey Frankel (eds.), *Managing Currency Crises in Emerging Markets*, Chicago: University of Chicago Press, pp. 11–30.

Cho, Dongchul and Kiseok Hong (2000), 'Currency Crisis of Korea: Internal Weakness or External Interdependence' in Shin (ed), *The Korean Crisis: Before and After*, Seoul: Korean Development Institute.

Cho, Soon (1994), *The Dynamics of Korean Economic Development*, Washington, DC: Institute for International Economics.

Cho, Yoon Je (1999), 'An Analysis of the Financial Liberalization Policies in the 90s and the Financial Crisis in Korea' (in Korean), *Journal of Korean Economy Studies*, **2**, pp. 61–86.

Cho, Yoon Je (2001a), 'What Have We Learned from the Korean Adjustment Program?' in David Coe and Se-Jik Kim (eds), *Korean Crisis and Recovery*, Seoul: International Monetary Fund and Korea Institute for Economic Policy, pp. 105–127.

Cho, Yoon Je (2001b), 'Reexamination of Economic Adjustment Policies, Based on the Korean Experience After Crisis,' paper presented to the workshop on Reexamination of Development Policies, Institute of Developing Economies, Keio University, March.

Cho, Yoon Je and Joon-Kyung Kim (1997), *Credit Policies and the Industrialization of Korea*, Seoul: Korea Development Institute.

Choe, H., B. Kho and R. Stulz (1998), 'Do Foreign Investors Destabilize Stock Markets? The Korean Experience in 1997,' Charles A. Dice Center for Research in Financial Economics Working Paper 98-6, Ohio State University.

Choe, Jang Jip (1998), 'Korea's Political Economy: Search for a Solution,' *Korea Focus*, **6** (2), pp. 1–20.

Choi, Doo-Yull (2002), *Asymmetric Regulations on Corporate Financing and the Currency Crisis* (in Korean), Seoul: Korea Economic Research Institute.

Choi, Gongpil (1999), 'The Korean Experience with Financial Crisis: A Chronology,' Financial Research Paper 99-06, Korea Institute of Finance.

Choi, Gongpil, et al. (1999), 'The Economic Prospects of the Second Half of 1999,' Seoul: Korea Institute of Finance.

Choi, Kyung-Soo (2001), 'The Causes of Increase in Non-Regular Employment and Policy Agenda in Korea,' unpublished manuscript, Seoul: Korea Development Institute.

Choi, Sung Noh (1996, 1998), *The Largest 30 Chaebols in Korea*, Seoul: Free Enterprise Institute.

Choi, Young-Ki (2002), 'Labor Reforms during Restructuring,' *Korea Journal*, **42**, pp. 100–128.

Choi, Young-Ki, Joon Kim, Hyo Rae Cho and Bum Sang Yoo (2001), *Labor Movement in Korea since 1987* (in Korean), Seoul: Korea Labor Institute.

Chopra, Ajai, Kenneth Kang, Meral Karasulu, Hong Liang, Henry Ma and Anthony Richards (2001), 'From Crisis to Recovery in Korea: Strategy, Achievements, and Lessons,' IMF Working Paper 01/154.

Chossudovsky, Michel (1997), *The Globalization of Poverty: Impacts of IMF and World Bank Reforms*, Penang: Third World Network.

Chung, Byong Hyou and Young Shik Yang (1992), *Korean Chaebols*, Seoul: Korea Development Institute.

Chung, Duck-Koo (2002), 'The Korean Financial Crisis in View of the Mismatch Phenomenon,' paper presented at the Center for Research on Economic Development and Policy Reform, Stanford University.

Claessens, Stijn, Simeon Djankov and Larry H.P. Lang (1998), 'East Asian Corporates: Growth, Financing and Risks Over the Last Decade,' unpublished manuscript, World Bank.

Claessens, Stijn, Simeon Djankov and Larry H.P. Lang (2000), 'East Asian Corporations – Heroes or Villains?' World Bank Discussion Paper 409.

Claessens, Stijn, Simeon Djankov and Giovanni Ferri (1999), 'Corporate Distress in East Asia: The Effect of Currency and Interest Rate Shocks,' unpublished manuscript, World Bank.

Cook, Maria L., Kevin J. Middlebrook and Juas M. Horcaritas (eds) (1994), *The Politics of Economic Restructuring: State–Society Relations and Regime Change in Mexico*, San Diego: Center for US–Mexican Studies, University of California, San Diego.

Corsetti, Giancarlo, Paola Pesenti and Nouriel Roubini (1998a), '"Paper Tigers:" A Model of the Asian Crisis,' NBER Working Paper 6783.

Corsetti, Giancarlo, Paola Pesenti and Nouriel Roubini (1998b), 'What Caused the Asian Currency and Financial Crisis?' NBER Working Paper 6834.

Crafts, Nicholas (1999), 'Implications of Financial Crisis for East Asian Trend Growth,' *Oxford Review of Economic Policy*, **15**, pp. 110–31.

Cronin, Richard P. (1998). *Asian Financial Crisis: An Analysis of U.S. Foreign Policy Interests and Options*, CRS Report 98-74, http://www.cnie.nle/crsreports/economics/econ-56.cfm.

Cumings, Bruce (1999), 'The Asian Crisis, Democracy, and the End of "Late" Development,' in T.J. Pempel (ed.), *The Politics of the Asian Economic Crisis*, Ithaca: Cornell University Press, pp. 17–44.

Daewoo Economic Research Institute (1993–98), *Surveys of Economic Activities of Korean Households*.

Danziger, Sheldon and Peter Gottschalk (1995), *America Unequal*, Cambridge, MA: Harvard University Press.

Dekle, Robert, Cheng Hsiao and Siyan Wang (1999), 'Interest Rate Stabilization of Exchange Rates and Contagion in the Asian Crisis Countries,' manuscript, University of Southern California.

Dekle, Robert, Cheng Hsiao and Siyan Wang (2001), 'Do High Interest Rates Appreciate Exchange Rates During Crises? The Korean Evidence,' *Oxford Bulletin of Economics and Statistics*, **63**, pp. 369–80.

DeLong, J. Bradford and Barry Eichengreen (2002), 'Between Meltdown and Moral Hazard: The International Monetary and Financial Policies of the Clinton Administration,' in Jeffrey A. Frankel and Peter R. Orszag (eds), *American Economic Policy in the 1990s*, Cambridge, MA: MIT Press, pp. 191–276.

Demirgüç-Kunt, Asli and Enrica Detragiache (1998), 'Financial Liberalization and Financial Fragility,' IMF Working Paper 98/83.

Demirgüç-Kunt, Asli and Ross Levine (1999), 'Bank-Based and Market-Based Financial Systems: Cross-Country Comparisons,' mimeo, World Bank.

Diamond, Douglas W. (1991), 'Monitoring and Reputation: The Choice between Bank Loans and Directly Placed Debt,' *Journal of Political Economy*, **99**, pp. 689–721.

Diamond, Larry (2001), 'Introduction,' in Larry Diamond and Marc F. Plattner (eds), The *Global Divergence of Democracies*, Baltimore and London: The Johns Hopkins University Press.

Dobson, Wendy and Pierre Jacquet (1998), *Financial Services Liberalization in the WTO,* Washington, DC: Institute for International Economics.

Dollar, David and Aart Kraay (2001), 'Growth is Good for the Poor,' Policy Research Working Paper 2587, World Bank.

Dong, Wonmo (1994), 'Civilian Democracy and the Politics of Leadership Change,' research paper presented to the Carnegie Council on Ethnics and International Affairs, International Seminar on Continuity and Change in Contemporary Korea: The Impact of Democratic Reform, New York.

Economist (1995), 'Frankenstein Economy,' **335**, pp. SS10–SS13.

Edwards, Franklin R. (1996), *The New Finance: Regulation and Financial Stability*, Washington, DC: AIE Press.

Edwards, Sebastian (1989), *Real Exchange Rates, Devaluation, and Adjustment: Exchange Rate Policy in Developing Countries*, Cambridge, MA: MIT Press.

Edwards, Sebastian (2001), 'Capital Mobility and Economic Performance: Are Emerging Economies Different?' NBER Working Paper 8076.

Eichengreen, Barry (1999), *Toward a New International Financial Architecture: A Practical Post-Asia Agenda*, Washington, DC: Institute for International Economics.

Eichengreen, Barry, Andrew K. Rose, and Charles Wyplosz (1995), 'Exchange Market Mayhem: The Antecedents and Aftermath of Speculative Attacks,' *Economic Policy*, **21**, pp. 249–312.

Evans, Peter B. (1976), *Dependent Development: The Alliance of Multinational, State, and Local Capital in Brazil*, Princeton, NJ: Princeton University Press.

Fechner, Harry H.E. and Alan Kilgore (1994), 'The Influence of Cultural Factors on Accounting Practice,' *International Journal of Accounting*, **29**, pp. 265–77.

Feldstein, Martin (1992), 'The Council of Economic Advisors and Economic Advising in the United States,' *Economic Journal*, **102**, pp. 1223–34.

Feldstein, Martin (1998), 'Refocusing the IMF,' *Foreign Affairs*, **77**, pp. 20–33.

Ferreira, F., G. Prennushi and M. Ravallion (2000), 'Protecting the Poor from Macroeconomic Shocks: An Agenda for Action in a Crisis and Beyond,' Policy Research Working Paper 2160, World Bank.

Financial Supervisory Service (1992–2001), *Annual Statistical Report*, Seoul: Financial Supervisory Service.

Financial Supervisory Service (2000), 'Press Release on the Review of Auditing Firms' Financial Statement,' Seoul: Financial Supervisory Service.

Financial Supervisory Service (2001), *Bank Management Statistics*, Seoul: Financial Supervisory Service.

Financial Supervisory Service (various years), *Monthly Financial Statistics Bulletin*, Seoul: Financial Supervisory Service.

Financial Supervisory Service (various years), *Financial Supervisory Information*, Seoul: Financial Supervisory Service.

Fischer, Stanley (1998a), 'The IMF and the Asian Crisis,' Forum Fund Lecture at UCLA.

Fischer, Stanley (1998b), 'Response: In Defense of the IMF, Specialized Tools for a Specialized Task,' *Foreign Affairs*, **77**, pp. 103–6.

Fischer, Stanley (1999), 'The Road to a Sustainable Recovery in Asia,' mimeo, Washington, DC: International Monetary Fund.

Fischer, Stanley (2001a), 'Exchange Rate Regimes: Is the Bipolar View Correct?' manuscript, Washington, DC: International Monetary Fund.

Fischer, Stanley (2001b), 'International Economic Policy Under the Clinton Administration,' Harvard University, http://www.imf.org/external/np/speeches/2001/062701.htm.

Fischer, Stanley and William Easterly (1990), 'The Economics of the Government Budget Constraint,' *World Bank Research Observer*, **5**, pp. 127–42.

Frankel, Jeffrey A. and Andrew K. Rose (1996), 'Currency Crashes in Emerging Markets: An Empirical Treatment,' International Finance Discussion Paper 534, Washington, DC: Board of Governors of the Federal Reserve.

Freedman, C. (1994), 'The Use of Indicators and of the Monetary Conditions Index in Canada,' in Tomas J.T. Balino and Carlo Cottarelli (eds), *Frameworks for Monetary Stability: Policy Issues and Country Experiences*, Washington, DC: International Monetary Fund.

Freeman, Richard B. (1999), *The New Inequality: Creating Solutions for Poor America*, Boston, MA: Beacon Press.

Furman, Jason and Joseph E. Stiglitz (1998), 'Economic Crises: Evidence and Insight from East Asia,' *Brookings Papers on Economic Activity*, **2**, pp. 1–135.

Gamarra, Eduardo A. (1994), 'Market-Oriented Reforms and Democratization in Latin America: Challenges of the 1990s,' in Smith, Acuna and Gamarra (1994a), pp. 1–15.

Garuda, Gopal (2000), 'The Distributional Effects of IMF Programs: A Cross-Country Analysis,' *World Development*, **28**, pp. 1031–51.

Gerlach, Stefan and Frank Smets (2000), 'MCIs and Monetary Policy,' *European Economic Review*, **44**, pp. 1677–700.

Gerschenkron, Alexander (1962), *Economic Backwardness in Historical Perspective*, Cambridge, MA: Harvard University Press.

Glick, Reuven and Michael Hutchison (1999), 'Banking and Currency Crises: How Common Are Twins?' Pacific Basin Working Paper Series 99-07, Federal Reserve Bank of San Francisco.
Gobat, J. (1998), 'Corporate Restructuring and Corporate Governance, Republic of Korea–Selected Issues' IMF Staff Country Reports 98/74.
Goldfajn, Ilan and Taimur Baig (1998), 'Monetary Policy in the Aftermath of Currency Crises: The Case of Asia,' IMF Working Paper 99/42.
Goldfajn, Ilan and Poonam Gupta (1999), 'Does Monetary Policy Stabilize the Exchange Rate Following a Currency Crisis?' IMF Working Paper 99/42.
Goldstein, Morris, Graciela Kaminsky and Carmen Reinhart (2000), *Assessing Financial Vulnerability: An Early Warning System for Emerging Markets*, Washington, DC: Institute for International Economics.
Gould, David M. and Steven B. Kamin (2000), 'The Impact of Monetary Policy on Exchange Rates During Financial Crises,' Board of Governors of the Federal Reserve System International Financial Discussion Paper 669.
Gray, S.J. (1988), 'Towards a Theory of Cultural Influence on the Development of Accounting Systems Internationally,' *Abacus*, **24**, pp. 1–15.
Haggard, Stephan (2000), *The Political Economy of the Asian Financial Crisis*, Washington, DC: Institute for International Economics.
Haggard, Stephan and Robert R. Kaufman (eds) (1992), *The Politics of Economic Adjustment*, Princeton, NJ: Princeton University Press.
Haggard, Stephan and Linda Low (2001), 'The Political Economy of Malaysian Capital Controls,' mimeo, University of California, San Diego.
Hahm, Joon-Ho (2002), 'The Government, Chaebol and Financial Institutions in Pre-Crisis Korea,' in Stephan Haggard, Wonhyuk Lim and Euysang Kim, *Economic Crisis and Corporation Restructuring in Korea: Reforming the Chaebol*, New York: Cambridge University Press, pp. 79–101.
Hahm, Joon-Ho and Frederic S. Mishkin (2000), 'The Korean Financial Crisis: an Asymmetric Information Perspective,' *Emerging Markets Review*, **1**, pp. 21–52.
Hahn, Chin-Hee (1999), 'Implicit Loss-Protection and the Investment Behavior of Korean Chaebols: An Empirical Analysis' (in Korean), *KDI Journal of Economic Policy*, **21**, pp. 3–52.
Hall, David and Roger T. Ames (1999), *The Democracy of the Dead: Dewey, Confucius, and the Hope for Democracy in China*, Chicago, IL: Open Court.
Hall, Peter (1986), *Governing the Economy: The Politics of State Intervention in Britain and France*, Oxford and New York: Oxford University Press.
Hallward-Dreimeier, Mary (2000), 'Firm-Level Survey Provides Data on

Asia's Corporate Crisis and Recovery', World Bank Policy Research Working Paper No. 2515.
Heller, Peter S. (1997), 'Aging in the Asian "Tigers": Challenges for Fiscal Policy,' IMF Working Paper 97/143.
Hirshman, Albert O. (1973), *Journeys Toward Progress: Studies of Economic Policy Making in Latin America*, New York: W.W. Norton and Co.
Hofstede, Geert H. (1995), *Cultures and Organizations*, New York: McGraw-Hill.
Hollingsworth, J. Rogers and Robert Boyer (eds) (1997), *Contemporary Capitalism: The Embeddedness of Institutions*, Cambridge: Cambridge University Press.
Hong, Kiseok and Aaron Tornell (2000), 'Recovery from a Crisis: Some Stylized Facts,' mimeo.
Hong, Wontack (1981), 'Export Promotion and Employment Growth in South Korea,' in Anne O. Krueger, Hal B. Lary, Terry Monson and Narongchai Akrasnee (eds), *Trade and Employment in Developing Countries*, Chicago: University of Chicago Press, volume 1, pp. 341–91.
Hood, Ron (2001), 'Malaysian Capital Controls,' World Bank Working Paper 2536.
Hoogvelt, Ankie (1997), *Globalization and the Postcolonial World: The New Political Economy of Development*, London: Macmillan Press.
Hoshi, Takeo and Anil Kashyap (1999), 'The Japanese Banking Crisis: Where Did It Come From and How Will It End?' NBER Working Paper 7250.
Hoshi, Takeo, Anil Kashyap and D. Scharfstein (1991), 'Corporate Structure, Liquidity and Investment: Evidence from Japanese Industrial Groups,' *Quarterly Journal of Economics*, **106**, pp. 33–60.
Hsieh, Chang-Tai (2002), 'What Explains the Industrial Revolution in East Asia? Evidence from the Factor Markets,' *American Economic Review*, **92**, pp. 520–46.
Huntington, Samuel P. (1991), *The Third Wave: Democratization in the Late Twentieth Century*, New York: Norman and London.
Hwang, In Hak (2001), 'An Empirical Study on *Chaebols*' Performance,' Seoul: Korea Economic Research Institute.
Hyun, Jin-Kwon (1996), 'Analysis of Disproportionate Land Ownership and Burden of Aggregate Land Tax' (in Korean), in *Tax Policy and Income Redistribution*, Seoul: Korea Institute of Public Finance.
Hyundai Economic Research Institute (HERI) (1998), *A Survey of Living and the Consciousness of the Middle Class in the IMF Period*, Seoul: Hyundai Economic Research Institute.
Hyundai Economic Research Institute (HERI) (1999), *A Survey of the Middle Class Consciousness*, Seoul: Hyundai Economic Research Institute.

International Monetary Fund (1994–2002), *International Financial Statistics*, Washington, DC: IMF.
International Monetary Fund (1999, 2002), *World Economic Outlook*, Washington, DC: IMF.
Jensen, Michael C. and William H. Meckling (1976), 'Theory of the Firm: Managerial Behavior, Agency Costs, and Ownership Structure,' *Journal of Financial Economics*, **3**, pp. 305–60.
Ji, Dong-Hyun (2000), 'Measures to Improve Bank Competitiveness by Enhancing Profitability' (in Korean), paper presented at the Korea Institute of Finance symposium on Improving Bank Competitiveness.
Joh, Sung Wook (1999), 'A Study on the Profitability of Korean Firms: The Effects of Conflicts of Interests among Shareholders,' *KDI Journal of Economic Policy* 1999.
Joh, Sung Wook (2000), 'Micro-dynamics of Industrial Competition: Evidence from Korean Manufacturing Plants,' *Policy Study 5*, Seoul: KDI.
Joh, Sung Wook (2001a), 'An Empirical Analysis of Chaebol Reform After the Crisis,' (in Korean), *Policy Study Series 15*, Joh: KDI.
Joh, Sung Wook (2001b), 'The Korean Corporate Sector: Crisis and Reform,' in Yui Kwon and Wiiliam Shepherd (eds), *Korea's Economic Prospects: From Financial Crisis to Prosperity*, Cheltenham, UK: Edward Elgar Publishing, pp. 116–32.
Joh, Sung Wook (2003), 'Corporate Governance and Firm Profitability: Evidence from Korea before the Economic Crisis,' *Journal of Financial Economics*, **68** (2), 287–322.
Joh, Sung Wook and Sang Dai Ryoo (2000) 'Evaluation of Changes in the Corporate Governance System of Korean Chaebols,' paper presented at the PAFTA conference.
Johnson, Simon (2002), 'Institutions, Corporate Governance, and Debt: What Have We Learned?' MIT Working Paper.
Johnson, Simon, Peter Boone, Alasdair Breach and Eric Friedman (2000), 'Corporate Governance in the Asian Financial Crisis,' *Journal of Financial Economics*, **58**, pp. 141–86.
Johnson, Simon, Rafael La Porta, Florencio Lopez-de-Silanes and Andrei Shleifer (2000), 'Tunneling,' *American Economic Review*, **90**, pp. 22–7.
Jomo, Kwame S. (2001), 'Capital Controls,' in Kwame Jomo (ed.), *Malaysian Eclipse: Economic Crisis and Recovery*, Singapore: Select Books Pte Ltd, pp. 199–215.
Jones, Leroy and Il SaKong (1980), *Government, Business, and Entrepreneurship in Economic Development: The Korean Case*, Studies in the Modernization of the Republic of Korea: 1945–1975, Cambridge, MA: Harvard University Press.

Jun, In Woo and Byeong-Ho Gong (1995), *Corporate Governance in Korea*, Seoul: Korea Economic Research Institute.

Jun, Joosung (2001), 'The Role of Public Finance in Overcoming the Economic Crisis' (in Korean), seminar paper, Korean Society of Public Finance Policy Symposium.

Jun, Joosung, Jinwoo Hwang and Youngsun Koh (2000), 'The Fiscal Balance Implications of Financial Restructuring' (in Korean), *Journal of Korean Economic Analysis*, **6**, pp. 173–200.

Jun, Sung-In (2002), 'Laws, Rules, and Old Habits in a New World: A Summary of Post-Crisis Institutional Changes,' *Korea Journal*, **42**, pp. 74–99.

Jwa, Sung-hee and Huh Can-guk (1998), 'Risk and Returns of Financial–Industrial Interactions: The Korean Experience,' KERI Working Paper 98-01, Seoul: Korea Economic Research Institute.

Kakwani, Nanak and Nicholas Prescott (2001), 'Impact of Economic Crisis on Poverty and Inequality in Korea,' mimeo.

Kakwani, Nanak and Hyun H. Son (1999), 'Economic Growth, Inequality, and Poverty: Korea and Thailand,' mimeo.

Kalleberg, Arne L. (1997), *Nonstandard Work, Substandard Jobs: Flexible Work Arrangements in the US*, Washington, DC: Economic Policy Institute.

Kaminsky, Graciela S. (1998), 'Currency and Banking Crises: The Early Warnings of Distress,' International Finance Discussion Paper 629, Board of Governors of the Federal Reserve System.

Kaminsky, Graciela S. and Carmen M. Reinhart (1999), 'The Twin Crises: The Causes of Banking and Balance-of-Payments Problems,' *American Economic Review*, **89**, pp. 473–501.

Kaminsky, Graciela S. and Carmen M. Reinhart (2000), 'On Crises, Contagion and Confusion,' *Journal of International Economics*, **51**, pp. 145–68.

Kaminsky, Graciela S. and Sergio Schmukler (1999), 'What Triggers Market Jitters? A Chronicle of the Asian Crisis,' International Finance Discussion Paper 634, Board of Governors of the Federal Reserve System.

Kaminsky, Graciela S., Saul Lizondo and Carmen M. Reinhart (1997), 'Leading Indicators of Currency Crises,' IMF Working Paper 97/79.

Kang, Byong H. (1998), 'Restructuring of Financial Institutions and the Corporate Sector in Korea,' *Journal of Asian Economics*, **9**, pp. 653–70.

Kaplan, Ethan and Dani Rodrik (2001), 'Did the Malaysian Capital Controls Work?' NBER Working Paper 8142.

Kapur, Devesh (1998), 'The IMF: A Cure or a Curse?' *Foreign Policy*, **111**, pp. 114–28.

Karl, Terry Lynn and Philippe C. Schmitter (1991), 'Modes of Transition in

Latin America, Southern and Eastern Europe,' *International Social Science Journal*, **128**, pp. 269–84.

Kawai, Masahiro (2000), 'The Resolution of the East Asian Crisis: Financial and Corporate Sector Restructuring,' *Journal of Asian Economics*, **11**, pp. 133–68.

Kawai, Masahiro, Ira Lieberman and William P. Mako (2001), 'Financial Stabilization and Initial Restructuring of East Asian Corporations: Approaches, Results and Lessons,' in Charles Adams, Robert E. Litan and Michael Pomerleano (eds), *Managing Financial and Corporate Distress: Lessons from Asia*, Washington, DC: Brookings Institution Press, pp. 77–135.

Keister, Lisa A. (2000), *Wealth in America: Trends in Wealth Inequality*, Cambridge: Cambridge University Press.

Kilpatrick, A. (2003), 'Structures to Support Stability and Growth: Some Observations Based on UK Experience', in G. de Brauwer and Y. Wang (eds), *Financial Governance in East Asia*, Routledge, London, pp. 50–82.

Kim, Byung-Kook (2001), 'The Politics of Financial Reform in Korea, Malaysia, and Thailand: Does Democracy Matter?' paper presented at the Annual Meeting of the American Political Science Association, San Francisco, California.

Kim, Byung-Kook and Jin-Young Suh (1999), 'The Politics of Reform in Korea: Dilemma, Choice and Crisis,' in Jin-Young Suh and Changrok Soh (eds), *The World After the Cold War: Issues and Dilemmas*, Seoul: Graduate School of International Studies, Korea University, pp. 17–53.

Kim, Chung-Yum (1997), 'Policymaking on the Front Lines: Memoirs of a Korean Practitioner, 1945–1979,' *Jung-Ang Daily Press*.

Kim, Dae Il (1997), 'Demand for College Education and Labor Market Outcomes in Korea,' paper presented at the APEC–HRD–NEDM–KDI International Seminar on Improving the Economic Performance of Education, Seoul: Korea Development Institute.

Kim, Dae Il (2000a), 'Marginal Participants and Unemployment' (in Korean), *Proceedings of Panel Discussions for the Analysis of the Korean Economy*, **6** (1), 1–57.

Kim, Dae Il (2000b), 'Unemployment Dynamics during the Period of Economic Crisis,' *International Economic Journal Economics Annual* (conference proceedings), Seoul: Korea International Economic Association.

Kim, Dae Il (2001a), 'The Pattern of Job Growth During the Period of Economic Crisis' (in Korean), *Journal of the Korean Econometric Society*, pp. 1–35.

Kim, Dae Il (2001b), 'Growth in Non-Regular Employment in Korea: Human

Resource Management vs. Cost-Reduction Hypothesis,' unpublished manuscript, Seoul National University.

Kim, Dae Il and Gyeong-Joon Yoo (2001), 'Labor Market Changes in Korea Since the Crisis,' paper presented at the KDI–EWC Conference on A New Paradigm for Social Welfare in the New Millennium, East–West Center, University of Hawaii.

Kim, Jeong-Han, Moo-Ki Moon and Jae-Sik Jeon (2001), *Analysis of Collective Agreements III* (in Korean), Seoul: Korea Labor Institute.

Kim, Jin-Wook and Changyong Park (2000), 'Changes in Poverty Accompanying the Economic Crisis' (in Korean), *The Public Economy*, **5**.

Kim, Joon Kyung (1991), 'Changes in Financial Market and Non-Performing Loans at Banks,' mimeo, Korea Development Institute.

Kim, Joon-Kyung (1999), 'Chaebols Ownership of NBFIs and Related Problems,' *KDI Economic Outlook*, **1** (4), pp. 83–94.

Kim, June-Il (1996), 'Business Cycles and GDP Gap' (in Korean), *KDI Policy Studies*, Korea Development Institute, **18**, pp. 217–70.

Kim, June-Il and Dongchul Cho (2002), *Business Forecasting Based on GDP Gap Estimation*, Seoul: Korea Development Institute.

Kim, Ky Won (2002), 'Corporate Restructuring: With an Emphasis on Chaebol,' *Korea Journal*, **42**, pp. 5–41.

Kim, Man Eum (1988), 'The Biased Personnel Recruitment has Created Regional Feelings,' *Shindong-A*, **380** (March) pp. 486–99.

Kim, Sang-Jo (2002), 'Financial Sector Reform in Korea: A Dilemma between "Bank-Based" and "Market-Based" System,' *Korea Journal*, **42**, pp. 42–73.

Kim, Seok-Joon (1999), 'IMF Regime and the Re-Formation of Class in Korea' (in Korean), *The Korean Society*, **2**, pp. 33–54.

Kim, Woochan and Yangho Byeon (2001), 'Restructuring Korean Banks' Short-Term Debts,' in David Coe and Se-Jik Kim (eds), *Korean Crisis and Recovery*, Washington, DC: International Monetary Fund and Korea: Korea Institute for Economic Policy, pp. 405–448.

Kim, Woochan and Shangjin Wei (1999), 'Foreign Portfolio Investors Before and During a Crisis,' NBER Working Paper 6968.

Kim, Wook-Joong (2002), 'A Study on the Degree of Concentration in the Korean Banking Industry,' *Bank of Korea Financial Studies Review*, **6**, pp. 21–44 (in Korean).

Kim, Yong-Ha (2000), 'Liabilities of Public Pensions and Measures for Financial Stability,' paper presented at the Annual Conference of the Social Welfare Association, Seoul.

Kim, Yong-Hak (1999), 'The Impact of Economic Crisis and the Trust Crisis: A Comparison of Empirical Indices Before and After the Crisis' (in Korean), *Studies in Social Development*, **5**, pp. 125–49.

Kim, Yong-Ho (1998), 'Korea,' in Wolfgang Sachsenroder and Ulike Frings (eds.), *Political Party Systems and Democratic Development in East Asia, Volume II: East Asia*, Aldershot, England: Ashgate, pp. 132–78.

Kolko, Joyce and Gabriel Kolko (1972), *The Limits of Power: The World and United States Foreign Policy, 1945–1954*, New York: Harper & Row.

Koo, Bonchun (1998), *Reform Measures for Korean Bankruptcy Reorganization and Composition*, Seoul: Korea Development Institute.

Koo, Hagen (ed.) (1995), *State and Society in Contemporary Korea*, Ithaca, NY: Cornell University Press.

Kook, C., Yungchul Park and J. Lee (1997), 'Investment Decision and Capital Cost of Korean Business Groups,' *Corporate Finance Review*, **13**, pp. 101–129.

Korea Fair Trade Commission (1997), 'Large Business Groups in 1997,' press release.

Korea Fair Trade Commission (1998a), 'Corporate Strategy for Financial Institutions to Resolve the Corporate Debt Guarantee Problem,' press release.

Korea Fair Trade Commission (1998b), *Large Business Groups and Designation of Business Groups with Debt Guarantee Restrictions*, Seoul: Korea Fair Trade Commission.

Korea Fair Trade Commission (1998, 2000) *White Book for Fair Trade Commission*, Seoul: Korea Fair Trade Commission.

Korea Fair Trade Commission (1999), '30 Largest Chaebols' Ownership Structure,' press release, Seoul: Korea Fair Trade Commission.

Korea Fair Trade Commission (various years), 'Debt Payment Guarantees,' press release, Seoul: Korea Fair Trade Commission.

Korea Fair Trade Commission (various years), *Large Business Groups*, Seoul: Korea Fair Trade Commission.

Korea Labor Institute (1995–2000), *Employment Insurance Data Base*, Seoul: Korea Labor Institute.

Korea Ministry of Finance and Economy (2000), Korea Financial Supervisory Commission, *White Paper on Restructuring Fund* (in Korean), Seoul: Korea Ministry of Finance and Economy.

Korea Ministry of Finance and Economy (2001), Public Fund Management Committee, *White Paper on Restructuring Fund Management* (in Korean), Seoul: Korea Ministry of Finance and Economy.

Korean Financial Supervisory Commission (2000), 'Second Stage Reform' (in Korean), Seoul: Korean Financial Supervisory Commission.

Kraay, Aart (2000), 'Do High Interest Rates Defend Currencies during Speculative Attacks?' World Bank Working Paper 2267.

Krasner, Stephen D. (1978), *Defending the National Interest*, Princeton, NJ: Princeton University Press.

Krueger, Anne O. and Jungho Yoo (2002), 'Falling Profitability, Higher Borrowing Costs, and Chaebol Finances During the Korean Crisis,' in David T. Coe and Se-Jik Kim (eds), *Korean Crisis and Recovery*, Washington, DC: International Monetary Fund, pp. 157–96.

Krugman, Paul (1994), 'The Myth of Asia's Miracle,' *Foreign Affairs*, **73**, pp. 62–78.

Krugman, Paul (1998), 'What Happened to Asia?' http://www.irvl.net/what_happened_to_asia.htm.

Kwack, Sung-yueng (1994), 'Rates of Return on Capital in the United States, Japan and Korea, 1972–1990,' in Sung-yueng Kwack (ed.), *The Korean Economy at a Crossroad*, Westport, CT: Praeger, pp. 57–71.

Kwack, Sung-yueng (1999), 'Total Factor Productivity Growth and the Sources of Growth in Korean Manufacturing Industries, 1971–1999,' unpublished manuscript.

Kwon, Soon-Won et al. (1992), *The Status of Distributional Inequality and Major Policy Issues* (in Korean), Seoul: Korea Development Institute.

Kwon, Soon-Won et al. (1998), *Combating Poverty: The Korean Experience*, Seoul: UNDP.

Lakonishok, Joseph, A. Schleifer and R. Vishny (1992), 'The Impact of Institutional Trading on Stock Prices,' *Journal of Financial Economics*, **32**, pp. 23–43.

Lane, Timothy, Atish Ghosh, Javier Hamann, Steven Phillips, Marianne Shulze-Ghattas and Tsidi Tsikata (1999), 'IMF-Supported Programs in Indonesia, Korea, and Thailand: A Preliminary Assessment,' Occasional Paper 178, Washington, DC: IMF.

La Porta, Rafael, Florencio Lopez-de-Silanes, Andrei Shleifer and Robert W. Vishny (1998), 'Law and Finance,' *Journal of Political Economy*, **106**, pp. 1113–55.

Leahy, Michael, Sebastian Schich, Gert Wehinger, Florian Pelgrin and Thorsteinn Thorgeirsson (2001), 'Contributions of Financial Systems to Growth in OECD Countries,' Economic Department Working Paper 280, Paris: OECD.

Lee, Byoung Ki (1998), *Debt Payment Guarantees of Korean Chaebols*, Seoul: Korea Economic Research Institute.

Lee, Byoung Ki (2000), *Investment Patterns of Korean Corporate Firms* (in Korean), Seoul: Korea Economic Research Institute.

Lee, Chung H. (1992), 'The Government, Financial System, and Large Private Enterprises in the Economic Development of South Korea,' *World Development*, **20**, pp. 187–97.

Lee, Chung H., Keun Lee and Kangkoo Lee (2000), '*Chaebol*, Financial Liberalization, and Economic Crisis: Transformation of Quasi-Internal Organization in Korea,' mimeo, University of Hawaii.

Lee, Dong Gull (2003), 'The Restructuring of Daewoo,' in S. Haggard, E. Kim and W. Lim (eds), *Chaebol Reform and Corporate Restructuring*, Cambridge: Cambridge University Press, pp. 150–80.

Lee, Dong Gull and Dae-Sik Kim (2001), 'Past, Present and Future of Banking Industry in Korea' (in Korean), in *Past, Present and Future of Financial Industries in Korea*, Seoul: Korea Institute of Finance.

Lee, In Kwon (2000), 'Excess Capacity and Big Deals,' in H. Jwa and I. Lee (eds), *Korean Chaebol in Transition: Road Ahead and Agenda*, Seoul: Korea Economic Research Institute, pp. 223–59.

Lee, Jong-Wha, Changyong Rhee and Kiseok Hong (2001), 'The Macroeconomic Adjustment during the Currency Crises' (in Korean), *Kyung Je Hak Yon K*, **49**, pp. 227–53.

Lee, Jong-Wha and Young Chul Park (2001), 'Recovery and Sustainability in East Asia,' NBER Working Paper 8373.

Lee, Jong-Wha and Changyong Rhee (2002), 'Macroeconomic Impacts of the Korean Financial Crisis: Comparison with the Cross-Country Patterns,' *World Economy*, **25**, pp. 539–62.

Lee, Jong Yoon (1987), *Formation of Business Groups and Evaluation*, Research Series 43-87-06, Korea Economic Research Institute, Seoul.

Lee, Joung-Woo and Seonglim Lee (2001a), 'Estimating Wealth Inequality in Korea' (in Korean), *Korean Journal of Development Economics*, **6**.

Lee, Joung-Woo and Seonglim Lee (2001b), 'Economic Crisis and Income Disparity: Income Inequality and Poverty Before and After the 1997 Crisis' (in Korean), *Kukje Kyongje Yongu*, **7**, pp. 1–28.

Lee, J. and Y. Lee (1998), 'Capital Structure of Korean Firms: Comparison of Chaebol Firms and Non-Chaebol Firms 1981–96,' paper presented at the Korean Meeting of Econometric Society.

Lee, Keun, Keunkwan Ryu and Jung Mo Yoon (2002), 'Long-Term Performance of Chaebols and Non-Chaebols in Korea.' biz.korea.ac.kr/~aicg/paper_2nd/LongTerm_Performance of.PDFA.

Lee, Soon Woo (1995), *Reorganization of Failing Firms*, Seoul: Jilritamgoo.

Leipziger, Danny M., David Dollar, Anthony F. Shorrocks and Soo-Yong Song (1992), *The Distribution of Income and Wealth in Korea*, Washington, DC: World Bank.

Levine, Ross (1996), 'Financial Development and Economic Growth,' Policy Research Working Paper 1678, World Bank.

Lim, Hyun-Chin (1985), *Dependent Development in Korea, 1963–1979*, Seoul: Seoul National University.

Lim, Hyun-Chin and Suk-Man Hwang (2000), 'Structural Adjustment, Social Realignment, and Coalition Change: From a Comparative Perspective,' paper presented at the 2000 Annual Meeting of American Sociological Association, Washington, DC.

Lim, Wonhyuk (2002), 'Corporate Peformance in Post-Crisis Korea,' mimeo, Korea Development Institute.

Lim, Youngjae (2003), 'Corporate Bankruptcy System and Economic Crisis in Korea,' in S. Haggard, W. Lim and E. Kim (eds), *Chaebol Reform and Corporate Restructuring*, Cambridge: Cambridge University Press, pp. 207–32.

Lingrin, Carl-Johan, T. Balino, C. Enoch, A. Gulde, M. Quintyn and L. Teo (2000), *Financial Sector Crisis and Restructuring, Lessons from Asia*, IMF Occasional Paper 188.

Mainwaring, Scott (1992), 'Transition to Democracy and Democratic Consolidation: Theoretical and Comparative Issues,' in Scott Mainwaring, Guillermo O'Donnell and J. Samuel Valenzuela (eds), *Issues in Democratic Consolidation: The New South American Democracies in Comparative Perspective*, Notre Dame, IN: University of Notre Dame Press, pp. 294–341.

Mako, William P. (2002a), 'Corporate Restructuring and Reform: Lessons from Korea,' in David Coe and Se-Jik Kim (eds), *Korean Crisis and Recovery*, Seoul: International Monetary Fund and Korea Institute for Economic Policy, pp. 203–228.

Mako, William P. (2002b), 'Korean Corporate Restructuring: Halfway There?' *Korea's Economy*, **18**, pp. 22–7.

Martin, Stephen (1993), *Advanced Industrial Economics*, Oxford: Blackwell.

Masson, Paul (1998), 'Contagion: Monsoonal Effects, Spillovers, and Jumps between Multiple Equilibria,' IMF Working Paper 98/142.

Masson, Paul (1999), 'Multiple Equilibria, Contagion, and the Emerging Market Crises,' IMF Working Paper 99/164.

McIlroy, John (1998), 'The Enduring Alliance? Trade Unions and the Making of New Labour, 1994–1997,' *British Journal of Industrial Relations*, **36**, pp. 537–64.

McKinnon, Ronald I. (1973), *Money and Capital in Economic Development*, Washington, DC: Brookings Institution.

McKinnon, Ronald (2000), 'The East Asian Dollar Standard: Life after Death?' *Economic Notes*, **29**, pp. 31–82.

Milesi-Ferreti, Gian Maria and Assaf Razin (1995), 'Determinants and Consequences of Current Account Reversals and Currency Crises,' NBER Conference on Currency Crises.

Ministry of Finance and Economy (1998), 'Press Release,' Gwacheon-City: Ministry of Finance and Economy.

Ministry of Finance and Economy (2000), Korea Financial Supervisory Commission, *White Paper on Restructuring Fund*, Gwacheon-City: Ministry of Finance and Economy.

Ministry of Finance and Economy (2001a), Public Fund Management Com-

mittee, *White Paper on Restructuring Fund Management*, Gwacheon-city: Ministry of Finance and Economy.
Ministry of Finance and Economy (2001a), *Report on the National Debt*, Gwacheon-City: Ministry of Finance and Economy.
Ministry of Finance and Economy (2001b), Republic of Korea, *Beyond the Financial Crisis, A Resilient Korean Economy*, Gwacheon-City: Ministry of Finance and Economy.
Ministry of Finance and Economy (2002), *A Plan to Redeem Restructuring Bonds*, Gwacheon-City: Ministry of Finance and Economy.
Ministry of Finance and Economy, *Financial Statistics Bulletin*, various issues, Gwacheon-City: Ministry of Finance and Economy.
Ministry of Finance and Economy, *Government Finance Statistics in Korea*, various issues, Gwacheon-City: Ministry of Finance and Economy.
Ministry of Labor (1987–2000), *Yearbook of Labor Statistics*, Seoul: Ministry of Labor Press.
Ministry of Labor (1996–2000), *Monthly Labor Statistics* (in Korean), Seoul: Ministry of Labor Press.
Ministry of Labor (2001), *Report to OECD*, Seoul: Ministry of Labor Press.
Ministry of Labor (1978–99), *Survey on Wage Structure*, micro-data files, Seoul: Ministry of Labor Press.
Ministry of Planning and Budget (2002), *Mid-Term Fiscal Plan*, Banpo-dong: Ministry of Planning and Budget.
Montes, Manuel F. (1998), *The Currency Crisis in Southeast Asia*, Singapore: Institute of Southeast Asia.
Moon, Hyungpyo and Gyeongjoon Yoo (1999), 'Future Policies of Unemployment and Welfare: With Focus on Productive Welfare' (in Korean), *KDI Policy Forum*, **146**.
Moon, Hyungpyo, Hyehoon Lee and Gyeongjoon Yoo (1999), 'Social Impact of the Financial Crisis in Korea: Economic Framework,' mimeo.
Nanto, Dick K. (1998), *The 1997–1998 Asian Financial Crisis*, CRS Report 97-1021.
National Statistical Office (1985–2002), *KOSIS Database*, KNSO: Korea.
National Statistical Office (1985–1999), *Survey on Economically Active Population*, micro-data files, KNSO: Korea.
National Statistical Office (1997–2000), *Korean Social Indicators*, KNSO: Korea.
National Statistical Office (2000), *Annual Report on Monthly Industrial Productions Statistics*, KNSO: Korea.
Nelson, Joan M. (1990), 'Introduction: The Politics of Economic Adjustment in Developing Nations,' in Joan M. Nelson (ed), *Economic Crisis and Policy Choice: The Politics of Adjustment in the Third World*, Princeton, NJ: Princeton University Press, pp. 3–32.

New York Times (1997), 'Crisis in South Korea: The Bailout,' 4 December.
New York Times (1997), 'Crisis in South Korea: The U.S. Role,' 4 December.
Noland, Marcus (2000), *Avoiding the Apocalypse: The Future of the Two Koreas*, Washington, DC: Institute for International Economics.
Noland, Marcus (2001), 'Economic Reform in Korea: Achievements and Future Prospects,' paper presented for the conference on Peace and Democracy in the Korean Peninsula, Seoul.
North, Douglas (1990), *Institutions, Institutional Change and Economic Performance,* Cambridge: Cambridge University Press.
O'Donnell, Guillermo (1992), 'Delegative Democracy,' University of Notre Dame, Kellogg Institute, Working Paper 41.
O'Donnell, Guillermo (1994), 'The State, Democratization, and Some Conceptual Problems (A Latin American View with Glances at Some Post-Communist Countries),' in Smith, Acuna and Gamarra (1994a), pp. 157–80.
O'Donnell, Guillermo (2001), 'Illusions about Consolidation,' in Larry Diamond and Marc Plattner, *The Global Divergence of Democracies*, Baltimore and London: The Johns Hopkins University Press, pp. 113–30.
OECD (1994), *Employment Outlook*, Paris: OECD.
OECD (1998), *OECD Economic Surveys 1998 Korea*, Paris: OCED.
OECD (1999), *OECD Economic Survey: Korea*, Paris: OECD.
OECD (2000), *Pushing Ahead with Reform in Korea: Labour Market and Social Safety Net Policies*, Paris: OECD.
OECD (2001), *OECD Economic Outlook,* **68**, p. 262.
Oh, Gyutaeg and Changyong Rhee (2001), 'Characteristics of the Post-Crisis Flow of Funds: A Study on the Corporate Bond Market' (in Korean), paper presented at the Congress of Economic Associations in Korea.
Ouchi, William (1981), *Theory Z: How American Business Can Meet the Japanese Challenge*, Reading, MA: Addison-Wesley.
Park, DaeKeun and ChangRyong Rhee (1998), 'Korean Currency Crisis: Development and Lessons,' Working paper #98-2, Hanyang University.
Park, Daekeun and In Choi (1999), 'Was the High Interest Rate Policy Effective to the Exchange Rate Stabilization?' (in Korean), *Analysis of the Korean Economy* (journal), Korea Institute of Finance, **5**, pp. 63–119.
Park, Won-Am and Gongpil Choi (1998), 'Predicting Korean Crisis: A Signals Approach' (in Korean), *Econometric Review*, **9**, Korean Econometric Society.
Park, Won-Am and Gongpil Choi (1999), 'Causes of the Korean Financial Crisis and Predictability' (in Korean), *International Economic Journey*, **5**, pp. 1–26.
Park, Yung Chul (1993), 'The Role of Finance in Economic Development in South Korea and Taiwan,' in Alberto Giovannini (ed.), *Finance and Devel-*

opment: Issues and Experience, Cambridge: Cambridge University Press, pp. 121–57.

Park, Yung Chul (1998), 'Financial Crisis and Macroeconomic Adjustments in Korea, 1997–98,' in Yung Chul Park (ed.), *Financial Liberalization and Opening in East Asia: Issues and Policy Changes*, Seoul: Korea Institute of Finance, pp. 11–69.

Park, Yung Chul (2001), *The East Asian Dilemma: Restructuring Out or Growing Out?* Princeton Essays in International Economics 223, International Financial Section, Department of Economics, Princeton University.

Park, Yung Chul and Jong-Wha Lee (2001), 'Recovery and Sustainability in East Asia,' NBER Working Paper 8373.

Park, Yung Chul and C.Y. Song (2001a), 'Institutional Investors, Trade Linkage, Macroeconomic Similarities and the Contagious Thai Crisis,' *Journal of the Japanese and International Economies*, 15, pp. 199–224.

Park, Yung Chul and C.Y. Song (2001b), 'Financial Contagion in East Asia: with a Special Reference to the Republic of Korea,' in K. Forbes and S. Claessens (eds), *International Financial Contagion*, Boston: Kluwer Academic Publishers, pp. 241–365.

Pastor, M. (1987), 'The Effects of IMF Programs in the Third World: Debate and Evidence from Latin America,' *World Development*, 15, pp. 365–91.

PBS Online Newshour (1998), 'Newsmaker: Secretary Rubin,' 16 January. (http://www.pbs.org/newshour/bb/asia/jan-june98/rubin_1-16.html).

Pencavel, John (1996), 'The Legal Framework for Collective Bargaining in Developing Economies,' policy paper, Center for Economic Policy Research, Stanford University.

Pereira, Carlos B., Jose Maria Maraval and Adam Przeworski (1994), 'Economic Reforms in New Democracies: A Social-Democratic Approach,' in Smith, Acuna and Gamarra (1994a), pp. 181–212.

Pieper, Ute and Lance Taylor (1998), 'The Revival of the Liberal Creed: The IMF, the World Bank, and Inequality in a Globalized Economy,' in Dean Baker et al. (eds), *Globalization and Progressive Economic Policy*, Cambridge: Cambridge University Press.

Polanyi, Karl (1957), *The Great Transformation: The Political and Economic Origins of Our Time*, Boston, MA: Beacon Press.

Presidential Committee for Better Quality of Life (2000), *Soduk Bunbae Gujo Gaesun (How to Improve the Structure of Income Distribution)*.

PriceWarterhouseCoopers (2001), *The Opacity Index*, http://www.opacityindex.com.

Putnam, Robert (1997), 'Democracy in America at Century's End,' in Alex Hadenius (ed.), *Democracy's Victory and Crisis*, Cambridge: Cambridge University Press, pp. 43–63.

Pyo, Hak-kil (1999), 'The Financial Crisis in Korea and its Aftermath,' unpublished manuscript, Seoul National University.

Radelet, Steven and Jeffrey D. Sachs (1998), 'The East Asian Financial Crisis: Diagnosis, Remedies, Prospects,' *Brookings Papers on Economic Activity*, **1**, pp. 1–74.

Rajan, Raghuram G. and Luigi Zingales (1998), 'Which Capitalism? Lessons from the East Asian Crisis,' *Journal of Applied Corporate Finance*, **11** (3), Fall, pp. 40–48.

Rew, Jung-Soon (2000), 'The Size of Poverty and the Standard of Living of the Poor' (in Korean), in Dong-Choon Kim (ed.), *Poverty in Korea since the Economic Crisis*, Seoul: Naman Publishing Co.

Rodrik, Dani (1998a), 'The Global Fix,' *The New Republic*, 2 November, p. 17–18.

Rodrik, Dani (1998b), 'Who Needs Capital-Account Convertibility?' in Peter Kenen (ed.), *Should the IMF Pursue Capital Account Convertibility?* Essays in International Finance 207, International Finance Section, Department of Economics, Princeton University, pp. 55–65.

Rubin, Robert E. (1998), 'U.S. Response to Asian Financial Crisis,' speech, Georgetown University.

Ruggie, John (1983) 'International Regime, Transactions, and Change: Embedded Liberalism in the Post War Economic Order,' in Stephen Krasner (ed.), *International Regime*, Ithaca: Cornell University Press.

Ryscavage, Paul (1999), *Income Inequality in America*, Armonk, NY: M.E. Sharpe.

Sachs, Jeffrey D. (1997), 'The Wrong Medicine for Asia,' *New York Times*, 3 November, p. A23.

Sachs, Jeffrey D., A. Tornell and A. Velasco (1996), 'Financial Crises in Emerging Markets: The Lessons from 1995,' *Brookings Papers on Economic Activity*, **1**, pp. 147–98.

Sakong, Il (1993), *Korea in the World Economy*, Washington, DC: Institute for International Economics.

Scharfstein, David and Jeremy Stein (1990), 'Herd Behavior and Investment,' *American Economic Review*, **80**, pp. 465–79.

Schedler, Andreas (2001), 'What is Democratic Consolidation?' in Larry Diamond and Marc Plattner, *The Global Divergence of Democracies*, Baltimore and London: The Johns Hopkins University Press, pp. 149–64.

Schinasi, Gary, J. and Mark S. Lutz (1991), 'Fiscal Impulse,' IMF Working Paper 91/91.

Schmitter, Phillip (1989), 'Corporatism is Dead! Long Live Corporatism,' *Government and Opposition*, **24**, pp. 54–73.

Schumpeter, Joseph (1952), *History of Economic Analysis*, New York: Oxford University Press.

Seok, Hyun-Ho (ed.) (1997), *Inequality and Justice in Korean Society* (in Korean), Seoul: Nanam Publishing Co.
Shaw, Edward S. (1973), *Financial Deepening in Economic Development*, New York: Oxford University Press.
Shigemi, Yosuke (1995), 'Asset Inflation in Selected Countries,' *Bank of Japan Monetary Economic Studies*, **13** (2), pp. 89–130.
Shiller, Robert J. (1995), 'Conversation, Information and Herd Behavior,' *American Economic Review Papers and Proceedings*, **85**, pp. 181–5.
Shin, Eun-Jong (2001), 'Unions, Government and the Politics of Industrial Relations in Korea,' Ph.D. dissertation, Michigan State University.
Shin, In-Seok (1998), 'A Study on the Origin of the Korean Currency Crisis,' *Policy Study 20*, Seoul: KDI.
Shin, In-Seok and Joon-Ho Hahm (1998), 'The Korean Crisis – Causes and Resolution,' KDI Working Paper 9805, Korea Development Institute.
Shin, Kwan-Ho (1999), 'Changes in Unemployment Rate and Natural Rate of Unemployment in Korea' (in Korean), in Fun-Koo Park (ed.), *Economic Crisis and Changes in the Structure of Unemployment*, Seoul: Korea Labor Institute Press, pp. 97–132.
Smith, William C., Carlos H. Acuna, and Eduardo A. Gamarra (eds) (1994a), *Latin American Political Economy in the Age of Neoliberal Reform: Theoretical and Comparative Perspectives for the 1990s*, New Brunswick and London: Transaction Publishers.
Smith, William C., Carlos H. Acuna and Eduardo A. Gamarra (eds) (1994b), *Democracy, Markets, and Structural Reform in Latin America: Argentina, Bolivia, Brazil, Chile, and Mexico*. New Brunswick and London: Transaction Publishers.
Smith, William C. and Roberto P. Korzeniewicz (eds) (1997), *Politics, Social Change, and Economic Restructuring in Latin America*, Boulder, CO: North–South Center Press.
Sohn, Jang-Kwon (1999), 'IMF and the Inequalities of Women' (in Korean), *Korean Society*, **2**, pp. 55–79.
Song, Ho-Keun (2001), 'Social Policy in Korea,' mimeo.
Stallings, Barbara, and Robert Kaufman (eds) (1989), *Debt and Democracy in Latin America*, Boulder, CO: Westview Press.
Stiglitz, Joseph (1999), 'Reforming the Global Financial Architecture: Lessons from Recent Crises,' *Journal of Finance*, **54**, pp. 1508–22.
Stiglitz, Joseph (2001), 'Globalization and Its Discontents: How to Fix What's Not Working,' lecture, IDPM, University of Manchester, UK, (http://idpm.man.ac.uk/idpm/stiglitz.html).
Stiglitz, Joseph (2002), *Globalization and Its Discontents*, New York: W.W. Norton & Company.
Strobel, Frederick R. (1993), *Upward Dreams, Downward Mobility: The*

Economic Decline of the American Middle Class, Savage, MD: Rowman and Littlefield.

Suh, Tongwoo (2001), 'Current Situation and Trends of Suicidal Deaths, Impulses and Attempts of Committing Suicides in Korea' (in Korean), *Studies in Health and Social Issues*, **21**, pp. 106–25.

Suk, Jae-Eun (2002), 'A Proposal for Reform of Public Pensions,' Korea Institute for Health and Social Affairs.

Takahashi, Kichinosuke, Yukiharu Kurokawa and Kazunori Watase (1984), 'Corporate Bankruptcy Prediction in Japan,' *Journal of Banking and Finance*, **8**, pp. 229–47.

Tanner, Evan (1999), 'Exchange Market Pressures and Monetary Policy: Asia and Latin America in the 1990s,' IMF Working Paper 99/114.

Taylor, J. (1993), 'Discretion versus Policy Rules in Practice', *Carnegie-Rochester Conference Series on Public Policy*, 39, 195–214.

Thompson, James D. (1967), *Organizations in Action: Social Science Bases of Administrative Theory*, New York: McGraw-Hill.

Tornell, Aaron (1999), 'Common Fundamentals in the Tequila and Asian Crises,' NBER Working Paper 7139.

Transparency International (TI), *Transparency Index*, http://www.transparency.org.

Truman, David D. (1971), *The Governmental Process: Political Interests and Public Opinion*, 2nd edn, New York: Knopf.

Valenzuela, J. Samuel (1992), 'Democratic Consolidation in the Post-Transitional Settings: Notion, Process, and Facilitating Conditions,' in Scott Mainwaring, Guillermo O'Donnell and J. Samuel Valenzuela (eds), *Issues in Democratic Consolidation: The New South American Democracies in Comparative Perspective*, Notre Dame, IN: University of Notre Dame Press, pp. 57–104.

Veltmeyer, Henry, James Petras and Steve Vieux (1997), *Neoliberalism and Class Conflict in Latin America: A Comparative Perspective on the Political Economy of Structural Adjustment*, London: Macmillan.

Vreeland, James R. (2001), 'The Effect of IMF Programs on Labor,' *World Development*, **30**, pp. 121–39.

Wade, Robert and Frank Veneroso (1998). 'The Asian Crisis: The High Debt Model vs. The Wall Street–Treasury–IMF Complex,' *New Left Review*, **228**, pp. 3–24.

Weisberg, Jacob (1998) 'Keeping the Boom From Busting,' *New York Times*, 19 July, sec. 6, p. 24.

Whang, Duck-Soon (2001), 'A Dynamic Analysis of Poverty after the Economic Crisis,' *Labor Policy Research*, **1**, pp. 31–59.

World Bank (2000a), 'External Shocks, Financial Crises, and Poverty in

Developing Countries,' in *Prospects for Development*, Washington, DC: World Bank.
World Bank (2000b), *East Asia: Recovery and Beyond*, Washington, DC: World Bank.
Yang, Joon-Mo (1999), 'A Study on Unemployment Fluctuation in Korea' (in Korean), in Fun-Koo Park (ed.), *Economic Crisis and Changes in the Structure of Unemployment*, Seoul: Korea Labor Institute Press, pp. 71–96.
Yee, Jaeyeol (1998), 'Democracy, Trust, and Social Capital,' *Kyegan Sasang*, **10** (2) (Summer), pp. 65–93.
Yonhap News Agency (2001), 'Restructuring Fund Burden to Top 2.52 Million Won Per Person.'
Yoo, Gyeong-Joon (1999a), 'Current Labor Market Development and Equilibrium Unemployment Rate' (in Korean), in Ministry of Labor (ed.), *Enhancing the Efficiency in Employment Promotion Policy*, Seoul: KDI Press, pp. 103–122.
Yoo, Gyeong-Joon (1999b), 'Unemployment Projection Based on the Okun Coefficient' (in Korean), *Korean Development Policy Report*, Seoul: KDI Press.
Yoo, Gyeong-Joon (2001), 'Changes in Income Distribution and Their Sources since the Economic Crisis' (in Korean), mimeo.
Yoo, Jung-ho (1994), 'South Korea's Manufactured Exports and Industrial Targeting Policy,' in Yang Shu-Chin (ed.), *Manufactured Exports of East Asian Industrializing Economics*, Armonk, NY: M.E. Sharpe, pp. 149–73.
Yoo, Kyung-Joo (2000), 'Changes in Income Distribution and Poverty in South Korea after IMF Bail-Out,' Korea Development Institute Working Paper.
Yoon, Yong-Man, et al. (1999), *Disparities of Land and House Ownership* (in Korean), Seoul: Haenam.
Yoon, Young-Kwan (1999), 'The East-Asian Economic Model and the World Capitalism: Focusing on the Concepts of the Market, State, and Institutions' (in Korean), in Young-Kwan Yoon and Kwang-il Paik (eds), *East Asia: The Political Economy of Crisis*, Seoul: Seoul National University Press, pp. 424–5.
Young, Alwyn (1998), 'Alternative Estimates of Productivity Growth in the NICs: A Comment on the Findings of Chang-Tai Hsieh,' NBER Working Paper 6657.
Zoellick, Robert B. (1998), 'A Larger Plan for Asia,' *Washington Post*, 6 January.

Index

Acceleration of Restructuring and Concrete Practice Plan, 325–26
Albright, Madeleine, 75
Anglo-American system, 249, 253, 286
Asian crisis, 4, 48, 49, 74, 80, 82, 83, 87, 88, 91, 94, 95, 137, 332, 333
Asian Development Bank (ADB), 76, 307
Asian Monetary Fund (AMF), 16, 73, 88
Atkinson, Caroline, 75
Auditing, 14, 19, 23, 33, 38, 133, 187, 196, 199, 204, 205, 207, 208, 259, 261, 262, 320, 326

Bank for International Settlements (BIS), 176, 183, 184, 187, 319, 320, 328
Bank of Korea, 8, 29, 61, 75, 78, 89, 102, 103, 159, 160, 166, 167, 258
Bank of Korea Act, 110
Banking crises, 8, 95, 291, 292, 294, 295, 296, 300, 301, 304, 306, 314, 339
Bankruptcy, 11, 15, 30, 32, 35, 37, 41, 51, 59, 89, 94, 129, 137, 160, 162, 176, 196, 199, 201, 203, 205, 209–12, 222–24, 242, 256, 287, 308, 321, 324
Bankruptcy Prevention Accord, 59
Banks, commercial, 7, 8, 13, 22, 32, 35, 42, 45, 52, 70, 77, 160, 172–81, 183–87, 201–03, 310, 320–23, 327, 328, 333, 341
Banks, merchant, 13, 32, 33, 42, 52, 53, 58, 70, 173, 175, 176, 178, 203, 321, 322
Berger, Sandy, 75
Big Deals, 13, 35, 40, 41, 212, 259, 325
Binary probit model, 59, 64–66, 300

Bureaucracy, 4, 57, 251, 252, 255, 256, 260

Camdessus, Michel, 77
Capital account liberalization, 9, 50, 318, 333, 334, 336, 339
Capital adequacy, 7, 57, 176, 183, 186, 187, 189, 241, 310, 319, 320, 328
Capital flows, 6, 48, 50, 66, 69, 88, 175, 308, 334
Cholla region, 279
Civil Service Commission, 260
Clinton Administration, 76, 77, 80, 81, 82, 87
Commercial bank portfolio structure, 178, 179
Competitiveness, 3, 19, 36, 50, 53, 58, 219, 247, 253, 254, 324, 330
Consumption, 4, 51, 124, 139, 140, 154, 166, 171, 245, 306–09
Contagion, international financial, 49, 57, 58, 69, 194, 318, 332–36, 339, 342, 343
Corporate bonds, 10, 33, 39, 169, 173–79, 183, 188
Corporate governance, 3, 13, 16, 18, 34, 35, 169, 187, 188, 194, 208, 209, 216, 239–242, 244, 245, 248, 258, 262, 311, 326, 338, 339, 342
Corporate restructuring, 14, 18, 180, 186, 194, 208, 221, 243, 275, 317, 318, 334, 342
Corporate Restructuring Agreement, 211, 325
Corporate Restructuring Coordination Committee, 325
Cumings, Bruce, 12, 82
Currency crisis, 60, 71, 89, 95, 98, 166, 167, 176, 199, 290–302, 306, 309, 314–316, 332, 338

369

Daewoo Group, 14, 15, 25, 37, 41, 138, 162, 177, 190, 208, 210, 211, 215, 216, 242, 258, 259, 319, 324–326, 341
Decentralization, Ch11, 16, 258–60, 268, 273, 278, 281, 282, 286, 289
Democracy, 251–253
Deposits, bank, 54, 175, 190
Dollar, US, 7, 8, 11, 31, 33, 34, 52, 57, 58, 70, 71, 77, 79, 91, 104, 105, 157, 160

East Asia, 19, 22, 49, 69, 71, 81, 163, 165, 167, 194, 195, 248, 253, 287, 288, 332, 333, 338, 342, 343
East Asian system, 253
Economic Planning Board (EPB), 265, 539
Electronics, 57, 208
Employment Insurance System (EIS), 117, 119, 122, 123
Europe, 16, 19, 30, 31, 157, 252, 263, 286, 287, 289
  France, 31, 78
  Germany, 31, 78, 206, 254, 282
  Portugal, 268
  Spain, 268
  Sweden, 95, 215, 254
  Switzerland, 192
  United Kingdom (UK), 31, 78, 81, 95, 147, 165, 224, 254, 282
Exports, 1–4, 31, 33, 50–52, 56, 60, 61, 65, 66, 70, 74, 81, 87, 162, 176, 202, 285, 296, 302, 304, 309, 330, 340
External borrowing, 50, 175, 240

Federal Reserve Board (FRB), 73–75, 78, 81, 167
Federation of Korean Trade Unions (FKTU), 219, 220, 263
Financial intermediation, 82, 193
Financial liberalization, 1, 5–7, 30, 55, 81, 88, 173, 183, 239, 245, 249
Financial sector, 5, 6, 8, 12, 13, 16, 26, 28, 30, 34, 36, 39, 42, 49, 52–54, 57, 81, 88, 89, 114–116, 118, 161, 172, 175, 176, 294, 201, 222, 229, 239, 241–44, 248, 259, 308, 310, 311, 317–19, 327, 339, 343

Financial sector restructuring, 35, 44, 45, 89, 114, 116, 124, 125, 128, 132, 162, 311, 318, 322, 323
Financial supervision, 14, 39, 44, 45, 49, 166
Fiscal consolidation, 114, 115, 118, 120, 125, 128, 133, 161
Fiscal policy, 17, 53, 113–117, 119, 120, 128, 132, 133
Fordism, 255
Foreign direct investment, 20, 88, 124, 276, 289, 302, 311, 312, 355
Foreign investors, 9, 28, 50, 59, 84, 101, 124, 188, 194, 221, 241, 308, 318, 320, 329, 330, 332

Geithner, Timothy, 74, 75, 78
Gini coefficient, 138, 140, 148, 149, 150, 151, 152, 162, 163, 229, 273, 274
Globalization, 81, 83, 157, 281, 282, 289
Government securities, 179, 180
Great Depression, 282
Greenspan, Alan, 73–75, 79, 82
Group of Seven (G-7), 98
Growth rate, 5, 8, 15, 50, 56, 89, 103, 115, 118, 122, 126, 127, 162, 291, 302, 304, 306, 307, 329, 341

Hanjin Group, 259
Hierarchy, 250–53, 255, 256, 279, 286
Hong Kong, 31, 32, 57, 71, 73, 74, 93, 254, 287, 320
Human capital, 223

IMF financial assistance, 291, 292, 294, 296–99, 301, 302, 314, 339, 340
Income distribution, 138–41, 147, 156, 162, 163
India, 315
Indonesia, 5, 6, 8, 10, 16, 31, 32, 57, 73, 74, 76, 83, 87, 88, 95–97, 166, 195, 287, 308, 315, 341
Industrial relations, 19, 218–20, 224, 230, 233, 234, 276
Inflation targeting, 17, 89, 102, 103
Interest rate policy, 11, 89, 91–94, 98, 101, 103, 108, 109, 166
Internal financing, 176, 177

Investment trust companies (ITCs), 14, 176, 177, 190, 322

Japan, 2, 3, 16, 18, 28, 30, 31, 32, 50, 54, 57, 73, 76, 78, 81, 82, 88, 105, 143, 146, 189, 245–47, 253–55, 261, 262, 287, 289, 309, 333, 338
Japanese commercial banks, 333
Job security, 218, 227, 230–33, 273

Keynesian policies, 270
Kia Group, 15, 25, 51, 59, 211
Kim Dae Jung, 12, 34, 79, 220, 248, 263, 267–71, 273, 275, 279, 281, 282, 288
Kim Young Sam, 49, 268, 270, 271, 279
Korea Asset Management Company(KAMCO), 128, 243, 311, 323, 341
Korean Confederation of Trade Unions (KCTU), 19, 220, 231, 232, 263
Korea Deposit Insurance Company (KDIC), 36, 128, 180, 311, 323
Korea First Bank, 13, 320
Korea Social Science Council, 134, 148
Korean crisis, 1, 5, 10, 32, 49, 57, 60, 64–66, 72, 81–83, 88, 159–61, 163, 194, 195, 245, 248
Korean Financial Supervisory Commission (FSC), 36, 259, 318, 320

Labor market, 12, 16, 18, 19, 89, 122, 123, 143, 155, 161, 163, 218, 219, 221, 224, 226, 234, 244, 246, 248, 273, 276, 338
Latin America, 73, 275, 289
  Nicaragua, 315
Lee Keun Yung, 75

Malaysia, 8, 31, 57, 71, 74, 95, 96, 315, 320, 334, 341
Mergers and acquisitions (M&As), 124, 186, 187, 188, 205, 208, 211, 215, 216, 247
Mexico, 52, 73, 76, 95, 96, 219, 315
Ministry of Defense, 271
Ministry of Finance and Economy (MOFE), 258, 318
Moral hazard, 27, 49, 54, 57, 58, 79, 123, 190, 239, 242, 321, 323, 331, 342

National Assembly, 269, 270, 278, 279
National Basic Livelihood Protection Law, 114
National Basic Security Livelihood Law, 123
National Intelligence Service, 271
National Pension Scheme, 129
National Revenue Service, 271
National Security Council, 73
Nonbank financial institutions (NBFI), 173–78, 181, 183, 203, 240, 246
Nonperforming Loans (NPLs), 28, 30, 35, 36, 42, 43, 45, 52, 53, 57, 70, 128, 129, 130, 183, 184, 186, 245, 310, 311, 317, 319–21, 323, 324, 330, 331, 341, 342
North Korea, 75, 80

Paul, Ron, 77
Philippines, 31, 74, 90, 91, 95–100, 315, 320
Poverty, 1, 2, 122, 137–39, 154–57, 162, 223, 273
Presidential Committee for Quality of Life, 138
Presidential Secretariat Office, 271
Profitability, 5, 8, 9, 13–16, 18, 27, 28, 30, 40, 45, 52–54, 57, 69, 183, 184, 186, 187, 189, 194–97, 202, 209, 216, 222, 240, 309, 311, 318–20, 327–30, 341

Recovery, 12, 13, 15, 17, 34, 37, 44, 48, 70, 96, 109, 113, 114, 117, 118, 123, 129–30, 224, 225, 228, 243, 248, 273, 292, 306, 309, 311, 312, 317, 318, 323, 325, 327, 329–31, 333–35, 338, 340, 341
Recovery rates, 128
Recurrence, 90, 290–92, 294, 297–99, 302–04, 306, 311, 312, 317, 340
Roh Tae Woo, 268
Rubin, Robert, 72–83, 87
Russia, 32, 74, 76

Sakakibara, Eisuke, 73
Securities companies, 42, 259, 322
Securities, financial, 8, 12, 18, 27, 41, 70, 124, 175, 178–80, 188, 190, 209, 241, 321, 322

Seoul Bank, 13, 320
Shareholders, 13, 14, 16, 18, 35, 42, 81, 169, 187, 196, 204, 205, 207–09, 212, 213, 215, 216, 242, 243, 245, 256, 258, 286, 320, 323, 324, 326, 334
Singapore, 31, 253, 254, 261, 262, 287, 315
Small and medium sized enterprises (SMEs), 324
Social Darwinism, 251
Social Equity Survey, 138
Social realignment, 267, 268
Social welfare, 114, 115, 122, 123, 132, 248, 273
South America, 158
  Argentina, 314
  Brazil, 74, 96, 314
  Chile, 95, 96, 243, 314
  Peru, 315
South Korea, 1, 2, 6, 72, 73, 75, 76, 81, 275, 276
Southeast Asia, 74, 286, 317
State Department, US, 73, 79, 80, 83
Steinberg, James, 76
Stock market, 6, 15, 18, 74, 182, 188, 213, 276, 322, 325, 332, 334
Supplemental Reserve Facility, 74

Taiwan, 31, 54, 57, 88, 195, 253, 254, 261, 262, 287
Tax revenue, 113, 162
Temporary Livelihood Program (TLP), 123

Thailand, 5, 6, 8, 10, 16, 31, 32, 57, 73, 76, 90, 91, 95–100, 166, 194, 195, 308, 316, 320, 341
Toyotaism, 253
Trade, international, 234
Transparency, 12, 14, 19, 34, 35, 41, 42, 45, 46, 53, 57, 69, 187, 207, 209, 244, 248–57, 261, 264, 286, 323, 326, 334
Tripartite Commission, 18, 19, 219, 220, 234, 263, 269, 270, 281
Truman, Edwin, 74

Unemployment, 1, 37, 39, 89, 115, 118, 137, 143, 147, 152, 218, 220–22, 224, 225, 260, 273, 275, 276, 295, 296, 304, 307, 318, 330
  insurance, 18, 119, 122, 223, 226
Unions, industrial, 19, 232, 233
Urban Household Income and Expenditure Survey (UHIES), 138, 140, 141, 154, 155

Wage Claim Guarantee Fund, 223
Wage differentials, 146, 147
Wall Street, 80–83, 87
  Treasury Complex, 81, 82, 87
Wealth inequality, 148, 156
World Bank, 74, 76, 137, 148, 273, 318, 326, 338, 343
World Wars, 30, 282

Zelikow, Daniel, 75